ACKNOWLEDGING CONSUMPTION

Today, parents, public transport users, hospital patients, everyone, is being called a 'consumer'. The term seems to have taken over political and economic debate. Yet only very recently have the social sciences woken up to the significance of these changes.

Acknowledging Consumption is a survey of the enormous number of writings on consumption produced over the last decade and demonstrates that the study of consumption is no academic bandwagon, but rather a belated acknowledgement of a fundamental transformation in the world.

This is an interdisciplinary project which provides new theories and critical analyses with contributions from the leading researchers in the field. There are chapters on consumption studies in anthropology, consumer behaviour, economics, geography, history, media studies, psychology and sociology.

This volume will provide the first substantive textbook on consumption studies. Each subject area includes a review of the literature, a general assessment of the impact of the new work on discipline as a whole, and ends with case studies exemplifying recent trends. It will be invaluable for students of consumption, students of the many disciplines covered in this book, and anyone interested in consumption.

Editor: Daniel Miller is Reader in Anthropology, University College London. He is the author of *Material Culture and Mass Consumption* (1987) and editor of *Unwrapping Christmas* (1993).

Contributors: Russell W. Belk, Department of Marketing, University of Utah; Colin Campbell, Department of Sociology, University of York; Ben Fine, School of Oriental and African Studies, London; Paul Glennie, Department of Geography, University of Bristol; Peter Jackson, Department of Geography, University of Sheffield; Peter Lunt, Department of Psychology, University College London; David Morley, Department of Media and Communication Studies, Goldsmiths' College, University of London; Nigel Thrift, Department of Geography, University of Bristol.

MATERIAL CULTURES
Interdisciplinary studies in the material construction of social worlds

Series Editors
Daniel Miller, Dept of Anthropology, University College London
Michael Rowlands, Dept of Anthropology, University College London
Christopher Tilley, Institute of Archaeology, University College London
Annette Weiner, Dept of Anthropology, New York University

ACKNOWLEDGING CONSUMPTION

A Review of New Studies

Edited by Daniel Miller

London and New York

First published 1995
by Routledge
11 New Fetter Lane, London EC4P 4EE

Simultaneously published in the USA and Canada
by Routledge
29 West 35th Street, New York, NY 10001

Reprinted 1996, 2001, 2002

Routledge is an imprint of the Taylor & Francis Group

Typeset in Stoodleigh, Devon by Florencetype Ltd., Stoodleigh, Devon
Printed and bound in Great Britain by Selwood Printing Ltd, Burgess Hill, West Sussex

British Library Cataloguing in Publication Data
A catalogue record for this book is available from the British Library

Library of Congress Cataloguing in Publication Data
Acknowledging consumption / edited by Daniel Miller.
p. cm. – (Material cultures)
Includes bibliographical references and index.
1. Consumption (Economics)   I. Miller, Daniel
II. Series.
HB820.A25 1995
339.4'7-dc20 94-37293

ISBN 0-415-10688-5 (hbk)
ISBN 0-415-10689-3 (pbk)

CONTENTS

FIGURES

CONTRIBUTORS

Russell W. Belk, David Eccles School of Business, Dept of Marketing, University of Utah.

Colin Campbell, Dept of Sociology, University of York, Heslington, York YO1 5DD.

Ben Fine, Centre for Economic Policy for Southern Africa, School of Oriental and African Studies, Thornhaugh Street, London WC1H OXG.

Paul Glennie, Dept of Geography, University of Bristol, Bristol BS8 1SS.

Peter Jackson, Dept of Geography, University of Sheffield, Western Bank, Sheffield S10 2TN.

Peter Lunt, Dept of Psychology, University College London, Gower Street, London WC1E 6BT.

Daniel Miller, Dept of Anthropology, University College London, Gower Street, London WC1E 6BT.

David Morley, Dept of Media and Communication Studies, Goldsmiths' College, University of London, New Cross, London SE14 6NW.

Nigel Thrift, Dept of Geography, University of Bristol, University Road, Bristol BS8 1SS.

CONSUMPTION AS THE VANGUARD OF HISTORY

A Polemic by Way of an Introduction[1]

Daniel Miller

THE CONSUMER AS GLOBAL DICTATOR

This introduction examines the evidence presented in the subsequent chapters that there has been a considerable and relatively sudden expansion of interest in the topic of consumption throughout the social sciences. I shall argue that this is not merely one more topic to be added to various subdisciplines or bandwagons of academic concern. Rather it is a remarkably delayed acknowledgement of social and economic transformations at a global level that had previously suffered from extraordinary academic neglect. My argument is that consumption has become the vanguard of history and that there are clear reasons why the social sciences should previously have failed to acknowledge this development. The remaining chapters provide the evidence that they are now starting to address the consequences of these changes through developing the required perspectives and research. The introduction is intended as an explicit return to the 'grand narrative' tradition, which ironically has become most derided just as the moment when it has become most authentic to history as global–local articulation.

The subsequent chapters provide much of the evidence to support such a strong statement. Although addressing a variety of disciplines, each with its own historical trajectory, what is striking in their juxtaposition within this volume is that the study of consumption does not seem to represent merely an additional accretion – an extra topic to add to a list of previous concerns. Rather, in many cases the topic of consumption seems to present a fundamental challenge to the basic premises that have sustained each discipline up to the present. That this should happen in a single discipline might call for little further comment, but that there seems to be emerging evidence for an 'across the board' sea-change suggests something rather more fundamental with regard to the significance of consumption itself. Such studies may not only cause us to rethink our conception of consumption but also point to the need for a radical rethinking of areas of already acknowledged importance such as economics and politics.

At first the significance of the new study of consumption seems to arise almost fortuitously out of particular histories of particular disciplines. Fine shows how neoclassical economics has used tautology and subterfuge to deny the presence of a consumer that would destroy its key premises, while even the more promising approaches from political economy are still radically challenged by a clear focus upon consumption. Campbell argues that what seemed to be merely a pendulum swing away from production-ist interests in sociology is actually a more profound questioning of the presumptions of the discipline as a whole. For psychology, Lunt suggests a similar potential but for now this remains only a 'pollutant' upon the purity of established psychology. Perhaps most surprising is Belk's argument that even marketing studies has only within the last decade started to repudi-ate formally an unholy mixture of economics and psychoanalysis in order to acknowledge consumers, replete with the complex social relations within which they practise actual consumption.

We can see therefore that each discipline has its own specific grounds for viewing these new studies as of particular importance. But in a sense this begs a larger set of questions. Why should anthropology have previously been so ensconced in this romantic antipathy to the world of goods? Why should economics have succeeded for so long as an ideological abstraction based on quite bizarre models of how social beings actually act in the world? Why have we been so ready to accept premises and beliefs that, once put under the perspective of consumption, come to look so patently absurd? In particular, why should this be so within academic disciplines that are supposed to have been more self-critical than mere colloquial discourse?

The answer I believe lies in the hegemonic control by two major political ideologies conventionally termed the 'right' and the 'left', which first defined themselves by mutual opposition but second combine in their opposition to the notion of consumption as a political activity. These ideologies developed through the cold war oppositions between socialist and market economies. But they are more than political parties. They have emerged as the paradigmatic dimension upon which are clustered most 'opinions' held by modern populations with regard to anything from political preference to general orientation and behaviour. Defining themselves largely by opposition, the right and the left were thereby enabled to act for many decades as relatively abstracted theoretical structures increasingly protected from their consequences for the daily life of mass populations. This situation has recently changed and the rise of an explicit concern with consumption is symptomatic of this change.

I want to argue that the key to the prior political consensus by opposi-tion and its protection from global realities was the rise to power of one particular academic discipline which attempted, where possible, to shift the world in the direction of increasing compliance with its abstract models. In short, modern politics has become a mere dependant of modern economics. What both resisted was historical change that threatens to make them increasingly impotent against the power of modern consumption processes. We are all brought up within the subsequent ideologies and it is therefore extremely difficult for us, as also for politicians, to acknowledge the degree to which economic instruments such as the International Monetary Fund and political parties of left and right are increasingly the agents, not of international capitalists so much as of international shopping. Both politicians and economists are, of course, having to rethink their roles in terms of global change. Thanks to the development of electronic communications, this is itself not mere pretension. Both in the financial centres, such as stock markets, and also in ordinary living rooms, computer screens and television may make global events closer to 'home' than neighbourhood events (e.g. Morley 1992: 270–289).

Occasionally, however, there are also meetings when in effect 'the globe' delegates individuals to negotiate political and economic interests in a forum which comes closer to the traditions of 'face to face' encounters. One such example was the conference in Rio in 1992, which was largely concerned with environmental change and development. Many anecdotes abound about this conference, but one is of particular importance for the present topic. Not long before the conference it is said that various Third World countries requested that the topic of First World consumption be placed high on the agenda. The reasons for this request were evident enough to those who made it. From their perspective, on the periphery of the world economy, they were often subject to the clear and unmitigated consequences of certain economic shifts that are much more muddied and confused when they occur in the metropolitan core. The change in one commodity price such as bananas or Bauxite can spell the difference between poverty and fortune for many such countries. In earlier periods producers knew little as to the forces that created shifts in such demand. A famine might arise in eighteenth-century India because a fashion for calico in Europe persuaded many peasants to give up growing food in preference for either growing more cotton or taking to weaving. When that fashion changed, for no apparent reason, the peasant starved.

Today, however, the links between First World 'taste' and Third World suffering are understood by the producing nations and it has become evident that increasingly their destiny has become, in effect, a secondary effect of shifts in First World consumption patterns. Furthermore it was also the unspoken premise to both First and Third World delegates at Rio that First World consumption was the primary problem with respect to those environmental issues that were the official focus of concern. First World consumption was not, however, discussed in Rio and according to the anecdote (pers. comm. Desmond McNeil) there was an informal agreement that the Third World would not raise this as an issue if reciprocally the First World did not raise the issue of population control.

When First World consumption does inevitably come on the agenda, it will expose one of the most severe problems of the contemporary world, which is an increasing deficit in the concept of democratic politics. Officially, politics in democratic societies is the supreme exercise of the sovereign will of the mass population through the ballot box. This creates every few years a rise to consciousness and responsibility among the population as to a crucial decision, the consequences of which they must live with for the next period of history (hence the common post-election car sticker 'Don't blame me, I didn't vote for them'). This then is the decision whose consequences are evident, the moment in which the population is itself politicised. In Trinidad (and I suspect elsewhere) there is a joke that makes the rounds at wedding receptions in which the best man notes that the wife will make all the unimportant decisions, such as the household budget, the children's schooling etc., while the husband will make the important decision, as to who will win the next election. To varying degrees in most democratic countries there is a similar division of 'significance' between the properly politicised and the daily mundane world, and this is very commonly based also on a conception of gender differentiation.

The truth of this joke lies in the burden of responsibility taken by the housewife in everyday decision-making with regard to the use of household income on household expenditure. It is evident to all that most such decisions are in themselves trivial: the choice between two brands of the same product or between a cosmetic and a household cleaner. This hardly seems to bear the same weight as a change in government and anyway is generally regarded as merely the tail-end of capitalist strategic planning for profitability. This particular tail, however, is increasingly wagging the dog. As capitalism has become more sophisticated, it has harnessed the new forms of communication and driven deeper into competitive commoditisation of ever more niches of ordinary life. In the major supermarket chains of First World countries, for example, the display consists of an extraordinary range of food and non-food items. The aggregate decisions of housewives are relayed on a daily basis as the nature of demand. The supermarkets themselves have been pushed towards a relatively low percentage of profit extraction. Indeed, bulk-buying warehouses such as Cost-Co are likely to drive profit margins in Britain still lower: while in the United States the success of these out-of-town warehouses which are developing for each product range is credited with the relatively cheap prices of goods compared to Europe. Such margins are acceptable since, given the high volume of sales, the final profits can be impressive. Although each chain attempts to tempt customers with innovations and strategic plans, in general it is both economies of scale and the speed by which they can respond to shifting aggregate 'taste' that is the key to their success. Today they are able to restock almost on a daily basis with instant knowledge of the pattern of purchases. Their ability to analyse purchasing patterns through point of sale electronics makes them also the vanguard of marketing research.

This volume of sales has become the apex to increasing vertical integration whereby the retailers become ever more dominant over distribution and indeed manufacture. The degree to which First World economies have become concentrated around relatively few key retail operations has varied. This is partly in relation to the differences between commodity fields (see Fine and Leopold 1993) and partly in relation to different state attitudes to what threaten to become close to oligopolies if not monopolies (see Wrigley 1993a; Wrigley 1993b). Furthermore this may not be evident to consumers, since retailers in, for example, clothing, divide into six or eleven different stores in order to segment the market (Crewe and Foster 1993). Through vertical integration it is retailers who inform marketing and advertising as to trends in demand, and this in turn is fed back to producers and designers who are told to come up with a new (e.g. low-fat, or conspicuously more safety-conscious, or less gendered) version of a familiar commodity in order to fulfil this aspiration. This represents a distinct shift from the period when producers determined their own priorities and looked for ways to persuade the population to purchase the result (e.g. Galbraith 1969). It also represents an increasing move from opposition to collusion between producers and consumers. We see here only the beginnings of a larger trend which should not be overgeneralised. As anyone who has worked in business will testify, there are plenty of instances where, despite all the information on consumption available, brand managers do their work without much of a clue as to how to interpret or respond to changes in demand.

Retailers in turn feed back the demands for increasing economies of scale and, as the delegates of Rio might have observed (had they been given the opportunity!), this results in quite extraordinary road haulage and other polluting consequences since an international division of labour and an international competition for low-priced commodities create individual supermarket products combining ingredients of astonishingly far-flung origins and varied zones of primary processing. Supermarket and chain-store competition also act to suppress farm and other production level prices to their minimum. Although they may face considerable opposition from producer interests, as reflected in the European Common Agricultural Policy, such resistance is increasingly regarded as a tired legacy of an older ideology which should be removed. The major supermarket chains are often quite effective at squeezing out the middleman through this vertical integration. In general they thereby favour the overproduction of basic foodstuffs across the globe to help force down prices through overcompetition between producing nations, while retaining the power to shift quickly their source of raw materials to whichever gives the lowest costs at that time. In Chapter 4 Fine provides a concise review of some key recent developments in food retailing and the increasing significance of retailing in the British economy as a whole. This provides an example of what Jackson and Thrift in Chapter 6 call international 'chains', which seem to have developed far more quickly than our ability to trace and analyse them. It is not surprising then that retailing has a prominent role in several other chapters of this volume, including that of Glennie (Chapter 5), where it provides the main case-study.

But it would be quite wrong to identify the supermarket manager as the 'villain' of the piece, as a replacement of the role of the 'top-hat' capitalist of Marxist rhetoric and political imagery. The supermarket may gain considerable profits, but this is based upon the increasing scale of the enterprise, alongside a profit margin that otherwise might be seen as quite low. Certainly top managers and shareholders may gain disproportionate material rewards from this process. Today, however, most of the 'value' extracted from labour does not take the form of profits, but is manifested in benefits to First World consumers. Prices in real terms for non-basic foodstuffs have often dropped. Retailers whose long-term perspective persuaded them to cut prices rather than take quick profits have generally increased market share and survived best (Hallsworth 1992: 43–49). But the improvement of value based on the rise of production efficiency and mass marketing is much more evident when price is broadened to the more general concept of convenience, where, as Becker and others noted, time is as important a measure of value as price. The majority of First World consumers have been almost entirely relieved of seasonality, of distance (once they possess a car) and of scarcity.

Supermarkets provide substances that would once have been rare and of prohibitive cost but now serve as mundane accompaniments for weekly purchasing. For the First World consumer, capitalism has in many respects 'delivered the goods', with vast increases in real wealth for all but a substantial minority. This is particularly the case when those benefits of welfare provision that are paid for by taxes on business are included. The rich of previous centuries might well look enviously at the possessions and mobility of the lower-middle class of today (this is not the less true for being a cliché). It is not just, as some suggest, a case of home commodities and appliances replacing the servants, since today it is the households of those who would once have been servants that also have the basic appliances and associated mass commodities. Overall low rewards for labour, while still creating handsome profits for transnational companies, are above all a means for ensuring low prices for consumers.

In the voluminous writings about post-Fordism there has certainly been considerable concern to document the shifts that have occurred in the global economy in recent decades. Yet it is remarkable how little acknowledgement is given to consumption. As Fine notes, this literature has re-established the assumed primacy of production that it was in part intended to critique. Consumption is either disregarded or reduced to postmodern style as a kind of ideological reflection of changes in production (as in Harvey 1989). An exception is Robin Murray, who pointed out 'The groundwork for the new system was laid not in manufacturing but in retailing' (Murray 1989: 42). He notes four related changes:

1 the ability of shops to use new information technology to match exactly supply to demand;
2 the market niching of stores now carefully differentiated by segments defined by marketing research and recognised by designers;
3 the dynamic forms of customisation with flexible automation;
4 the degree of subcontracting by new firms such as Benetton.

What is missing even here, however, is the acknowledgement that retailing was in turn responding to the new forms of demand that preceded such commercial movements. This is the demand that followed from a global shift towards the pluralism of 'roots', 'regionalism', 'identity politics', 'religious revivals' and other anti-modernist movements that arose very quickly after 1968. This preceded and made essential the development of computer aided technology as providing the appropriate flexibility in production and distribution. It is this phenomenon that is misunderstood in most of the writings on postmodernism.

This does not mean that consumption has somehow overcome capitalism. Such a conclusion would have to assume that the interests of capitalism are necessarily opposed to those of consumer demand. Instead it may be that this new power of consumers actually assists capitalism's search for profits. Instead of having to put considerable time and money into finding markets for goods and persuading consumers to buy, a manufacturing and distribution system that largely responds to consumers makes considerable potential savings in storage, in advertising and in reducing wasted investment. Theoretically, then, a demand-led capitalism should increase its potential profitability. In practice, as noted above, it is more likely that the benefits would largely be shunted into better value for consumers. None of this represents an argument in itself in favour of capitalism, since all of this would also be the case for an alternative system for the provision of goods and services, such as the state. It is equally true that the state suffered at least as much as capitalism in a previous era from being production-led rather than demand-led. What we are documenting here is a shift in power from production to consumption, irrespective of the forms of distribution and the behaviour of capital and states *per se*.

The market ideologists claim it is the market itself that has delivered the goods which require a demand for goods that is prior and autonomous, and they contrast this achievement with production-led socialism. To make this claim they have to ignore the long period during which capitalism was just as keen as the state to create consumers as 'the market' upon which they could dump whatever they chose to produce. Historically both the market and the state have had to respond to a shift towards consumer power for which neither they, nor 'right' or 'left' politics can take credit.

These changes affected politics on two fronts. The First World consumer 'votes' on a daily basis for cheap goods through the competitive mechanisms of capitalism forcing down prices. The same priorities are echoed in formal political voting, where increasingly it is the promise of lower taxes and lower prices that is used to appeal to the voter, often in the forms of electoral bribes and electoral lies. This leads to a 'democratic deficit'. This exists within First World countries where it may produce two-thirds living in relative affluence and up to one-third living in poverty. This is because a relatively well-off majority with a secure political control has no need to pay regard to what can become an increasingly impoverished group within its own society. The poor have little chance of significantly altering the government and any violent protest by them is largely utilised to justify their oppression.

The second form taken by the democratic deficit lies in the distance between First World consumers and Third World producers. The former can vote for a government that to some extent expresses their desires and safeguards their demand for more goods at cheaper prices. By contrast the Third World producers, if they have a vote at all, can only vote as part of the far less significant democratic forum of their own country. Their government is increasingly unable to influence even the local economy that is subservient to the shifts in the larger global economy. They are competing with other developing countries to produce goods at the lowest costs, thereby suppressing wages. But even this may not be sufficient to compete with some First World agricultural producers who pay higher wages but use highly capital-intensive technologies to undercut their rivals.

Of course there is a great variety of consumers divided by many social attributes. For the purpose of this polemic, however, I want to select one image to stand for the idea of a consumer. This is the First World housewife, such as from Western Europe or North America. The number of households in these areas represented by a nuclear family and the traditional 'housewife' role is steadily declining, although this may be compensated for by the rise of such figures in newly industrialised countries. I do not know what proportion of purchasing is made by such housewives, and furthermore it is important to incorporate consumption by institutions and not just by individuals (whether male or female). Nevertheless there are grounds for focusing upon this stereotypical figure. This is partly because in popular culture (from misogynistic newspaper strip cartoons to television sitcoms) the mythic figure of the housewife dominates the image of consumption. The other justification for this reification is because I want to argue (see pp. 34–9) that the housewife in many respects epitomises the contradictions of contemporary consumer power. It is by focusing upon the housewife as the global dictator that the ironies of power may be most directly confronted. It is ironic in the sense that the housewife is often stereotyped as herself both modest and denigrated. She commands little respect in the social world she inhabits. Her labour in shopping, her skills of thrift and comparative purchasing are largely disregarded and unvalorised. Yet it is she (or at least the consumption she stands for) who may have displaced the top-hat capitalist as the aggregate 'global dictator'. She thereby stands as the potential objectification of tremendous fear and power for the peasantries of the developing world, who are increasingly aware how far their life-chances are dependent upon her.

There are still further complexities to this relationship. It would be easy enough to render this conclusion in terms of the exploitation of poor countries by rich countries, but, as with Marx's original formulation, it is better to understand this phenomenon in terms of fundamental contradictions rather than the working out of particular interests. This conclusion becomes evident when we look within the developing world. In my own research in Trinidad I am investigating the nature of shopping within that island (Miller forthcoming). This is a community that is much closer to the problems of the vulnerability of commodity prices (especially the price of oil) than most First World countries, yet the contradiction of labour and consumption is equally evident here. The people of this island have clear political imperatives and desires, including relative economic and political power and autonomy. In general, however, their decisions as consumers do not reflect these political interests but not surprisingly favour the global economy's search for the cheapest possible prices, irrespective of the consequences for labour. In relation to the wedding day joke, it seems that the bride has the last laugh. This is because her 'little' decision-making in day-to-day consumption effectively renders the 'big' political decision-making of her husband quite impotent. The government he chooses loses all autonomy to increasingly powerful bodies, such as the International Monetary Fund (IMF), which constrain what any local state may do. The IMF takes this action in the name of providing the cheapest goods to the consumer, including here the Trinidadian housewife who responds favourably to any lowering of prices.

This suggests that the issue may be less one of some First World instrumentalist desire to exploit (though this may be there) than one of the fundamental contradictions that would equally apply within a developing country had it the consumer power to express this. That the contradiction lies within and not just between nations is not true simply of the developing world. Also in First World countries there is an increasingly common scenario in which the primary victim of capitalism and the primary beneficiary may be one and the same person: that is, the housewife in her other guise as worker or unemployed. This would be the case where the political and economic priorities that are being 'voted' for by careful shopping act to undermine the demands of the same shopper in bidding

9

for higher wages or a secure job. Clearly, to comprehend the contemporary world order we need rather more sophisticated forms of analysis which, as in Hegelian Marxism, focus upon contradiction.

A theorising of this concept of the consumer as global dictator might come from some synthesis of Foucault and de Tocqueville. Foucault certainly raised critical analysis from a more simplistic concept of power easy to locate and identify. The concept of power that is of concern here is much closer to that formulated by Foucault. Foucault pushed the concept of power beyond its association with 'ideology' and the control of some interest groups over others, to refashion it as more diffuse but also ambivalent. But Foucault achieves this sophistication at the expense of our ability to locate power at all, rendering it a rather abstracted almost ethereal presence, associated by his students with that much abused term 'discourse', which although at first located in institutions seems almost to transcend them. This dehumanising of the very concept of power does us no service, since power remains all too humanly located. Today real power lies unequivocally with us, that is with the waged consumers of the First World. This is not a unitary phenomenon; there are forms of power as resource that may be especially associated with those who have had access to the kind of educational capital that produces the readers and writers of books such as this one. The key to economic power lies in the mass shopping population (which also votes in the major democracies of the First World), supplemented as I will argue later by the theoretical models of the discipline of economics.

Power is, however, not just resource, and here Foucault is of considerable assistance. It is when we understand that power is today located above all in consumers, such as the housewife, that we realise that we need a much more sophisticated concept of power: a power that can be repressive as well as enabling to those who wield it, and a power that is central to the constitution of desire. In a sense rather analogous with Marx's critique of Hegel, one may suggest that Foucault made a major advance through his understanding that the nature of power has radically shifted, but failed to appreciate the proper site of this new form of power, leaving it a largely abstract philosophical contention that reified the historical transformations that have taken place. What is required is a materialist grounding of Foucault that shows that the new diffuse ambivalent nature of power is all too real, being increasingly located among ourselves as mass.

This diffusion of power was facilitated by what de Tocqueville presciently understood as both the culture and effects of democracy. He was one of the first writers to conceive of power as not only being present in the majority but also as itself a form of tyranny over them.

> In the first place I see an innumerable multitude of men, alike and equal, constantly circulating around in pursuit of the petty and banal pleasures with which they glut their souls. Each one of them,

10

withdrawn into himself, is almost unaware of the fate of the rest. Mankind for him, consists in his children and his personal friends. As for the rest of his fellow citizens, they are near enough, but he does not notice them. He touches them but he feels nothing. He exists in and for himself. . . . Over this kind of men stands an immense, protective power which is alone responsible for securing their enjoyment and watching over their fate. That power is absolute, thoughtful of detail, orderly provident and gentle. . . . It gladly works for their happiness but wants to be the sole agent and judge of it.

(de Tocqueville 1969: 691–692)

This overarching power is held as an expression of the same mass population in its form as governance.

Both Foucault and de Tocqueville point the way to a new understanding of power as diffuse and ambivalent, simultaneously liberating and oppressive. But both took highly conservative stances towards it, evidently despising the vulgar acts of ordinary people as of interest only in as much as they are expressive of this massivity of power. If anything, Foucault remains considerably more distant than the figure who preceded him by more than a century, in coming to appreciate and respect the nature of mundane daily desire. I would prefer to argue, however, in that same spirit with which Marx welcomed capitalism in the *Communist Manifesto*, that these developments have many positive consequences and are the necessary foundation for any future progressive developments in the world.

Those capitalists who are directly involved in production and distribution (who might be termed commodity capitalists) have thereby become in many ways much less significant as decision-makers. Rather they have been transformed into international managerial elites competing through their ability to harness and extract profits out of a process that has gone out of their control. Their higher echelons certainly continue to make exorbitant salaries but these are minor compared to what we (for example, the massive middle class) extract by way of low prices. In modern market and political rhetoric, services are increasingly also seen as pseudo-commodities, where clients are turned into customers and the organisation of supply is supposed to model business practice. There remains, however, a group of capitalists who might be called 'finance capitalists', who do not deal with such processes but exist parasitically on the necessity for ever-increasing abstraction in money forms, through the speculative manipulation of risk and debt. These finance capitalists have if anything increasing importance, though in the relatively sealed arenas of financial capitals, rather than in direct relation to the flow of commodities from production to consumption. They are better understood therefore as parasitical (and para-statal as noted by Thrift and Leyshon, unpublished) rather than controlling capitalists. Though in alliance with pension funds, insurance funds and real

11

estate speculators, they intrude sufficiently to have effectively destroyed the fabric of several First World cities (e.g. Davis 1990 on Los Angeles; Zukin 1982 on New York), and can have a quite detrimental effect on specific retailing enterprises (Hallsworth 1992: 121–132).

THE POWER OF ECONOMICS

The politician is in practice as much the servant of the consumer as of the capitalist. Previously politics was about a variety of goals, many of them raised to the level of ideals as socialists strove with welfare statists and various conservatisms for a vision of society. Today, by contrast, a prediction made by the members of the Frankfurt School half a century ago seems to have been largely fulfilled: elections are now fought increasingly over the issue of who can most efficiently manage the economy, in short who can provide the resources to households to buy and in turn 'deliver the goods'. For the householder there may well be little remaining concern with any ideological contention between the state and the market as good or bad forms of distribution in themselves, although that is the terrain that politicians continue to dispute. I suspect that the elector is more concerned with the consequences of such distributive systems for themselves. Privatisation is accepted if the public is persuaded that the service it provides will improve, but not as an ideological commitment, since the state will equally be preferred if privatisation is found to result in the elimination of valued services to the consumer.[2]

If politicians continue to ignore these shifts in power and remain absorbed in ideological debates over the relative merits of the state and market *per se*, then the institution which has in effect best isolated politics from having to come to terms with history is the academic discipline of economics. Fine puts forward the argument that it was the rise to power of economists that has been largely responsible for the long neglect of consumption. He is surely correct, but I wish to add to this a possibly more extreme view, which is to suggest that the discipline of economics has achieved unprecedented power in the world today in large measure precisely because it has justified the complete neglect of the topic of consumption. It was very apt that one of the first books on alternative approaches to consumption (Douglas and Isherwood 1979) should have begun with a critique of conventional economists' views on the topic.

By economists I refer to those individuals who are indoctrinated through the various and abundant academic institutions that teach degree and postgraduate courses under the title of 'economics'. Although, as in all academic subjects, there are vast differences internal to the discipline – between say pure monetarists and neo-Keynesians – as Fine points out in Chapter 4 with respect to consumption, there is little to distinguish them. I shall in this section generalise a complex and heterogeneous discipline in a manner that may make its practitioners squirm. But given that many of the problems I am concerned with here result from the economist's modelling of the 'aggregate' consumer, I do not feel we need take to heart any protest about the degree to which I am choosing to pillory an 'aggregate' economist!

In general this aggregate economist holds to a model of the consumer as an individual who make a choice of goods based on particular functional requirements, exercising rational decision-making techniques to maximise his or her self-interest so that the choices made represent individual needs. Such premises are vital to the discipline for a number of reasons. First, they establish an unquestioned moral foundation which implies that all economic mechanisms that help supply goods to people are positive since people consist of unmet needs which goods requite. Second, they imply that consumption is not influenced by factors such as advertising or emulation, or even other consumption choices, which might distort this process of rational self-interest. Third, they imply that no further enquiry is necessary into the actual practices of consumption since economists need only be concerned with aggregate demand.

The bizarre nature of these premises, which accord with no serious attempt to describe actual social behaviour, depends upon the development of a discipline which cut itself off from social studies. In its repudiation of political economy, it also refused the challenge of those, such as Marx, who were primarily concerned with discovering the social relations that were hidden by economic relations. Economists' ethereal repudiations of the world were not confined to models of consumption. The same discipline developed, through its neoclassical tradition, equally abstract notions of pure trade, *laissez-faire* production systems and so forth, which consigned most existing institutions such as the state to the category of 'distortions'. Thus several generations of economists have been inculcated in the belief that the world in which they live is to be treated as a series of messy distortions to a system of other-worldly abstractions, providing a hermetic theory of ideal worlds of a purity rarely achieved in pre-secular religious beliefs. However, as with world religions, the internal disputations within economics appear to the economist so profound as to represent the very antithesis of a system of closure.

The 'power' of economists, unlike that of consumers, is relatively simple to characterise. It lies closer to the pre-Foucaultian notion of ideology. Given the discrepancy between economic theory and the world, economists could be said to have power to the degree that they have been enabled to transform human practices so that these increasingly come into correspondence with the premises of the discipline. Again the extent of this power is most clearly exemplified from the perspective of the developing world. With the collapse of colonialism many states assumed that in achieving independence they would be relatively autonomous sovereign political units able to take decisions about how their society and economy might proceed. In practice almost all such states today have come under the control of a combination of the International Monetary Fund and the World Bank. These two institutions have to an extent come together with the advent of 'policy based lending' by the latter in the 1980s (Mosley *et al.* 1991). This means that in recent years the conditionality of lending procedures has made it seem that the aim has been to effect largely political changes in the direction of liberal government. Some 'conspiracy theorists' have viewed these institutions as merely the executive branch of the United States or other similar political interests. If, however, the precise demands made by these institutions on particular states are examined, it is more evident that they translate as closely as possible to the demands of academic economic theory. That is to say, they take up each country at a phase when it has achieved levels of international debt that, in effect, renders it 'bankrupt', and they then act as supra-state 'receivers' that extend borrowing rights under certain conditions.

These conditions include the elimination of as many 'distortions' as can be achieved without the state collapsing into violent repudiation. This translates as pure *laissez-faire* economies without price controls, without protection for local industry, with free currency exchange, with privatisation of state companies, with a running down of the state sector, and with the removal of state constraints on free trade, on business practices and on employment conditions. This formula has been applied with equally disastrous results to states as small as Jamaica and as large as Russia. Although I would not wish to deny that in some cases some of these measures have proved successful, on the whole these policies may rank among the primary causes of suffering in the world today. It ensures, for example, that any state-supported institutions that might ameliorate the negative consequences of transitions to pure market relations, such as educational programmes for the unemployed, are cut. The results, which have been documented in countless countries, are that a given, for example African, state is faced with the most immediate and most brutal consequences of the purity of these economic equations.

Although proto-institutions such as GATT claim to achieve similar effects on a larger scale, to date we find that a whole raft of developing countries is every year coming closer to the economists' dreams of a pure economy. Meanwhile First World states maintain protectionism and narrow state interests most often directed against the Third World. The ability vastly to increase, in effect, oppression and poverty in the Third World is however only one sign of the power of economics. Equally significant has been the inculcation of economic models as political beliefs. In the last two decades there have arisen strategies that take the name of particular politicians, such as 'Thatcherism' and 'Reaganomics'. Such terms imply that these represent political philosophies and strategies. This is not the case – neither of these politicians had the capacity for original conceptualisation. When Margaret Thatcher stated that there is no such thing as society, but only individuals, she did so because she had increasingly absorbed a particular premise of economics and represented it as politics. These movements represent a high point in the transformation of one into the other. The situation in both cases is similar. The left tries to imagine the IMF as a political (e.g. American) interest, with *laissez-faire* as largely a cover for discretionary intervention by powerful states. By contrast, the right tries to imagine its hero and heroine as political ideologists, rather than merely the ciphers to economists. My argument is, however, that both are little more than direct translations of the same set of economic premises. These premises are derived from a specific ideology, which, as the Frankfurt School noted, probably in turn has its roots in the particular form of positivist epistemologies espoused by disciplines such as economics and psychology (see Lunt, Chapter 7).

This power of economics is further facilitated by the bifurcation in capitalism noted above. As global profitability is increasingly sucked into consumption providing excellent value for the First World consumer, the capitalist who works with the production and distribution of commodities is rendered mere midwife to the birth of this new form of power. By contrast, there remains the finance capitalist who plays a more active role in facilitating the transformation of the world by economists towards its premises. The capitalist as speculator is favoured by the increasing dominance of highly sophisticated and abstract economic theory. This is because they deal with money (or 'futures') at their most abstract level. They are thereby following what Simmel (1978) showed to be a tendency evident in one side of the dialectical property of money itself as abstraction (the other side to which is the particularity of consumption). In as much as speculators can use their freedom of financial flows to break down 'distortions', they help to assist in this hegemony of economic theory. An example is the power of speculators such as Soros to undermine national currencies as reflections of the particularity of national interests.

A similar trajectory may be traced in the development of the socialist world. Once again we find, over more than half a century, a particular economic model of the world increasingly rendering politics subservient to its interests, here based around state control rather than market control. Socialist economics had no more to say about the consumer than did liberal economics. The major differences (when seen from the hindsight of 1994) are that historical transformations caught up with existing communist regimes in a way that has not yet become so explosively evident within capitalist regimes.

State socialism collapsed,[3] despite in some cases clear achievements in the direction of egalitarianism, because of its failures with respect to two main issues. The first is easily identified as a political failure. It was the greater attraction of at least an ideal of democratic voting systems as the exercise of the aggregate population as sovereign body. The second is less evident as a 'vote', though in many respects that is what is embodied in the choices made on a daily basis by consumers as decision-makers. This expresses a desire to have power in relation to both government services and the goods provided through the market. What was rejected was what became seen as a culture of shortages that laid bare the arrogance of an idealised economic system, which nevertheless stimulated desire for goods because it constantly justified itself as the motor behind a supposedly ever-rising standard of living (Humphrey forthcoming). That this system had become unable even to conceive of the consumer as a source of values was increasingly evident. The refusal of production forces to consider the requirements, the imperatives and indeed the priorities of consumers, which was symbolised for Drakulic (1992) by the inability of Eastern European regimes to produce a satisfactory sanitary napkin, seems to have been as much a factor as democratic ideals in the final repudiation of Marxist regimes.

While Marxism declines, partly because it is understood as a subservience of practising institutions to idealised notions of pure economic beliefs, the symmetrical trajectory that occurs under the guise of 'capitalism' is bolstered by the collapse of its erstwhile adversary. Curiously, with the decline of Marxism the social sciences seem to lose interest in the explicit study of capitalism, which becomes almost the 'taken for granted' backdrop of social and cultural life as critical studies dissolve into cultural studies. By contrast, the new study of consumption should lead inexorably to the direct study of capitalism, since almost all attempts to understand consumption as practice come up against the absurdities of the neoclassical model of consumption that is increasingly used to justify both political and economic changes in the contemporary world.

There are reasons why this has not happened so far. Indeed, it is often argued that the study of consumption consists in some measure of a refusal to engage with the macro-world of politics and economics. It is likely that this would be the case in the early stages of a new study of consumption as reported in this volume. This is because such studies (as noted by several contributors to this volume) represent a pendulum swing away from the neglect of consumption as a practice in favour of the study of production relations favoured by socialist ideology. But as a more mature phase of consumption studies is reached (as I hope is starting to be reflected in this volume), I would predict the opposite effect. It was the Marxist study of capitalism that in a sense failed, because it largely projected on to practising capitalism large-scale theoretical models often as far from actual practice as neoclassical theory. It is with the decline of Marxism that practising capitalism with its variance is revealed. The profound critical studies of its emergence and development are not matched by sensitive attention to its contemporary forms and variants. The study of consumption should thereby be increasingly articulated with, and not become an opposition to, the study of the mechanisms by which goods are produced and distributed. There are likely to be many crucial links between what would thereby emerge as the diverse cultures of capitalism and the diverse worlds of consumption that will be discussed below. When research was sealed within the conflict of 'left' and 'right', it was the refusal to study consumption (because it was assumed that we knew what it was) that contributed to the refusal to study capitalism (because it was assumed that we knew what it was).

In contemporary politics the term 'consumer' looms large, and many are the changes pressed upon the economy and performed in the name of the 'consumer' and of 'consumer choice'. In practice this is the fictive consumer of economic models, the aggregate of desocialised, individual, rational choice-makers, the source of whose demands or desires is understood as entirely irrelevant to politics as it was already to economics. It is thereby economics that alleviates any potential burden upon politicians to be concerned with actual consumption, since economics has provided politics with a pseudo consumer constituted by the notion of 'choice'. The effect of this is twofold. On the one hand this rhetoric is not without some potential benefit to the consumer. It provides a basis by which their power may be acknowledged as the partial arbiters of state and commercial services and, as will be argued, it is important that progressive political parties do not reject this stance simply because they see it as arising out of a now defunct trajectory of 'right' versus 'left' rhetoric. On the other hand, this appeal to consumption emerging out of neoclassical economics is a consumer homogenised as choice, but also as mere choice.

There is a profound irony to this political development. While in politics consumption becomes synonymous with choice, I have argued that there is a much better definition of consumption that focuses on the opposite aspect of consumption as lack of choice (Miller 1987). To be a 'consumer' as opposed to being a producer implies that we have only a secondary relationship to goods. This secondary relationship occurs when people have to live with and through services and goods that they did not themselves create. The consumer society exists when, as in industrial societies today, most people have a minimal relationship to production and distribution such that consumption provides the only arena left to us through which we might potentially forge a relationship with the world.

Campbell notes that in the social sciences the term 'consumption' has become increasingly pervasive. We are being encouraged to think of people who watch films or go to schools as 'consumers' rather than audiences and students. As is often the case in such shifts in the language of legitimation, this represents a movement in ideology with specific political implications. Increasingly in market-driven politics, all action is being termed consumption choice. No account is made of the relative access to resources that make choices illusory or real, whether this is monetary or educational capital. There need be no concern with the imperatives behind consumption, the moralities, the experiential aspects of consumption or its responsibilities, since all these are discounted by the economists' notion of individual rationalities that simply secure self-interested needs through choice. Furthermore, this political ideology increasingly asserts only an image of individual consumers and the market, ignoring collective consumption and state provision. This is true even when, as in Britain, the government may have centralised provision at the same time as explicitly lauding the advantages of the market over the state.

To conclude this representation of the 'problem' of contemporary consumption, current political development rests upon current economic models. This interdependence is based upon a bizarre conception of the consumer, which protects politics from having to confront either the nature or the increasing power of consumption. Instead politics projects an aggregate of individuals who remain below the level of political concern except as assumed needs to be met by the efficiency of supply. At the level of the global economy, economic theory harnesses consumption as aggregate demand in order to attempt a transformation of the world into a pure system where all goods are made at their cheapest site of production in order that First World consumers in effect obtain the cheapest supplies of goods and companies are enabled thereby to maintain their profitability. The First World politician presents him or herself as the primary facilitator of this process and therefore privileges consumer choice as the final adjudication of all political acts, a finality that is, however, intended to be constantly deferred. One is tempted to suggest that there is a spectre haunting the world today – the spectre of the flesh and blood consumer!

The above account rests upon a notion of the aggregate or the mass. This is what allows for the present scenario and also dehumanises consumption as a process which should be used for our self-construction as humanity. This is a phase that has parallels with what Hegel called 'the unhappy consciousness', when we understand consumption to be something of significance in cultural development but only as a distant, removed phenomenon that oppresses us rather than as a source of our liberation towards citizenship. To move forward in a dialectic based upon reason requires an attempt to break down the terminologies of 'aggregate' and 'mass' and to delve deeply into the nature of consumption as a social, cultural and moral project. The premise for such a position is, of course, a reaffirmation both of the dialectic as the basis for understanding social change and of reason as the only proper foundation for progressive thinking (for a profound defence of this stance, see Rose 1993).

To challenge the hegemony of a system of representation that increasingly acts upon the world to make it adhere to its beliefs must therefore commence with a refusal to accept its image of the consumer. Furthermore we cannot hope to analyse critically this form of power without starting from the point of confession, which is the acknowledgement that we ourselves wield it. This is not only in theory but in practice. It is not the proletariat today whose transformation of consciousness would liberate the world, but the consumer. Where Hegel saw the consciousness of the philosopher as providing the resolution of suffering as distance in the world, Marx (and later Lukács) saw the proletariat as the point of a new perspicacity that would reveal the true mechanisms by which historical forces were transforming modernity. Today it is the process of consumption itself that must be engaged, through an act of self-revelation, into taking responsibility for the power that it wields without consciousness, and therefore largely without responsibility. Where once it was the language and practice of capitalists that were seen as the main barriers to consciousness, today it is the obfuscation embedded in the abstract models of economists which performs the fetishistic art of appearing to represent the world and thereby denying knowledge of its actual transformations.

At present 'homo economicus' is a powerful tool of ideological legitimation for academic, politician and consumer. But it remains so far from the actual practice of consumption that it is unlikely that many consumers or many economists actually believe this representation, even though they find it expedient to defend it. Indeed, as will be shown in the next section, this model is constantly countered by another discourse of quite contradictory clichés about the 'consumer society'. The social scientist who wishes to advance any kind of progressive understanding of society has already a responsibility to criticism. The mere sense that this is an entirely daft model of existing social action already leans one in the direction of attack. This should only be strengthened by the knowledge that the present collusion acts to the constant detriment of those who suffer from the democratic deficit. These include both the substantial minority within First World democracies and most of the developing world. It is no coincidence that most of the chapters in this book include some specific criticism of economists' approaches to consumption.

I have suggested that this historical movement may be regarded as progressive, in as far as it provides the foundation for at least formulating some ideas of how societies might develop in the future. In short, this historical shift should and will lead to the replacement of socialism as a political ideal in favour of a more feasible and more progressive formulation. The possibilities of a progressive role for consumption as a transcendence of what is currently regarded as politics is described in the penultimate section of this introduction. But any such 'ambitions' for a future progressive consumption remain far from a description of the present. Today consumption is more the problem than the solution.

THE MYTHS OF CONSUMPTION

If the above representation is accepted, it helps to explain why until the 1980s there was remarkably little by way of a sustained attempt to characterise either the imperatives behind consumption or its fundamental nature, either as general phenomenon or as local process. The continued reliance upon Veblen to characterise consumption is ample witness as to how little writing of consequence has emerged in the period since Veblen's time. Although this changed in the 1980s with a growing interest in Simmel, Benjamin and others, the yawning gap left in academic analysis has been amply filled with colloquial beliefs. Most people have abundant things to say about consumption and these have gradually crystallised around a large number of core clichés and myths as to the 'true' nature of consumer societies. Not surprisingly these bear no relation to the kind of economistic assumptions made in the dominant fraction of academic work. Instead the clichés are taken up by what might be called the dominated fraction of social science. Thus in writings about postmodernism spawned from the work of Baudrillard, Jameson and the like, these clichés often become the premises of their attempts to represent contemporary social and cultural norms. Rather than challenge the key myths, they exploit and perpetuate them.

The hegemonic political ideologies have also favoured the plethora of myth-making about consumer society, since these tell us that we already know what mass consumption is 'about'. As Hebdige (1988: 45–76) documented, this denigration is equally prevalent among those who regard themselves as right-wing and left-wing. This again supports one of the contentions of the Frankfurt School, which was that there were many key points of common ideology in the rise of this structure of politics by oppositional definition. As a result there can be few topics in which most of the population and most academics share a set of ideological assumptions which bear so little resemblance to any scholarly information we have on a particular subject. Without an explicit repudiation of these clichés, it will remain very difficult to embark on any considered attempt to characterise the actual imperatives behind consumption.

In a sense these myths form a 'package' that characterises the fundamental 'nature' of consumer society, but they may conveniently be broken down into four major groups comprising nineteen clichés. In addition to these myths there are two main assertions about the morality of consumption without which a section intended to 'remove dead wood' would certainly be incomplete. I want to suggest that while some of these may be reasonable characterisations of particular social groups or, more often, partial tendencies within these particular groups, none of them can reasonably be linked to an intrinsic property of the process of consumption itself as an act of objectification through the medium of goods.

One of the key problems in analysing consumption is that to attack these assumptions about the nefarious effects of consumerism is taken as a defence of either capitalism or inequality. This is entirely mistaken: it is merely hypocrisy to attack the prevalence of poverty, and at the same time to pretend (as many of these myths proclaim) that we are merely stunted by our wealth. I write as a middle-class academic literally 'enjoying' resources and access to goods which few elites of previous generations would have contemplated, and as a member of the 'global dictatorship' described above. I cannot but think that an elimination of poverty which gave others equal access to such empowering forces would be a moral and progressive change in the world. The acknowledgement of consumption need not detract from the critique of inequality and exploitation, but this critique is foundering precisely because the enormous consequences and attractions of consumption are left out of the analysis. Facing up to and learning from the experience of being middle-class consumers may assist rather than prevent the foundation of a critique of poverty.

Myth 1: Mass Consumption Causes Global Homogenisation or Global Heterogenisation

This comprises five main assertions:-

1 That the world of commodities has destroyed significant differences between peoples.
2 The opposite idea that the world of consumption is a postmodern condition that has destroyed the basis for significant cultural homogeneities.
3 That commodities are the prime force behind Americanisation.
4 That consumption is intrinsically linked to capitalism and the dominance of capitalism.
5 That consumer culture is an aspect of an overall erosion of culture *per se*.

Such theories tend to pick up those bits of consumer culture that suit their premises. Thus homogenisation is 'proved' by the existence of brands such as Coca-Cola or Levi jeans. While such brands are indeed global and gain their significance precisely as objectifications of a superordinate sense of global, they are a small proportion of actual branded goods. More generally, goods and brands can be shown to have had considerable difficulty homogenising around the idea of Europe let alone the globe. Recent anthropological research has also shown that identical goods may relate to quite different issues in varied local contexts. Similarly while one can observe in some instances the breaking up of Fordist uniformities into postmodern reassertions of locality, there exists simultaneously the growth of new global identities such as in 'world music' or around international media.

It is therefore remarkably easy to find 'evidence' for both increasing homogenisation and heterogenisation, since both of these processes are certainly occurring in the world today. While it is therefore reasonable to examine new technologies and goods to investigate how far they lend themselves to either of these two processes, consumption itself is more commonly the form taken by them and their means of expression. It is not, in and of itself, a causative presence. This is particularly true of Americanisation, which has become an important ideological symbol but is increasingly untrue as a characterisation of the vast transnational corporations. These are as likely to be based in Europe, in the Pacific Rim or to an often unremarked extent even to be emergent from developing countries.

It might seem more reasonable to see capitalism as itself increasingly dominant in the modern world. But to accept that this is an inevitable consequence of mass consumption is to accept capitalism's own assertion that it is the only structure capable of providing the goods for mass consumption. Partly this derives from a natural tendency to assume that wealth is simply a reflection of the desire for goods. As noted in the anthropological chapter (see Chapter 8), there is evidence that peoples who have never had many possessions show a greater desire for goods than the materialistic West. Indeed, the very concept of poverty rests upon the opposed assumption, which is that many people who don't have goods desire them. Any system that opposes itself to capitalism, unless it embraces asceticism as a creed, will tend to promise the capacity to provide such goods today. Various societies developed mass goods (e.g. medieval China, see Hamilton and Lai 1989) without the typical infrastructure and ideology of capitalism. In Chapter 5 Glennie uses historical materials to demonstrate how often cultures of consumption preceded mass markets, rather than being produced by them. It is clearly of some importance in considering alternatives to capitalism that these be at least imagined as equally proficient in serving consumer imperatives. My representation of the relationship between consumption and capitalism in the first half of this introduction is therefore a reflection on a historical dialectic, not evidence for the intrinsic propensity of consumption.

The idea that 'consumer culture' is a misnomer, being a state other than that of 'culture', implies that the new diversities and forms of sociality found in consumer cultures are somehow diminished with respect to earlier forms. This represents a typical dualism which asserts a kind of static 'tradition' that has never existed. Indeed, the one 'tradition' that seems remarkably common even from centuries ago is that each generation regards the new generation as a significant decline in true values from themselves. In general the myth of cultural erosion emphasises both consumption as the repudiation of local history and a refusal to regard new forms of diversity as aspects of 'culture'.[4] Both of these assumptions relate to the wider myth of consumption as an opposition to sociality and authenticity which will be discussed below.

Myth 2: Consumption is Opposed to Sociality

This myth comprises three main assertions:-

1 That consumption is premised on materialism as an unreasonable desire for goods.
2 That consumption is opposed to sociality since it is premised on a concern for goods which replaces a previous concern for people.
3 That we are increasingly dominated by the world of goods and are thereby diminished in our humanity.

This myth relies upon one of the principal foundations of the modern ideology of Western philosophy, one which achieved clarity for the first time during the French Revolution. This is based upon the reification of the person as a replacement of the divine in constituting the proper measure of all things. As Sennett (1976) noted, this represented also a marked shift in the conceptualisation of things. Whereas previously people were adjudged according to 'stations' in life revealed by their appearance, now appearance could be often viewed as a misleading 'act' which mystified the true nature of personhood which lay deep within. Indeed, one of the styles of the post-revolutionary period was a near nakedness, asserting the idea of the truth of the natural person as against the artifice of manufactured appearance.

Since the French Revolution this ideology has asserted itself most clearly in a myth of the past, or of the primitive, who is the possessor of true unmediated sociality. The climax of this ideology comes with the debates over postmodernism, which renders all consumption as a reification opposed to true persons. We are now only mannequins for the world of objects as produced by capitalism. In essence the more persons are manifested through objects the more they have lost their fundamental personhood.

As with a number of these myths about consumption, this depends upon a notion of some prior historical state which, in this case, was of relatively pure sociality. Anthropology which is often looked to for the characterisation of this state does indeed have as its core topic the study of kinship as the 'essence' of sociality. However, one of the founding figures of anthropology demonstrated some time ago the absurdity of the dualism between person and object upon which this myth depends. Mauss's classic book *The Gift* does not start with the best-known example, of how an object exchanged between two persons creates a relationship between them of reciprocal obligation (Mauss 1966: 8–10), and therefore the object carries 'person'-like properties. Rather the first example is of persons (in this case children) who are used themselves as gifts to create solidarity within a larger kindred, in which case persons are exchanged as having 'thing'-like properties (ibid.: 6–8). Throughout this early section Mauss is showing that in non-capitalist societies the relationship of object and person is so close that the distinction is often blurred. Modernity arises with the separation into a sense of 'pure' personhood, not with a greater subservience to objects.

In my own research in London (Miller 1988), I found evidence for an association that I expect may be quite common. It is those persons who found they were best able to express their relationships through their manipulation of their material worlds who formed the closest social networks, while those who felt unvalorised in their social relations also felt impotent with respect to any manipulation of their material culture. Of course, there are pathologies of fetishism in which people become obsessed with goods which have no redolence of social relations about them, but ironically it may be far more often the narcissistic obsession with personhood which detracts from social relations, not the materialism which is often an expression of social relations through a process of objectification.

Similarly the use of persons to objectify moral projects often takes the form of essentialism and racism as 'types' of person are credited with certain key characteristics – the 'Irish' are this or the 'blacks' are that. In many respects the use of objects to generalise human characteristics and values is a progressive rather than a regressive tendency. The condemnation of consumption often begins by noting the increasing use of consumer stereotypes such as 'yuppie' to characterise people. These authors fail even to consider the possible advantages of such labelling over the previous prevalent tendency to consider it quite sufficient to label people by occupation as 'docker' or 'secretary', which as Gortz (1982) pointed out, reflected largely the unchallengeable dictates of business projected on to a subservient population.

Myth 3: Consumption is Opposed to Authenticity

This myth comprises five main assertions:-

1 That the rise of consumption represents a loss of authenticity.
2 That consumption is an act of free choice.
3 That the relationship of consumption contrasts with that of production by being intrinsically more superficial.
4 That mass consumption has seen a rise in irrational desires which replace an earlier more utilitarian and rational relationship to material culture.
5 That a rise in mass consumption is necessarily to be opposed to involvement in production.

Behind many of these assertions lies the idea that at some earlier period humanity lived in a firm relationship to the world around it, within which it was socialised as part of larger cosmological, moral and utilitarian projects. Today, by contrast, we simply choose/purchase our worlds with a largely ephemeral and irrational lack of genuine concern. Of course, there have been changes and it is probably true that fashion, style and other more transient forms of relationship to goods have become more common for more people, but we must be careful as to how we interpret such changes. Similarly many of the constraints of socialisation and circumstance remain with us. Consumers may exercise some degree of choice as part of their activity of consumption, but equally often they are forced to consume governmental services such as public housing and public medicine or indeed live with a paucity of goods that must be appropriated as their mode of life, but are far from some pure expression of their will as an act of choice.

Current research suggests that the simple gulf drawn between 'traditional' times and the present has been overdrawn. Consumer culture is often found today to carry with it many more of the cosmological concerns that were developed in older periods, as in the transformation of Pacific societies (Thomas 1991). Similarly we may recognise that new, sometimes unprecedented forms of cultural difference may be just as significant (authentic) to people, since it is not just today that traditions have been 'invented'. The Renaissance was no less important just because it was a pastiche of 'classical' styles that preceded it by more than a millenium.

The problem with a concern with objects that are more transient, or a concern with the surface of style, is that it comes up against one of the fundamental tenets of classical Western philosophy – the critique of superficiality. Most respected European and North American philosophical traditions, and the more colloquial ideologies associated with them, assume what might be called a 'depth' ontology. This implies that 'being' is some unchanging deep interior, often associated with roots, which is held against and opposed to the sense of surface or façade. This ideology clearly infects debates about modernism in the opposition to façade but most especially the debate over postmodernism, where lack of depth and constancy is the principal accusation held against modern life. But there is no reason why important issues of identity, and indeed of ontology, should not be conceptually located in both more transient and more surface-orientated modes. For at least one group of Trinidadians the concern with style is quite evidently profound because there is a very different relationship between surface and being. Indeed, their most common accusation against other Trinidadians is precisely that they are given to storage and interiorisation. This is regarded as the primary source of their anti-social nature. Henry Louis Gates (1988) provides just one recent argument for such a critique of the connotations of the term superficial, and there are others more particular to the circumstance of Trinidad (for details see Miller 1994).

One of the most bizarre clichés about shopping and modern mass consumption is the assumed unprecedented nature of those irrationalist and fantastic desires associated with it. I would not for a moment deny that shopping is an enchanted domain, but the discourse appears to imply that this is to be held against some other, or some previous, relation to material culture which was strictly functionalist. It is as though our interest in material culture would be pragmatic and related to some concept of basic needs and true interests were it not for the blandishments of capitalism. Sociologists, in particular, almost inevitably write about consumption as though contemporary society were a decline from some earlier state in which our main relationship to objects was constructed through some form of utility or need (as in vulgarised versions of the term 'use-value'). But whether we recall contemporary Melanesian cultivation of long yams or seventeenth-century Netherlanders' concern with tulips, an abstract principle of utility and basic need is something of a cultural rarity. It is extremely hard to find evidence for merely functional or utilitarian relations to material culture in any non-industrial society. Even in an impoverished peasant village in South Asia, an analysis of everyday earthenware found functional efficiency to be of far less concern than other criteria for determining the precise shape and form of mundane material culture (Miller 1985: 51–74). If anything, it is the abstraction of pure function which is unprecedented.

Finally there is an assumption that the rise of mass consumption means a fall in our involvement with production which, through a combination of 'vulgar' Marxism and aesthetic ideals of creativity, has continually been seen as the primary site for the proper creation of authenticity. I have argued (Miller 1987: 178–217) that consumption is, a priori, potentially a more suitable process than production for social construction in industrialised societies, and that Marx and the Victorians were quite wrong to privilege production. But even if we were to agree with their premise, one could question the assumed decline in production-related activities. Certainly it is the case that workers' involvement in factory and agrarian labour has markedly declined. These represent, however, simply the coercive requirement for individuals to earn a living, and any attachment to such labour is often more a sense of acquiescence than identity. By contrast, the new regimes of leisure have allowed a massive democratisation of production as most people have increased opportunities to be creative with respect to some form of labour which previously was dominated by services. Whether this labour is in car-care, cake decoration, do-it-yourself or hobbies, there has arisen a plethora of pursuits in which people buy small-scale production facilities (e.g. beer making equipment) and from that point take over those production activities with which they choose to be involved. It would seem to be a very weird kind of Marxism which came to view pure commoditised industrial wage-labour as a 'better' source of authenticity than self-selected, decommodified processes of production practised by the mass population. The point being of course that consumption, so far from being opposed to production, increasingly involves production at those points when the consumer prefers to be involved in creative labour. It is only ethnographic studies, such as by Finnegan (1989) on music-making in the English town of Milton Keynes, that reveal just how widespread is mass participation in creative activities.

Myth 4: Consumption Creates Particular Kinds of Social Being

This myth comprises six main assertions:-

1 That consumers tend naturally towards emulation as their main mode of social relation.
2 That consumers tend naturally towards competition over status as their main mode of social relation.
3 That consumer societies are necessarily more individualistic than other societies.
4 That consumers are given to conspicuous consumption and display as against other kinds of sociality.
5 That the consumer society is necessarily more hedonistic than other societies.
6 That consumption is naturally an inegalitarian process that acts of itself to create relative disempowerment.

What these six assertions have in common is that they confuse the characterisation of a particular consumer society with an assumed characterisation of the intrinsic nature of consumption itself. Let us pretend that the primary image of a consumer society were not (as in practice it usually is) the United States, but Norway. There is no reason why this should not be the case since Norwegians have as high a standard of living and seem just as devoted to mass consumption as North Americans. It is clearly problematic to attempt to characterise a 'national' character, but if we refer only to some ethnographic work on a region of Norway (e.g. Gullestad 1984, 1992) then the following generalisations about consumer society would seem to follow.

First mass consumption is highly normative and is clearly concerned to avoid status competition at all costs in, for example, the interior decoration of the home. Consumption is therefore opposed to individualism but largely concerned with community approbation and remains at a generalised level rather than permitting any form of individualistic conspicuous consumption. Consumption therefore becomes an instrument of relatively rigid egalitarian morality, and while it would be unfair to call it 'dour', it is certainly only in small measure given to hedonistic concerns. From the perspective of Norway, these would become the established implications of living within a predominantly consumer society.

27

In order to argue against these generalisations about the intrinsic 'nature' of consumer society, we would have to assume that somehow Norway was not a 'proper' consumer society, or was inevitably going to become more like the United States. This is, of course, nonsense. It is merely that the most influential texts were far more concerned with the problems of particular cultural contexts and attempted to project consumption as the 'cause' of these characteristics, while refusing to allow for comparative analysis either of consumer societies or indeed of capitalism itself. De Tocqueville was able to formulate most of these traits described in these myths as typical of American society long before there was any conception of ubiquitous shopping malls. Even within those societies that are characterised by Veblenesque traits, such as status competition and emulation, it is possible to suggest that key forms that have previously been assumed to assert these values, and to be handmaidens of capitalist desire to stimulate such competition, may on closer study be found to relate to quite different social concerns. An example would be Christmas, which has been taken to be a festival celebrating hedonism and materialism, but which on closer inspection may be seen to be often quite opposed to materialism, though open to appropriation by capitalist interests (see various papers in Miller 1993).

Finally, in addition to the myths of consumption, there has developed in academia as much as in the colloquial world of discourse an increasingly meaningless debate as to the morality of goods. This seems to depend almost entirely on whether consumption is seen as a passive process reflecting producer interests or an active process representing consumer interests. This leads to two main arguments:

Assertion A: Consumption is Bad

This approach derives from ideological positions that project on to consumption an unholy mixture of left asceticism and right conservatism that want consumption to be nothing more than a symbol of the 'fall' of humanity from some earlier state of grace (Hebdige 1988: 45–76). Many of the previous 'myths' are simply extensions of this fundamental position. The manner by which this morality of consumption derives from an opposition between the notion of an 'active' and a 'passive' consumer is particularly well dealt with by Morley in Chapter 9 on media studies. The specific implications drawn from this position are criticised (above) through the various myths to which it gives rise.

Assertion B: Consumption is Good

Equally problematic, and less fully covered in the above section, is a much more recent phenomenon that renders the consumer as paragon of creative individualism. In this vein the consumer becomes a kind of artist of popular culture, painting on the canvas of our world a tapestry of colourful subcultures in an explosion of celebratory 'identities'. This trajectory of consumer characterisation is evident in the development of cultural studies, popular culture studies, media studies, anthropology, etc. Absurdly, consumption becomes 'the transgressive tactics of the weak' (de Certeau 1984: xviii–xx). My own work is properly subject to critique in as much as it may have favoured this tendency. Similarly important historical work on English working-class culture associated with Williams (e.g. 1961) and Thompson (e.g. 1963) which attempted to construct a more informed and realistic view of the history of popular culture, has tended to be developed into this same romantic celebration of all such culture as 'creativity' and 'resistance'. In most of these cases, the trend has probably arisen as a 'pendulum' swing in the repudiation of many of the assertions discussed in this section. Of course, there are cases where consumption can clearly be shown to have had positive consequences for the consumer, or even transgressive ones, quite apart from the utilitarian benefits obtained, and it was well worth insisting on this possibility when it was largely being denied. But I suspect that it is far more common for the tactics of the weak to be concerned with gaining access to resources than in using acts of consumption as some kind of 'resistance'.

The idea that most consumer empowerment is a result of resistance to the forces that create commodities is highly implausible. As an academic I am 'empowered' when a new software package allows me to replace some very tedious and repetitive action, which previously took up a great deal of my time. I may now delegate this operation (e.g. spelling corrections) to the far swifter and more reliable mechanisms of my computer.[5] But this empowerment is based on my acquiescence to the product – learning to obey the strict instructions without mistakes. Acts of 'resistance', such as the computer virus, have not proved particularly enabling. Computer work stations may, of course, be used to foster unpleasant forms of secretarial work, but less so than the endless rows of clerks copying figures by pen that disfigured the workscape at the turn of the century.

Increasingly writers who once ascribed to Marxist dismissals of consumption developed a variant of culture studies that will often wax lyrical about consumption as the site of resistance to capitalism, but thereby ignores any negative impact of consumption itself. Ironically, as Belk's chapter suggests, it is researchers in the field of business studies (which until recently would never have thought to criticise the world of business and consumption) who are now developing highly critical perspectives on consumption from feminist, neo-Marxist and other perspectives.

Today the need is clearly for a more mature phase of consumption studies. The infant consumer studies must learn to transcend such simplistic

29

images of the 'bad' and the 'good' breast (consumer). Indeed, any attempt merely to read off consumption as 'good' or 'bad' seems to miss the key point of recent history. It has become about as useful a task as trying to determine whether kinship is 'good' or 'bad'. Consumption is simply a process of objectification – that is, a use of goods and services in which the object or activity becomes simultaneously a practice in the world and a form in which we construct our understandings of ourselves in the world. In my own work I have focused on the manner by which people appropriate the objects of consumption to construct moral projects, not necessarily intended by the producers (an approach originally inspired by Hebdige 1988: 77–115). It is important to distinguish this point from the moral adjudication on consumption. I would continue to maintain that consumption is much more autonomous of business intentions and manipulations of the symbolic potential of commodities than was previously thought. This is of little concern to business, which deals with sales and not the subsequent histories of the object sold – for them consumption is only about purchase.

What does not follow is that, because the project represented is thereby more 'true' to the consumer, this is of itself a good thing. Indeed, one could envisage an object which is being sold on the slogan that it helps liberate women from some aspect of drudgery and can be seen to have that potential. This same object may then be appropriated within the world of consumption as a class marker for the denigration of those who did not know about it. The object has been 'appropriated' by the consumer but for a more nefarious purpose than that intended by the distributor! Consideration of consumption has been torn apart by the conventional polarity of 'right' and 'left' politics. This meant that it was either evil, or a form of resistance, depending only upon its relationship to capitalism. There was no attempt to suggest either that business might produce progressive goods with progressive implications or that consumers might independently produce morally indefensible imperatives and appropriations. Again this debate prevented, rather than encouraged, any attempt to investigate the nature of consumer imperatives, since it merely projected a 'politicised' stance upon consumption acts.

WHAT IS CONSUMPTION?

The previous section seems essential to a proper consideration of the nature and imperatives of contemporary consumption because otherwise our field of vision is hopelessly cluttered with the spent shells of spent ideologies. If we are therefore to engage with the consumer as social being, to provide empathy and respect, as the foundation for observational encounter, then we must first strip away these assertions as to the assumed nature of this activity.

Attempts to construct precise definitions in social studies are, contrary to many expectations, as often a barrier as an aid to understanding, imposing constraints rather than liberating enquiry, and leading to rather pedantic arguments about semantics. None of the contributors to this volume reduces consumption merely to acts of purchase – which is that definition that suits business, since it is the only consumer act that affects their profitability. Furthermore it is essential that the term consumption includes the reception of state services as well as the products of the market; otherwise we would not be able to consider the lessons to be learnt from lack of attention to consumption in regimes where most goods and services came from the state. Similarly we would not be helped by following the colloquial use of the term, which tends to restrict it to individuals. This is because consumption may often be the public act of the crowd, or the state appropriation of an importation. Even with respect to daily purchasing of goods, this more often involves the 'moral economy' of the household than merely an individual agent.

An alternate approach to the definition of consumption is to examine the meaning the term might have within a particular historical conjecture. Clearly, little purpose would be served by simply projecting it on to a society whose concepts of being and exchange are radically different, as in Strathern's (1988) portrayal of Melanesian populations. We need to be sensitive to the possibility that consumption represents a kind of activity quite different in North China to Argentina, or for women as opposed to men, within a given region.

I would, however, argue that such relativism needs to be tempered by the academic requirement to generalise as a means to analysis. The salience and poignancy of acts of consumption may have both increased and altered in recent years as a result of developments in industry, trade and bureaucracy. This has led to the development of large-scale rationalisation in institutions and bureaucracies which at least take on the aura of impersonality and anonymity with respect to their workers and clients. This means that people increasingly come to face the world in a secondary relation, in which they do not themselves identify with the institutions that produce and distribute goods and services. To that extent they increasingly see themselves as consumers as opposed to producers. I have argued elsewhere (Miller 1987) that this establishes one of the main imperatives behind much modern consumption, which is an attempt by people to extract their own humanity through the use of consumption as the creation of a specificity, which is held to negate the generality and alienatory scale of the institutions from which they receive goods and services. This generalisation may not hold in certain circumstances, either because people continue to identify closely with large-scale institutions (such as many Scandinavians' positive sense of the welfare state in the 1970s), or because they have unusual confidence in their abilities to appropriate, and feel

31

relatively little estrangement from the market (as I have found, contrary to my expectations, in Trinidad). Nevertheless, as a generality regarding the global significance of consumption, I would stand by this theory.

Another example that suggests a more generalised development of a new sense of consumption comes from the rise of the green movement. The ubiquity and rapid growth of 'green' consciousness must have resulted in another major increase in people's self-conception as consumers. In this case, however, it is not necessarily just a sense of consumers opposed to producers but also an image of us as the consumers of a set of finite resources constituted by the 'natural' resources of the globe as a whole. It shows the flexibility of the term consumption. Where the source of goods was not a consideration, the term consumption did not exploit the semantic potential of the idea that something is thereby consumed. With the rise of green consciousness, however, this semantic element is brought into play as an integral part of the term consumption, which becomes self-conscious about the finality of the resources that are thereby removed by the act of consumption.

This suggests that rather than attempting to define consumption, we need to be sensitive to the dynamic fields within which it shifts its meaning and to refuse the more constraining uses of the term. Nevertheless this liberalism might lead to an unwelcome conclusion which would lead to the dismissal of the term itself. Some have suggested that the kind of work represented in this book is a sort of category mistake, a reification of a process, which is really just a mystifying façade for a more authentic object of concern. For example, Friedman (1994) in a recent volume on consumption implies that to focus so squarely upon this topic is to miss an important point, which is that modern consumption is 'really' about 'identity'. We are as it were remaining within a fetishised concern with objects, media, etc., when we ought to be looking at the problematics of identity as the crucial topic of modernity. Others have tried to reduce consumption to topics such as time management or access to knowledge; and as Belk's chapter shows, consumption studies may be used to explore any number of fashions in academic analysis. A common reductionism is performed by simply privileging one of the contextualising social dimensions, that is to say consumption is 'really' about class/gender/ethnicity, etc., or at least that it ought to be.

To take Friedman as a representative of this tendency, I would argue that this is a mistaken criticism for two reasons. The first is that as anthropologists are increasingly becoming aware (Strathern 1991), almost any topic can become the context for another. If, for example, we accepted his suggestion and tried to reduce consumption to identity, we would find the same accusation of reification still applies. As Kapferer (forthcoming) has recently argued (following in part Foucault), the plethora of current discussions about multiple identities, plural identities, or indeed just identity, fails to acknowledge that the concept of identity itself arose in alignment with the development of modern bureaucracy. For bureaucracies, it has been increasingly important to establish clear attributes of personhood that could be registered and responded to. These become projected as people's 'identities', be these ethnic, class, national, religious or some other. In short, to reduce consumption to identity is not only to pass the buck, but to replace one reification with what is possibly a still more problematic one.

Of course, to render any topic as the focus of our analysis is in some sense to 'reify' it, but as long as there is an understanding that this is a necessary stage in the academic process of analysis, such reification may be no bad thing. Equally important would be the second argument that this particular topic has contemporary significance, and not just (as would be the case of identity) undoubted salience. In an introduction that has started with the argument that consumption is indeed the vanguard of history, this is obviously not a particularly burdensome responsibility. The topic of consumption is critical today because it has become the fulcrum of dialectical contradiction. On the one hand, consumption appears as the key contemporary 'problem' responsible for massive suffering and inequality. At the same time it is the locus of any future 'solution' as a progressive movement in the world, by making the alienatory institutions of trade and government finally responsible to humanity for the consequences of their actions.

There are then generalities that can usefully be made with respect to the topic of consumption, but when consumption becomes almost as ubiquitous as kinship, then generality is likely to be matched by ever more diverse specificity. Indeed, this relationship between increasing specificity and increasing generality is a hallmark of dialectical analysis. Specificity is equally important since it is what lifts consumption studies out of the abuses that psychological and economic theories have rendered possible, and forces us to be concerned with the particular imperatives behind consumption acts. This is the relativistic antidote to the easily generated universals to which any branch of studies is subject. The best source of such relativism is the detailed enquiry into particular cases. Examples in this volume show that consumption may be employed as central to the production of difference, as in framing off multiple and plural identities, but equally may be an act of totalisation where individuals or groups locate themselves unambiguously in the semiotics of an object or commodity sign. Consumption may be dictated by a restless search to find the right objectification of 'success' or 'modernity' but equally can just be the 'other' to asceticism or experienced as the stability of comfort and 'self-evident' utilitarian need. Consumption revolves around a vast number of object worlds each with its specific tendencies. There is a whole subdiscipline constituted by the history of drugs (such as tea, coffee, tobacco and alcohol) which were central to the articulation of mass consumption and colonialism (Goodman 1994). Today there are often relatively autonomous regimes of clothing, foodstuffs and high technology, each of which produces its own studies (see Fine, Chapter 4). There is also a particular concern with the 'pathologies' of consumption, which may address issues as diverse as shoplifting, drug abuse and materialism.

Consumption as a topic cannot therefore be usefully defined. Rather it must be followed as dialectic between the specificity of regions, groups and particular commodity forms on the one hand, and the generality of global shifts in the political economy and contradictions of culture on the other. The most convincing studies of consumption, such as by Schama (1987) and Simmel (1978), are probably those that most fully enunciate the centrality of contradiction in the projects and imperatives that are carried by this practice. It follows that, in the next section on the housewife as consumer, I am not trying to comprehend all the possible collective and varied forms of consumption practice. Rather I am taking one particular instance, which may be regarded as of particular significance, in order to exemplify the kinds of contradiction that are thrown up by the study of consumption.

THE HOUSEWIFE

Early on in this introduction it was suggested that the quintessence of power in the modern world lies objectified in the image of the First World housewife. Indeed, I termed the housewife a global dictator in recognition of the sheer authority that the collective decision-making, which she stands for, now exercises. This is hardly likely to be an intuitive (or indeed a popular) assertion, and I argued that it required a transformation of the ideas of Foucault and de Tocqueville to comprehend the nature of this new form of power. The housewife may stand as the key figure in both my negative and positive reading of the historical position of contemporary consumption. She commands the fate of developing countries as one of poverty or relative affluence. But she also commands the progressive activity by which consumption is used to extract culture as the self-construction of humanity from the intractable but essential institutions of the modern world, such as the market or bureaucracy.

I recognise, of course, that consumption is not synonymous with housewifery. There are many men who are primary consumers for households, and much infrastructure and provisioning that is purchased by institutions rather than individuals. Nevertheless, while in most cases not the consumer, she continues to stand as image for consumer decision-making. In many countries the housewife is far more than a figure of speech and there remain (or are now coming into being) vast numbers of women for whom such generalisations may usefully be retained as a description of the obligations they are required to fulfil. It is likely that, especially since the development of feminism, many individual females will be struggling with the burden of normative expectations that the term 'housewife' projects upon her. This then becomes a specific example of the general problem of releasing the contradictions and experience of consumers from the aggregate categories that they either know of, as in this case, or which are projected upon them at a level they rarely encounter, as in the statistical models of economists.

What is of particular note is that over the last two decades there has been built up an image of housewives which may be generalised from aggregate observational material mainly derived from feminist academics. This generality built up from the ground could hardly be further removed from the common assumptions and assertions as to the nature either of power, or of consumption, which has been projected on to her from ideological debates. This disparity is perhaps the reason it has been so hard to discover her role as the fulcrum of modernity.

Take, for example, the economists' vision of the intensely individualistic, maximising rationalist who seeks pure utility in independent choices within the world of goods. Take, in addition, the colloquial picture of the intensely competitive, status-seeking, emulator, as superficial as she is unauthentic. When studies have been made of the consumption imperatives of housewives in, for example, London, then an entirely different picture is drawn (from Oakley 1976 to Wallman 1984). The flesh and blood housewife emerges as one of the least individualistic of the social beings of the First World. Her source of desire is largely repressed by modest subservience within larger projects. The best characterisation of the source of these concerns is probably captured in the term 'the moral economy of the home',[6] in which the act of consumption is addressed to the objectification of those values that arise out of the dynamics of family life within the domestic sphere. This should not be assumed to be some collapse into the private domain of some previous ideal collectivity. As mass observation showed for Britain, true 'neighbourhoods' of the Ealing comedies variety were always pretty thin on the ground.

It is increasingly in the array of commodities as brought to life in the consumption practices of the household that moral, cosmological and ideological objectifications are constructed to create the images by which we understand who we have been, who we are, and who we might or should be in the future. It is the sheer scale of the object world which assists us in making it increasingly possible for these to be merely partial connections, bits and pieces of often contradictory 'habiti' rather than the more systematic habitus of traditional socialisation analysed by Bourdieu (1977). Furthermore, as almost all studies of housewifery since Oakley's pioneering work have demonstrated, this is one of the least valorised, most lowly and most commonly denigrated practices of the modern world. The self-effacing, normative, moral and aesthetic concerns of housewifery reveal starkly the absurdities of economic theory and the barrenness of colloquial accounts of consumption. The very concept of 'choice' is revealed to be very far from some autonomous, independently generated act. Rather it is a limited condition that bears the burden of histories of social category formation in terms of class, gender and other parameters, the normative adjudication of families and peers, and the pressure of business attempts to ensure their particular profitability. Meanwhile politics and, as the Trinidadian joke demonstrates, sometimes almost the entire male population, has often been sequestered in the cause of denigrating the nature of this consumer power.

This suggests that the exercise of power which derives from consumption is not experienced as empowerment in the daily life of those who wield it. Indeed, while shopping and consumption may be a source of considerable pleasure, it may equally be regarded as the source of considerable anxiety. Housewives are given the burden of provisioning for their household. This is a task whose skills are commonly uncredited but whose failures, as in a lack of thrift, or forgetting to replace some mundane item such as toilet paper, may quickly become the source of blame. Even the considerable power of finance capital in the political economy finds its echo in the increasing importance of credit and debt within these regimes of pleasure and anxiety for those dealing with household budgets. To view the housewife as the possessor of power in the world today is then to appreciate her burden, and to appreciate that power today may be as oppressive to those who wield it as to those who do not.

Though not experienced as a source of power, it does not follow that the housewife lacks insight into her situation, nor that she fails to exercise power in its diffused daily context. It has often been assumed that the First World housewife is unwittingly shoring up oppressive institutions because she is beaten by the sheer magnitude of capitalist advertising, etc. The real problem may be much greater – it is possible that the housewife is responding with far more perspicacity than the average academic, in understanding the conditions of her existence. This is shown in the actions she takes to foster the positive and ameliorate the negative consequences of consumption, through those practices at which experience has skilled her. From her position the housewife has a dual interest. One is to extract the maximum quantity of value, in the sense of the cumulative productive capacity of workers and machines, through insisting on as low prices as possible. Her success is evident in that she has overtrumped capitalism to replace the capitalist as the main instrument for extracting value to the benefit of her household. But, in addition, she has to negate dialectically this sense of value as abstracted labour at the same moment that she obtains it, by transmuting it as far as possible into 'value' in the colloquial sense of that term. She has to create through consumption the moral and affective qualities that sustain and reproduce social relations using a variety of social mechanisms (such as the gift discussed in Chapter 2 by Belk). This may often involve either the appropriation of the meaning given to goods by producers or the creative construction of her social relations through consumption processes. Consumption is more than merely a shift or appropriation in meaning (for which see McCracken 1988: 71–89). It is a process of objectification (Miller 1987).

At present we can discern in political economy the macro-effects of aggregate shopping (and the transformation of state provision), but we have little research that would allow us better to comprehend this crucial moment in the history of value. Sociology and cultural studies, in particular, have poured forth accounts of consumer imperatives. They describe a new self-reflexive, materialistic, hedonistic desire. This is backed by a mixture of esoteric theories of postmodernity and psychoanalysis. These are projected on to housewives and other consumers in what has become a largely self-perpetuating discourse. To choose between these and the economist's projections of individual maximisers is an unpleasant task. If a single factor may be discerned as of overwhelming importance today, it is probably that old-fashioned 'virtue' of thrift. Apart from some consumer behaviour literature and the odd television programme such as 'The Price is Right', there is little respect paid to housewives' knowledge of comparative pricing. Yet this may well still be a vital part of the moral economy of the home as well as an important element of rivalry and status competition between housewives. Current transformations in retailing are in the direction of what seem to be universally disliked, out-of-town bulk-buying warehouses. These may successfully challenge the promotion of shopping as a pleasant leisure experience through aggressive competition on price.

This suggests that while academics have assumed that the appeal of capitalism is to 'vices' such as hedonism and materialism, such an inference is neither demonstrated nor likely. It is equally possible that the prime motivation is thrift, which is regarded by the consumer as a virtue. Much, if not most consumption may be the search for good value through low prices for commodities and services regarded as household necessities. Furthermore, in closing the circle from housewifery back to political economy, it may be noted that it is the same virtue to which appeal is made by politicians who favour free markets as serving the 'thrifty', 'sensible' housewife. Similarly GATT is advocated by politicians on almost the sole criterion that it will produce the lowest possible priced goods from the global economy to the consumer. Arguments about the decline in actual housewifery make little difference to this powerful rhetoric directed to her image.

We await the kind of qualitative studies that could show whether the key consumer imperative retains continuity with older concerns for thrift. That is the housewife's objectification of the household as a locus retaining value, which is then expressed in monetary terms. If this turns out to be the case, it is far from the economist's vision of individual choice, but equally distant from cultural critique of materialism and self-indulgent subjectivities. Indeed, the problem may be that modern writers are keen to associate something that has such harmful effects through its involvement with capitalism with an imperative that can also be despised and that they do not have to associate themselves with. It may be, however, that the situation is more complex and contradictory and that the dominant consumption imperative which justifies Third World and other oppressions is precisely what these same writers might regard as the anti-materialistic 'virtue' lacking in the modern consumer!

At present housewives' consumption seems to reflect a perspicacity of action rather than theory. But in keeping with a materialist grand narrative, one might well expect such a shift in the material foundations of culture to have a commensurate effect in the field of ideology. I want to suggest that this effect may be demonstrated in the phenomenon of feminism. While it is common for anthropologists to analyse 'other' people's cosmologies in terms of shifts that the people in question do not themselves use to legitimate their beliefs, this is a strategy that is rarely turned back on to ourselves. The rise of feminism is therefore most often regarded as the subjective 'coming to consciousness' of oppression, by women. But by the canons of feminism, women have been oppressed in many times and places without any equivalent movement to consciousness. One reading of this shift in global cosmology might relate it closely to the historical movements that have been documented here. If consumption is indeed the vanguard of history then, by implication, it is women in particular who have radically transformed the world.

I suspect that this might well have been evident, but for a fortuitous historical conjunction (which of course is how history usually happens!). There is increasing historical evidence that the nineteenth century saw the development, across much of Western Europe, of a powerful consumer cooperative movement, which in some countries rivalled the productionist equivalent. Furlough (1991) shows that in France women were not permitted the leadership roles that they took elsewhere, but women were certainly central to the mass activity that this movement represented. That this never developed into a political movement, as predicted by Gide (1921) and others, was perhaps in part a result of the rise of Marxism to hegemony in the formation of what became global radical politics. It was the male proletariat who was handed the torch of progressive movements while the bourgeois female was rendered as probably the least appropriate objectification of radicalism. As a result there has arisen a vast gulf between the continued rise of women as the consumers who wield power in the political economy and their valorisation. As consumers, their practices continue to be trivialised at the expense of 'true' politics.

Given these discrepancies between historical change and the experience of power, it may not be too fanciful to see the rise of feminism as predicated upon precisely this separation. It is not that women did not have power, but that there was no experience or acknowledgement of power, at precisely the time when a new kind of diffused and contradictory power was in fact accruing to them. This rendered ever more exposed an ideology that lionised an effort by workers to gain a few more pounds a week by opposing employers in heroic strikes, but took no account of the skills of a consumer in saving the household the same few pounds a week by the development of the requisite abilities. Feminism is then a change in consciousness founded upon a historical development, but as a displaced, vicarious expression of this change. It expresses a desire that this new form of power be matched with some experience of more conventional senses of power.

This transformation may not apply solely to women. The diaspora black population of the First World had its own historical reasons for eschewing identification through production and the institutions of distribution, at an earlier stage than most other populations. This may have led to a particular reliance on forms of consumption for the self-construction of social relations. The black diaspora population therefore emerges as the vanguard of certain consumer skills such as in creative style and modernity (Gilroy 1993; Miller 1994). Again this may lead to a contradiction where many black subcultures have refined skills at the techniques of power, but there is tremendous resistance from dominant ideologies to the valorisation of such skills which are used rather to denigrate populations. Thus women and blacks as generic categories suffer from very similar forms of denigration, being seen as inherently more superficial and materialistic than the 'properly' politicised fractions of the population.

POLITICISED CONSUMPTION OR PROGRESSIVE CONSUMPTION?

If my argument for consumption as the vanguard of history is even partially accepted, it remains extraordinary how limited has been its impact on contemporary politics. In Britain, the Labour party has spent most of the last two decades in opposition. During this period many of the fundamental tenets of the socialism with which it was associated have been thrown into doubt. Not surprisingly the party has been explicitly casting around for significant new ideas as to how to bring itself up to date with the issues that seem of concern to the population, and to the new sources of power in the contemporary global–local world. Despite this, very little indeed is said about consumption. As a result the seizure of this term by the political right under Margaret Thatcher as a Conservative banner went almost unchallenged. Thatcherism, though economically disastrous in Britain, retained enough rhetoric force to be used to justify similar changes around the world. I believe that the Conservative rhetoric on this topic was fraudulent. It correctly pointed out the importance of consumption as the point of consequences for the working of state and market. But it simply followed economistic reasoning to claim that the market was the authentic voice of consumer choice, while divesting local politics of its power and emptying it into a combination of market forces and more centralised political control.

I suspect, however, that the Conservative rhetoric was a political success in as much as simply by making claims to represent the consumer, the party was able to articulate a general sense of the importance of this issue as a neglected area of power, in such a way that rhetoric counted for more than action in securing support. Indeed, this might well have been the ideological gambit that sufficiently swung the electorate so that the Conservative party achieved a third term success in 1992. Since this suggests that consumption is already influential in the political arena, it makes even more culpable those with other political concerns who have failed to address its potential. I do not want to exaggerate this neglect: there has been some concern on the left of politics with issues that only just stop short of the nature of consumption *per se*. These would include debates over market socialism, the development of radical left-wing local government from the Greater London Council to Bologna, and magazines such as *Marxism Today* that took an explicit interest in the possibilities of consumption as radical action.

I have argued throughout this introduction that there is a specific resistance by politics to the actual process of consumption, since the trivialisation of consumer action is important to the maintenance of respect for conventional political power. Consequently the major strategy of those with an interest in consumption has been to 'politicise' consumption. An example may be found in the recent growth of interest in the history of consumption in the United States. On the whole it is where consumers acted as a form of political resistance, for example through the organisation of a consumer boycott, which has been excavated from the archives. This comes to stand in much the same relation to history as the key 'strike' has held as a sign of the coming to political maturity for the (more commonly male) proletariat in labour history. Similarly the idea of a politics of consumption tends most readily to be associated with consumerism, for example, green movements, arguments over shopping hours or the work of consumer protection agencies to ensure both good value and proper safety levels in consumer goods.

No one with an interest in consumption would wish to decry such activities. Consumerism as an activist movement remains one of the most powerful critical points in assessing the consequences of capitalism. From the legacy of Ralph Nader in the United States, through consumer movements in Malaysia, to the consumer cooperatives of Japan, to the green movements of Western Europe, the politicised form of consumption concern has become increasingly fundamental to the formation of many branches of alternative politics. As might be expected of the one remaining region of responsible politics, the Scandinavians have taken a lead in thinking through the pragmatics of consumer policy. Nevertheless it is vital not to view consumption as simply important when it is politicised, but also to consider the implications of these movements for our imagination of politics.

At several points in this introduction I have suggested that the increasing domination of consumption may prove ultimately progressive even at the moment when it seems most oppressive. This may seem to reflect the hubris of Marx's confidence that capitalism would be superseded by communism. But there are many reasons why the progressive potential of consumption as the continuation of history as contradiction appears both more feasible and more likely than the ideal of communism as the end of history. First, a political radicalism based on the possibilities of consumption has to be mainly concerned with the consequences of the economy rather than reifying its mechanisms. It is the consumer, both as the totality of social beings and as individual citizen, who becomes the proper arbiter of macro worlds, since this is the point at which economic institutions have direct implications for ordinary humanity. The rhetoric of consumer choice is therefore progressive in as far as it can be transformed into the actuality of persons with the resources to become empowered, arbitrating the moralities of institutions that provide goods and services. It is entirely proper that political adjudication is moved from the site of production and competing mechanisms of distribution to the moment of human consequence in the act of consumption.

The second advantage of consumption is that it is a relatively autonomous and plural process of cultural self-construction. There is no single or proper way to consume. The imperatives of consumption may be as varied as the cultural contexts from which consumers act. Consumption stands for the diversity of 'local' social networks that maintain their differences in the face of the homogenisation of institutions and mechanisms of production and distribution. The failure of previous political philosophies has often been in the prescriptive and constraining models of human action. Socialism, in practice, attempted as a political act to homogenise the population. By comparison an emphasis upon consumption is an acknowledgement of the potential and creative power of diverse human groups to make of their resources what they will. Indeed, consumption stands among other things for the necessity for humility by both theory and politics in the face of actual social diversity, which should be neither over-controlled, nor over-generalised. But contra to theories of postmodernism, which also acknowledge the importance of pluralism, this approach to consumption is based on respect for consumption as empowerment. It is not the Conservative

41

ridicule of the 'superficial' and inchoate mass, by which debates about post-modernism reveal themselves as merely the legacy of disappointment in the failures of modernist movements such as socialism or utopianism.

Finally consumption allows room for a morality of egalitarianism that posits equality at a more appropriate place within societal self-construction than that postulated by socialism. Marx's translation of Hegel was based on the reification of labour as the moment by which humanity created itself as social being. This successfully created a powerful ideology based upon a very specific reading of the implications of dialectical thought manifesting itself as universal truth. As Strathern (1988) has argued, another society need neither conceptualise nor experience work in this way. Consumption is the vanguard of history partly because the situation that Marx assumed as premise has actually declined as a generalisation of the experience of most persons in the First World. People have found that an identity constructed through consumption is far more empowering and controllable than that which is dependent upon their placement within ever larger systems of production over which they have little control (Gortz 1982). There is a clear preference for consumers to be able autonomously to employ their resources for the self-construction of their individual and social identity, rendering their place in work as no more than a necessary constraint created by their obligation to earn a living. It is therefore equality at the point of access to resources for the self-construction of consumers that becomes the proper point of arbitration of egalitarian moralities. Of course, the end point may not be equal as consumers dispose of resources for better or worse.

FROM RIGHTS TO RESPONSIBILITIES TO CITIZENSHIP

The debates that centred around the journal *Marxism Today* and the manifesto of *New Times* (Hall 1989) were unusual in giving recognition to the vanguard position of consumption in a potential progressive movement. As Hall notes:

> There has been an enormous expansion of 'civil society', related to the diversification of social worlds in which men and women now operate. At present, most people only relate to these worlds through the medium of consumption. But, increasingly we are coming to understand that to maintain these worlds at an advanced level requires forms of collective consumption far beyond the restricted logic of the market.
>
> (Hall 1989: 129)

There have been other routes from Marxism into consumption. Bourdieu (1984), for example, preserves the primacy of at least a variety of class-based analysis through his work on taste.

On the whole the debate about citizenship, as an increasingly important element in future politics, has concentrated upon the idea of rights (e.g. Turner 1993). These are defined broadly as including access to the resources and knowledge without which a claim to rights is likely to be empty. The concern with the rights of consumers can, however, lead to a number of different consequences. The British Conservative government uses the rhetorical legitimation of rights to inculcate a massive expansion of 'auditing' almost entirely directed in Britain to public institutions. The principle of accountability through auditing seems entirely reasonable, but at present this has been mainly used to funnel power to a managerial cadre, mostly concerned with easily quantifiable reporting. It has thereby become merely an instrument in the darker side of the 'Dialectic of Enlightenment'. This represents the imposition of a narrow view of rationalisation which suppresses the humanity of those institutions it controls.

Clearly, accountability needs to be redirected in two ways. First, to turn it into an instrument of consumers, rather than of managers, with resources directed to providing information and infrastructure to those who wish to seek redress. Second, auditing from the point of view of consumption needs to be as much directed against private and commercial distributive systems as against public ones. The British public have not seen even a pretence to redress against private companies grow alongside that of their increasing supposed authority with respect to state enterprises. Finally this 'authority' of the consumer itself needs to be kept in check, since, as with any other form of institutionalised power, it can itself become a regressive force acting against the longer term interests of consumers (see various papers in Keat, Whiteley and Abercrombie 1994).

The key to a successful implementation of consumer-related auditing is that it should transcend the current ideologies of right and left. These merely presume what mechanism best serves the consumer, that is the market or state respectively. What most needs to be challenged at present is the assumption that a concern with consumers always means a move from state to market provision. Instead these have to be seen as alternatives adjudicated by their consequences. The debates on market socialism (e.g. Le Grand and Estrin 1989) have suggested that both have advantages. So it is likely that the provision of most goods and services would work best as a combination of the two, each acting to ensure the other does not 'reify' its interests at the expense of its consequence for consumers.

In a sense, however, this concern with rights is the least problematic issue in considering the future. Even though it may be politically extremely hard to secure, it is conceptually easy to envisage. What is more problematic is the corollary of rights, which is responsibilities. Yet responsibility is just as important as rights to the fulfilment of Hall's imagined route to citizenship through consumption. In a sense this is the hardest part of *New Times* for those committed to traditional politics, because it requires an

43

abandonment of power and control by political institutions of whatever complexion. Pluralism as a banner is in essence a faith that freedom will be circumscribed by responsibility, given the right conditions. The democratic state mostly prefers to see itself as the collective expression of responsibility translated into the moralities of law and adjudication. As de Tocqueville noted: 'It gladly works for their happiness but wants to be the sole agent and judge of it' (de Tocqueville 1969: 691–692). It is this which is challenged by pluralist consumption.

It is then in the dialectic between rights and responsibilities that we should see the ideal of consumer citizenship, manifested as much in institutions as in individuals. Unfortunately the current literature on citizenship seems almost entirely concerned with a political discussion as to the proper relationship of the citizen to the state. What has thereby been seriously neglected is a consideration of the proper relationship of citizen to the market. The neglect of this issue has left the field wide open for a quite different position, which equates consumer interest solely with the market. In practice this is an idealised concept of pure market which rarely describes the conditions of actual markets (Dilley 1992).

An excellent example of this argument was recently put forward by Saunders (1993), who tries to demonstrate that liberal citizenship based around the market is inherently superior to collectivist models. He argues that the tradition of rights (as derived from Marshall), which asserts the need for a welfare state as providing an equal foundation for citizenship, should be superseded. In its stead he advocates a voucher system, which thereby shows trust in the citizen to choose the best provision from the market. As such he acknowledges his precedents in Christian concepts of free will and conservative arguments (by Burke and others) for small, historically given nodes of sociality, such as church and village. Although he claims to be arguing for the interests of the consumer, the argument is really the same tired political debate about the market versus the state. Saunders assumes that it is the market which provides the foundation for plurality. He ignores the decades during which the market crushed plurality in favour of modernist homogenisation to suit industrial profitability. Then it was socialist bureaucracies such as the Greater London Council that came closest to fostering the kind of 'from the roots' voluntary groupings that he claims to favour.

I do not want to suggest that the state is necessarily superior to the market as a distributor, but only that a true concern with consumers would let the consequences be the judge. Furthermore writers on state provision today also show equal concern with mechanisms to curb state power. By contrast, writers such as Saunders who proclaim the market show no concern at all with the need to curb clear abuses of the market such as the provision of unsafe, poor value, monopolistic or addictive goods through the repetition of false claims.

Fortunately there is a good chance that the right wing will finally be hoist with its own petard when the growth of consumer power, which they use rhetorically, actually becomes the main force in opposing the *laissez-faire* policies they assume it should espouse. At the moment popular emphasis is still on escape from an overbearing state, but once this is achieved it is likely to turn increasingly to the need to submit an abusive market to juridical control. Over the twentieth century, various populations have differed in what they see as the bounds of the market, and at any given time an issue such as surrogate wombs, or gun control, will pull activities in or out of market relations. Through all this there remains considerable respect for professional expertise as the delegation of responsibility for making choices and in some areas for centralised as opposed to market distribution. As in educational systems, consumers may prefer to delegate, rather than exercise, the responsibilities of choice, even in the face of governments who want to use them to oppose professional expertise (see Keat 1994 for a general discussion of this issue).

Where both right and left seem to agree is that over-centralised government creates a frame in which consumption is almost bound to be irresponsible. Indeed, liberal decentralisation of choice to the consumer merely accentuates a problem where (as in neoclassical economic theory) it is individuals who are supposed to make decisions out of self-interest in a sphere completely separated from that of collective responsibility. Even Saunders admits that citizenship cannot be built from purchase alone. In effect, both conservatives and the left come together in envisaging users who desire to take responsibility for and become involved in the consumption of services and in the responsible delegation of responsibilities, whether educational or leisure pursuits. There is a clear parallel here with a recent argument for 'reconnecting taxation' (Mulgan and Murray 1993), which claims to help citizens to acknowledge their responsibilities by simplifying and specifying the relationship between taxes and the benefits which these taxes fund.

If, however, politicians attempt to modify their assumption of power, and instead provide facilities for groups to emerge (even when these are not those that reflect their own political ideals as to how such groups should be), then this may allow space through which consumption can increasingly recognise itself as responsibility. As compared to the socialist proletariat, a 'republic of consumers' is more unwieldy, more anarchic, more fortuitous, less dogmatic, but possibly more enabling. At present we retain a conceptual dualism by which rationality is tied to the goal of homogeneity, and pluralism is seen as some kind of pure resistance, or even an opposition to rationality.

By contrast, given our understanding of social relations and the importance of small-scale, encompassable sociality, we should come to acknowledge that it is pluralism which best expresses the rationality of a sensible

45

politics within a mass society. Responsibility must include self-imposed limitation on action, which is most likely to be accepted when the oppressive consequences of mere freedom are experienced. What is then required is for consumers to choose to have less choice. In short the final aim of modern consumption must be to give up something of the burden of freedom for the sacrament of law and professional adjudication, which ensures equity and the actualisation of rights.

In practice, politics translates this philosophical imperative as the requirement to act as a balance between, on the one hand a pluralism of consumer worlds that should not be homogenised into a statist vision of proper life, and on the other hand the mechanisms that protect such pluralistic social networks and represent their interests against the reified institutions of both the market and the bureaucratic state. The one should not, of course, be at the expense of the other. What Mulgan calls 'weak power structures' (1989: 347–363) and Saunders 'platoons', by which pluralist bodies are empowered with respect to their own smaller worlds, need to be complemented by ever larger, more macro bodies such as European or United Nations regulatory bodies, which can provide protection against agents of the scale of nations and transnational companies. Contrary to the expectations of the radical right, it seems to be the relatively wealthy middle classes, with considerable resources, which seem to support consumer associations, which attempt to lobby for greater regulation to limit the market, through insisting upon safety standards and other requirements that protect the consumer.

Most such debates have been highly parochial and largely ignore the considerable diversity that already exists in the relationship of consumers to the market rather than to the state. There is a vast difference between Japan, Sweden and the United States in terms of how citizens view the market. One example of this relationship, not well known in the West, is the Japanese consumer cooperative movement. This is probably the most powerful such movement yet seen. One author suggests that it now accounts for a third of all consumer purchases in that country (Clammer 1992). Here the power of corporations to organise lives from the top down is becoming increasingly matched by the power of people to combine as flesh and blood aggregate (as opposed to hypothesised aggregate) to ensure that consumption reflects the values of consumers and not that of corporations. I have, however, possibly maligned the state by seeing such moves as necessarily coming from below. In Sweden, during the period of social democracy, there is considerable evidence that it was a benign state that achieved such unusual levels of positive association with its citizenship that it became the main proponent of political action mediated through consumption-based institutions (Pestoff 1988).

In Western Europe the most explicit attempt to construct a new relationship between consumption and the market has come through the green movement. Where greens have tried to mobilise under conventional political banners, their success has been limited and, after peaking in the 1980s, seems to be in decline. But their influence on everyday 'voting' of consumers seems, by contrast, to be increasing. Green ideology is an interesting reflection of the global–local articulations which should be the core of any new consumer responsibilities. On the one hand, it is based around planetary resources and the superordinate concept of a planetary citizenship. On the other hand, it expresses a conservative localism of the 'village green' ethos. It is not surprising therefore that it is most successful precisely in the new articulations that act to link the local and the global, for example, the use of household moralities and actions to influence the branding claims of transnational products or national policy on recycling.

The green movement is commonly considered as an anti-consumption movement, but in many respects it is more realistically viewed as the vanguard of new forms of consumption. In many respects it appears as the 'global' version of the same ideology of thrift in opposition to the squandering of resources that may well remain the main justification for most acts of shopping. As it becomes a mass movement, its mystical relationship to a reified notion of nature becomes tempered by a more rationalistic concern with the defetishism of goods. This shows increasing awareness of the consequence of goods for peoples as well as for the planet's natural resources. In practice, 'green' food choices seem more often to be actualised by fear of consequences for the consumer's body rather than abstract planetary health. Nevertheless this movement shows some signs of transcending simple self-interest and at least reconceptualising this linkage between the healthy and moral individual and a healthy and moral world. Thus 'moral investments' in finance seem to have arisen more readily as a movement from 'green' rather than 'red' political consciousness. For similar reasons it is today often green activists who proclaim the most strident egalitarianism. It is in recognition of the significance of the goods that money buys (for good as well as for bad) that we may regenerate the demand for equality in access to goods and services.

These concerns probably also reflect the increasing power of domestic moralities projected on to the larger world. In the world of consumption, morality as charity (even if only limited to recycling) seems to have begun at home. It is possible (though it cannot be assumed) that this will be a major route by which the housewives' practical perspicacity and morality will become transformed into more abstracted and theoretical concerns. This is essential if, in this polemic, we are even to conceive of closing the circle – that is bringing this investigation of the flesh and blood housewife back to the questions of Third World poverty with which I started. I would suggest that at present consumption is, contrary to most assumptions, a highly moral activity. But this is a morality based largely around the ethical

47

issues of home and family, and is only sometimes a leap into a generic sense of the 'green' world. It is also, despite in recent debates becoming almost restricted to the 'market', often a collective act and still often made in relation to a state provision. What is required is a 'middle-range' morality, which reinscribes on to the surface of commodities their consequences for producers, often from the developing world. Given the democratic nature of most First World societies, this will require a transformation of consciousness with the acceptance of wider responsibilities among the middle classes of the First World. The move to green consumption suggests that this is not impossible, but it is more likely that the initial impetus is going to come much more from attempts to exert pressure by the oppressed, than some philanthropic turn of heart by the oppressors. If it is accepted that consumption is the vanguard of history, then it is here that any change in power has to take place. The first move has to be a transfer of profits from First World consumers to Third World producers as increased prices for raw materials.

Though consumers have prised power out of a realm of production, they have thereby abrogated responsibility even for themselves in their 'otherness' as the human capital of institutions (e.g. as wage-labour or clients of bureaucracies). Thus the actions they take as consumers rarely acknowledge their consequences for their status as workers. This suggests that there is a profound sense in which a reconciliation of the global economy is none other than a reconciliation of the dialectical contradiction that exists within an increasing number of persons. Even in the global economy, we cannot escape the foundational ethical principles by which taking responsibility for others is the same process by which we take responsibility for ourselves.

CONCLUSION TO THE POLEMIC

The argument of this polemic is for the increasing importance of consumption in both the global economy and the local extraction of value. That commerce may be becoming more consumption-led is *not* to suggest that capitalism has become more benign. It is merely that profitability may be more efficiently created through collusion with consumers rather than spending the money to attempt to transform consumers. Equally this does *not* necessarily mean that the results are more benign, since this depends upon the imperatives behind consumer demand (think of some of the governments that populations have voted for!). What it does mean, however, is that there is a radical shift emerging in the political economy which needs to be researched and its consequences understood. It also means that consumption has become the key domain through which future political options must be developed. Although I have argued that consumption is a more suitable site for the construction of human values than production and distribution, there is no particular reason for optimism here. There is a considerable distance between sectional interest collusion between consumer societies and business on the one hand, and the formation of a responsible, moral citizenship concerned with the consequences of its demands.

Nevertheless it is important at least to formulate strategies for feasible progressive movements. Predicting the future is a hazardous exercise, but my expectation is that the roots of consumerism which Gide and others saw in the experience of France in the nineteenth century will be highly prescient. Whether clothed in green, red or some other symbolic armature, it is likely to be the bourgeois female not the working-class male who will become the progressive force in the first stage of the next millennium.

I write this polemic not as a Marxist, but as someone who believes that 'Marxists' in the end failed the challenge Marx set them. Marx attempted to live up to the Hegelian concept of the dialectic which demanded a perspective on history that transcended most previous forms of analysis. Marx therefore turned the analysis of his own time into a historical moment, set within a dynamic whose consequences for social relations were changing as he wrote. This implied an unfolding analysis shifting as each future was appropriated by theory. He avoided the hubris of extended prediction so that the concept of actual communism, for example, is little more than a rhetorical gesture. Unfortunately, some of those who followed developed a largely static 'Marxism' (although there are many exceptions), which emphasised communism as a kind of 'end of history', reflecting the original hubris of Hegel's phenomenology as the end of philosophy.

Instead, what was required was a succession of thinkers each prepared to employ dialectical perspectives in order to rethink radically their predecessors in the light of their own times. The legacy for today is a requirement to rethink our present and once again reflect on the consequences for social relations. This may also mean emphasising elements, such as feasible consequences for the near future, that Marx neglected. While Marx emphasised critique and homogenising categories, we might wish to concentrate upon what might be positively enacted and pluralism. Today we require a massive shift in our conception away from easy targets, such as the capitalist, or the politician who convinced herself that she was the inventor of a politics which was really just the destructive premise of monetarist economics. Instead we must turn to much more diffuse and ambivalent targets. At the time of Marx the main thrust of history as dialectic was recognised as the opposing interests of discrete groups representing labour and capital respectively. Indeed, partly as a result of Marx's influence, people were increasingly objectified as the representatives of these opposed classes. Today, by contrast, the contradictions of dialectical development are increasingly manifested within individuals, whether of the First or Third Worlds, in their dual existence as labour and consumer. The emphasis upon consumption today does not therefore resolve the contradictions analysed by Marx but rather extends them.

Marx at least attempts to formulate his economic analysis on the basis of the social meaning of persons and things, even if this laudable goal was not always consistently realised in his political economy. His economic analysis was also intended ultimately to serve political goals. Today we may feel that economics cannot be relied upon to serve some assumed historical movement, but rather politics must be wrested away from economic control to proclaim its own goals. Similarly we need to start by excavating our own social relations and our relationship to the major institutions of the modern world. It is these that give rise to our imperatives as consumers and in turn cause us unwittingly to find ourselves at the commanding heights of the global economy.

The varied 'local' cultures of consumption and business are not remnants to be eliminated by a new global hegemony, but the motor behind abstracted, aggregate and finally global changes. This is a progressive development because, if we can rise to consciousness in our consumption activities as the vanguard of history, then there is at least the glimmer of hope that responsibility could confront irresponsibility in citizenship, and morality could confront the amorality of the market. The task of the new study of consumption remains therefore the original goal of the Enlightenment, which is a rational morality born of consciousness.

THE IMPERATIVES OF RESEARCH

This conclusion suggests a particular significance for the chapters that follow. The failure of Marx's grand narrative was that it grounded its theory in the abstractions of economics and led to modernist, homogenising models of social relations. A new grand narrative must therefore be in dialectical tension with the actual development of social relations, which is our present time as a moment in social history. We need to uncover the possibilities of consumption as much from empirical research as from theory. This implies a respect for existing society, for example, the possibility that housewives may have shown greater perspicacity in determining what consumption might become than have purely academic models. The evidence that arises from the following chapters, which reveal as it were the flesh and blood of pluralistic consumption, is therefore the essential complement to a grand narrative that proclaims pluralism as the future of consumption.

Each contributor to this volume has a particular disciplinary stance from which to view the eruption of consumption as a theoretical issue upon the previous premises of that discipline. Often they depend upon particular traditions of analysis or even particular kinds of evidence as, for example, the particular role of probate reports in historians' studies of consumption reported by Glennie. None can be assumed to share my belief in consumption as the vanguard of history. Most would regard this introduction as taking an 'extremist' position to which they would not subscribe. All have their specific perspectives upon the light shed on actual consumption practices by the research that their disciplines have so far engaged upon. I have mainly used their insights into the surprisingly significant impact that consumption studies may have for academic disciplines. But these chapters are principally interested in how their academic disciplines contribute to the understanding of consumption.

In order to make this contribution, these disciplines are having to swim against a recent tide of academic fashion. Twenty years ago movements such as structuralism and Marxism insisted that we did not take at face value the self-expression of those we study. Rather we were told to construct analytical and abstract models that excavate hidden foundations to social life under a neo-realist epistemology. By contrast, in recent years these strategies have been repudiated by those who claim they represent the intrusive projections by rationalistic authority over the life-worlds of ordinary people. Instead researchers are now expected neither to impose nor to delve, but merely to facilitate the expression of those whose voices had previously been disregarded. The ideal contemporary research in disciplines such as anthropology consists then of a series of unedited 'conversations' with as much concern for the author's voice as for those who are in conversation with the author. The result is a return to the most vulgar positivism that equates verbal legitimation by the actor with the imperative behind action. Unfortunately this relies upon an absurdly simple notion of agency. As Campbell notes, we require this exposure to language and the reasons given by consumers, but we also require extensive knowledge as to consumption as action in context.

Instead I would argue that consumption research needs to be more not less intrusive, more not less analytical, more not less observational. To understand consumption imperatives means being saturated in the lives of ordinary people, perhaps especially housewives, and at the same time aware of the macro forces emanating from business and the state that operate upon them. It is the contradictory, inconsistent mess of ordinary mundane worlds that is so often absent in writings on both consumption and commerce. Nor am I arguing for the abandonment of generalised aggregate representations. This chapter in one sense divides between a first half that is mainly concerned with the consequences of demand, and a second half that starts to delve into the question of the sources of demand. For the former it is often necessary to construct models of aggregate consumers. The problem is that under the influence of economists, the desire for the aggregate as an expression of the consequences of demand has been at the expense of any research into the sources of demand. This has permitted the development of theoretical models that are so distant

51

from actual consumption as to have become an extraordinarily destructive ideology.

Jackson and Thrift note for geographical studies, and Campbell for post-modernist sociology, that there is an enormous weight of recent literature that projects upon consumption practices both theoretical and moral dualisms, with very little corresponding research on actual consumers. This suggests that to talk of the 'moral economy of the home' requires being present in the home: an intrusive, almost voyeuristic, presence in that most private and boundary-maintaining of domestic spaces, which is where power is today increasingly constituted. Such new research might help to demolish the rhetorical generalised 'housewife', standing for consumption, which I have employed in this introduction. Morley in his case-studies on both media-watching and on media technology as commodity, together with Lunt's description of Livingstone's work on domestic technologies, indicate the degree to which researchers are starting to provide a more sophisticated and informed portrait of consumption and gender within the social relations of the private household.

Simultaneously this means challenging another set of boundaries, which are imposed by business and the production and distribution spheres that provide mass goods and services. To think that we have studied capitalism by reading off the semiotics of advertising is self-delusion. We need to be inside business examining it with the same intensity and scrutiny as might be employed inside the home. Observation should be made on media production (as in Morley, Chapter 9 of this volume), or agro-industry (as in Jackson and Thrift, Chapter 6; and Fine's Chapter 4) in a spirit of critical, comparative, moral and analytical perspectives which transcends narrow positivism. Neither the 'global' nor the 'local' aspects of mass consumption can be comprehended through projecting on to the other. Yet this is exactly what we have tended to do in the past. Those with knowledge of business have invented an abstract aggregate consumer. Those involved in everyday social relations project an abstract instrumental business practice.

Fortunately, the unknown nature of consumption as mass practice is emerging through the cracks in a curtain of assumed knowledge. A whole series of both colloquial and academic clichés, which previously informed us as to what mass consumption was 'about', are riven by critical enquiry on one side and the sheer perversity of social actors who refuse to conform to expectations on the other. At present we are only just coming out of a period in which the reliance upon surveys, hypothesis testing and uni-versalistic psychological premises meant that our understanding of the moralities, values and imperatives in consumer action has been limited. These methods, while possibly essential in natural science, seem to have largely stymied investigation in the social sciences – though not entirely, since Lunt (see Chapter 7) provides some positive examples, even as he criticises the genre.

Although this book is organised by 'discipline', common to all chapters is an appeal for consumption studies that transcend disciplinary parochialism and reconstitute themselves as interdisciplinary, using methods and theories from whatever source provides the quality of ideas and materials that are needed. Indeed, I believe we would all wish this volume to help kick-start interdisciplinary work on consumption. Equally impressive is the consensus emerging around the repudiation of abstract theory, whether as positivistic equation testing or postmodern projections. Instead there is the desire for an immersion in the complex worlds of existing consumption, in order then to return to generalised, analytical but also informed theory.

Throughout this introduction it has been suggested that the key to progressive consumer studies is disaggregation. Any of the traditional parameters of social analysis such as class, ethnicity and gender can be challenged and rethought through the perspective of consumption as practice. But equally the individual consumer is disaggregated as they are found, not to comprise some clear coherent cultural imperatives, but often partially connected, partially formulated, and quite contradictory sources of value and desire. What an individual consumer creates through clothing may be quite inconsistent with their expressive use of the car. The same household uses the living room to objectify their understanding of nostalgic tradition and their kitchen for a brash aggressive modernism. This disaggregation of the consumer parallels Fine's call for a disaggregation of forms of provision and Jackson and Thrift on the disaggregation of sites of consumption. This does not mean that we reflect pluralism by shifting from relatively clear concepts such as 'class' to emulate vague marketing notions of lifestyle (see Campbell on the problems with these). Rather the analysis of class already contained questions of available resources and (in its Weberian form) questions of status and exclusion that need to be preserved in the development of what may well be necessarily new and more complex approaches to social classification.

At present the concept of the consumer is becoming fetishised as mere purchaser. Retailers using the new information from electronic point of sale smart cards are able increasingly to pinpoint consumer behaviour and relate it to micro-area defined by the census and other contextual variables. But this is led by a commercial desire to construct persons reduced to their buying behaviour. Social research, by contrast, should not be averse to using such information, but its primary purpose is to ensure that all other aspects of consumption, its collective nature, its concern with state services, and its intimate place in value creation should render purchase as merely one element in social characterisation. Our purpose should be to defetishise the consumer by rendering the social welfare of persons, whether in their form as consumers or workers, as pre-eminent in their characterisation.

What is required of research is something that starts by transcending dualisms of good and bad, or symbolic versus utilitarian consumption. A dialectical perspective that understands the link between emerging differentiation or specificity and new forms of totalisation and generality is best suited to this transcendence of dualism. It proceeds by rearticulating the sundered local and global. On the one hand we observe the manner by which both individuals and groups objectify themselves and their values through their material culture and consumption acts. The aim is to reveal the humanity of this process. But this must be reattached to the study of the micro and macro projects of commerce and states and behind them the labourers who produce the goods and services. By recognising consumption as the vanguard of history, we acknowledge the massive influence of consumption upon the political economy, while acknowledging the political economy inscribed in the historical projects given to people as consumers. It is the work of consumer research to elucidate such processes in all their complexity, and on that basis to provide the foundation for an informed political debate that can move beyond the established clichés about consumers and consumer societies. The goal is to achieve the knowledge, the consciousness and the confidence required to attack and remove from the world the curse of economistic certitudes.

NOTES

1 I have used the term polemic here in order to justify what might otherwise be seen as unsupported assertions in the body of the text. The introduction is written in order to suggest that there has been a radical transformation in the world which justifies the title of this chapter and to consider the way the world would look if I am correct in my arguments. Because, however, I suspect few would go as far as I have done in the claims made, there has been relatively little work to date which would allow these assertions to be made with confidence. I suggest that we require this leap of imagination (or if I am correct, perspicacity) which might then provoke academics in various disciplines to determine how far this portrait of the modern world might be justified. I obviously imply a commitment of my own to work in the future towards this goal.
    I am very grateful for many critical comments on this piece by colleagues and by my postgraduate students. In particular I would like acknowledge written comments from Ben Fine, Peter Jackson, Beverley Holbrook, Mike Rowlands and Nigel Thrift. I would confirm that none of these commentators (and probably most of the contributors to this book) can be assumed to feel particularly sympathetic to my arguments.
2 This is clearly speculative on my part. At present research is still concerned to document public approval or disapproval of state versus privatised institutions, rather than the degree to which a population would otherwise be much concerned about the distinction itself.
3 I would include China here, since although the government retains the strong centralism of communist (and indeed pre-communist) regimes, there has been a radical shift in economic philosophy which mirrors the shift to market forces elsewhere.
4 I use the term culture here in accordance with a definition given elsewhere

(Miller 1987) which renders it synonymous with 'objectification' by which people are enabled to construct themselves as social beings in the same process by which they construct their world.

5 This section should not be viewed as my attempt to escape blame for my poor orthography as evident in my writing!

6 For the background of this term see Cheal (1989); for an example of its usage in the study of consumption see Silverstone, Hirsch, Morley (1992).

BIBLIOGRAPHY

Bourdieu, P. (1977) *Outline of a Theory of Practice*, Cambridge: Cambridge University Press.

Bourdieu, P. (1984) *Distinction*, London: Routledge and Kegan Paul.

Cheal, D. (1989) 'Strategies of resource management in household economies: moral economy or political economy?' in R. Wilk (ed.) *The Household Economy*, Boulder, Col.: Westview.

Clammer, J. (1992) 'Aesthetics of the self: shopping and social being in contemporary urban Japan', in R. Shields (ed.) *Lifestyle Shopping*, London: Routledge.

Crewe, L. and Foster, Z. (1993) 'Markets, design and local agglomeration: the role of the small independent retailer in the workings of the fashion system', in *Society and Space* 11(2): 213–229.

Davis, M. (1990) *City of Quartz*, London: Verso.

De Certeau, M. (1984) *The Practice of Everyday Life*, Berkeley: University of California Press.

De Tocqueville, A. (1969) *Democracy in America*, New York: Anchor Books.

Dilley, R. (1992) 'Contesting markets', in R. Dilley (ed.) *Contesting Markets*, Edinburgh: Edinburgh University Press, pp. 1–34.

Douglas, M. and Isherwood, B. (1979) *The World of Goods*, London: Allen Lane.

Drakulic, S. (1993) *How We Survived Communism and Even Laughed*, London: Vintage.

Fine, B. and Leopold, E. (1993) *The World of Consumption*, London: Routledge.

Finnegan, R. (1989) *The Hidden Musicians*, Cambridge: Cambridge University Press.

Friedman, J. (1994) 'Introduction', in J. Friedman (ed.) *Consumption and Identity*, London: Harwood Academic Press.

Furlough, E. (1991) *Consumer Cooperation in France*, Ithaca, NY: Cornell University Press.

Galbraith, K. (1969) *The New Industrial State*, Harmondsworth: Penguin.

Gates, H. L. (1988) *The Signifying Monkey*, Oxford: Oxford University Press.

Gide, C. (1921) *Consumers' Co-operative Societies*, New York: Haskell House Publishers.

Gilroy, P. (1993) *The Black Atlantic*, London: Verso.

Goodman, J. (1994) *Tobacco in History*, London: Routledge.

Gortz, A. (1982) *Farewell to the Working Class*, London: Pluto Press.

Gullestad, M. (1984) *Kitchen-Table Society*, Oslo: Universitetsforlaget.

Gullestad, M. (1992) *The Art of Social Relations*, Oslo: Scandinavian University Press.

Hall, S. (1989) 'The meaning of New Times', in S. Hall and M. Jacques (eds) *New Times*, London: Lawrence and Wishart.

Hallsworth, A. (1992) *The New Geography of Consumer Spending*, London: Bellhaven Press.

Hamilton, G. and Lai, C.-K. (1989) 'Consumption without capitalism: consumption and brand names in late Imperial China', in H. Rutz and B. Orlove (eds) *The Social Economy of Consumption*, Lanham: University Press of America, pp. 253–279.

Harvey, D. (1989) *The Condition of Postmodernity*, Oxford: Blackwell.

Hebdige, D. (1988) *Hiding in the Light*, London: Routledge.

Humphrey, C. (forthcoming) 'Consumers in Moscow', in D. Miller (ed.) *Worlds Apart: Modernity through the Prism of the Local*, London: Routledge.

Kapferer, B. (forthcoming) 'Bureaucratic erasure: identity, resistance and violence. Aborigines and a discourse of autonomy in a North Queensland town', in D. Miller (ed.) *Worlds Apart: Modernity through the Prism of the Local*, London: Routledge.

Keat, R. (1994) 'Scepticism, authority and the market', in R. Keat, N. Whiteley and N. Abercrombie (eds) *The Authority of the Consumer*, London: Routledge.

Keat, R., Whiteley, N. and Abercrombie, N. (eds) (1994) *The Authority of the Consumer*, London: Routledge.

Le Grand, J. and Estrin, S. (eds) (1989) *Market Socialism*, Oxford: Clarendon Press.

McCracken, G. (1988) *Culture and Consumption*, Bloomington, Ind.: Indiana University Press.

Mauss, M. (1966) *The Gift*, London: Cohen and West.

Miller, D. (1985) *Artifacts as Categories*, Cambridge: Cambridge University Press.

Miller, D. (1987) *Material Culture and Mass Consumption*, Oxford: Blackwell.

Miller, D. (1988) 'Appropriating the state on the council estate', *Man* 23: 353–372.

Miller, D. (ed.) (1993) *Unwrapping Christmas*, Oxford: Oxford University Press.

Miller, D. (1994) *Modernity: an Ethnographic Approach*, Oxford: Berg.

Miller, D. (forthcoming) *Capitalism: an Ethnographic Approach*.

Morley, D. (1992) *Television Audiences and Cultural Studies*, London: Routledge.

Mosley, P., Harrigan, J. and Toye, J. (1991) *Aid and Power: the World Bank and Policy Based Lending*, London: Routledge.

Mulgan, G. (1989) 'The power of the weak', in S. Hall and M. Jacques (eds) *New Times*, London: Lawrence and Wishart.

Mulgan, G. and Murray, R. (1993) *Reconnecting Taxation*, London: Demos.

Murray, R. (1989) 'Fordism and Post-Fordism', in S. Hall and M. Jacques (eds) *New Times*, London: Lawrence and Wishart, pp. 38–53.

Oakley, A. (1976) *Housewife*, Harmondsworth: Penguin.

Pestoff, V. (1988) 'Exit, voice and collective action in Swedish consumer policy', *Journal of Consumer Policy* 11: 1–27.

Rose, G. (1993) *Judaism and Modernity*, Oxford: Blackwell.

Saunders, P. (1993) 'Citizenship in a Liberal society', in B. Turner (ed.) (1993) *Citizenship and Social Theory*, London: Sage.

Schama, S. (1987) *The Embarrassment of Riches*, London: Fontana.

Sennett, R. (1976) *The Fall of Public Man*, Cambridge: Cambridge University Press.

Silverstone, R., Hirsch, E. and Morley, D. (1992) 'Information and communication technologies and the moral economy of the home', in R. Silverstone and E. Hirsch (eds) *Consuming Technologies*, London: Routledge.

Simmel, G. (1978) *The Philosophy of Money*, London: Routledge and Kegan Paul.

Strathern, M. (1988) *The Gender of the Gift*, Berkeley: University of California Press.

Strathern, M. (1991) *Partial Connections*, Savage: Rowman and Littelfield.

Thomas, N. (1991) *Entangled Objects*, Cambridge, Mass.: Harvard University Press.

Thompson, E. P. (1963) *The Making of the English Working Class*, New York: Vintage.

Thrift, N. and Leyshon, A. (unpublished) 'A phantom state? The de-traditionalisation of money, the international financial system and international financial centres'.

Turner, B. (ed.) (1993) *Citizenship and Social Theory*, London: Sage.

Wallman, S. (1984) *Eight London Households*, London: Tavistock.

Williams, R. (1961) *Culture and Society*, Harmondsworth: Penguin.

Wrigley, N. (1993a) 'Antitrust regulation and the restructuring of grocery retailing in Britain and the USA', *Society and Space* 11: 727–749.

Wrigley, N. (1993b) 'Abuses of market power? Further reflections on UK retailing and the regulatory state', *Society and Space* 11: 1545–1557.

Zukin, S. (1982) *Loft Living*, Baltimore: Johns Hopkins University Press.

2

STUDIES IN THE NEW CONSUMER BEHAVIOUR

Russell W. Belk

I The emergence and transformation of consumer behaviour research

THE BEGINNINGS OF A DISCIPLINE OF CONSUMER BEHAVIOUR RESEARCH

Market-based trading, selling, buying and consuming existed for thousands of years before such phenomena became a subject of academic enquiry and instruction. Only as production, communication, sales and consumption became mass processes involving large institutions did behavioural investigations of these activities begin. The genealogy of the body of research to be reviewed in this chapter may be simply sketched: economics begat marketing which begat consumer behaviour research which begat 'the new consumer behaviour research'. Marketing courses were first taught in American universities in 1902 (Bartels 1976). By 1908 the Harvard Business School had been established. But it was not until the late 1920s and early 1930s that the academics who taught these courses began to regard themselves chiefly as marketing scholars rather than as economists. During the 1930s the creation of the American Marketing Association and the *Journal of Marketing* signalled marketing academics' formal separation from economics, but, as will be seen, not necessarily from its ideological influence.

The development of an academic discipline of consumer behaviour within the marketing departments of colleges of commerce and business began in the 1950s. Earlier in the century in North America and Europe, advertising and marketing research firms began to study the consumer in order to market consumer goods more successfully. For example, during the late 1920s and early 1930s in Vienna, Paul Lazarsfeld and his colleagues conducted consumer survey research investigating tea consumption, shoe-purchasing, film-going, noodle-eating, and other everyday consumption experiences of interest to business clients (Fullerton 1990, 1994). The academic marketing departments that developed at about this time had a more applied and behavioural focus than the economics departments from which they emerged. Improving mass marketing efficiency and effectiveness as well as training future marketing managers were the avowed goals of the new marketing academics. But as Tucker (1967) noted, marketing academics studied consumers as fishermen study fish rather than as marine biologists might. Within this micro perspective consumer needs were seen as innate rather than socially constructed or marketer influenced, and marketers sought to 'hook' consumers by offering a product or service that met these needs better than competitors' offerings. Thus, the initial consumer research within these marketing departments stressed objective product and service benefits and did not stray far from the conception of rational economic man.

This emphasis on the economic man changed temporarily in America during the 1950s when depth interviewing and projective methods from psychoanalysis began to be applied within what came to be known as motivation research. Such research was conducted both by industry (in marketing research, advertising and specialised motivation research agencies) and within academic marketing departments at respected US universities (Newman 1992). Motivation research examined the more latent emotional meanings of a variety of consumer goods, with the primary focus still being on how to sell branded products more effectively (Dichter 1964). Ernest Dichter, the creator of the major motivation research agency, was trained in Freudian psychology at the University of Vienna. He advised clients that men buy convertibles as substitute mistresses, that housewives symbolically give birth when they bake a cake, and that the safety razor will not be supplanted by the electric razor because it provides a fantasy fulfilment of the Freudian death wish. Vance Packard's *Hidden Persuaders* (1957) raised public fears that such motivation research had manipulative potential by tapping consumer's subconscious desires, and its publication was a key factor causing motivation research to decline in academic respectability (Durgee 1991; Holbrook 1988b; Stern 1990).

The other major cause of the decline of motivation research in academic marketing departments was the rise of 'scientific' experimentation and the multivariate revolution of the 1960s. Borrowing both methods and concepts from psychology, laboratory research on consumers began to examine various persuasive techniques and the effects of promotion, pricing, product design, packaging and physical distribution on consumers, based primarily on paper and pencil manipulations of these variables and scaled responses. The result of this 'scientific' revolution was a re-rationalization of the dominant view of the consumer. Starting in the late 1960s, the reigning model became that of consumer-as-information-processor. Much like a computer, the consumer was seen as acquiring and processing information to assist in making decisions about which brand to acquire in a particular product or service category (e.g. Bettman 1979). Consumer researchers working within this model have joined cognitive researchers in psychology and every four years the *Annual Review of Psychology* publishes a consumer psychology review article authored by someone in a marketing department (e.g. Cohen and Chakravarti 1990; Tybout and Artz 1994). Early textbooks in consumer behaviour were largely framed in terms of information processing, although they also attempted to incorporate topics of culture, subculture, group processes, social class, family influences, learning and personality (e.g. Nicosia 1966; Engel, Kollat and Blackwell 1968; Howard and Sheth 1969).

The emerging field of consumer research was further legitimated by the founding of the Association for Consumer Research in 1969 and the establishment of the *Journal of Consumer Research* in 1974. While consumer behaviour research remained within the business school and marketing department, these developments marked a disciplinary separation from marketing – a separation that in other ways parallels the earlier discipli-nary separation of marketing from economics. ACR became the focal organisation of consumer researchers and quickly grew to approximately 1,200 (now 1,500) members, primarily from American academic marketing departments with a few from other academic departments, industry and government, and a minority portion of members from other countries. Both *JCR* and the proceedings of the annual ACR conference, *Advances in Consumer Research*, remain the primary outlets of consumer behaviour research by those in academic marketing departments, and recently ACR has established a second conference held outside of the US every other year. Consumer research has become the intellectual centre of academic marketing departments and produces the largest number of PhD disser-tations in the field each year. Much of this consumer research retains the strong rationality biases inherited from economics and the strong micro biases inherited from marketing. Nevertheless, there are important signs of change.

THE EMERGENCE OF THE NEW CONSUMER BEHAVIOUR

Beginning in the 1980s, alternative perspectives in consumer research began to emerge. Because these alternative perspectives necessarily contrast with the older perspectives in the field and because researchers in academic mar-keting departments have tended to align themselves with either traditional or emergent views, it is useful to contrast 'the new consumer behaviour' with the old.

As summarized in Figure 2.1, the new consumer behaviour differs from the old both methodologically and substantively. Philosophically it rejects positivist tenets in favour of a broader array of epistemologies, ontologies and axiologies. Predictably, this participation in the broader paradigm shift

Old Perspective	New Perspective
Positivist	Non-positivist
Experiments/Surveys	Ethnographies
Quantitative	Qualitative
A priori theory	Emergent theory
Economic/Psychological	Sociological/Anthropological
Micro/Managerial	Macro/Cultural
Focus on buying	Focus on consuming
Emphasis on cognitions	Emphasis on emotions
American	Multicultural

Figure 2.1 Old versus new perspectives in consumer behaviour research

occurring within the social sciences has stirred resistance from those committed to positivist consumer research. Nevertheless, non-positivism has won respect in the discipline of consumer behaviour and a public façade of methodological pluralism prevails (e.g. Hunt 1991; Lutz 1989). Both the *Journal of Consumer Research* and the Association for Consumer Research invite and publish positivist as well as non-positivist research. With information processing experiments and experiential consumption ethnographies abutting one another in the journals, it seems likely that the latest shift to the new consumer behaviour from the old is not yet complete. Ultimately the incommensurate assumptions of the underlying research paradigms and conflicting objectives of the two sets of researchers are likely to foster a further split. Whether or not the business school allows this degree of non-managerial, self-critical, macro focus among the consumer researchers it houses remains to be seen.

Several events nourished the development of a new consumer behaviour in schools of business. During the 1980s a number of anthropologists, sociologists and literary critics joined marketing departments that were seeking to broaden their perspectives. Prominent among this group are Eric Arnould, Janeen Costa, Jeffrey Durgee, Annamma Joy, John Sherry and Barbara Stern. It is also not lost upon some in marketing that other disciplines like those represented elsewhere in this book were beginning to become very interested in the consumer. While nominally the *Journal of Consumer Research* is interdisciplinary and sponsored by a dozen different organisations in various behavioural sciences, in practice it continues to publish primarily the work of those in marketing departments. It is therefore important that these departments have begun to broaden internally. It is also important to the substantive course of the new consumer behaviour research that the more vigorous debates in the field (see the introduction to the next section) have pitted positivism against non-positivism and that the substantive shifts occurring simultaneously have seemed less troublesome. This may be the case partly because beginning in the 1960s the marketing subfields of macro marketing, social marketing, consumer policy and marketing history have helped to legitimise macro and non-managerial topics in marketing departments. These subfields clearly retain a minority status, but they are each viable and accepted specialities. The changing external environment has also helped support the shift in substantive agendas. As the world becomes more global, a more multicultural set of concerns begs for attention. Basic consumption issues are raised as multinational marketers enter the so-called Third World, sometimes with disastrous results as illustrated by infant formula marketing. Basic consumption issues are also raised as economic systems change from variants of communism to variants of capitalism. Even transient media events like the rise of the yuppie focus attention on basic macro consumption issues of materialism. Just as a business operating in a single country can no longer afford to ignore events in the rest of the world, a marketing academic studying consumption can no longer afford to ignore the broader consumption issues being raised in other disciplines.

Removed from the sterile assumptions of the laboratory or anonymous scaled attitude measures, the new consumer behaviour precipitates the unavoidable conclusion that consumers are not mere automatons who receive information inputs and produce brand choice outputs that maximise satisfaction. Rather they are socially connected human beings participating in multiple interacting cultures. Social class is not just a classificatory variable with which to segment the market for clothing and other consumer goods, but is rather a consumption reality, involving wealth and poverty, haves and have-nots, hegemonic control, core and periphery cultures and subcultures, and desires and frustrations. A family is not a decision-making consumption unit, but a fragile and symbolically rich human group relating to one another in ways that are increasingly mediated by consumption. And a product like an automobile is not just a transportation vehicle but a vehicle for fantasy, fun, prestige, power, pollution, carnage, sex, mobility, connection, alienation, aggression, achievement, and the host of cultural changes it brings in its wake. As marketing and consumption become increasingly dominant parts of the human landscape, the new consumer behaviour attempts to understand how consumption relates to the rest of human existence.

II A review of the new consumer behaviour literature

The seeds of the paradigm shift occurring within consumer behaviour research can be found in a number of seminal papers (Anderson 1983, 1986, 1989; Hudson and Ozanne 1988; Ozanne and Hudson 1989; Peter 1991; Peter and Olson 1989). Several conferences and workshops sponsored by the American Marketing Association focused on alternative philosophies of science in the 1980s (e.g. Bush and Hunt 1982; Anderson and Ryan 1984). A number of chapters in volumes edited by Brinberg and Lutz (1986), by Bagozzi, Dholakia and Firat (1987), and by Kumcu and Firat (1988) address themselves to 'radical' philosophies in consumer research as well. Reactions against this paradigm shift are found in similar sources (e.g. Calder and Tybout 1987, 1989; Cooper 1989; Hunt 1989; Siegel 1988). The shift in perspectives was crystallised by debates within the Association for Consumer Research conferences on whether a business perspective was good or bad for consumer research (Holbrook 1985; Jacoby 1985a, 1985b) and whether marketers should be the ultimate consumers of such research (Belk 1986; Clayton 1986; Fennell 1986; Hirschman 1986b; Holbrook 1986). Belk's (1987c) presidential address to ACR, urged that the pre-paradigmatic field adopt a more macro focus on human well-being and the effects of marketing and consumption activities on culture. More recently, ACR presidential addresses have argued for greater use of the humanities (Holbrook 1990), more attention to 'the dark side' of consumer behaviour, such as drug addiction (Hirschman 1991c), and more consideration of social issues, such as homelessness (Andreasen 1993).

Interdisciplinary conferences were initiated and co-sponsored by the Association for Consumer Research in the areas of history (Tan and Sheth 1985), aesthetics (Hirschman and Holbrook 1981), fashion (Solomon 1984), and semiotics (Umiker-Sebeok 1987). In 1986 two dozen consumer researchers from the US and Canada spent the summer on a qualitative research project that moved from Los Angeles to Boston. The project was widely attended within the discipline and culminated in conference papers (e.g. Belk 1987e, 1988b; Belk, Wallendorf, Sherry, Holbrook and Roberts 1988; Holbrook 1988a; Sherry 1987, Wallendorf 1987), journal articles (Belk, Sherry, and Wallendorf 1988; Belk, Wallendorf, and Sherry 1989), an edited book (Belk 1991a), and a videotape (Wallendorf and Belk 1987). In 1989 the Association for Consumer Research published its first monograph, which significantly is a volume of interpretive research (Hirschman 1989).

In the 1990s it has become clear that the new consumer behaviour has established itself beside the old. The number of researchers and publications within the more macro non-positivist framework continues to grow and further ACR-co-sponsored conferences have been held on the topics of materialism (Rudmin and Richins 1992), gender and consumption (Costa 1991, 1993a), and marketing and international development (Kumcu, Firat, Karafakroğlu, Karabulut, and Oluç 1986; Littlefield and Csath 1988; Dholakia and Bothra 1991; Dominguez 1993). Macro consumer behaviour books (Belk 1995; Belk and Dholakia 1995; Costa 1994; Costa and Bamossy 1995; Hirschman and Holbrook 1992; Holbrook 1993; Otnes and Beltramini 1995; Shultz, Belk and Ger 1994), texts

(Solomon 1992) and review chapters (Sherry 1991) continue to proliferate as well. In addition to written text, visual ethnography is emerging within consumer research (Heisley and Levy 1991; Heisley, McGrath and Sherry 1991; Wallendorf and Belk 1987). And a variety of non-positivist research methods continues to be championed within the new consumer research including critical theory (Murray and Ozanne 1991), ethnography (Sanders 1987), historical analysis (Firat 1987; Fullerton 1987; Kumcu 1987; Smith and Lux 1993), literary criticism (Stern 1989a, 1989b), naturalistic enquiry (Hirschman 1986a; Belk, Sherry and Wallendorf 1988), phenomenology (Churchill and Wertz 1985; Durgee 1987; Fennell 1987; Thompson, Locander and Pollio 1989), psychoanalytic methods (Holbrook 1988b), projective methods (Rook 1988) and semiotics (Mick 1986, 1989).

In a sense the 'discovery' of non-positivist research methods in consumer research has opened a Pandora's box full of 'new' substantive questions to be investigated. During this transitional period, even the new consumer research continues to carry a legacy of the prior psychological focus on the individual, but it simultaneously shows evidence of increasing attention to cultural and societal issues. The areas reviewed below, of necessity, only partly represent the emerging agenda of consumer research topics. They should serve, however, collectively to characterise the multiple projects of those involved in the new consumer behaviour research movement.

CONSUMPTION SYMBOLISM

The oldest of the new consumer behaviour topics, with roots in early motivation research, counters economic assumptions of the utilitarian, price-conscious, information-processing consumer with evidence of the non-literal meanings that marketers and consumers jointly create and find in consumer goods and services. Thorstein Veblen's (1899) influential work on status symbols is an earlier influence in this area, but more recent work finds that consumption can also convey age, gender, ethnicity, personality, mood and other symbolic information. In large-scale urban environments with multiple social roles, our choices of clothing, vehicles, homes, foods, drinks, magazines, fragrances, pets, entertainments and alterations to our body all convey information to us and others about who we are (e.g. Belk, Bahn and Mayer 1982; Hirschman 1986c; Holman 1981; Kleine and Hubbert 1993; Levy 1981, 1986; McCracken 1986; Sanders 1985; Schouten 1991b). Not simply as individual items, but as part of consumption constellations (or Diderot unities – McCracken 1989b), these goods define and express lifestyles (Solomon and Assael 1987; Solomon 1988). The consumption symbolism of gifts is a related area of consumer research explored below. The work on consumption symbolism has been part of the effort to envision a more experiential, less mechanised, and less cognitively rational consumer than the consumer-as-information-processor (Belk 1987b; Holbrook 1987; Holbrook and Hirschman 1982).

PROPERTY AND POSSESSIONS

Another important part of the new consumer behaviour with old roots is the focus on what it means to own something or say that it is ours. In this case the behavioural foundation was laid by William James (1890) with further work in the 1930s (Beaglehole 1932; Isaacs 1935; see Rudmin, Belk and Furby 1987). The role of property and possessions in defining the self is succinctly summarised in a consumer culture: you are what you possess. Consumer research into the phenomena of property and possessions has developed the concepts of possessions as extensions of self, as links to individual and aggregate sense of past, and as sources of self-completion (Belk 1988a, 1991b; Rudmin 1991). Other work has examined how these meanings differ across cultures and how possessions allow us to shed, transport and create meanings across locales when we move from one place to another (Belk 1992b; Joy and Dholakia 1991; Mehta and Belk 1991). In addition the concept and implications of object attachment have been examined, including feelings of personal gain and loss through object acquisition and disposition (Adelman 1992; Ball and Tasaki 1992; Belk 1992a; Gulerce 1991; McAlexander 1991; McAlexander, Schouten, and Roberts 1993; Pavia 1993; Roberts 1991; Sayre 1994; Schouten 1991a; Schultz, Kleine, and Kernan 1989). The meaning of possessions to the self is considered further in section III.

CONSUMPTION FESTIVALS AND RITUALS

Social festivals and rituals involving consumption raise issues involving family, society and culture that go beyond the narrow assumption that the consumer is an autonomous individual. To date consumer research has focused primarily on North American and European consumption festivals, although it is apparent that some of these festivals have an increasingly global presence. This is perhaps most true of Christmas celebrations and attendant gift-giving. Issues investigated in this context include gender roles and Christmas shopping (Fisher and Arnold 1990; Otnes, Lowrey and Kim 1993; Sherry and McGrath 1989), the role of Santa Claus in consumer socialisation (Belk 1987a), and material versus non-material meanings of the holiday (Belk 1989, 1993a; Belk and Bryce 1993; Hirschman and LaBarbara 1989). Valentine's Day has been examined with regard to gender issues (Otnes, Ruth and Milbourne 1994). The American Thanksgiving has been found to be a celebration of abundance and the family with strong gender role differences (Wallendorf and Arnould 1992). And Hallowe'en has been found to involve sex role socialisation, commercial appropriation, and battles between chaos and control taking place within a symbolic ritual of rebellion (Belk 1990, 1994b; Levinson *et al.* 1992).

The ritual substratum of such aggregate consumption celebrations as well as less prominent aspects of group and individual consumer life have been examined via concepts such as sacredness, liminality and pilgrimage in such diverse contexts as grooming (Rook 1985; Rook and Levy 1983; Wallendorf and Nelson 1987), clothing (Solomon and Anand 1985), home decoration (McCracken 1989a), collecting (Belk, Wallendorf, Sherry and Holbrook 1991), money use (Ahuvia 1992; Ahuvia and Adelman 1993; Belk and Wallendorf 1990), time use (Bergadaà 1990; Chebat and Venkatesan 1993; Schroeder *et al.* 1993), theme park visitation (O'Guinn and Belk 1989), nouveau riche consumption (Costa and Belk 1990), use of security service symbols (Rook 1987b), use of informal markets (Belk, Sherry and Wallendorf 1988; Herrmann 1991, 1993; Sherry 1990a, 1990b), tourism (Belk and Costa 1991), motorcycling (Schouten and McAlexander 1992), skydiving (Celsi, Rose and Leigh 1993), river rafting (Arnould and Price 1993), sports spectating (Holt 1993), consumption of performances (Deighton 1992; Durgee, Holbrook and Sherry 1991), coming out at debutante balls (Escalas 1993), and gift-giving (Sherry 1983). Possession, exchange, grooming and divestment rituals have all received conceptual attention (McCracken 1986). Besides work on grooming and exchange rituals, divestment rituals have received some empirical attention (Heisley, Cours and Wallendorf 1993; Young 1991; Young and Wallendorf 1989). And Boorstin's (1968, 1973) contention that consumers gain a sense of community through shared brand choices and consumption loyalties has recently received some support (Friedman 1991; Friedman, Abeele and De Vos 1993).

CRITICAL PERSPECTIVES

While micro consumer behaviour studies focus on the impact of the marketing mix (product, price, promotion and physical distribution) on consumer purchase behaviour, macro consumer behaviour studies have increasingly focused on societal consumption problems, consumer resistance strategies and dysfunctional consumption. Conceptual frames for many of these investigations derive from critical theoretic (Frankfurt School), feminist, Marxist and postmodern or post-structuralist perspectives (e.g. Bristor and Fischer 1993; Firat 1991b, 1992; Firat and Venkatesh 1993; Hirschman 1993; Murray and Ozanne 1991; Rogers 1987; Van Raaij 1993; Venkatesh 1992). Such criticism is not unusual in religion, humanities and older social sciences, but the still small critical voice is a recent phenomenon within the business school. The masculine and capitalist biases of older consumer research are seen in its decontextualised positivist methods, its behavioural manipulation, prediction, and control objectives, and its masculine rationality in modelling the consumer as a purposeful agent with little concern with or for others (Bristor and Fischer 1991, 1993; Hirschman 1991a, 1993; Venkatesh 1991). In addition, gender stereotypes have been shaped and reinforced by marketers and the role of production has been masculinised and valorised while the role of consumption has been feminised and denigrated (Firat 1991a; Stern 1993).

Much, though not all, of the consumer behaviour work on consumer materialism and consumer culture has adopted a critical perspective (e.g. Belk 1982, 1983, 1985, 1988c; Bond 1992; Costa 1990; Ross 1991; Rudmin 1992; Venkatesh 1992; Venkatesh and Swamy 1994; Wright and Larsen 1992). Investigations of efforts to reduce consumption-related environmental pollution have largely supplanted the study of energy conservation efforts that proliferated following the OPEC oil embargo of the early 1970s (e.g. Dobscha 1993; Olney and Bryce 1991), although studies of attempts to discourage private automobile use continue (e.g. Hutton and Markley 1991). Marketer invasion of consumer privacy is another area that has begun to receive some attention (Goodwin 1991). And the under-consumption problems of homelessness, poverty and starvation have been addressed by a small number of consumer research studies (Chin 1992; Hill 1991; Hill and Stamey 1990; Pfeiffer 1992).

Work on consumer resistance strategies in the face of proliferating consumer culture goes beyond the postmodern critique to consider active attempts by consumers to withstand or counteract such cultural forces. Strategies include consumer boycotts, cooperative movements, voluntary simplicity, market and advertising critiques, and the transformation of mass-produced objects into individuated possessions and experiences (Burke, Milberg and Smith 1993; Garrett 1987; Herrmann 1993; Kilbourne 1992; Peñaloza and Price 1993; Pollay 1993; Putnam and Muck 1991; Rudmin and Kilbourne 1995). Recently consumer resistance to marketed images of female beauty has also begun to be considered (Bristor and Fontenelle 1993; Gainer 1993).

Dysfunctional consumer behaviours examined include alcohol use (Lastovika, Murry, Joachimsthaler, Bhalla and Scheurich 1987), illegal drug use (Hirschman 1992), smoking (Pollay and Lavack 1993), prostitution (Hirschman 1991b; Østergaard 1993), compulsive buying (Faber 1992; Faber, O'Guinn and Krych 1987; Nataraajan and Goff 1991; O'Guinn and Faber 1989; Shapiro 1993), gambling (Burns, Gillett, Rubinstein and Gentry 1990), dysfunctional eating (Grunert 1993), and AIDS risk-taking (Cooper-Martin and Stephens 1990; Middlestadt 1993). While most of these harmful consumption behaviours have also been examined by researchers in other fields, the work on compulsive buying thus far appears relatively unique to consumer research with only limited attention in the psychiatric literature. Like the similarly unique self-gift investigations noted in the part of section III on gift-giving, compulsive buying is intended to be self-medicative. However, the effects of indulging these uncontrollable urges to shop and buy are often extremely dysfunctional for these consumers and their families. Compulsive buying also differs in this respect from impulse buying, which tends to be more benign (Rook 1987a; Rook and Hoch 1985; Thompson, Locander and Pollio 1990).

CULTURAL STUDIES

Traditionally consumer research has been focused on American and, to a lesser degree, European consumption. In recent years more cross-cultural and cross-subcultural research has emerged although the number of such studies is still quite small. The subcultural studies have examined consumption patterns among Jews (Hirschman 1981), Mormons (Belk 1992b, 1994a), WASPs (Hirschman 1988), American Indians (Gilster 1993); Indian-Americans (Joy and Dholakia 1991; Mehta and Belk 1991), Korean-Americans (Lee and Um 1992), Hispanic-Americans (Peñaloza 1994; Peñaloza and Gilly 1986; Reilly and Wallendorf 1984, 1987; Wallendorf and Nelson 1987; Wallendorf and Reilly 1983a, 1983b), French- and English-speaking Canadians (Chebat and Venkatesan 1993), and Gypsy, Hungarian and majority Romanians (Belk and Paun 1995). Food, clothing, housing, home decor, automobiles, shopping, banking, personal care product use and holiday celebrations are among the consumption differences examined in these studies.

Cross-cultural comparisons as well as studies of single cultures have also been conducted by consumer researchers. Examples of cross-cultural studies include studies of selected traditional cultures (Arnould and Wilk 1984; Belk 1984, 1988c; Wilk 1987), comparisons of cultures at different levels of economic development (Belk and Ger 1990; Ger, Belk, and Lascu 1993; Jolibert and Fernandez-Moreno 1983; Schroeder et al. 1993; Thøgersen 1993; Wallendorf and Arnould 1988), comparisons of cultures at similar levels of economic development (Bamossy and Dawson 1991; Dawson and Bamossy 1990; Englis, Solomon and Olofsson 1993), comparison of host and guest perceptions in cross-cultural tourism (Costa 1993b), and semiotic and content analytic comparisons of advertising in different cultures (Belk and Pollay 1985; Englis, Solomon and Olofsson 1993; Tse, Belk and Zhou 1989). Single-country studies have been conducted in countries including China (Belk and Zhou 1986), Niger Republic (Arnould 1989), Nepal (Belk 1993b), Japan (Brannen 1992; Sherry and Camargo 1987), Greece (Costa 1989), Turkey (Ger 1992); Ireland (James and James 1985; Wilson 1993, 1995), and India (Belk and Mehta 1991; de Pyssler 1992; Venkatesh and Swamy 1994). In addition, the demise of communism and the subsequent adoption of market-based capitalism has fostered a number of studies examining the consumption impact of these changes (e.g. Boski 1992; Damjan 1993; Dietl 1993; Gubin, Young,

Osipov and Kostioutchenko 1993; Lofman 1993; Manrai and Manrai 1993; Pecotich and Shultz 1993; Shultz, Belk and Ger 1994; Witkowski 1993). These ethnographies in transitional economies make clear that whatever role consumer desire may have had in precipitating this wave of conversion to capitalism, the changes have hardly brought about a consumer paradise in these countries. And some work has examined George Gerbner's (Gerbner, *et al.* 1986) cultivation hypothesis regarding the media-based anticipatory consumption socialisation of immigrants prior to immigration (Lee 1989; O'Guinn, Lee, and Faber 1986; Peñaloza 1989). Nevertheless, consumer behaviour research remains predominantly the study of the American consumer.

III   Two case-studies

GIFTS AND GIFT-GIVING

A key consumption phenomenon through which we relate to each other and help weave the web of culture is through gift-giving. In gift-giving, consumer research joins older anthropological research (e.g. Malinowski 1922; Mauss 1925) in confronting issues of egoism versus altruism and symbolic interpersonal communication. Gift-giving has been examined as a form of communication, social exchange, economic exchange, socialisation and luxury expenditure (Banks 1979; Belk 1976, 1979; Garner and Wagner 1991; Pandya and Venkatesh 1993). In addition to the gift-giving contexts of the consumption rituals noted in section II, gift-giving has also been examined in the contexts of weddings (Fisher and Gainer 1991; Lowes, Turner and Wills 1971; McGrath 1993; Otnes and Lowrey 1993), baby showers (Fischer and Gainer 1993), birthdays (McGrath and Otnes 1993), funerals (Mallard 1992, 1993), hospitality thank-you gifts (Rucker, Freitas and Dolstra 1994), gifts for no occasion (Scammon, Shaw and Bamossy 1982), and *omiyage* gifts by returning Japanese tourists (Rucker *et al.* 1986; Witkowski and Yamamoto 1991). Gender comparisons and gift shopping ethnographies confirm that choosing gifts in the West remains 'women's work' (Coon and Belk 1991; McGrath 1989, forthcoming; Rucker, Freitas, Murray and Prato 1991; Sherry and McGrath 1989; Wolfinbarger and Gilly 1991). Contrary to obligatory ritual expressions of joy and thanks, gift-giving and gift receipt have sometimes been found to be frustrating, resented or hostile acts (McGrath, Sherry and Levy 1993; Otnes, Lowrey and Kim 1993; Sherry, McGrath and Levy 1992, 1993). While the majority of this work has been conducted in a North American context, some research has begun to explore cultural differences in gift-giving (e.g. Beatty, Kahle and Horner 1991; James and James 1985; Jolibert and Fernandez-Moreno 1983; Green and Alden 1988).

Although these studies have generally assumed an exchange model of gift-giving, work in a dating gift context has identified three different models that may be operative: economic exchange, social exchange and romantic love (Belk and Coon 1993). The romantic love model involves non-reciprocal altruistic gifts given as expressions of emotions. A summary of the differences between the exchange paradigm of the first two models and the agapic (unselfish) love paradigm in which the latter is embedded is seen in Figure 2.2. Compared to the exchange models of gift-giving, the agapic love paradigm involves idealisation and singularisation of the beloved, inattention to gift cost, passion, altruism and submissiveness by the giver, as well as gifts with predominantly expressive significance and without reciprocal obligations. The agapic love paradigm includes not only romantic love, but also parental or familial love, religious love of God, and brotherly or neighbourly love. While the paradigm has been found to supplement rather than supplant the exchange model in accounting for patterns of dating gift-giving, it represents a substantial departure from exchange assumptions that dominate the social sciences.

A more egoistic side of gift-giving has also been detected in consumer research: self-gifts. Self-gifts are rewards and therapeutic mood-enhancing 'gifts' we present to ourselves, often as a part of motivational self-bargaining in a rhetoric of deservingness (Faure and Mick 1993; McKeage 1992; McKeage, Richins and Debevec 1993; Mick 1991; Mick and DeMoss 1990a, 1990b, 1993). A small self-gift might involve a reader rewarding

Exchange Paradigm	Agapic Love Paradigm
Instrumental (designed and purposive)	Expressive (spontaneous and celebratory)
Rational (dispassionate)	Emotional (passionate)
Pragmatic	Idealistic
Masculine	Feminine
Reciprocal gifts	Non-binding gifts
Egoistic	Altruistic
Giver-dominant (seeks control)	Giver-submissive (abandons control)
Money is relevant (economically or symbolically)	Money is irrelevant
Gifts singularise objects	Gifts singularise recipient

Figure 2.2 Differences in exchange and agapic love paradigms
Source: Belk and Coon (1993)

herself with a cola after completing a chapter, while larger self-gifts might involve a university student rewarding himself with an automobile upon completion of a degree. These processes of self-reward may be characteristic of consumer societies in which consumers engage in a mental accounting of entitlements or just rewards (Hoch and Lowenstein 1991; Thaler 1985) and model their self-gifts after the more delayed gratifications thought to obtain in religious visions of heaven for the faithful (McDannell and Lang 1988). It has also been observed that parental material rewards to children (Belk 1988a) and contemporary gifts supposedly bestowed by Santa Claus in return for 'good' behaviour (Belk 1987a) invoke a similar reward paradigm, and that such reinforcement may prepare children to self-reward themselves as adults. We give ourselves gifts not only to reward 'deserving' behaviour, but also as a therapeutic device to cheer ourselves up when we have done badly, are lonely, or are in a bad mood. Just as Spradley (1970) found in his study entitled 'You Owe Yourself a Drunk', mood-altering gifts of alcohol, drugs, food and music are often chosen for such therapeutic purposes. Linking this phenomenon to compulsive buying, one study has found that the use of therapeutic self-gifts may become compulsive for some consumers (Shapiro 1993). And where guilt over self-indulgence discourages self-gifts, the possibility exists that a pair (or larger group) of gift-givers can fulfil each other's gift requests in such a way that interpersonal giving effectively becomes self-gift-giving (Belk 1993a; Olshavsky and Lee 1993). Both therapeutic self-gifts and (especially) reward self-gifts make more dramatic strategic use of consumer goods than is assumed by utilitarian views of consumer choice.

CONSUMPTION AND THE SELF

A second area of new consumer behaviour research that also directly opposes utilitarian views of behaviour is that of the meanings of consumption for self-definition and expression. The initial consumer research suggestion of the links between consumption and sense of self was the work of Sidney Levy (e.g. Levy 1959, 1967). An early line of research seeking to understand these meanings attempted to find correspondence between product image and self-image by comparing scores on a common set of attributes used to measure each (see Sirgy's 1982 review). While some moderate relationships were found between perceived characteristics of chosen brands and both actual and ideal self-concepts, the measurement procedures used were restricted to utilitarian attitude measures, the focus was only on consumption meanings at the moment of purchase, and the understanding of the meanings of consumption that resulted were accordingly constrained. A more promising avenue of enquiry distinguishes between low- and high-involvement consumption and seeks to demonstrate that the personal meanings of consumption are greater in the case of high-involvement products. There is some evidence that

71

enduring involvement with a product category like automobiles or clothing results in greater use of such products to define the self (Bloch and Bruce 1984; Bloch and Richins 1983), although some types of product involvement appear temporary (Richins and Bloch 1986). Another line of enquiry suggests that certain types of consumer goods that are likely to be highly meaningful for the self have a secular sacred character (Belk, Wallendorf and Sherry 1989). Such sacred things may have become so through contagious contact with the numinous (e.g. relics of star musicians (O'Guinn 1991), souvenirs from transcendent experiences (Gordon 1986)), through ritual (e.g. bequeathing and inheriting, acquiring for a collection), or through their singularity (e.g. quintessential brands, gifts from loved ones). These goods are retained and cherished because of their extraordinary status and their implications for self-definition. Their sacredness may be preserved through sustaining rituals and they may need to go through a 'cooling off' such as putting a child's former infant clothes away for a while so they will be cool enough in meaning to allow disposition (McCracken 1986).

A further conception of the relationship between consumption and the self is that certain goods may come to be seen as extensions of the self (Belk 1988a). These things extend our grasp, our abilities or our ego. They provide a sense of mastery of the environment, others and the self. They are expressive and aid feelings of identity, continuity and even immortality. And they often provide us with a sense of past – both individual and shared with others (Belk 1991b). Such things may become a part of self through appropriating and controlling them, creating or buying them, knowing them, becoming habituated to or contaminated by them, or by literally incorporating them into self. Collections, companion animals, money, other people, gifts and body parts may all be part of the extended self, as well as musical instruments, homes, vehicles, clothing, photographs, souvenirs, jewellery, furniture, and a variety of other important objects we own. Evidence suggests that we better care for and safeguard such highly cathected possessions (Belk 1987d).

Consider, for example, our companion animals (Hirschman 1994; Robins, Sanders and Cahill 1991; Sanders 1990, 1993). When a dog or cat is first acquired it is likely to be largely fungible with its same-sex litter mates. But after we have lived with this pet for a period of time, cared for it, given it a name, watched it grow, and mutually adapted to each other's idiosyncrasies, it is no longer at all interchangeable with its siblings. As with our children, we tend to treat a compliment or insult to our pet as a compliment or insult to our selves and we make excuses when the animal publicly misbehaves (Sanders 1990). The process of mourning that may accompany the death of a companion animal is often similar to that which accompanies the death of a family member (Belk 1988a, 1992a). In all significant respects, such a pet is a part of self.

Another example of extended self is found in the meaning of collections to collectors (Belk, Wallendorf, Sherry and Holbrook 1991; Formanek 1991; Olmsted 1991). Collecting entails deep involvement with certain sets of possessions. It is a behaviour that is widely distributed across ages, genders and social classes, although the particular objects collected tend to differ within such strata (Belk and Wallendorf forthcoming). Besides acting as extensions of self, collections may even promise collectors a type of immortality if their collections are preserved in their names after death. During life, collections of even such humble objects as beer cans take on (to the collector) a sacred or magical character which transcends the here and now and markedly distinguishes the items in a collection from other consumption objects. These objects may also extend the collector's sense of self to include the other times, people and places with which they share a provenance. And the social sanction generally granted the activity of collecting, elevates and legitimises acquisitiveness into an art or science (Danet and Katriel 1989). While collecting may provide feelings of prestige, accomplishment and collegiality to the collector, it can also result in asocial and addictive behaviours. Like gift-giving, collecting presents a distilled microcosm of consumption that informs significant issues in the broad study of consumer behaviour.

CONCLUSION

One conclusion that emerges clearly from these two case-studies is that consumption has both good and bad consequences for the individual and society. While quantitative studies of materialism consistently find a moderate negative relationship between materialistic traits and individual feelings of well-being (e.g. Belk 1985; Richins and Dawson 1992), it is clear that contemporary consumption is too complex to warrant a simple good/bad judgement. In fact, it has been suggested that the passionate custodial relationship that some consumers like collectors may have with selected possessions is object-centred more than self-centred and may transcend materialism (Belk and Coon 1993; Shimp and Madden 1988). While such possessions are clearly implicated in the construction of self, at the same time they may become a self-transcendent vehicle. It is clear from these cases that those who give gifts and compete to acquire collectible objects are using consumption to mediate human relationships. Property and possessions in these roles can act as either a glue binding us together in love or as objects provoking jealousy, hatred and rivalry. Such powerful interpersonal emotions in consumption point to further inadequacies in the dispassionate and lifeless utilitarian models of consumption.

The literature reviewed in this chapter suggests that the new consumer behaviour research is creating a very different model of the consumer than the information processing rational consumer who is at the core of more traditional consumer research. In the past decade the agenda of consumer behaviour research topics has enlarged and become less managerial and more societal in nature. Consumer research is in the early stages of theory development and continues to draw more on other disciplines than these disciplines draw on it. Carrying the academic stigma of a business school affiliation, the new consumer researchers seem, in part, to be collectively striving for academic legitimacy and a sense of social responsibility in their work. More than this is involved in the shift from the old consumer behaviour however. Whereas previous consumer behaviour research sought to expand upon the lingering legacy of economic assumptions about consumption, the new consumer behaviour research challenges these assumptions. Whereas previous research sought primarily to advance marketing management, emerging consumer research takes a distanced and sometimes critical perspective on marketing management. And whereas traditional consumer behaviour research sought to predict and control consumer brand purchases, the new consumer behaviour research seeks to understand consumption processes in a broad, literal and contextual sense. Time will tell how successful these efforts will be, but the early results are promising.

REFERENCES

Adelman, Mara (1992) 'Rituals of adversity and remembering: the role of possessions for persons and community living with AIDS', in *Advances in Consumer Research*, vol. 19, John F. Sherry, Jr. and Brian Sternthal (eds), Provo, UT: Association for Consumer Research, pp. 401–403.

Ahuvia, Aaron C. (1992) 'For love of money: materialism and product love', in *To Have Possessions: A Handbook on Ownership and Property*, Floyd Rudmin (ed.), Corte Madera, CA: Select Press (Special issue of *Journal of Social Behavior and Personality*, 6 (6): 188–198).

Ahuvia, Aaron C. and Mara B. Adelman (1993) 'Market metaphors for meeting mates', in *Research in Consumer Behavior*, vol. 6, Janeen Costa and Russell W. Belk (eds), Greenwich, CT: JAI Press, pp. 55–84.

Anderson, Paul F. (1983) 'Marketing, scientific progress, and scientific method', *Journal of Marketing*, 47 (Fall): 18–31.

Anderson, Paul F. (1986) 'On method in consumer research: a critical relativist perspective', *Journal of Consumer Research*, 13 (September): 155–173.

Anderson, Paul F. (1989) 'On relativism and interpretivism – with a prologomenon to the "Why" question', in *Interpretive Consumer Research*, Elizabeth C. Hirschman (ed.), Provo, UT: Association for Consumer Research, pp. 10–13.

Anderson, Paul F. and Michael J. Ryan (eds) (1984) *Scientific Method in Marketing*, Chicago: American Marketing Association.

Andreasen, Alan R. (1993) 'A social marketing research agenda for consumer behavior researchers', in *Advances in Consumer Research*, vol. 20, Leigh McAlister and Michael L. Rothschild (eds), Provo, UT: Association for Consumer Research, pp. 1–5.

Arnould, Eric J. (1989) 'Preference formation and the diffusion of innovations: cases from Zinder Province, Niger Republic', *Journal of Consumer Research*, 16

(September): 239–267.

Arnould, Eric J. and Linda L. Price (1993) 'River magic: extraordinary experience and the extended service encounter', *Journal of Consumer Research*, 20 (June): 24–45.

Arnould, Eric J. and Richard Wilk (1984) 'Why do the natives wear Adidas?', in *Advances in Consumer Research*, vol. 11, Thomas Kinnear (ed.), Provo, UT: Association for Consumer Research, pp. 748–752.

Bagozzi, Richard P., Nikhilesh Dholakia, and A. Fuat Firat (eds) (1987) *Philosophical and Radical Thought in Marketing*, Lexington, MA: Lexington Books.

Ball, A. D. and L. H. Tasaki (1992) 'The role and measurement of attachment in consumer behavior', *Journal of Consumer Psychology*, 1: 155–172.

Bamossy, Gary and Scott Dawson (1991) 'A comparison of the culture of consumption between two Western cultures: a study of materialism in the Netherlands and United States', *European Marketing Academy Conference Proceedings*, vol. 2: 147–168.

Banks, Sharon K. (1979) 'Gift-giving: a review and an interactionist perspective', in *Advances in Consumer Research*, vol. 6, William Wilkie (ed.), Ann Arbor, MI: Association for Consumer Research, pp. 319–324.

Bartels, Robert (1976) *The History of Marketing Thought*, 2nd edn, Columbus, OH: Grid.

Beaglehole, Ernest (1932) *Property: A Study in Social Psychology*, New York: Macmillan.

Beatty, Sharon E., Lynn R. Kahle and Pamela Horner (1991) 'Personal values and gift-giving behaviors: a study across cultures', *Journal of Business Research*, 22 (March): 149–157.

Belk, Russell W. (1976) 'It's the thought that counts: a signed digraph analysis of gift-giving', *Journal of Consumer Research*, 3 (December): 155–162.

Belk, Russell W. (1979) 'Gift-giving behavior', in *Research in Marketing*, vol. 2, Jagdish N. Sheth (ed.), Greenwich, CT: JAI Press, pp. 95–126.

Belk, Russell W. (1982) 'Acquiring, possessing, and collecting: fundamental processes in consumer behavior', in *Marketing Theory: Philosophy of Science Perspectives*, Ronald F. Bush and Shelby D. Hunt (eds), Chicago: American Marketing Association, pp. 185–190.

Belk, Russell W. (1983) 'Worldly possessions: issues and criticisms', in *Advances in Consumer Research*, vol. 10, Richard P. Bagozzi and Alice M. Tybout (eds), Ann Arbor, MI: Association for Consumer Research, pp. 514–519.

Belk, Russell W. (1984) 'Cultural and historical differences in concepts of self and their effects on attitudes toward having and giving', in *Advances in Consumer Research*, vol. 11, Thomas Kinnear (ed.), Provo, UT: Association for Consumer Research, pp. 753–760.

Belk, Russell W. (1985) 'Materialism: trait aspects of living in the material world', *Journal of Consumer Research*, 12 (3) December: 265–280.

Belk, Russell W. (1986) 'What should ACR want to be when it grows up?', in *Advances in Consumer Research*, vol. 13, Richard J. Lutz (ed.), Provo, UT: Association for Consumer Research, pp. 423–424.

Belk, Russell W. (1987a) 'A child's Christmas in America: Santa Claus as deity, consumption as religion', *Journal of American Culture*, 10 (1) Spring: 87–100.

Belk, Russell W. (1987b) 'A modest proposal for creating verisimilitude in consumer-information-processing models and some suggestions for establishing a discipline to study consumer behavior', in *Philosophical and Radical Thought in Marketing*, Richard P. Bagozzi, Nikhilesh Dholakia and A. Fuat Firat (eds),

Lexington, MA: Lexington Books, pp. 361–372.

Belk, Russell W. (1987c) 'Happy thought: presidential address', in *Advances in Consumer Research*, vol. 14, Melanie Wallendorf and Paul Anderson (eds), Provo, UT: Association for Consumer Research, pp. 1–4.

Belk, Russell W. (1987d) 'Identity and the relevance of market, personal, and community objects', in *Marketing and Semiotics: New Directions in the Study of Signs for Sale*, Jean Sebeok (ed.), Berlin: Mouton de Gruyter, pp. 151–164.

Belk, Russell W. (1987e) 'The role of the Odyssey in consumer behavior and in consumer research', in *Advances in Consumer Research*, vol. 14, Melanie Wallendorf and Paul Anderson (eds), Provo, UT: Association for Consumer Research, pp. 357–361.

Belk, Russell W. (1988a) 'Possessions and the extended self', *Journal of Consumer Research*, 15 (September): 139–168.

Belk, Russell W. (1988b) 'Qualitative analysis of data from the consumer behavior Odyssey: the role of the computer and the role of the researcher', in *Proceedings of the Division of Consumer Psychology*, Linda Alwitt (ed.), Washington, DC: American Psychological Association, pp. 7–11.

Belk, Russell W. (1988c) 'Third World consumer culture', in *Marketing and Development: Toward Broader Dimensions*, Erdoğan Kumcu and A. Fuat Firat (eds), Greenwich, CT: JAI Press, pp. 103–127.

Belk, Russell W. (1989) 'Materialism and the modern U.S. Christmas', in *Interpretive Consumer Research*, Elizabeth C. Hirschman (ed.), Provo, UT: Association for Consumer Research, pp. 136–147.

Belk, Russell W. (1990) 'Halloween: an evolving American consumption ritual', in *Advances in Consumer Research*, vol. 17, Gerald Gorn, Marvin Goldberg and Richard Pollay (eds), Provo, UT: Association for Consumer Research, pp. 508–517.

Belk, Russell W. (ed.) (1991a) *Highways and Buyways: Naturalistic Research from the Consumer Behavior Odyssey*, Provo, UT: Association for Consumer Research.

Belk, Russell W. (1991b) 'Possessions and the sense of past', in *Highways and Buyways: Naturalistic Research from the Consumer Behavior Odyssey*, Russell W. Belk (ed.), Provo, UT: Association for Consumer Research, pp. 114–130.

Belk, Russell W. (1992a) 'Attachment to possessions', in *Place Attachment*, Irwin Altman and Setha M. Low (eds), New York: Plenum Press, pp. 37–62.

Belk, Russell W. (1992b) 'Moving possessions: an analysis based on personal documents from the 1847–1869 Mormon migration', *Journal of Consumer Research*, 19 (December): 339–361.

Belk, Russell W. (1993a) 'Materialism and the making of the modern American Christmas', in *Unwrapping Christmas*, Daniel Miller (ed.), Oxford: Oxford University Press, pp. 75–104.

Belk, Russell W. (1993b) 'Third World tourism: panacea or poison? The case of Nepal', *Journal of International Consumer Marketing*. 5 (1): 27–68.

Belk, Russell W. (1994a), 'Battling worldliness in the new Zion: mercantilism versus homespun in 19th century Utah', *Journal of Macromarketing* 14 (Spring): 9–22.

Belk, Russell W. (1994b), 'Carnival, control, and corporate culture in contemporary Halloween celebrations', in *Halloween*, Jack Santino (ed.), Knoxville, TN: University of Tennessee Press, pp. 105–132.

Belk, Russell W. (1995), *Collecting in a Consumer Society*, London: Routledge.

Belk, Russell W., Kenneth D. Bahn and Robert N. Mayer (1982) 'Developmental recognition of consumption symbolism', *Journal of Consumer Research*, 9 (June): 4–17.

Belk, Russell W. and Wendy Bryce (1993) 'Christmas shopping scenes: from modern miracle to postmodern mall', *International Journal of Research in Marketing*, 10 (August): 277–296.

Belk, Russell W. and Gregory S. Coon (1993) 'Gift-giving as agapic love: an alternative to the exchange paradigm based on dating experiences', *Journal of Consumer Research*, 20 (December): 393–417.

Belk, Russell W. and Janeen Arnold Costa (1991) 'A critical assessment of international tourism', *Proceedings of the Third International Conference on Marketing and Development*, Ruby Roy Dholakia and Kiran C. Bothra (eds), Calcutta: Indian Institute of Management, pp. 371–382.

Belk, Russell W. and Nikhilesh Dholakia (eds) (1995) *Consumption and Marketing: Macro Dimensions*, Belmont, Cincinnati, OH: Southwestern.

Belk, Russell W. and Güliz Ger (1990) 'Measuring and comparing materialism cross-culturally', in *Advances in Consumer Research*, vol. 17, Gerald Gorn, Marvin Goldberg and Richard Pollay (eds), Provo, UT: Association for Consumer Research, pp. 186–192.

Belk, Russell W. and Raj Mehta (1991) 'Special possessions and their meanings in West Central India', *Proceedings of the Third International Conference on Marketing and Development*, Ruby Roy Dholakia and Kiran C. Bothra (eds), Calcutta: Indian Institute of Management, pp. 162–171.

Belk, Russell W. and Magda Paun (1995) 'Ethnicity and consumption in Romania', in *Marketing, Consumption, and Ethnicity*, Janeen Costa and Gary Bamossy (eds), Newbury Park, CA: Sage.

Belk, Russell W. and Richard W. Pollay (1985) 'Materialism and status appeals in Japanese and U.S. print advertising: an historical and cross-cultural content analysis', *International Marketing Review*, December.

Belk, Russell W., John Sherry and Melanie Wallendorf (1988) 'A naturalistic inquiry into buyer and seller behavior at a swap meet', *Journal of Consumer Research*, 14 (March): 449–470.

Belk, Russell W. and Melanie Wallendorf (1990) 'The sacred meanings of money', *Journal of Economic Psychology*, (March): 35–67.

Belk, Russell W. and Melanie Wallendorf (forthcoming) 'Of mice and men: gender identity in collecting', in *The Material Culture of Gender/The Gender of Material Culture*, Kenneth Ames and Katharine Martinez (eds), Ann Arbor, MI: University of Michigan Press.

Belk, Russell W., Melanie Wallendorf and John Sherry (1989) 'The sacred and the profane in consumer behavior: theodicy on the Odyssey', *Journal of Consumer Research*, 16 (June): 1–38.

Belk, Russell W., Melanie Wallendorf, John F. Sherry, Jr. and Morris B. Holbrook (1991) 'Collecting in a consumer culture', in *Highways and Buyways: Naturalistic Research from the Consumer Behavior Odyssey*, Russell W. Belk (ed.), Provo, UT: Association for Consumer Research, pp. 178–215.

Belk, Russell W., Melanie Wallendorf, John F. Sherry, Jr., Morris B. Holbrook and Scott Roberts (1988) 'Collectors and collecting', in *Advances in Consumer Research*, vol. 15, Michael Houston (ed.), Provo, UT: Association for Consumer Research, pp. 548–553.

Belk, Russell W. and Nan Zhou (1986), 'Emerging consumer culture in the PRC', in *The Role of Marketing in Development: Global, Consumer, and Managerial Issues*, Erdoğan Kumcu, A. Fuat Firat, Mehmet Karafakroğlu, Muhitin Karabulut, and Mehmet Oluç (eds), Muncie, IN: Ball State University Press, pp. 137–145.

Bergadaà, Michelle M. (1990) 'The role of time in the action of the consumer',

Journal of Consumer Research, 17 (December): 289–302.

Bettman, James R. (1979) *An Information Processing Theory of Consumer Choice*, Reading, MA: Addison Wesley.

Bloch, Peter H. and Grady D. Bruce (1984) 'Product involvement as leisure behavior: the case of automobiles and clothing', in *Advances in Consumer Research*, vol. 11, Thomas Kinnear (ed.), Provo, UT: Association for Consumer Research, pp. 197–201.

Bloch, Peter H. and Marsha L. Richins (1983) 'A theoretical model for the study of product importance perceptions', *Journal of Marketing*, 47 (Summer): 69–81.

Bond, E. J. (1992) 'Materialism as a fundamental mistake about value', in *Meaning, Measure, and Morality of Materialism*, Floyd Rudmin and Marsha Richins (eds), Provo, UT: Association for Consumer Research, pp. 164–166.

Boorstin, Daniel J. (1968) 'The consumption community', in *The Consuming Public*, G. McClellan (ed.), New York: H. W. Wilson.

Boorstin, Daniel J. (1973) *The Americans: The Democratic Experience*, New York: Random House.

Boski, Pawel (1992) 'Culture consequences to market economy: stability of anti-materialist orientation in Polish mentality', in *Meaning, Measure, and Morality of Materialism*, Floyd Rudmin and Marsha Richins (eds), Provo, UT: Association for Consumer Research, pp. 14–30.

Brannen, Mary Yoko (1992) 'Cross-cultural materialism: commodifying culture in Japan', in *Meaning, Measure, and Morality of Materialism*, Floyd Rudmin and Marsha Richins (eds), Provo, UT: Association for Consumer Research, pp. 167–180.

Brinberg, David and Richard J. Lutz (eds) (1986) *Methodological Perspectives in Consumer Research*, New York: Springer Verlag.

Bristor, Julia M. and Eileen Fischer (1991) 'Objectivity and gender in consumer research: a feminist deconstructionist critique', in *Gender and Consumer Behavior Conference Proceedings*, Janeen Arnold Costa (ed.), Provo, UT: Association for Consumer Research, pp. 115–123.

Bristor, Julia M. and Eileen Fischer (1993) 'Feminist thought: implications for consumer research', *Journal of Consumer Research*, 4 (March): 518–536.

Bristor, Julia and Suzana de M. Fontenelle (1993) 'Feminine representations in beauty advertising: the paradox of liberation', in *Gender and Consumer Behavior Second Conference Proceedings*, Janeen Arnold Costa (ed.), Provo, UT: Association for Consumer Research, p. 195.

Burke, Sandra J., J. Milberg and N. Craig Smith (1993) 'The role of ethical concerns in consumer purchase behavior', in *Advances in Consumer Research*, vol. 19, John F. Sherry, Jr. and Brian Sternthal (eds), Provo, UT: Association for Consumer Research, pp. 119–122.

Burns, Alvin C., Peter L. Gillett, Marc Rubinstein and James W. Gentry (1990) 'An exploratory study of lottery playing, gambling addiction and links to compulsive consumption', in *Advances in Consumer Research*, vol. 17, Marvin E. Goldberg, Gerald Gorn and Richard W. Pollay (eds), Provo, UT: Association for Consumer Research, pp. 298–305.

Bush, Ronald F. and Shelby D. Hunt (eds) (1982) *Marketing Theory: Philosophy of Science Perspectives*, Chicago: American Marketing Association.

Calder, Bobby J. and Alice M. Tybout (1987) 'What consumer research is . . .', *Journal of Consumer Research*, 14 (June): 551–563.

Calder, Bobby J. and Alice M. Tybout (1989) 'Interpretive, qualitative, and traditional scientific empirical consumer behavior research', in *Interpretive Consumer Research*, Elizabeth C. Hirschman (ed.), Provo, UT: Association for Consumer

Research, pp. 199–208.

Celsi, Richard L., Randall L. Rose and Thomas W. Leigh (1993) 'An exploration of high-risk leisure consumption through skydiving', *Journal of Consumer Research*, 20 (June): 1–23.

Chebat, Jean-Charles and M. Ven Venkatesan (1993) 'Time orientation and Canadian consumer behavior: case of French and English speaking Canadians', in *Advances in European Consumer Research*, vol. 1, W. Fred Van Raaij and Gary J. Bamossy (eds), Provo, UT: Association for Consumer Research, pp. 24–27.

Chin, Elizabeth (1992) 'Toward a documentation of the consumer lives of inner city children', in *Meaning, Measure, and Morality of Materialism*, Floyd Rudmin and Marsha Richins (eds), Provo, UT: Association for Consumer Research, pp. 102–109.

Churchill, Scott and Frederick Wertz (1985) 'An introduction to phenomenological psychology for consumer research: historical, conceptual, and methodological foundations', in *Advances in Consumer Research*, vol. 12, Elizabeth C. Hirschman and Morris B. Holbrook (eds), Provo, UT: Association for Consumer Research, pp. 550–555.

Clayton, Alden (1986) 'Research as a voyage of discovery', in *Advances in Consumer Research*, vol. 13, Richard J. Lutz (ed.), Provo, UT: Association for Consumer Research, pp. 425–426.

Cohen, Joel B. and Dipankar Chakravarti (1990) 'Consumer psychology', *Annual Review of Psychology*, Palo Alto, CA: Annual Reviews, Inc., 41: 243–248.

Coon, Gregory S. and Russell W. Belk (1991) 'Men and women on dating and gift-giving: same planet, different worlds', *Gender and Consumer Behavior Conference Proceedings*, Janeen Arnold Costa (ed.), Provo, UT: Association for Consumer Research, pp. 94–103.

Cooper, Lee G. (1989) 'Do we need critical relativism?: Comments on "On Method in Consumer Research"', *Journal of Consumer Research*, 14 (June): 126–127.

Cooper-Martin, Elizabeth and Debra Lynn Stephens (1990) 'AIDS prevention through consumer communication: ideas from past and current research', in *Advances in Consumer Research*, vol. 17, Marvin E. Goldberg, Gerald Gorn and Richard W. Pollay (eds), Provo, UT: Association for Consumer Research, pp. 288–293.

Costa, Janeen Arnold (1989) 'On display: social and cultural dimensions of consumer behavior in the Greek Soloni', in *Advances in Consumer Research*, vol. 16, Thomas K. Srull (ed.), Provo, UT: Association for Consumer Research, pp. 562–566.

Costa, Janeen Arnold (1990) 'Toward an understanding of social and world systemic processes in the spread of consumer culture: an anthropological case study', in *Advances in Consumer Research*, vol. 17, Marvin E. Goldberg, Gerald Gorn and Richard W. Pollay (eds), Provo, UT: Association for Consumer Research, pp. 826–832.

Costa, Janeen Arnold (ed.) (1991) *Gender and Consumer Behavior Conference Proceedings*, Provo, UT: Association for Consumer Research.

Costa, Janeen Arnold (ed.) (1993a) *Second Gender and Consumer Behavior Conference Proceedings*, Provo, UT: Association for Consumer Research.

Costa, Janeen Arnold (1993b) 'Tourism as consumption precipitate: an exploration and example', in *Advances in European Consumer Research*, vol. 1, W. Fred Van Raaij and Gary J. Bamossy (eds), Provo, UT: Association for Consumer Research, pp. 300–306.

Costa, Janeen Arnold (1994) *Gender and Consumer Behavior*, Newbury Park, CA: Sage.

Costa, Janeen Arnold and Gary Bamossy (eds) (1995) *Marketing, Consumption, and Ethnicity*, Newbury Park, CA: Sage.

Costa, Janeen Arnold and Russell W. Belk (1990) 'Nouveaux riches as quintessential Americans: case studies of consumption in an extended family', in *Advances in NonProfit Marketing*, vol. 3, Russell W. Belk (ed.), Greenwich, CT: JAI Press, pp. 83–140.

Damjan, Janez (1993) 'Consumer behavior in transforming socialist countries: the case of Slovenia', in *Advances in European Consumer Research*, vol. 1, W. Fred Van Raaij and Gary J. Bamossy (eds), Provo, UT: Association for Consumer Research, pp. 236–243.

Danet, Brenda and Tamara Katriel (1989) 'No two alike: the aesthetics of collecting', *Play and Culture*, 2 (3): pp. 253–277.

Dawson, Scott and Gary Bamossy (1990) 'Isolating the effect of non-economic factors on the development of consumer culture: a comparison of materialism in the Netherlands and the United States', in *Advances in Consumer Research*, vol. 17, Gerald Gorn, Marvin Goldberg and Richard Pollay (eds), Provo, UT: Association for Consumer Research, pp. 182–185.

Deighton, John (1992) 'The consumption of performance', *Journal of Consumer Research*, 19 (December): 362–372.

Dholakia, Ruby Roy and Kiran C. Bothra (eds) (1991) *Proceedings of the Third International Conference on Marketing and Development*, Calcutta: Indian Institute of Management.

Dichter, Ernest (1964) *Handbook of Consumer Motivations*, New York: McGraw-Hill.

Dietl, Jerzy (1993) 'Dilemmas of the consumption and consumer behavior in the postcommunist countries', in *Advances in European Consumer Research*, vol. 1, W. Fred Van Raaij and Gary J. Bamossy (eds), Provo, UT: Association for Consumer Research, pp. 5–17.

Dobscha, Susan (1993) 'Women and the environment: applying eco-feminism to environmentally-related consumption', in *Advances in Consumer Research*, vol. 19, John F. Sherry, Jr. and Brian Sternthal (eds), Provo, UT: Association for Consumer Research, pp. 36–40.

Dominguez, Luis (ed.) (1993) *Proceedings of the Fourth International Conference on Marketing and Development*, Coral Gables, FL: University of Miami.

Durgee, Jeffrey (1987) 'Phenomenology: new methods for asking questions and interpreting results', in *Advances in Consumer Research*, vol. 14, Melanie Wallendorf and Paul Anderson (eds), Provo, UT: Association for Consumer Research, p. 561.

Durgee, Jeffrey (1991) 'Interpreting Dichter's interpretations: an analysis of consumer symbolism in "The Handbook of Consumer Motivations"', in *Marketing and Semiotics: Selected Papers from the Copenhagen Symposium*, Hanne H. Larsen, David G. Mick and Christian Alsted (eds), Copenhagen: Handelshøjskolens Forlag, pp. 52–74.

Durgee, Jeffrey, Morris B. Holbrook and John F. Sherry, Jr. (1991) 'The delivery and consumption of vacation performances', in *Highways and Buyways: Naturalistic Research from the Consumer Behavior Odyssey*, Russell W. Belk (ed.), Provo, UT: Association for Consumer Research, pp. 131–140.

Engel, James F., David Kollat and Roger D. Blackwell (1968) *Consumer Behavior*, New York: Holt, Rinehart and Winston.

Englis, Basil G., Michael R. Solomon and Anna Olofsson (1993) 'Music television as teen image agent – a preliminary report from the United States and Sweden', in *Advances in European Consumer Research*, vol. 1, W. Fred Van Raaij and Gary J. Bamossy (eds), Provo, UT: Association for Consumer Research, pp. 449–450.

Escalas, Jennifer Edson (1993) 'The consumption of insignificant rituals: a look at debutante balls', in *Advances in Consumer Research*, vol. 20, Leigh McAlister and Michael L. Rothschild (eds), Provo, UT: Association for Consumer Research, pp. 709–716.

Faber, Ronald (1992) 'Money changes everything: compulsive buying from a biopsychosocial perspective', *American Behavioral Scientist*, 35 (July/August): 809–819.

Faber, Ronald, Thomas O'Guinn and Raymond Krych (1987) 'Compulsive consumption', in *Advances in Consumer Research*, vol. 14, Melanie Wallendorf and Paul Anderson (eds), Provo, UT: Association for Consumer Research, pp. 132–135.

Faure, Corinne and David Glen Mick (1993) 'Self-gifts through the lens of attribution theory', in *Advances in Consumer Research*, vol. 20, Leigh McAlister and Michael L. Rothschild (eds), Provo, UT: Association for Consumer Research, pp. 553–556.

Fennell, Geraldine (1986) 'Extending the thinkable: consumer research for marketing practice', in *Advances in Consumer Research*, vol. 13, Richard J. Lutz (ed.), Provo, UT: Association for Consumer Research, pp. 427–432.

Fennell, Geraldine (1987) 'Things of heaven and earth: phenomenology, marketing, and consumer research', in *Advances in Consumer Research*, vol. 12, Elizabeth C. Hirschman and Morris B. Holbrook (eds), Provo, UT: Association for Consumer Research, pp. 544–549.

Firat, A. Fuat (1987) 'Historiography, scientific method, and exceptional historical events', in *Advances in Consumer Research*, vol. 14, Melanie Wallendorf and Paul Anderson (eds), Provo, UT: Association for Consumer Research, pp. 435–438.

Firat, A. Fuat (1991a) 'Consumption and gender: a common history', in *Gender and Consumer Behavior Conference Proceedings*, Janeen Arnold Costa (ed.), Provo, UT: Association for Consumer Research, pp. 378–386.

Firat, A. Fuat (1991b) 'The consumer in postmodernity', in *Advances in Consumer Research*, vol. 18, Rebecca Holman and Michael Solomon (eds), Provo, UT: Association for Consumer Research, pp. 70–76.

Firat, A. Fuat (1992) 'Fragmentations in the postmodern', in *Advances in Consumer Research*, vol. 19, John F. Sherry, Jr. and Brian Sternthal (eds), Provo, UT: Association for Consumer Research, pp. 203–205.

Firat, A. Fuat and Alladi Venkatesh (1993) 'Postmodernity: the age of marketing', *International Journal of Research in Marketing*, 10 (August).

Fischer, Eileen and Stephen J. Arnold (1990), 'More than a labor of love: gender roles and Christmas gift shopping', *Journal of Consumer Research*, 17 (December): 333–345.

Fischer, Eileen and Brenda Gainer (1991) 'I shop therefore I am: the role of shopping in the social construction of women's identities', in *Gender and Consumer Behavior Conference Proceedings*, Janeen Arnold Costa (ed.), Provo, UT: Association for Consumer Research, pp. 350–357.

Fischer, Eileen and Brenda Gainer (1993) 'Baby showers: a rite of passage in transition', in *Advances in Consumer Research*, vol. 20, Leigh McAlister and Michael L. Rothschild (eds), Provo, UT: Association for Consumer Research, pp. 320–324.

Formanek, Ruth (1991) 'Collectors reveal their motivations', in *To Have Possessions: A Handbook on Ownership and Property*, Floyd Rudmin (ed.), Corte Madera,

CA: Select Press (Special issue of *Journal of Social Behavior and Personality*, 6 (6): 275–286).

Friedman, Monroe (1991) *A 'Brand' New Language: Commercial Influences in Literature and Culture*, New York: Greenwood Press.

Friedman, Monroe, Piet Vanden Abeele and Koen De Vos (1993) 'Boorstin's consumption community concept: a tale of two countries', *Journal of Consumer Policy*, 16 (1): 35–60.

Fullerton, Ronald (1987) 'Historicism: what it is, and what it means for consumer research', in *Advances in Consumer Research*, vol. 14, Melanie Wallendorf and Paul Anderson (eds), Provo, UT: Association for Consumer Research, pp. 431–434.

Fullerton, Ronald (1990) 'The art of marketing research: selections from Paul F. Lazarsfeld's "Shoe Buying in Zurich" (1933)', *Journal of the Academy of Marketing Science*, 18 (Fall): 319–327.

Fullerton, Ronald (1994) 'Tea and the Viennese: a pioneering episode in the analysis of consumer behavior', in *Advances in Consumer Research*, vol. 21, Christopher Allen and Deborah Roedder-John (eds), Provo, UT: Association for Consumer Research.

Gainer, Brenda (1993) 'Fear and sin: images of fat in contemporary culture', in *Gender and Consumer Behavior Second Conference Proceedings*, Janeen Arnold Costa (ed.), Provo, UT: Association for Consumer Research, p. 197.

Garner, Thesia I. and Janet Wagner (1991) 'Economic dimensions of household gift giving', *Journal of Consumer Research*, 18 (December): 368–379.

Garrett, Dennis E. (1987) 'The effectiveness of marketing policy boycotts: environmental opposition to marketing', *Journal of Marketing*, 51 (April): 46–57.

Ger, Güliz (1992) 'The positive and negative effects of marketing on socioeconomic development: the Turkish case', *Journal of Consumer Policy*, 15 (December): 229–254.

Ger, Güliz, Russell W. Belk and Dana-Nicoleta Lascu (1993) 'The development of consumer desire in marketizing and developing economies: the cases of Romania and Turkey', in *Advances in Consumer Research*, vol. 20, Leigh McAlister and Michael L. Rothschild (eds), Provo, UT: Association for Consumer Research, pp. 102–107.

Gerbner, George, Larry Gross, Michael Morgan and Nancy Signorelli (1986) 'Living with television: the dynamics of the cultivation process', in *Perspectives on Media Effects*, Jennings Bryant and Dorf Zillmann (eds), Hilldale, NJ: Lawrence Erlbaum, pp. 17–40.

Gilster, Elisabeth (1993) 'Telling stories: a sociolinguistic analysis of language use in a marketplace', in *Advances in Consumer Research*, vol. 20, Leigh McAlister and Michael L. Rothschild (eds), Provo, UT: Association for Consumer Research, pp. 83–88.

Goodwin, Cathy (1991) 'Privacy: recognition of a consumer right', *Journal of Public Policy & Marketing*, 10: 149–166.

Gordon, Beverly (1986) 'The souvenir: messenger of the extraordinary', *Journal of Popular Culture*, 20 (3): 135–146.

Green, Robert T. and Dana L. Alden (1988) 'Functional equivalence in crosscultural gift-giving in Japan and the United States', *Psychology and Marketing*, 5 (Summer): 155–168.

Grunert, Suzanne C. (1993) 'On gender differences in eating behavior as compensatory consumption', in *Gender and Consumer Behavior Second Conference Proceedings*, Janeen Arnold Costa (ed.), Provo, UT: Association for Consumer Research, pp. 74–87.

Gubin, Oleg I., Melissa Martin Young, Alexander G. Osipov and Natasha Kostioutchenko (1993) 'Social control versus social stability: a conceptualization of contradictory goals and hybrid outcomes on ethnic relations, consumer satisfaction, and entrepreneurship in the former USSR', in *Advances in European Consumer Research*, vol. 1, W. Fred Van Raaij and Gary J. Bamossy (eds), Provo, UT: Association for Consumer Research, pp. 89–96.

Gulerce, Aydan (1991) 'Transitional objects: a reconsideration of the phenomenon', in *To Have Possessions: A Handbook on Ownership and Property*, Floyd Rudmin (ed.), Corte Madera, CA: Select Press (Special issue of *Journal of Social Behavior and Personality*, 6 (6): 187–208).

Heisley, Deborah D., Deborah Ann Cours and Melanie Wallendorf (1993) 'The structural dimensions of the inter-generational transfer of possessions', paper presented at the Annual Conference of the Association for Consumer Research, Nashville, TN, October.

Heisley, Deborah D. and Sydney J. Levy (1991) 'Autodriving: a photoelicitation technique', *Journal of Consumer Research*, 18 (December): 257–272.

Heisley, Deborah D., Mary Ann McGrath and John F. Sherry, Jr. (1991) '"To everything there is a season": a photoessay of a farmer's market', in *Highways and Buyways: Naturalistic Research from the Consumer Behavior Odyssey*, Russell W. Belk (ed.), Provo, UT: Association for Consumer Research, pp. 141–166.

Herrmann, Gretchen M. (1991) 'Women's exchange in the American garage sale: giving gifts and creating community', in *Gender and Consumer Behavior Conference Proceedings*, Janeen Arnold Costa (ed.), Provo, UT: Association for Consumer Research, pp. 234–243.

Herrmann, Gretchen M. (1993) 'His and hers: gender and garage sales', in *Gender and Consumer Behavior Second Conference Proceedings*, Janeen Arnold Costa (ed.), Provo, UT: Association for Consumer Research, pp. 88–98

Herrmann, Robert O. (1993) 'The tactics of consumer resistance: group action and marketplace exit', in *Advances in Consumer Research*, vol. 20, Leigh McAlister and Michael L. Rothschild (eds), Provo, UT: Association for Consumer Research, pp. 130–134.

Hill, Ronald Paul (1991) 'Homeless women, special possessions and the meaning of "home": an ethnographic case study', *Journal of Consumer Research*, 18 (December): 298–310.

Hill, Ronald Paul and Mark Stamey (1990) 'The homeless in America: an examination of possessions and consumption behaviors', *Journal of Consumer Research*, 17 (December): 303–321.

Hirschman, Elizabeth C. (1981) 'American Jewish ethnicity: its relationship to some selected aspects of consumer behavior', *Journal of Marketing*, 45 (Summer): 102–110.

Hirschman, Elizabeth C. (1986a) 'Humanistic inquiry in marketing research: philosophy, method, and criteria', *Journal of Marketing Research*, 23 (August): 237–249.

Hirschman, Elizabeth C. (1986b) 'Marketing, intellectual creativity, and consumer research', in *Advances in Consumer Research*, vol. 13, Richard J. Lutz (ed.), Provo, UT: Association for Consumer Research, pp. 433–435.

Hirschman, Elizabeth C. (1986c) 'The creation of product symbolism', in *Advances in Consumer Research*, vol. 13, Richard J. Lutz (ed.), Provo, UT: Association for Consumer Research, pp. 327–331.

Hirschman, Elizabeth C. (1988) 'Upper class WASPs as consumers: a humanistic inquiry', in *Research in Consumer Behavior*, vol. 3, Elizabeth Hirschman and Jagdish N. Sheth (eds), Greenwich, CT: JAI Press, pp. 115–148.

Hirschman, Elizabeth C. (ed.) (1989) *Interpretive Consumer Research*, Provo, UT: Association for Consumer Research.

Hirschman, Elizabeth C. (1991a) 'A feminist critique of marketing theory: toward agentic-communal balance', in *Gender and Consumer Behavior Conference Proceedings*, Janeen Arnold Costa (ed.), Provo, UT: Association for Consumer Research, pp. 324–340.

Hirschman, Elizabeth C. (1991b) 'Exploring the dark side of consumer behavior: metaphor and ideology in prostitution and pornography', in *Gender and Consumer Behavior Conference Proceedings*, Janeen Arnold Costa (ed.), Provo, UT: Association for Consumer Research, pp. 303–314.

Hirschman, Elizabeth C. (1991c) 'Secular morality and the dark side of consumer behavior: or how semiotics saved my life', in *Advances in Consumer Research*, vol. 18, Rebecca Holman and Michael Solomon (eds), Provo, UT: Association for Consumer Research, pp. 1–4.

Hirschman, Elizabeth C. (1992) 'The consciousness of addiction: toward a general theory of compulsive consumption', *Journal of Consumer Research*, 19 (September): 155–179.

Hirschman, Elizabeth C. (1993) 'Ideology in consumer research, 1980 and 1990: a Marxist and feminist critique', *Journal of Consumer Research*, 19 (March): 537–555.

Hirschman, Elizabeth C. (1994) 'Consumers and their companion animals', *Journal of Consumer Research*, 20 (March): 616–632.

Hirschman, Elizabeth C. and Morris B. Holbrook (eds) (1981) *Consumer Esthetics and Symbolic Consumption*, Ann Arbor, MI: Association for Consumer Research.

Hirschman, Elizabeth C. and Morris B. Holbrook (1992) *Postmodern Consumer Research: The Study of Consumption as Text*, Newbury Park, CA: Sage.

Hirschman, Elizabeth C. and Priscilla LaBarbara (1989) 'The meaning of Christmas', in *Interpretive Consumer Research*, Elizabeth C. Hirschman (ed.), Provo, UT: Association for Consumer Research, pp. 136–147.

Hoch, Stephen J. and George F. Lowenstein (1991) 'Time-inconsistent preferences and consumer self-control', *Journal of Consumer Research*, 17 (March): 492–507.

Holbrook, Morris B. (1985) 'Why business is bad for consumer research: the three bears revisited', in *Advances in Consumer Research*, vol. 12, Elizabeth C. Hirschman and Morris B. Holbrook (eds), Provo, UT: Association for Consumer Research, pp. 145–156.

Holbrook, Morris B. (1986) 'Whither ACR? Some pastoral reflections on bears, Baltimore, baseball, and resurrecting consumer research', in *Advances in Consumer Research*, vol. 13, Richard J. Lutz (ed.), Provo, UT: Association for Consumer Research, pp. 436–441.

Holbrook, Morris B. (1987) 'O, consumer, how you've changed: some radical reflections on the roots of consumption', in *Philosophical and Radical Thought in Marketing*, Richard P. Bagozzi, Nikhilesh Dholakia and A. Fuat Firat (eds), Lexington, MA: Lexington Books, pp. 156–177.

Holbrook, Morris B. (1988a) 'Steps toward a psychoanalytic interpretation of consumption: a meta-meta-analysis of some issues raised by the consumer behavior Odyssey', in *Advances in Consumer Research*, vol. 15, Michael J. Houston (ed.), Provo, UT: Association for Consumer Research, pp. 537–542.

Holbrook, Morris B. (1988b) 'The psychoanalytic interpretation of consumer behavior: I am an animal', in *Research in Consumer Behavior*, vol. 3, Elizabeth Hirschman and Jagdish N. Sheth (eds), Greenwich, CT: JAI Press, pp. 149–178.

Holbrook, Morris B. (1990) 'The role of lyricism in research on consumer emotions: Skylark, have you anything to say to me?', in *Advances in Consumer Research*, vol. 17, Marvin Goldberg, Gerald Gorn and Richard W. Pollay (eds),

Provo, UT: Association for Consumer Research, pp. 1–18.

Holbrook, Morris B. (1993) *Daytime Television Gameshows and the Celebration of Merchandise: The Price is Right*, Bowling Green, OH: Bowling Green State University Popular Press.

Holbrook, Morris B. and Elizabeth C. Hirschman (1982) 'The experiential aspects of consumption: consumer fantasies, feelings, and fun', *Journal of Consumer Research*, 9 (September): 132–140.

Holman, Rebecca H. (1981) 'Product use as communication: a fresh appraisal of a venerable topic', in *Review of Marketing 1981*, Ben M. Enis and Kenneth J. Roering (eds), Chicago: American Marketing Association, pp. 106–119.

Holt, Douglas B. (1993) 'Examining the descriptive value of "ritual" in consumer behavior: a view from the field', in *Advances in Consumer Research*, vol. 19, John F. Sherry, Jr. and Brian Sternthal (eds), Provo, UT: Association for Consumer Research, pp. 213–218.

Howard, John A. and Jagdish N. Sheth (1969) *The Theory of Buyer Behavior*, New York: Wiley.

Hudson, Laurel A. and Julie L. Ozanne (1988) 'Alternative ways of seeking knowledge in consumer research', *Journal of Consumer Research*, 14 (March): 508–521.

Hunt, Shelby D. (1989) 'Naturalistic, humanistic, and interpretive inquiry: challenges and ultimate potential', in *Interpretive Consumer Research*, Elizabeth C. Hirschman (ed.), Provo, UT: Association for Consumer Research, pp. 185–198.

Hunt, Shelby D. (1991) 'Positivism and paradigm dominance in consumer research: toward critical pluralism and rapprochement', *Journal of Consumer Research*, 18 (June): 32–44.

Hutton, R. Bruce and Frank Markley (1991) 'The effects of incentives on environmentally-friendly behaviors: a case study', in *Advances in Consumer Research*, vol. 18, Rebecca H. Holman and Michael R. Solomon (eds), Provo, UT: Association for Consumer Research, pp. 697–702.

Isaacs, Susan (1935) 'Property and possessiveness', *British Journal of Medical Psychology*, 15 (1): 69–78.

Jacoby, Jacob (1985a) 'Serving two masters: perspectives on consulting', in *Advances in Consumer Research*, vol. 12, Elizabeth C. Hirschman and Morris B. Holbrook (eds), Provo, UT: Association for Consumer Research, p. 144.

Jacoby, Jacob (1985b) 'The vices and virtues of consulting: responding to a fairy tale', in *Advances in Consumer Research*, vol. 12, Elizabeth C. Hirschman and Morris B. Holbrook (eds), Provo, UT: Association for Consumer Research, pp. 157–163.

James, Alice and William L. James (1985) 'Gift-giving in rural Ireland: an analysis of reciprocity', in *American Marketing Association Educators' Conference Proceedings*, Robert F. Lusch, *et al.* (eds), Chicago: American Marketing Association.

James, William (1890) *The Principles of Psychology*, vol. 1, New York: Henry Holt and Company.

Jolibert, Alain J. and Carlos Fernandez-Moreno (1983) 'A comparison of French and Mexican gift-giving practices', *Advances in Consumer Research*, vol. 10, Richard Bagozzi and Alice Tybout (eds), Ann Arbor, MI: Association for Consumer Research, pp. 191–196.

Joy, Annamma and Ruby Roy Dholakia (1991) 'Remembrances of things past: the meaning of home and possessions of Indian professionals in Canada', in *To Have Possessions: A Handbook on Ownership and Property*, Floyd Rudmin (ed.), Corte Madera, CA: Select Press (Special issue of *Journal of Social Behavior and Personality*, 6 (6): 385–402).

Kilbourne, William E. (1992) 'On the role of critical theory in moving toward voluntary simplicity', in *Meaning, Measure, and Morality of Materialism*, Floyd Rudmin and Marsha Richins (eds), Provo, UT: Association for Consumer Research, pp. 161–163.

Kleine, Susan Schultz and Amy R. Hubbert (1993) 'How do consumers acquire a new food consumption system when it is vegetarian?', in *Advances in Consumer Research*, vol. 20, Leigh McAlister and Michael L. Rothschild (eds), Provo, UT: Association for Consumer Research, pp. 196–201.

Kumcu, Erdoğan (1987) 'A historical perspective framework to study consumer behavior and retailing systems', in *Advances in Consumer Research*, vol. 14, Melanie Wallendorf and Paul Anderson (eds), Provo, UT: Association for Consumer Research, pp. 439–441.

Kumcu, Erdoğan and A. Fuat Firat (eds) (1988) *Marketing and Development: Toward Broader Dimensions*, Greenwich, CT: JAI Press.

Kumcu, Erdoğan, A. Fuat Firat, Mehmet Karafakroğlu, Muhitin Karabulut and Mehmet Oluç (eds) (1986) *The Role of Marketing in Development: Global, Consumer, and Managerial Issues*, Muncie, IN: Ball State University Press.

Lastovika, John L., John P. Murry, Jr., Erich A. Joachimsthaler, Gaurav Bhalla and Jim Scheurich (1987) 'A lifestyle typology of model young male drinking and driving', *Journal of Consumer Research*, 14 (September): 257–263.

Lee, Wei-Na (1989) 'The mass-mediated consumption realities of three cultural groups', in *Advances in Consumer Research*, vol. 16, Thomas K. Srull (ed.), Provo, UT: Association for Consumer Research, pp. 359–366.

Lee, Wei-Na and Koong-Hyang Ro Um (1992) 'Ethnicity and consumer product evaluation: a cross-cultural comparison of Korean immigrants and Americans', in *Advances in Consumer Research*, vol. 19, John F. Sherry, Jr. and Brian Sternthal (eds), Provo, UT: Association for Consumer Research, pp. 429–436.

Levinson, Stacey, Stacey Mack, Dan Reinhardt, Helen Suarez and Grace Yeh (1992) 'Halloween as a consumption experience', in *Advances in Consumer Research*, vol. 19, John F. Sherry, Jr. and Brian Sternthal (eds), Provo, UT: Association for Consumer Research, pp. 219–228.

Levy, Sidney J. (1959) 'Symbols for sale', *Harvard Business Review*, 37: 117–124.

Levy, Sidney J. (1967) 'Mammon and psyche', in *Explorations in Consumer Behavior*, Montrose S. Sommers and Jerome B. Kernan (eds), Austin, TX: University of Texas Bureau of Business Research, pp. 119–133.

Levy, Sidney J. (1981) 'Interpreting consumer mythology: a structural approach to consumer behavior', *Journal of Marketing*, 45 (Summer): 49–61.

Levy, Sidney J. (1986) 'Meanings in advertising stimuli', in *Advertising and Consumer Psychology*, vol. 3, Jerry Olson and Keith Sentis (eds), New York: Praeger, pp. 214–226.

Littlefield, James E. and Magdolna Csath (eds) (1988) *Proceedings of the Second International Conference on Marketing and Development*, Blacksburg, VA: Virginia Tech University.

Lofman, Brian (1993) 'Consumers in rapid transition: the Polish experience', in *Advances in European Consumer Research*, vol. 1, W. Fred Van Raaij and Gary J. Bamossy (eds), Provo, UT: Association for Consumer Research, pp. 18–22.

Lowes, Bryan, J. Turner and Gordon Wills (1971) 'Patterns of gift-giving', in *Explorations in Marketing Thought*, Gordon Wills (ed.), London: Bradford University Press, pp. 82–102.

Lutz, Richard J. (1989) 'Presidential address, 1988 – Positivism, naturalism and pluralism in consumer research: paradigms in paradise', in *Advances in Consumer Research*, vol. 16, Thomas Srull (ed.), Provo, UT: Association for Consumer

Research, pp. 1–8.

McAlexander, James H. (1991) 'Divorce, the disposition of the relationship, and everything', in *Advances in Consumer Research*, vol. 18, Rebecca H. Holman and Michael R. Solomon (eds), Provo, UT: Association for Consumer Research, pp. 43–48.

McAlexander, James H., John W. Schouten and Scott D. Roberts (1993) 'Consumer behavior and divorce', in *Research in Consumer Behavior*, vol. 6, Janeen Arnold Costa and Russell W. Belk (eds), Greenwich, CT: JAI Press, pp. 55–84.

McCracken, Grant (1986) 'Culture and consumption: a theoretical account of the structure and movement of the cultural meaning of consumer goods', *Journal of Consumer Research*, 13 (June): 71–84.

McCracken, Grant (1989a) 'Homeyness: a cultural account of one constellation of consumer goods and meaning', in *Interpretive Consumer Research*, Elizabeth C. Hirschman (ed.), Provo, UT: Association for Consumer Research, pp. 168–183.

McCracken, Grant (1989b) 'The Diderot effect: reflections on why goods run in packs', paper presented at the Annual Conference of the Association for Consumer Research, New Orleans, LA, October.

McDannell, Colleen and Bernhard Lang (1988) *Heaven: A History*, New Haven, CT: Yale University Press.

McGrath, Mary Ann (1989) 'An ethnography of a gift store: trappings, wrappings, and rapture', *Journal of Retailing*, 65 (Winter): 421–449.

McGrath, Mary Ann (1993) 'Communal exchange: intergenerational giving of wedding gifts', paper presented at American Marketing Association Winter Marketing Educators' Conference, Newport Beach, CA, February.

McGrath, Mary Ann (forthcoming) 'Gender differences in gift exchanges: new directions from projections', *Psychology and Marketing*.

McGrath, Mary Ann and Cele Otnes (1993) 'Children's understanding of birthday parties: a study of gender differences', in *Gender and Consumer Behavior: Second Conference Proceedings*, Janeen Arnold Costa (ed.), Provo, UT: Association for Consumer Research, p. 151.

McGrath, Mary Ann, John F. Sherry, Jr. and Sidney J. Levy (1993) 'Giving voice to the gift: the use of projective techniques to recover lost meanings', *Journal of Consumer Psychology*, 2 (2): 171–192.

McKeage, Kim K. R. (1992) 'An exploratory investigation of the role of materialism in self-gifts', in *Meaning, Measure, and Morality of Materialism*, Floyd Rudmin and Marsha Richins (eds), Provo, UT: Association for Consumer Research, pp. 140–148.

McKeage, Kim K. R., Marsha Richins and Kathleen Debevec (1993) 'Self-gifts and the manifestation of material values', in *Advances in Consumer Research*, vol. 20, Leigh McAlister and Michael L. Rothschild (eds), Provo, UT: Association for Consumer Research, pp. 359–364.

Malinowski, Bronislaw (1922) *Argonauts of the Western Pacific*, London: E. P. Dutton.

Mallard, Kina (1992) 'An examination of gift exchange at funerals', paper presented at the Annual Conference of the Association for Consumer Research, Vancouver, BC, October.

Mallard, Kina (1993) 'Men in mourning: gift receipt and funeral planning from a male point of view', paper presented at the Annual Conference of the Association for Consumer Research, Nashville, TN, October.

Manrai, Lalita A. and Ajay K. Manrai (1993) 'Complaints and compliments about service encounters: a comparison of American and Bulgarian consumers', in *Advances in European Consumer Research*, vol. 1, W. Fred Van Raaij and Gary J. Bamossy (eds), Provo, UT: Association for Consumer Research, pp. 97–101.

Mauss, Marcel (1925) *The Gift: Form and Functions in Archaic Societies*, London: Cohen and West.

Mehta, Raj and Russell W. Belk (1991) 'Artifacts, identity, and transition: favorite possessions of Indians and Indian immigrants to the United Sates', *Journal of Consumer Research*, 17 (March): 398–411.

Mick, David Glen (1986) 'Consumer research and semiotics: exploring the morphology of signs, symbols, and significance', *Journal of Consumer Research*, 13 (September): 196–213.

Mick, David Glen (1989) 'Contributions to the semiotics of marketing and consumer behavior', in *The Semiotic Web: A Yearbook of Semiotics*, Thomas A. Sebeok and Jean Umiker-Sebeok (eds), Berlin: Mouton de Gruyter.

Mick, David Glen (1991) 'Giving gifts to ourselves: a Gramassian analysis leading to testable propositions', in *Marketing and Semiotics: Selected Papers from the Copenhagen Symposium*, Hanne H. Larsen, David G. Mick and Christian Alsted (eds), Copenhagen: Handelshøjskolens Forlag, pp. 142–159.

Mick, David Glen and Michelle DeMoss (1990a) 'To me from me: a descriptive phenomenology of self-gifts', in *Advances in Consumer Research*, vol. 17, Gerald Gorn, Marvin Goldberg and Richard Pollay (eds), Provo: Association for Consumer Research, pp. 677–682.

Mick, David Glen and Michelle DeMoss (1990b) 'Self–gifts: phenomenological insights from four contexts', *Journal of Consumer Research*, 17 (December): 322–332.

Mick, David Glen and Michelle DeMoss (1993) 'Further findings on self-gifts: products, qualities, and socioeconomic correlates', in *Advances in Consumer Research*, vol. 19, John F. Sherry, Jr. and Brian Sternthal (eds), Provo, UT: Association for Consumer Research, pp. 140–146.

Middlestadt, Susan E. (1993) 'Encouraging discussion with partners and building negotiation skills: HIV prevention strategies for women in relationships in Brazil, Tanzania and Indonesia', in *Advances in Consumer Research*, vol. 20, Leigh McAlister and Michael L. Rothschild (eds), Provo, UT: Association for Consumer Research, pp. 297–301.

Murray, Jeff B. and Julie L. Ozanne (1991) 'The critical imagination: emancipatory interests in consumer research', *Journal of Consumer Research*, 18 (September): 129–144.

Nataraajan, Rajan and Brent G. Goff (1991) 'Compulsive buying: toward a reconceptualization', in *To Have Possessions: A Handbook on Ownership and Property*, Floyd Rudmin (ed.), Corte Madera, CA: Select Press (Special issue of *Journal of Social Behavior and Personality*, 6 (6): 287–306).

Newman, Joseph W. (1992) 'Some observations of a developing field', in *Advances in Consumer Research*, vol. 19, John F. Sherry, Jr. and Brian Sternthal (eds), Provo, UT: Association for Consumer Research, pp. 12–14.

Nicosia, Francesco (1966) *Consumer Decision Processes*, Englewood Cliffs, NJ: Prentice-Hall.

O'Guinn, Thomas C. (1991) 'Touching greatness: the Central Midwest Barry Manilow Fan Club', in *Highways and Buyways: Naturalistic Research from the Consumer Behavior Odyssey*, Russell W. Belk (ed.), Provo, UT: Association for Consumer Research, pp. 102–111.

O'Guinn, Thomas and Russell W. Belk (1989) 'Heaven on earth: consumption at Heritage Village, USA', *Journal of Consumer Research*, 15 (September): 227–238.

O'Guinn, Thomas C. and Ronald J. Faber (1989) 'Compulsive buying: a phenomenological exploration', *Journal of Consumer Research*, 16 (September): 147–157.

O'Guinn, Thomas C., Wei-Na Lee and Ronald J. Faber (1986) 'Acculturation: the impact of divergent paths on buyer behavior', in *Advances in Consumer Research*, vol. 13, Richard J. Lutz (ed.), Provo, UT: Association for Consumer Research, pp. 579–583.

Olmsted, A. D. (1991) 'Collecting: leisure, investment, or obsession?', in *To Have Possessions: A Handbook on Ownership and Property*, Floyd Rudmin (ed.), Corte Madera, CA: Select Press (Special issue of *Journal of Social Behavior and Personality*, 6 (6): 287–306).

Olney, T. J. and Wendy Bryce (1991) 'Consumer responses to environmentally based product claims', in *Advances in Consumer Research*, vol. 18, Rebecca H. Holman and Michael R. Solomon (eds), pp. 693–696.

Olshavsky, Richard W. and Dong Hwan Lee (1993) 'Self-gifts: a metacognition perspective', in *Advances in Consumer Research*, vol. 20, Leigh McAlister and Michael L. Rothschild (eds), Provo, UT: Association for Consumer Research, pp. 547–552.

Østergaard, Per (1993) 'Segmenting prostitutes' needs for information about AIDS: a field study', in *Advances in Consumer Research*, vol. 20, Leigh McAlister and Michael L. Rothschild (eds), Provo, UT: Association for Consumer Research, pp. 565–569.

Otnes, Cele and Richard Beltramini (eds) (1995) *Gift-Giving*, Bowling Green, OH: Bowling Green State University Popular Press.

Otnes, Cele and Tina M. Lowrey (1993) '"Til debt do us part: the selection and meaning of artifacts in the American wedding', in *Advances in Consumer Research*, vol. 20, Leigh McAlister and Michael L. Rothschild (eds), Provo, UT: Association for Consumer Research, pp. 325–329.

Otnes, Cele, Tina M. Lowrey and Young Chan Kim (1993) 'Gift selection for easy and difficult recipients: a social roles interpretation', *Journal of Consumer Research*, 20 (September): 229–244.

Otnes, Cele, Julie A. Ruth and Constance C. Milbourne (1994) 'The pleasure of being close: men's mixed feelings about participation in Valentine's Day gift exchange', in *Advances in Consumer Research*, vol. 20, Chris T. Allen and Deborah Roedder John (eds), Provo, UT: Association for Consumer Research.

Ozanne, Julie L. and Laurel A. Hudson (1989) 'Exploring diversity in consumer research', in *Interpretive Consumer Research*, Elizabeth C. Hirschman (ed.), Provo, UT: Association for Consumer Research, pp. 1–9.

Packard, Vance (1957) *The Hidden Persuaders*, New York: Pocket Books.

Pandya, Anil and Alladi Venkatesh (1993) 'Symbolic communication among consumers in self-consumption and gift giving: a semiotic approach', in *Advances in Consumer Research*, vol. 19, John F. Sherry, Jr. and Brian Sternthal (eds), Provo, UT: Association for Consumer Research, pp. 147–154.

Pavia, Teresa (1993) 'Dispossession and perceptions of self in late stage HIV infection', in *Advances in Consumer Research*, vol. 17, Gerald Gorn, Marvin Goldberg and Richard Pollay (eds), Provo: Association for Consumer Research, pp. 425–428.

Pecotich, Anthony and Clifford J. Shultz (1993) 'Vietnam revisited: observations and emergent themes in consumer behavior since the implementation of market reforms', in *Advances in European Consumer Research*, vol. 1, W. Fred Van Raaij and Gary J. Bamossy (eds), Provo, UT: Association for Consumer Research, pp. 233–235.

Peñaloza, Lisa (1989) 'Immigrant consumer acculturation', in *Advances in Consumer Research*, vol. 16, Thomas K. Srull (ed.), Provo, UT: Association for Consumer Research, pp. 110–118.

Peñaloza, Lisa (1994) 'Atravasando fronteras/border crossings: Mexican immigrant consumer acculturation', *Journal of Consumer Research*, 21 (June): 32–54.

Peñaloza, Lisa and Mary Gilly (1986) 'The Hispanic family: consumer research issues', *Psychology and Marketing*, 3 (4): 291–303.

Peñaloza, Lisa and Linda L. Price (1993) 'Consumer resistance: a conceptual overview', in *Advances in Consumer Research*, vol. 20, Leigh McAlister and Michael L. Rothschild (eds), Provo, UT: Association for Consumer Research, pp. 123–128.

Peter, J. Paul (1991) 'Philosophical tensions in consumer inquiry', in *Handbook of Consumer Behavior*, Thomas S. Robertson and Harold H. Kassarjian (eds), Englewood Cliffs, NJ: Prentice-Hall, pp. 533–547.

Peter, J. Paul and Jerry C. Olson (1989) 'The relativist/constructionist perspective on scientific knowledge and consumer research', in *Interpretive Consumer Research*, Elizabeth C. Hirschman (ed.), Provo, UT: Association for Consumer Research, pp. 24–28.

Pfeiffer, Wayne C. (1992) 'Material culture and the food supply', in *Meaning, Measure, and Morality of Materialism*, Floyd Rudmin and Marsha Richins (eds), Provo, UT: Association for Consumer Research, pp. 158–160.

Pollay, Richard W. (1993) 'Media resistance to consumer resistance: on the stonewalling of "Adbusters" and Advocates', in *Advances in Consumer Research*, vol. 20, Leigh McAlister and Michael L. Rothschild (eds), Provo, UT: Association for Consumer Research, p. 129.

Pollay, Richard W. and Anne M. Lavack (1993) 'The targeting of youths by cigarette marketers: archival evidence on trial', in *Advances in Consumer Research*, vol. 20, Leigh McAlister and Michael L. Rothschild (eds), Provo, UT: Association for Consumer Research, pp. 266–271.

Putnam, Todd and Timothy Muck (1991) 'Wielding the boycott weapon for social change', *Business and Society Review*, 78 (Summer): 5–8.

de Pyssler, Bruce (1992) 'The cultural and political economy of the Indian two-wheeler', in *Advances in Consumer Research*, vol. 19, John F. Sherry, Jr. and Brian Sternthal (eds), Provo, UT: Association for Consumer Research, pp. 437–442.

Reilly, Michael and Melanie Wallendorf (1984) 'A longitudinal study of Mexican-American assimilation', in *Advances in Consumer Research*, vol. 11, Thomas Kinnear (ed.), Provo, UT: Association for Consumer Research, pp. 735–740.

Reilly, Michael and Melanie Wallendorf (1987) 'A comparison of group differences in food consumption using household refuse', *Journal of Consumer Research*, 14 (September): 289–294.

Richins, Marsha L. and Peter H. Bloch (1986) 'After the new wears off: the temporal context of product involvement', *Journal of Consumer Research*, 13 (September): 280–285.

Richins, Marsha L. and Scott Dawson (1992) 'A consumer values orientation for materialism and its measurement: scale development and validation', *Journal of Consumer Research*, 19 (December): 303–316.

Roberts, Scott D. (1991) 'Consumer responses to involuntary job loss', in *Advances in Consumer Research*, vol. 18, Rebecca H. Holman and Michael R. Solomon (eds), Provo, UT: Association for Consumer Research, pp. 40–42.

Robins, Douglas M., Clinton R. Sanders and Spencer E. Cahill (1991) 'Dogs and their people: pet-facilitated interaction in a public setting', *Journal of Contemporary Ethnography*, 20 (April): 3–25.

Rogers, Everett M. (1987) 'The critical school and consumer research', in *Advances in Consumer Research*, vol. 14, Melanie Wallendorf and Paul Anderson (eds), Provo, UT: Association for Consumer Research, pp. 7–11.

Rook, Dennis W. (1985) 'The ritual dimension of consumer behavior', *Journal of Consumer Research*, 12 (December): 251–264.

Rook, Dennis W. (1987a) 'The buying impulse', *Journal of Consumer Research*, 14 (September): 189–199.

Rook, Dennis W. (1987b) 'Modern hex signs and symbols of security', in *Marketing and Semiotics: New Directions in the Study of Signs for Sale*, Jean Umiker-Sebeok (ed.), Berlin: Mouton de Gruyter, pp. 239–246.

Rook, Dennis W. (1988) 'Researching consumer fantasy', in *Research in Consumer Behavior*, vol. 3, Elizabeth Hirschman and Jagdish N. Sheth (eds), Greenwich, CT: JAI Press, pp. 247–270.

Rook, Dennis W. and Stephen J. Hoch (1985) 'Consuming impulses', in *Advances in Consumer Research*, vol. 12, Elizabeth C. Hirschman and Morris B. Holbrook (eds), Provo, UT: Association for Consumer Research, pp. 23–27.

Rook, Dennis W. and Sidney Levy (1983) 'Psychological themes in consumer grooming rituals', in *Advances in Consumer Research*, vol. 10, Richard P. Bagozzi and Alice M. Tybout (eds), Provo, UT: Association for Consumer Research, pp. 329–333.

Ross, Stuart A. (1991) 'Freedom from possession: a Tibetan Buddhist view', in *To Have Possessions: A Handbook on Ownership and Property*, Floyd Rudmin (ed.), Corte Madera, CA: Select Press (Special issue of *Journal of Social Behavior and Personality*, 6 (6): 415–426).

Rucker, Margaret, Susan Kaiser, Mary Bamy, Debra Brumett, Carla Freeman and Alice Peters (1986) 'The imported export market: an investigation of foreign visitors' gift and personal purchases', in *Developments in Marketing Science: Proceedings of the Academy of Marketing Science*.

Rucker, Margaret, Anthony Freitas, Deborah Murray and Harriet Prato (1991) 'Gender stereotypes and gift failures: when the sweet don't want sweets', in *Gender and Consumer Behavior Conference Proceedings*, Janeen Arnold Costa (ed.), Provo, UT: Association for Consumer Research, pp. 244–252.

Rucker, Margaret, Anthony Freitas and Jamie Dolstra (1994) 'A toast for the host? The male perspective on gifts that say "thank you"', in *Advances in Consumer Research*, vol. 20, Chris T. Allen and Deborah Roedder John (eds), Provo, UT: Association for Consumer Research.

Rudmin, Floyd (1991) *To Have Possessions: A Handbook on Ownership and Property*, Corte Madera, CA: Select Press (Special issue of *Journal of Social Behavior and Personality*, 6 (6)).

Rudmin, Floyd (1992) 'Materialism and militarism: De Tocqueville on America's hopeless hurry to happiness', in *Meaning, Measure, and Morality of Materialism*, Floyd Rudmin and Marsha Richins (eds), Provo, UT: Association for Consumer Research, pp. 110–120.

Rudmin, Floyd, Russell W. Belk, and Lita Furby (1987) *Social Science Bibliography on Property, Ownership, and Possession: 1580 Citations from Psychology, Anthropology, Sociology, and Related Disciplines*, Monticello, IL: Vance Bibliographies.

Rudmin, Floyd and William E. Kilbourne (1995) 'The meaning and morality of voluntary simplicity: history and hypotheses on deliberately denied materialism', in *Consumption and Marketing: Macro Dimensions*, Russell W. Belk and Nikhilesh Dholakia (eds), Cincinnati, OH: Southwestern.

Rudmin, Floyd and Marsha Richins (eds) (1992) *Meaning, Measure, and Morality of Materialism*, Provo, UT: Association for Consumer Research.

Sanders, Clinton R. (1985) 'Tattoo consumption: risk and regret in the purchase of a socially marginal service', in *Advances in Consumer Research*, vol. 12, Elizabeth C. Hirschman and Morris B. Holbrook (eds), Provo, UT: Association for Consumer Research, pp. 17–22.

Sanders, Clinton R. (1987) 'Consuming as social action: ethnographic methods in consumer research', in *Advances in Consumer Research*, vol. 14, Melanie Wallendorf and Paul Anderson (eds), Provo, UT: Association for Consumer Research, pp. 71–75.

Sanders, Clinton R. (1990) 'The animal "Other": self-definition, social identity and companion animals', in *Advances in Consumer Research*, vol. 17, Gerald Gorn, Marvin Goldberg and Richard Pollay (eds), Provo: Association for Consumer Research, pp. 662–668.

Sanders, Clinton R. (1993) 'Understanding dogs: caretakers' attributions of mindedness in canine–human relationships', *Journal of Contemporary Ethnography*, 22 (July): 205–226.

Sayre, Shay (1994) 'Possessions and identity in crisis: meaning and change for victims of the Oakland firestorm', in *Advances in Consumer Research*, vol. 21, Chris T. Allen and Deborah Roedder-John (eds), Provo, UT: Association for Consumer Research.

Scammon, Debra L., Roy T. Shaw and Gary Bamossy (1982) 'Is a gift always a gift? An investigation of flower purchasing across situations', *Advances in Consumer Research*, vol. 9, Andrew Mitchell (ed.), Ann Arbor, MI: Association for Consumer Research, pp. 531–536.

Schouten, John W. (1991a) 'Personal rites of passage and the reconstruction of self', in *Advances in Consumer Research*, vol. 18, Rebecca H. Holman and Michael R. Solomon (eds), Provo, UT: Association for Consumer Research, pp. 49–51.

Schouten, John W. (1991b) 'Selves in transition: symbolic consumption in personal rites of passage and identity reconstruction', *Journal of Consumer Research*, 17 (March): 412–425.

Schouten, John W. and James H. McAlexander (1992) 'Market impact of a consumption subculture: the Harley-Davidson Mystique', *European Advances in Consumer Research*, Gary Bamossy and Fred Van Raaij (eds), Provo, UT: Association for Consumer Research, pp. 389–393.

Schroeder, Jonathan E., M. Ven Venkatesan, John K. Wong and Beverlee Anderson (1993) 'Social time perspective and cross-cultural consumer behavior: a framework and some results', in *Advances in European Consumer Research*, vol. 1, W. Fred Van Raaij and Gary J. Bamossy (eds), Provo, UT: Association for Consumer Research, pp. 18–23.

Schultz, Susan E., Robert E. Kleine, III and Jerome B. Kernan (1989) '"These Are a Few of My Favorite Things": toward an explication of attachment as a consumer behavior construct', in *Advances in Consumer Behavior*, vol. 16, Thomas K. Srull (ed.), Provo, UT: Association for Consumer Research, pp. 359–366.

Shapiro, Jon M. (1993) 'Compulsive buying and self-gifts: a motivational perspective', in *Advances in Consumer Research*, vol. 20, Leigh McAlister and Michael L. Rothschild (eds), Provo, UT: Association for Consumer Research, p. 557.

Sherry, John F., Jr. (1983) 'Gift-giving in anthropological perspective', *Journal of Consumer Research*, 10 (September): 157–168.

Sherry, John F., Jr. (1987) 'Keeping the monkeys away from the typewriters: an anthropologist's view of the consumer behavior Odyssey', in *Advances in Consumer Research*, vol. 14, Melanie Wallendorf and Paul Anderson (eds), Provo,

UT: Association for Consumer Research, pp. 370–373.

Sherry, John F., Jr. (1990a) 'A sociocultural analysis of a Midwestern flea market', *Journal of Consumer Research*, 17 (June): 13–30.

Sherry, John F., Jr. (1990b) 'Dealers and dealing in a periodic market: informal retailing in ethnographic perspective', *Journal of Retailing*, 66 (Summer): 174–200.

Sherry, John F., Jr. (1991) 'Postmodern alternatives: the interpretive turn in consumer research', in *Handbook of Consumer Behavior*, Thomas S. Robertson and Harold H. Kassarjian (eds), Englewood Cliffs, NJ: Prentice-Hall, pp. 548–591.

Sherry, John F., Jr. and Eduardo Camargo (1987) '"May Your Life Be Marvelous": English language labeling and the semiotics of Japanese promotion', *Journal of Consumer Research*, 14 (September): 174–188.

Sherry, John F., Jr. and Mary Ann McGrath (1989) 'Unpacking the holiday presence: a comparative ethnography of two gift stores', in *Interpretive Consumer Research*, Elizabeth C. Hirschman (ed.), Provo, UT: Association for Consumer Research, pp. 148–167.

Sherry, John F., Jr., Mary Ann McGrath and Sidney J. Levy (1992) 'The disposition of the gift and many unhappy returns', *Journal of Retailing*, 68 (1): 40–65.

Sherry, John F., Jr., Mary Ann McGrath, and Sidney J. Levy (1993) 'The dark side of the gift', *Journal of Business Research*, 28 (November): 225–244.

Shimp, Terence A. and Thomas J. Madden (1988) 'Consumer–object relations: a conceptual framework based analogously on Sternberg's triangular theory of love', in *Advances in Consumer Research*, vol. 15, Michael Houston (ed.), Provo, UT: Association for Consumer Research, pp. 163–168.

Shultz, Clifford, Russell W. Belk and Güliz Ger (eds) (1994) *Consumption in Marketizing Economies*, Greenwich, CT: JAI Press.

Siegel, Harvey (1988) 'Relativism for consumer research? (Comments on Anderson)', *Journal of Consumer Research*, 15 (June): 129–132.

Sirgy, Joseph (1982) 'Self-concept and consumer behavior: a critical review', *Journal of Consumer Research*, 9 (December): 287–300.

Smith, Ruth Ann and David S. Lux (1993) 'Historical method in consumer research', *Journal of Consumer Research*, 19 (March): 595–610.

Solomon, Michael R., (ed.) (1984) *The Psychology of Fashion: From Conception to Consumption*, New York: Lexington Books.

Solomon, Michael R. (1988) 'Mapping product constellations: a social categorization approach to symbolic consumption', *Psychology and Marketing*, 5 (3): 233–258.

Solomon, Michael R. (1992) *Consumer Behavior: Buying, Having, and Being*, Needham Heights, MA: Allyn and Bacon.

Solomon, Michael R. and Punam Anand (1985) 'Ritual costumes and status transition: the female business suit as totemic emblem', in *Advances in Consumer Research*, vol. 13, Elizabeth C. Hirschman and Morris B. Holbrook (eds), Provo, UT: Association for Consumer Research, pp. 315–318.

Solomon, Michael R. and Henry Assael (1987) 'The forest or the trees? A Gestalt approach to symbolic consumption', in *Marketing and Semiotics: New Directions in the Study of Signs for Sale*, Jean Umiker-Sebeok (ed.), Berlin: Mouton de Gruyter, pp. 189–218.

Spradley, James P. (1970) *You Owe Yourself a Drunk: An Ethnography of Urban Nomads*, Boston: Little, Brown.

Stern, Barbara (1989a) 'Literary criticism and consumer research: overview and illustrative analysis', *Journal of Consumer Research*, 16 (December): 322–334.

Stern, Barbara (1989b) 'Literary explication: a methodology for consumer research', in *Interpretive Consumer Research*, Elizabeth C. Hirschman (ed.), Provo, UT: Association for Consumer Research, pp. 48–59.

Stern, Barbara (1990) 'Literary criticism and the history of marketing thought', *Journal of the Academy of Marketing Science*, 18 (4): 239–336.

Stern, Barbara (1993) 'Feminist literary criticism and the deconstruction of ads: a postmodern view of advertising and consumer responses', *Journal of Consumer Research*, 19 (March): 536–566.

Tan, Chin Tiong and Jagdish N. Sheth (eds) (1985) *Historical Perspective in Consumer Research: National and International Perspectives*, Singapore: Association for Consumer Research.

Thaler, Richard (1985) 'Mental accounting and consumer choice', *Marketing Science*, 4 (Summer): 199–214.

Thøgersen, John (1993) 'Wasteful food consumption: trends in food packaging and waste', in *Advances in European Consumer Research*, vol. 1, W. Fred Van Raaij and Gary J. Bamossy (eds), Provo, UT: Association for Consumer Research, pp. 434–439.

Thompson, Craig J., William B. Locander and Howard R. Pollio (1989) 'Putting consumer experience back into consumer research: the philosophy and method of existential-phenomenology', *Journal of Consumer Research*, 16 (September): 133–146.

Thompson, Craig J., William B. Locander and Howard R. Pollio (1990) 'The lived meaning of free choice: an existential-phenomenological description of everyday consumer experiences of contemporary married women', *Journal of Consumer Research*, 17 (December): 346–361.

Tse, David, Russell W. Belk and Nan Zhou (1989) 'Becoming a consumer society: a longitudinal and cross-cultural content analysis of print ads from Hong Kong, the People's Republic of China, and Taiwan', *Journal of Consumer Research*, 15 (March): 457–472.

Tybout, Alice M. and Nancy Artz (1994) 'Consumer psychology', *Annual Review of Psychology*, 45, Palo Alto, CA: Annual Reviews, Inc., pp. 131–169.

Umiker-Sebeok, Jean (ed.) (1987) *Marketing and Semiotics: New Directions in the Study of Signs for Sale*, Berlin: Mouton de Gruyter.

Van Raaij, W. Fred (1993) 'Postmodern consumption: architecture, art, and consumer behavior', in *Advances in European Consumer Research*, vol. 1, W. Fred Van Raaij and Gary J. Bamossy (eds), Provo, UT: Association for Consumer Research, pp. 550–558.

Veblen, Thorstein (1899) *The Theory of the Leisure Class: An Economic Study of Institutions*, New York: Macmillan.

Venkatesh, Alladi (1991) 'Feminist science and consumer research', in *Gender and Consumer Behavior Conference Proceedings*, Janeen Arnold Costa (ed.), Provo, UT: Association for Consumer Research, pp. 87–88.

Venkatesh, Alladi (1992) 'Postmodernism, consumer culture, and the society of the spectacle', in *Advances in Consumer Research*, vol. 19, John F. Sherry, Jr. and Brian Sternthal (eds), Provo, UT: Association for Consumer Research, pp. 199–202.

Venkatesh, Alladi and Sugana Swarmy (1994) 'India as an emerging consumer society: a critical perspective', in *Consumption in Marketizing Economies*, Clifford Shultz, Russell W. Belk and Güliz Ger (eds), Greenwich, CT: JAI Press, pp. 193–224.

Wallendorf, Melanie (1987) 'On the road again: the nature of qualitative research on the consumer behavior Odyssey', in *Advances in Consumer Research*, vol. 14, Melanie Wallendorf and Paul Anderson (eds), Provo, UT: Association for

Consumer Research, pp. 374–375.

Wallendorf, Melanie and Eric Arnould (1988) '"My Favorite Things": A cross-cultural inquiry into object attachment', *Journal of Consumer Research*, 14 (March): 531–547.

Wallendorf, Melanie and Eric Arnould (1992) '"We Gather Together": consumption rituals of Thanksgiving Day', *Journal of Consumer Research*, 18 (June): 13–31.

Wallendorf, Melanie and Russell W. Belk (1987) *Deep Meaning in Possessions: Qualitative Research from the Consumer Behavior Odyssey* (videotape), Cambridge, MA: Marketing Science Institute.

Wallendorf, Melanie and Daniel Nelson (1987) 'An archaeological examination of ethnic differences in body care rituals', *Psychology and Marketing*, 3 (January): 273–289.

Wallendorf, Melanie and Michael Reilly (1983a) 'Distinguishing culture of origin from culture of residence', in *Advances in Consumer Research*, vol. 10, Richard Bagozzi and Alice Tybout (eds), Ann Arbor, MI: Association for Consumer Research, pp. 699–701.

Wallendorf, Melanie and Michael Reilly (1983b) 'Ethnic migration, assimilation and consumption', *Journal of Consumer Research*, 10 (3): 292–302.

Wilk, Richard (1987) 'House, home, and consumer decision making in two cultures', in *Advances in Consumer Research*, vol. 14, Melanie Wallendorf and Paul Anderson (eds), Provo, UT: Association for Consumer Research, pp. 303–307.

Wilson, Thomas M. (1993) 'Consumer culture and European integration at the Northern Irish border', in *Advances in European Consumer Research*, vol. 1, W. Fred Van Raaij and Gary J. Bamossy (eds), Provo, UT: Association for Consumer Research, pp. 293–299.

Wilson, Thomas M. (1995) 'Blurred borders: local and global consumer culture in Northern Ireland', in *Marketing, Consumption, and Ethnicity*, Janeen Arnold Costa and Gary Bamossy (eds), Newbury Park, CA: Sage.

Witkowski, Terrence H. (1993) 'The Polish consumer in transition: shopping Warsaw's street vendors and open air markets', in *Advances in European Consumer Research*, vol. 1, W. Fred Van Raaij and Gary J. Bamossy (eds), Provo, UT: Association for Consumer Research, pp. 13–17.

Witkowski, Terrence H. and Yoshito Yamamoto (1991) '*Omiyage* gift purchasing by Japanese travelers in the U.S.', in *Advances in Consumer Research*, vol. 18, Rebecca H. Holman and Michael R. Solomon (eds), Provo, UT: Association for Consumer Research, pp. 123–128.

Wolfinbarger, Mary Finley and Mary C. Gilly (1991) 'The influence of gender on gift-giving attitudes: (or, are men insensitive clods?)', in *Gender and Consumer Behavior Conference Proceedings*, Janeen Arnold Costa (ed.), Provo, UT: Association for Consumer Research, pp. 323–333.

Wright, D. and Val Larsen (1992) 'Material values and the Book of Mormon', in *Meaning, Measure, and Morality of Materialism*, Floyd Rudmin and Marsha Richins (eds), Provo, UT: Association for Consumer Research, pp. 50–56.

Young, Melissa Martin (1991) 'Dispossession of possessions during role transitions', in *Advances in Consumer Research*, vol. 18, Rebecca H. Holman and Michael R. Solomon (eds), Provo, UT: Association for Consumer Research, pp. 31–39.

Young, Melissa Martin and Melanie Wallendorf (1989) 'Ashes to ashes, dust to dust: conceptualizing consumer disposition of possessions', in *Proceedings of the American Marketing Association Summer Educators' Conference: Marketing Theory and Practice*, Terry L. Childers *et al.* (eds), Chicago: American Marketing Association, pp. 33–39.

3

THE SOCIOLOGY OF CONSUMPTION

Colin Campbell

I   The significance of the study of consumption for sociology

THE DEVELOPMENT OF A SOCIOLOGY OF CONSUMPTION

In 1978 Robert Mayer published an article in the *American Behavioral Scientist* entitled 'Exploring sociological theories by studying consumers' in which he noted that the increasingly voiced suggestion that marketers and consumer researchers could profitably make more use of sociological concepts could equally be matched by calls for sociologists to pay more attention to individuals in their role as consumers. He claimed that 'sociologists have much to gain from focusing their empirical studies on consumers', and that 'the study of consumption is a useful setting for the testing and expansion of sociological theories' (ibid.: 600). Whilst there is little evidence to suggest that many sociologists took much notice of Mayer's remarks at the time, they can be seen, from the perspective of the 1990s, to have had a certain prophetic ring to them. Not that there has in fact been any rush to 'test' sociological theories by examining consumer behaviour, but there does now exist within the discipline a fairly widespread appreciation of the importance of focusing attention upon the sphere of consumption.

One of the first sociologists in Britain to recognise this was Peter Saunders, who ten years later, issued a very similar call to Mayer's suggesting that sociology needed a 'new research agenda' called 'the sociology of consumption' (Otnes 1988). Although to some extent echoing Mayer in suggesting that economic, political and cultural insights could be gained by treating consumption as a principal research site, Saunders went further by suggesting that it was time for sociology to throw off the old production-dominated paradigm in favour of a new, consumption-oriented one. He continued to develop this theme in subsequent publications, arguing that in place of the old Marxist analysis of a conflict between classes differentially related to the means of production, sociologists should recognise the fundamental conflict which exists between producers and consumers (Saunders 1990). For Saunders it was 'no longer axiomatic that class location is the fundamental basis of material life chances' (Saunders 1986: 319); rather the crucial divisions related to different modes of consumption, especially that between the socialised and privatised forms in such spheres as housing and transport.

Predictably enough perhaps, Saunders' work sparked off a lively debate, one in which he has come under fierce attack (Warde 1990b; Hamnett 1989; Sullivan 1989; Burrows and Butler 1989), principally on the grounds of his apparently unqualified endorsement of consumption and uncritical championing of consumer rights. But it should be noted that he does not focus on the nature of consumption itself but rather studies the contrasting social and political contexts in which it occurs, substituting categories of consumer for the traditional concept of social class. Hence it has been suggested that he is not so much correcting the production bias of Marxist analyses as proposing his own equally general theory of industrial societies (Warde 1990b).

Given that Saunders' background was in urban sociology and the sociology of work (Saunders 1986), it is understandable that the debate which he initiated was at first confined to these subfields of the discipline. However, not only did such views have obvious political significance in Thatcherite Britain, but to challenge the traditional view of the nature of social class in modern society was necessarily to query the orthodox opinions of the majority of contemporary British sociologists. Consequently it was not long before this debate reached a wider audience and in doing so became a critical factor in the development of a British sociology of consumption. This event can probably be dated to 1990, in which year not only was there a special issue of the British Sociological Association's journal *Sociology* (vol. 24, no. 1) devoted to the topic of consumption, but the organisation's annual conference also took 'Consumption and Class' as its central theme. A selection of these papers was subsequently published under the heading *Consumption and Class: Divisions and Change* (Burrows and Marsh 1992). However, the Saunders-inspired debate over class, consumption and modes of provision was not the only factor leading up to the emergence of a sociology of consumption in Britain. This – what one might call the largely 'economic' or 'material' perspective on consumption – clearly played an important part, yet there was another factor at work, one which has been at least as influential, although it involved approaching consumption from a very different perspective, one which stressed its character as a 'cultural' and 'psychological' phenomenon.

This strand of sociological analysis has its origins in traditional culture theory, especially in that perspective on modern mass culture which represents it as basically a 'consumer culture'. This essentially elitist critique existed in both a right-wing and a left-wing form in the 1950s and 1960s, with Leavisites and neo-Marxist Critical Theorists equally eager to condemn such components of mass culture as popular music and advertising. This has proved an influential intellectual inheritance, one which many academics have found difficult to throw off. However this critique was always marked by a general detachment from and indeed even an ignorance of, the reality of popular culture, relying heavily (especially in the British context) upon a suspicion of American cultural influences. Thus even those who ostensibly espoused non-elitist, traditional forms of popular culture, such as Richard Hoggart, tended to share the pessimistic vision of a culture in the process of being destroyed by transatlantic 'consumerist' values. 'Consumer culture' was, from this perspective, identified with an exploitative, alienating, modern, capitalist culture, and regarded as embodying selfish, dehumanising and materialist values.

Gradually this perspective became modified during the 1970s and 1980s in the face of a new form of culture theory; one that was in closer contact with ordinary people and their cultures (or more usually subcultures) and hence had a firmer ethnographic base. Thus a new generation of researchers found that the supposed 'mass culture' was in reality more of a patchwork of micro-cultures, many of which were genuinely popular creations, expressive of the real concerns and aspirations of ordinary people. This popular culture tradition of study (which gained much of its impetus in Britain from the Birmingham Centre for Contemporary Cultural Studies), evolved out of the critical theory tradition but tended to see 'protest' or 'resistance', rather than compliance or despair, in the cultural forms adopted by ordinary people. Thus Ioan Davies (1993: 142) describes British cultural studies in the 1970s as being, at least in part, a 'consumerist critique' in which work on 'the popular' dealt with consumerism as a form of resistance against a traditional, elitist culture and the society which it represented (see Hall and Jefferson 1976; Turner 1990). The cultural ethnographers who undertook this research tended to focus on aspects of youth culture, especially fashion, style, popular music and fiction (Hebdige 1979, 1988; Fiske 1989; Willis 1978, 1990), and their principal message was that the ordinary 'consumer' was not a passive and easily manipulated creature, but an active, critical and creative person; someone who adapted and moulded material acquired through the mass media to their own ends by means of a diverse range of everyday, creative and symbolic practices. By studying the 'real' consumer of popular products in this way, rather than the stereotypical, exploited and manipulated person portrayed in critical theory, cultural studies laid the basis for a genuine sociology of the consumer of cultural products.

At the same time, the rise of feminism was also having an impact on the development of a sociology of consumption. In retrospect it seems inevitable that feminism should make a significant contribution in this respect because it had long been assumed (rightly or wrongly) that most 'consumers' were women. Thus, to the extent that feminists set out to render women more 'visible' in both sociological theory and research, then this would logically lead more or less directly into the study of such central consumption-related topics as fashion, the body, shopping and household management (see Carter, in McRobbie and Nava 1984). Where feminism combined with the new popular culture ethnography, this focus on consumerism was particularly pronounced (Nava 1987, 1992).[1]

However, there was also another factor at work, one associated with a new and very different style of cultural analysis. This surrounded the debate over the 'condition' or 'culture' of postmodernity. A term originally used by architects to suggest the dissolution of any distinction between the high culture style of modernism and popular, vernacular, cultural traditions, it has since been applied to all areas of culture and in such diverse ways that a standard or common usage is hard to detect. As Burrows and Marsh (among others) have noted, postmodernism consists of 'a somewhat loose collection of ill-defined notions' (Burrows and Marsh 1992: 6). The important theorists of postmodernity are generally recognised to be Jean-François Lyotard (1979) and Fredric Jameson (1991). The key idea that connects their work is that of the fragmentation of culture and the increased importance of symbol over substance in everyday life (see Harvey 1989; Connor 1989). What is significant in this context, however, is the importance which these theorists of postmodernity attach to consumption and the fact that they tend to associate a postmodern society with a consumer society, an equation that has subsequently been adopted by many other writers (see Kaplan 1987; Featherstone 1991). Consequently a concern with consumption as a symbolic rather than an instrumental activity is a thread that unites writers as diverse as Lyotard, Jameson and Baudrillard. In fact, it is the latter's essay on consumer society, rather than the ideas of Lyotard or Jameson, which has probably had a more direct impact on the emerging sociology of consumption. From the perspective of Baudrillard's post-Marxist semiotic view of modern life, contemporary society is essentially a consumer society. What individuals can be regarded as consuming, however, is less products and services than their meanings or 'emancipated signs'; that is signs which no longer have any fixed referent. This results in a vast system of hyper-reality in which any object can, in principle, take on any meaning. The journal *Theory, Culture and Society* has served as a major organ for the dissemination of the views of these, mainly continental, apostles of postmodernism, and its special issue on consumer culture in 1983, together with its editor Mike Featherstone's subsequent publications (1988, 1990), have played a significant part in popularising this approach to 'consumption'. However, it is important not to forget that these postmodern theories generally have little by way of empirical support, suggestive though they might be, and consequently constitute a questionable basis for an emergent sociology of consumption.

Although one can claim that the contemporary sociology of consumption in Britain has something of a mixed parentage, these are the two broad strands which have combined to give it its present form; an 'economic-materialist' one emerging principally out of urban sociology and the sociology of work on the one hand, and an essentially 'psychological-cultural' one emerging out of critical theory, cultural studies and the debate over postmodernism on the other. These two very different approaches to consumption have now, in the climate of the 1990s, begun to mix and mingle to form that diverse body of observation and analysis that currently passes for 'the sociology of consumption'.[2]

In one sense it could be said that developments over the past two decades have resulted in the sociology of consumption being thrust into the limelight. This is because it has become a commonplace for people to express the view that contemporary society is a 'consumer society', with a predominantly 'consumer culture'. That is to say, 'a society organised around the consumption, rather than the production of goods and services' ('Consumer Society', *Blackwell's Dictionary of Twentieth-Century Social Thought*, 1993). This is presumed to mean not merely that the economy is structured around the selling and promoting of goods more than it is around their production, but also that members of such a society treat high levels of consumption as indicative of social success and personal happiness and hence choose consuming as their overriding life goal. Whether most sociologists actually believe that this is an accurate description of contemporary British society or not, they are nevertheless forced to acknowledge the widespread existence of such views.

Consequently the sociology of consumption is now necessarily at the centre of disciplinary concerns and its rise signals a general reordering of the saliency of different topic areas within the discipline. Increasingly that which was formerly considered central is now viewed as marginal (most noticeably the world of work and employment, but also and more controversially, the phenomenon of social class itself), whilst topics long regarded as insignificant, if not actually trivial and frivolous, such as fashion, advertising and shopping, are now considered critical to an understanding of contemporary 'postmodern' society. Clearly, the latter change should be welcomed, for these phenomena have been unduly neglected for too long. However, it is important to recognise that their study is primarily justified because they are significant components of human life, yielding experiences that are meaningful and important to those who 'follow fashion', or who 'live to shop', and not simply because any information gained may serve to illustrate the (itself fashionable) thesis of postmodernity. Much more questionable is the larger claim that *all* topic areas of interest to sociologists, ones which have generally been studied within a production, that is to say class-based, paradigm, are today best studied within a consumption one. It is this argument which has provoked such a vigorous response to Peter Saunders' claims and his explicit challenge to what he sees as the privileging of 'the formal workplace and workplace relations' by so many sociologists (1988: 142). At the same time, it is what makes the arguments of the postmodernists so disturbing as they foreground the isolated individual, juggling with assorted signs and symbols in a never-ending attempt to construct and maintain identity in a fragmented and ever-changing environment. Looked at in this light, the emerging sociology of consumption takes on the character, not merely as a critique of traditional productionist paradigms, but of sociology in general.

THE PROSPECTS FOR A SOCIOLOGY OF CONSUMPTION

One of the central difficulties facing anyone attempting to review work in the sociology of consumption is that, as a result of the trends outlined above, a loose 'consumerist' perspective is now commonly employed to frame the discussion in many different areas within the discipline. Thus work on popular culture or the media is commonly presented in such a way as to foreground the extent to which individuals should be viewed as 'consumers' of products rather than simply as participating in cultural activities, or as the 'consumers' of films or television programmes rather than simply as an 'audience' for them. To this extent, the language of consumption has become widely adopted in areas of research which formerly appeared to manage perfectly well without it. To what extent employing the term 'consumer' carries with it any implication of the presence of a perspective distinctive of the sociology of consumption is another matter. But then it is first necessary to attempt to define consumption and hence outline what is in effect the proper concern of such a field of study.

Several attempts have been made both to define and delineate the topic of consumption within the framework of the discipline of sociology (see Saunders in Otnes 1988; Miller 1987; Campbell 1987; Warde in Burrows and Marsh 1992). The difficulty here, given the diverse influences upon this field, is that since each of these tend to be closely tied to the specific background and interests of the particular author concerned, no one formulation has succeeded in gaining widespread acceptance. Not that defining consumption is in any case an easy matter since it is hard to overcome its accepted popular and professional usage to refer to an exclusively economic activity. Yet the assumptions contained in such usage, especially the idea that these activities can be identified by the analyst without reference to the subject's understanding of 'what he or she is doing', together with the presumption that 'consumption' and 'production' are necessarily exclusive categories, are ones that many sociologists might want to query. On the other hand, some sociologists, in their understandable frustration with economic usage, have fallen into the trap of substituting functionalist definitions for the traditional ones, applying the term 'consumption' to that activity which serves to enhance an individual's status or confirm or construct their identity. This practice is equally unhelpful, obscuring as it does the difference between activities that aim to achieve these goals and those that do in fact realise them, as well as that between 'consumption' proper and its functional alternatives. Perhaps, therefore, for the time being at least, it would be sensible to employ a simple working definition, one that identifies consumption as involving the selection, purchase, use, maintenance, repair and disposal of any product or service.[3] Now it is important to note that while purchase may be direct and personal, effected through the marketplace, it may also be indirect and impersonal, such as that effected through taxation; whilst it is also important to recognise that this definition embraces services as well as goods. Both these dimensions are sometimes overlooked in those treatments of consumption that adopt a primarily Marxist 'commodities' approach (see Lee 1993). Indeed, as Alan Warde has suggested (1990b), the mode of provision of a good or service, whether it is effected through the market, the state or even supplied privately, is itself an important feature of the phenomenon of consumption and ought itself to be the subject of sociological enquiry.

When considering the classic theoretical tradition that bears on consumption, one tends to think first of the contributions of Veblen and Simmel, and to a lesser degree perhaps, those of Marx and Weber. Certainly the major contributions would appear to be those of Veblen on conspicuous consumption (1925), Simmel on fashion and money (1957, 1978), Malinowski on the kula (1922), Boas on the potlatch (1944), Mauss on the gift (1976), Marx on commodity fetishism, use and exchange value (1971, 1973), Sombart on luxury (1967), and Weber on status groups and the Protestant ethic (1958, 1978). Yet it is not clear how far the theoretical contributions of these writers actually inform contemporary discussions of consumption. Certainly they are commonly cited, but it is unusual for their theories to be discussed at length, let alone used to analyse or interpret data. Thorstein Veblen is an excellent case in point since his theory of conspicuous consumption is probably the most widely referred to of all theories in this field (especially by academics in other disciplines, such as historians: see Stone 1982; Burke 1987). Yet it is rarely Veblen's specific theory, with its unqualified emphasis on the manifestation of 'pecuniary strength', which is appealed to, but rather a simplified and amended version featuring 'taste'. Whilst, in addition, the many difficulties and ambiguities of interpretation contained within it are rarely mentioned (for a discussion of some of these see Campbell 1987).[4] Simmel, by contrast, has received more attention, probably because, unlike Veblen, he has some enthusiastic supporters among the present generation of sociologists (see Frisby 1981). Consequently he is commonly cited as the source of insights into aspects of contemporary consumerism, especially in regard to the phenomena of fashion and the *flâneur*, as well as the aesthetic and stylistic dimensions of modern, urban life more generally (see, for an example, Bocock 1993). Weber's work is also widely recognised as pertinent to an understanding of a consumer society, mainly because his concept of a status group appears to refer to those who share a common lifestyle and consequently can be viewed as embodying a consumption-based rather than a production-based criterion of social differentiation. However, it is important to note that for Weber, individuals who occupied the same status situation were simply people who were accorded equal 'honour', that is to say prestige or esteem, in the eyes of others. Unlike Veblen, he did not presume that there was any single source of honour in modern society even though status differences might well be expressed in differentiated 'styles of life' (Gerth and Mills 1970: 186–188).

In this connection one can observe that it is more common to find sociologists drawing on contemporary theorists, such as Erving Goffman or Pierre Bourdieu, and especially upon such theorists of postmodernity as Baudrillard, Jameson or Maffesoli, than upon the more classical theorists mentioned above. Thus, in the Rob Shields' edited volume *Lifestyle Shopping* (1992), although contributors refer to Marx, Veblen and Simmel, the theorists who receive the most attention are Michael Bakhtin, Walter Benjamin, Erving Goffman, Henri Lefebvre and Michel Maffesoli. However, it is interesting to reflect on the extent to which these writers can properly be judged to have advanced theories of consumption, as they are principally theorists of culture, or more commonly, of postmodernity. Baudrillard probably has the best claim to be considered a 'theorist of consumption' since he builds directly upon Marx's concept of the 'commodity'. However, he modifies Marx's original usage by drawing upon semiotics in order to stress the significance of the 'commodity-sign' rather than the commodity itself. Thus, he argues that in capitalist societies, consumption should be understood as a process in which only the signs attached to goods are actually consumed, and hence that commodities are not valued for their use but understood as possessing a meaning that is determined by their position in a self-referential system of signifiers.

Probably the most important contemporary theorist of consumption proper is Pierre Bourdieu, whose work, *Distinction: A Social Critique of the Judgement of Taste*, first published in France in 1979 and only available in English since 1984, bears comparison, in character and importance, with Veblen's *Theory of The Leisure Class* (Veblen 1925). In stark contrast to most of the theorists of postmodernity mentioned above, Bourdieu's theory derives from, and is supported by, ample empirical material concerning people's 'taste'. He uses this to develop a complex thesis in which he stresses the centrality of consumption practices (especially the manifestation of taste) in the creation and maintenance of social relationships of domination and submission. Like Veblen he emphasises the hierarchical nature of the status system of modern society, but, unlike Veblen, Bourdieu plays down material possessions, stressing instead the importance of the individual's possession of symbolic or cultural capital and the way in which this can be put to use to display taste. There is, none the less, the same emphasis upon competition between individuals for the scarce resource of status as one finds in Veblen, with the addition of a subtle analysis of the character and historical development of the various *champs*, or markets, in which this takes place. Unlike Veblen, however, Bourdieu recognises that there are inherent limitations on an individual's chances of succeeding in moving up through such a system as a consequence of their 'habitus', or personal cultural inheritance, and that not even newly acquired wealth will necessarily enable individuals to advance their status.

II   A review of the sociological literature

Having identified consumption as any activity involving the selection, purchase, use, maintenance, repair and disposal of any product or service, it will be useful to employ these divisions, if loosely, in a review of the relevant sociological literature. In fact, not all of these topics have been adequately researched, with maintenance, repair and disposal especially neglected. But then even the selection, purchase and use of goods and services has been the subject of more speculative assertion than empirical enquiry.[5] At the same time, it is necessary to be aware of the two contrasting sociological traditions that have been identified as combining to constitute the present state of the sociology of consumption, as these cross-cut these divisions such that each aspect of consumption may be studied from either perspective.

THE SELECTION AND PURCHASE OF GOODS: SHOPPING

The selection and purchase of goods (in addition to services, if perhaps to a lesser degree) is commonly envisaged as achieved through the central consumer activity of 'shopping'. In view of this, it is something of a surprise to discover how little attention sociologists have devoted to the study of this activity, especially in view of the significance which it is accorded in most theories of consumer society. There is, however, a growing literature on the retail environment (see especially Gardner and Sheppard 1989), one which relies heavily on both historical studies of shopping in general (Adburgham 1964), of the department store (see M. Miller 1981; Williams 1982; Laermans 1993), or of the shopping arcade (Geist 1983); or, alternatively, upon the work of geographers and town planners (see Goss 1993). It is interesting to note in this connection the extent to which the shopping-mall appears to have a special significance for the consumption-as-culture theorists. Typically treated as if it were the very embodiment of the postmodern condition, the distinctive nature of the activities under-taken within its walls is characteristically presumed by the sociologist with-out the benefit of any evidence gleaned from shoppers themselves (see Shields 1992). Analyses such as these, which treat the department store and the shopping mall as if they were cultural phenomena, might be judged suggestive (see Chaney 1983, 1990; Shields 1992) but they hardly serve as a substitute for a detailed examination of the central consumer activity of shopping. Research that does possess this more empirical focus includes George and Murcott's note on strategies for managing embarrassment when shopping for sanitary towels and tampons (1992), as well as, if to a lesser extent, Mary Douglas' spirited defence of shopping as a social exclusion activity (1992). Yet the most useful contribution to date (at least in the British context) is probably the Lunt and Livingstone (1992) volume, *Mass Consumption and Personal Identity*.

In fact, this volume constitutes a fascinating contrast with the Shields volume mentioned earlier, for whilst the latter collection is a good illus-tration of that theoretically inspired and characteristically speculative approach typical of the 'postmodern' sociologist of consumption, the Lunt and Livingstone book represents a more 'economistic' approach which treats consumption as if it were a more mundane phenomenon concerned largely with resource allocation.[6] Not that such a perspective is to be deplored, since the information supplied (the results of analysing nearly 400 questions asked to a sample of around 300 people) represents a valuable addition to our understanding on such topics as spending patterns, the use of credit, debt management and household budgeting. (See also Lunt and Livingstone 1991a, 1991b; whilst further material on debt and the use of credit can be found in Drury and Ferrier 1984; Ford 1988; Gardner and Sheppard 1989.) By contrast, the majority of essays in the Shields volume focus on issues concerning image, identity, the gaze and voyeurism, especially in those contemporary public spaces devoted to shopping such as atriums and malls; whilst these comments rest on little more than the sociologists' own observations and speculations.

The Lunt and Livingstone concern with the use of material resources has a natural corollary in the work of those sociologists who focus on the patterns of use with respect to the scarce resource of time. Those who have applied time-budget analysis to the selection of goods and services include Gronmo and Lavik (1988) and Gershuny (Gershuny 1982; Gershuny and Jones 1987). Since this work reveals that the British have doubled the time devoted to shopping over the past thirty years,[7] it provides further justifi-cation (if any were needed) for devoting more attention to studying the phenomenological and experiential dimensions of this activity. However, virtually the only example of this kind to date is the work of the Canadians Prus and Dawson (1991), who focus on the means through which the 'social process' of shopping is accomplished. In their interviews with shoppers they encountered a sharp divide between those who viewed this as an enjoyable, 'recreational' activity and those for whom it was a 'laborious' activity akin to work itself. Employing a symbolic interactionist perspective, they explain this contrast in terms of differences in the manner in which the shopper's self is 'incorporated' into the activity. Their work is undoubtedly a useful first step in the direction of a proper ethnography of shopping, although the emphasis on the nature of self-involvement is probably more comprehensible when related to the wider social roles (especially gender) of the shoppers (see, for example, Campbell 1993b, 1994).

THE USE OF PERISHABLE GOODS: FOOD AND DRINK

As far as the use of goods is concerned, one naturally thinks first of those most basic of all consumption activities, eating and drinking. Obviously a central part of any sociology of consumption, the sociology of food has, as Beardsworth and Keil observe, been something of a 'lacuna' within the discipline (Beardsworth and Keil 1990: 139). There has, however, been some progress in recent years owing largely to the significant contributions made by Anne Murcott (1984, 1988), Stephen Mennell (1985) and Elisabeth Furst (Furst et al. 1991). Mennell's work in particular deserves mention, since by building on the historical analysis of Norbert Elias (1982, 1983), he has demonstrated how taste, and even appetite itself, can be shaped by broad social, political and economic processes. In fact, this reflects a general trend in which sociologists working in this field can be said to have benefited considerably from the valuable work of both social historians (Driver 1983; Mintz 1985; Schwartz 1986; Levenstein 1988) and social anthropologists (Lévi-Strauss 1969, 1978; Douglas 1975, 1984; Goody 1982; Harris 1986). Here too one can detect much the same division as noted earlier between that fundamentally materialist approach that focuses on food as related to issues of diet or nutrition, on the one hand, and that which treats food (or 'foodways') as codes or symbolic systems capable of semiotic or structural analysis on the other.

However, there is also a more distinctly sociological approach, one that focuses upon food provision within the household and its structuring by age, gender or life cycle (Kerr and Charles 1986; Charles and Kerr 1988). On the basis of material gained through interviews and diaries, information was obtained about the food and drink habits of some two hundred families in the North of England. This showed how sexual divisions and power relations affect the pattern of food distribution within the family, such that the distribution of meat, for example, is undertaken in accordance with a hierarchy in which men occupy first place, women second, and children third. In addition to demonstrating how the consumption of food and drink is structured by age and sex, Charles and Kerr also reveal the importance attached to the 'proper meal', the universality of the distinction between foods that 'are good for you' and those that are pleasant to consume, the widespread nature of nutritional ignorance, and the fact that many women, in an effort to remain slim and attractive, are engaged in a 'permanent struggle against food'.

This work is important, not merely because it lays the foundation for a sociology of food consumption, but also because in the process it serves to unlock the 'black box' of the family. As Close and Collins have observed, the idea that the modern family's relationship with the economy operates to a large degree through its function as a unit of consumption is accepted by a wide range of writers (Close and Collins 1985). Indeed, it is common to encounter the claim that the 'unity' of the modern family has been 'restored around its function not of production but of consumption' (M. Young and P. Wilmot, *The Symmetrical Family*, cited in Close and Collins 1985: 21). But such an argument often implies that the family or 'household' is regarded as if it constituted a single unit of consumption, and although this is the approach typically adopted in classical economics – in which households are effectively treated as if they were individuals – this ignores those complex intra-familial processes which in practice directly affect consumption. For, as the work of Charles and Kerr demonstrates, it is necessary to understand decision-making processes within the family if one is fully to understand how it functions as a consumption 'site'. Others whose research adds to our understanding of these intra-familial processes, especially as they relate to consumption and finance, include Branner and Wilson (1987), Gail Wilson (1987), Jan Pahl (1989) and Vogler and Pahl (1993); whilst mention should also be made of Peter Corrigan's valuable study of clothing and the family economy. Finally, some mention should be made of the fact that much consumption of food and drink also occurs outside the family. To date, Joanne Finkelstein's examination of the phenomenon of 'dining out' (1989) is one of the few studies in this field, and although intriguing in outlining the extent to which restaurant eating can be viewed as a branch of the entertainment industry, she does not succeed in charting the socio-demographic or social structural features of this phenomenon in quite the way that Charles and Kerr have done for 'dining in'.

Discussion of food and drink leads naturally enough to the topic of the body, since the original referent for the term 'consumption' was to those basic processes through which humans keep themselves alive. Hence it is quite understandable that the growth of a sociology of consumption should bring with it a new interest in the human body, or at least an interest in the processes of 'embodiment' (Bourdieu 1984) or 'corporeality' (Falk 1994). Consequently a focus on the primary consumption processes of eating and drinking is understandably matched by an interest in the body itself. As early as 1982 Mike Featherstone noted the importance of the body in modern consumer culture. Yet despite the very obvious basis of consumption in processes that arise within the body, much of the recent writing on this topic is more concerned with the image of the body than with its biological reality; both the image that consumers have of their own corporeality and those representations of the body contained in the culture at large. This has meant that the human body has been considered more as a medium of expression, or as an object for aesthetic contemplation, or even as the model for self-construction (Falk 1994), than in terms of its direct connection with eating and drinking. Of course, these different perspectives are not necessarily unrelated to the study of primary consumption processes, as there are many ways through which they may be connected. Nevertheless, there would seem to be a need for more empirical studies of these primary activities, as well as others, such as washing, exercising and using make-up, which involve individuals in interacting with their own bodies.

THE USE OF MATERIAL GOODS

When we come to consider the use of non-consumable goods, we find that sociologists have paid surprisingly little attention to the interaction of individuals with their possessions. Consequently we know very little about what individuals actually do with the goods they purchase, let alone about the time spent in the maintenance, repair or even the disposal of their possessions. Grant McCracken has called attention to what he calls 'possession rituals' and 'grooming rituals', whilst observing that consumers 'spend a good deal of time cleaning, discussing, comparing, reflecting, showing off, and even photographing many of their new possessions' (McCracken 1985). Yet despite the obvious truth of this assertion, few sociologists have chosen to study these practices. One exception would be Oakley's studies of housework (Oakley 1976) which provides some clues about the significance of such tasks as the washing and ironing of clothes, as well as the general cleaning of furniture, furnishings and other household objects. Yet the fact that these activities were framed within the context of 'housework' somewhat masks the extent to which the individuals engaged in them might have regarded themselves as interacting with prized personal possessions. Consequently Moorhouse's study of hot-rod enthusiasts (Moorhouse 1991) is valuable in filling this gap, since in this instance the subjects of the study were individuals who had both purchased the object in question and devoted themselves enthusiastically to its care and 'grooming'. What

Moorhouse demonstrates is that the essence of hot-rodding is buying and *using* automobiles and that the enthusiasts involved, far from being passive, manipulated consumers of a 'mass culture' item, used their vehicles as a means of personal self-expression and creativity; spending long hours building, mending and transforming their possessions. Unfortunately, even in this study, the absence of interviews and the reliance on correspondence in hot-rod magazines, means that the consumer's voice is still only heard 'at second-hand'.

In fact, for direct, detailed information on how people relate to their material possessions, it is necessary to turn to social psychology, where there is an established literature embodying the results of first-hand research (see Csikszentmihalyi and Rochberg-Halton 1981; Rudmin 1991; Dittmar 1992). From this it is possible to discern the significance which possessions play in socialisation and the development of the self; how they can function as symbolic expressions of an individual's identity; as well as something about the socio-demographic differentiation in evaluating material objects. Thus we learn that the young are more likely to value toys, televisions and stereos, whilst the old place a greater value on photographs and other 'sentimental' objects valued for their associations or memories. We also discover that, in general, males place a greater value on technology than do females (Csikszentmihalyi and Rochberg-Halton 1981). This is a useful contribution, but since the focus is largely on attitudes towards goods rather than upon patterns of interaction with purchased objects, whilst it is not always clear precisely how 'value' arises out of such interaction, there is still a need for a more sociological perspective on possessions.

One class of objects which sociologists do not appear to have overlooked is clothing, since there now exists a considerable literature on 'the sociology of fashion', although it is important to note that this field has largely been the exclusive concern of those sociologists who have adopted the psychological-cultural mode of analysis. Writers from Veblen and Simmel down to Barth and Bourdieu all concentrate on the distinguishing functions of clothes – that is to say on clothing as a 'code' or system of 'meanings' – whilst the more material strand is noticeably missing. At the same time, the examination of how individuals interact with clothing has been closely associated with the study of 'fashion' and hence with issues of imitation, emulation and the diffusion of innovation. Consequently, although some sociologists have sought to rebut the popular Veblen–Simmel model of fashion innovation (see Campbell 1992; King 1963; Davis 1992), it is still widely invoked as if it represented an explanation of how and why individuals interact with goods. In fact, not only is there considerable doubt about whether 'fashion' is an important consideration in the minds of clothes consumers, but there is little support for either the 'trickle-down' thesis or the stress on emulative motives. There are many examples of 'trickle-up' fashions, such as the frock-coat (Fine and Leopold 1990) and blue jeans (Davis 1992); whilst the stress on emulative motives as an explanation of fashion tends to take the form of a circular argument (see Campbell 1987: 49–57), whilst also lacking empirical backing (see Campbell 1993a).

What is more, sociologists still present observer-based analyses of clothing, with the result, as Peter Corrigan has observed (Corrigan 1993), that the 'wearer perspective' is generally ignored. All too often, those who represent clothing as a system of meaning employ historical material to draw conclusions about the way in which clothing may be employed today (see Finkelstein 1991); or alternatively employ material from highly distinctive youth groups or subcultures to support claims about the function of clothing in general (Lurie 1981). The problem, however, is that clothing, in the form of fashion, is an essentially ambiguous system, one which generally employs 'undercoding' (Davis 1992), whilst 'what it says' varies over time and depends critically on who is doing the decoding. Davis provides a useful and much needed balance to the over-concentration on observer-analysis of meaning by exploring the production and distribution stages in the fashion process. However, like most other analysts he focuses on the presumed connection between fashion and identity, tracing what he calls cultural 'fault lines' of collectively experienced identity, and relates these to fashion changes in contemporary society. It remains the case, as Elisabeth Wilson has stressed, that there is still no adequate theory that explains why people 'follow fashion', or indeed, in general what function or functions fashion can be said to perform (Wilson 1985).

THE USE OF INTANGIBLE GOODS AND SERVICES

Finally, something needs to be said about the consumption of intangible goods, such as information or images. As we have already seen, many theories of consumption (more especially those advanced by sociologists of a postmodernist persuasion), espouse theories that represent all consumption as, in effect, a process in which 'meaning' rather than tangible objects are actually 'consumed'. Be that as it may, the necessities of eating and drinking as well as the purchase and use of cars, clothes, washing machines, furniture and the like does involve people in exchanging money for real objects in a way that is not the case when people enjoy a pleasant view or watch a film. For in the latter cases the 'good' that is purchased is an experience rather than a material object. Viewed in this light the interaction of individuals with all sources of information or images, whether via the mass media, computerised data systems, the telephone or fax machine, or directly through their own senses when viewing artefacts in museums and art galleries, listening to music at concerts, or even simply 'enjoying the sights' as a tourist, becomes, in effect, 'consumption'. This is certainly the view taken by Silverstone and Hirsch (1992) in their study of the way in which information and communication technologies impact on the domestic sphere. Here, in echoes of the Charles and Kerr study mentioned earlier, the black box of the family is once again unpacked to reveal those intra-familial processes which structure consumption practices and how these may in turn influence not only technological innovation but also popular images of technological products. However, such a perspective leads inevitably to a position in which it becomes impossible to exclude not just the study of advertising and audience research from an all-embracing soci-ology of consumption, but also, and more controversially, the sociology of entertainment and spectator sports, and even the sociology of the arts and media studies in general. Perhaps such fields of study could benefit from a 'consumer' frame of analysis, but the suspicion must arise that in attempt-ing to encompass so large and diverse a range of topic areas, the sociology of consumption may lose whatever meaningful or distinctive character it is in the process of developing.

III Consumption: Why the meaning is not a message

Consumer goods may serve to fulfil a wide range of personal and social functions. Fairly obviously, they commonly serve to satisfy needs or indulge wants and desires. In addition they may serve to compensate the individ-ual for feelings of inferiority, insecurity or loss, or to symbolise achieve-ment, success or power. They also commonly serve to communicate social distinctions or reinforce relationships of superiority and inferiority between individuals or groups. They can also, on some occasions, express attitudes or states of mind, or communicate specific messages from one person to another. Finally they may be instrumental in creating or confirming an individual's sense of self or personal identity. All these possibilities have been canvassed in the wide variety of theories that can be said to have a bearing on consumption. Yet it is noticeable that in contemporary socio-logical discussions not all these perspectives are equally represented. Generally we may say that special emphasis tends to be placed on those theories that relate consumption to issues of identity and, within this, to those that represent consumption as an activity which conveys information about the consumer's identity to those who witness it. Indeed, we can be more specific still and identify theories that represent the consumer as actually preoccupied with conveying specific 'meanings' or 'messages' about his or her identity (or 'lifestyle') to others, as those currently predominant within the discipline.

In general this would seem to be because sociologists have been per-suaded that modern industrial societies have evolved in such a way that individuals are presented, effectively for the first time, with the possibility of choosing their identity by varying their pattern of consumption. What is commonly argued is that changes in production techniques associated with post-Fordism, together with ever-greater differentiation in the identification and targeting of market sectors, have led to a significant move away from mass consumption and towards an ever-wider diversity of consumption patterns. Quoting from Stuart and Elizabeth Ewen's book, *Channels of Desire*, Mike Featherstone suggests that such changes can be summed up in the phrases 'Today there is no fashion: there are only *fashions*', 'No rules, only choices', 'Everyone can be anyone' (Featherstone 1991: 83, italics in original). Thus, in contrast to the comparative fixity of a hierarchical system of social status groups, the claim is that there is now a completely 'open' system, one in which an individual is free self-consciously to choose to manifest any of the multitude of lifestyles on offer; and 'lifestyle' is the key term in such theories. Very much 'in vogue' as Featherstone suggests, it is usually employed to connote

> individuality, self-expression, and a stylistic self-consciousness. One's body, clothes, speech, leisure pastimes, eating and drinking preferences, home, car, choice of holidays, etc. are to be regarded as indicators of the individuality of taste and sense of style of the owner/consumer.
>
> (Featherstone 1991: 83)

Thus, because of the wide range and character of goods and services currently on offer in the marketplace, and consequently the considerable choice which this presents to consumers, individuals are regarded as free to select an identity for themselves. The consumption pattern that they select, whether represented by their choice of car or clothes, house, furnishings or leisure-time pursuits, can therefore be regarded as indicative not simply of their 'self-identity', but of how they wish others to regard them. Indeed, because George Herbert Mead's thesis concerning the dependence of self-images upon the attitudes of others is generally presumed to be valid, changing one's consumption habits in order to indicate a new identity to others is presumed to be the only way in which consumers can effectively adopt a new one for themselves.

Now, in part, this tendency to assume that the members of modern (or postmodern) society can be more adequately categorised, not on the basis of old production-style criteria such as occupation, educational qualifications or income, but rather by 'lifestyle', has gained considerable impetus because of recent developments in the fields of advertising and marketing. These professions now typically class people on consumption criteria, often employing what Gardner and Sheppard refer to as 'psychographic techniques', that is 'a way of looking at future market segments by attitudes and lifestyle' (Gardner and Sheppard 1989: 217). Market researchers increasingly make use of geo-demographic databases to construct profiles of 'consumer types' based on different 'lifestyles'. These profiles may include types such as 'working-class stay at homes', 'young upwardly-mobile' and 'well-off-retired', or the 'co-op, club and colliery', and 'families in the sky' (see Steve Flowers, 'Information Overload', *Guardian*, 10 Nov. 1993). Or the categories may focus on attitudes and values toward contemporary issues, such as conservation and the environment, with the consequent identification of different varieties of 'greens' (see Gardner and Sheppard 1989: 224). In general one may say that marketers have moved over the past ten to twenty years from categorising people by class and purchasing power, firstly to demographics and life-stages, and then increasingly to consumption patterns and 'lifestyle'. However, it was probably with the appearance of the 'yuppie' that the wider public first became aware of this change (see J. Burnett and A. Bush, 'Profiling the Yuppie', *Journal of Advertising Research*, April 1986; J. L. Hammond, 'Yuppies', *Public Opinion Quarterly* 50, 1986). This move has culminated in advertisers abandoning the old socio-economic classifications of A, B, C1, C2, D in favour of lifestyle categories, on the grounds that 'It is now misleading to relate life-styles simply to income or occupation' (Neil Tharpar, 'Advertisers usher in classless society', *Independent on Sunday*, 6 March 1994). In the light of these developments, there must be a strong suspicion that sociologists, in accepting that it is valid to change from using older 'objective' criteria such as occupation or income to these newer 'subjective' ones, are merely following a fashion, effectively taking their cue from the advertisers and market researchers, rather than modifying their views as a consequence of their own research findings.

However, there may well be good reasons for believing that it is unwise of sociologists to build theories of modern consumer behaviour around the concept of 'lifestyle'. For whilst lifestyle-based categories may be of value in the context of marketing and advertising, there is little evidence to suggest their sociological significance. In the first place it is important to note that even the marketing 'lifestyle' categories are still commonly built around discriminators – such as age, marital status, employment status, or stage of the life-cycle – which are 'objective' criteria and not simply features of a consumption pattern. For, not surprisingly, market researchers are well aware that age, employment status and life-cycle position are major factors influencing disposable income and hence purchasing power. Consequently it is still rare for individuals to be categorised on lifestyle variables alone. Second, when more 'subjective' factors are taken into account, as for example in the development of categories of 'green' consumer, the criteria employed relate more to differences in people's values than to differences in taste. This is clearly critical because although individuals may easily develop new tastes, there is much evidence to suggest that the values that people hold do not change much throughout their lifetime. Both these considerations suggest that the majority of consumers are not actually in a position freely to adopt a new lifestyle (or identity) simply by the expedient of changing their consumption patterns; either because of the limitations imposed by their objective circumstances or because to do so would require them to undergo the equivalent of a 'conversion' experience.

In the light of this conclusion it is easy to understand why so much emphasis is placed upon 'youth' in those theories which present consumption as guided by a desire to adopt a 'lifestyle' (see, for example, Langman 1992: 59–61). For not only is 'youth' (especially perhaps adolescence) necessarily a life-cycle stage in which experimentation with identity is a central concern, but it is also a stage when individuals generally have little in the way of regular, fixed financial commitments. Very often lacking a career, if not permanent employment, as well as dependants, property-maintenance payments or mortgages, youth is in an ideal position to 'play' with identities. In addition, they are more likely than 'adults' to be in need of reassurance concerning their identity from their peers, and consequently to engage in the 'other-directed' activities of 'viewing and being seen'. However, it is still necessary to note that, even here, the identities on offer frequently consist of merely one or two subcultural alternatives which are themselves set within clear class boundaries; ones which are experienced by the individual as both objective and subjective (that is internalised values) constraints on their choice. This would suggest that it is unwise to treat the identity-experimentation characteristic of youth as if it were in fact typical of the conduct of modern consumers as a whole. This danger may be most apparent when generalisations are made on the basis of studies of working-class or lower-middle-class youth, but there is a similar danger of treating the attitudes and practices of certain sections of the affluent middle class, for example yuppies, or the *nouveaux riches*, as if they too were typical of consumers as whole.

But there are yet deeper problems with the 'lifestyle' or 'consumption as indicative of identity choice' thesis; ones that surround the suggestion that consumption carries distinct meanings, in the form of 'messages' about identity, to those in a position to witness it. Veblen was the first theorist to suggest that an act of consumption might carry such a message and he was very explicit about what it might be. He considered that it indicated something about the consumer's 'pecuniary strength'. In other words, observers, because of their knowledge of how much things cost, would be able to assess an individual's wealth (and hence in Veblen's terms, social status) from the purchased goods which they displayed. This thesis is problematic enough, given that people's knowledge of the price of goods is far from perfect, whilst the casual observer is often not in a position to judge the 'expensiveness' of items that are conspicuously displayed. Yet modern theories generally presume that consumer goods carry more complex messages than this one, and what is more, they assume that consumer and observer share a common understanding of the 'language' in which they are conveyed. Both must be judged highly dubious assumptions.

It has become almost routine for theorists to employ a communicative act or expressive paradigm when focusing on consumption; with the consequence that consumer actions are not viewed as real events involving the allocation or use of material resources (or even as transactions in which money is exchanged for goods and services) so much as symbolic acts or signs: acts which do not so much 'do something' as 'say something', or more properly, perhaps, 'do something through saying something'. This communicative act paradigm – in which talk or language more generally is the model for all action – is one common to theorists as diverse in other ways as Veblen, Goffman, Bourdieu, Barthes and Baudrillard. Now in one sense the perception that individuals may employ material objects to send messages to others and thus to symbolise or express an existing social relationship or to mark a new one, is something of a platitude in the social sciences. Indeed, it is easy to illustrate this perspective by reference to inheritance practices, the giving of dowries, indeed gift-giving in general, or to 'hosting' (that is, entertaining) and the like. One can indeed 'say it with flowers' (and with other things); that is to say, convey love, affection, gratitude, or the like (the precise message depending on the circumstances surrounding the gift) to one or more other people.[8] However, in these instances not only is it the case that actual objects are transferred to specific targeted others, but such acts are themselves usually clearly situated in time and space, something which helps to determine their 'meaning'. By contrast, sending a message to largely unknown and generally unspecified others merely by a process of displaying or using goods, and often without the assistance of specifically designated display situations, is a rather different matter.

There are several important distinctions which often become confused when the 'meaning' of goods is under discussion. The first concerns the difference between the fact that actions are intelligible and the assumption that they have an agreed meaning; the second concerns the confusion between possessing a meaning and constituting a message; and the third, the confusion between receiving a message and intending to send one. Now one could reasonably claim that most actions that individuals perform are usually intelligible to other fully socialised members of the same culture. Consequently it is rare for anyone to be completely mystified by the goods that others have purchased or by the way that they are being utilised. This is not the same, however, as claiming that all, or even most members of that society would be in a position to agree on what 'meaning' should be attributed to the fact that a particular individual has purchased a pair of blue jeans or chooses to wear them to go shopping. For such conduct does not possess a given meaning in contemporary British society, in the way, for example, that a bride wearing a white dress on her wedding day has a given and widely understood meaning. This is not to say that blue jeans do not carry a range of associations and indeed market researchers devote a good deal of time and effort to discovering precisely what these might be. But this does not mean that the activity of wearing them can be compared in any way with uttering a word or even giving a hand signal. For in this case, there is simply no commonly agreed code (let alone a 'language') which would allow any such 'message' to be decoded.

This is not to deny that cultural categories or even cultural principles cannot be 'encoded' in clothes or indeed in goods generally. The anthropological evidence here is strong (see, in particular, Bogatyrev 1971; McCracken 1985). Yet the case is more easily made for traditional or non-literate societies than it is for modern, complex industrial ones. Here, as McCracken's research has shown, the more that individuals try to employ clothing as a language, that is by making their own combinations of items to construct a personal 'ensemble', the less successful it is as a means of communication (McCracken 1988: 55–70). What is more, the essentially fixed nature of a person's appearance renders any 'dialogue' or 'conversation' through clothes an impossibility. Typically, individuals 'read' clothing as if it were a single Gestalt, whilst they employ a very limited range of nouns and adjectives to categorise those portrayed. No attempts are made to 'read' outfits in a linear sense or to detect novel messages. Indeed, only when individuals wear conventional 'outfits' of the kind that correspond to existing social stereotypes (such as 'housewife', 'businessman' or 'hippie') can a 'language code' be read at all.

What is more, the fact that one individual may be able to perceive some 'meaning' (in the sense of clues about 'identity') in the consumption activities of another does not imply either that other observers would discern similar 'meanings' in that activity, or that the meanings discerned correspond to those the consumer intended to convey (if indeed they intended to convey any) through their conduct. In fact, there is a considerable gulf between the wide range of possible meanings which an observer might claim that they can discern in the consumption activities of an individual and the very limited and highly general messages which any individual can possibly hope to succeed in conveying consciously and deliberately to others solely by means of their deployment of consumer goods. Thus despite the many claims that there is a 'language' of goods, especially of clothes (see in particular Lurie 1981), this metaphor, as Davis (1992) has argued most forcibly, is deeply misleading.

None of this should be taken as implying that the material objects that individuals possess or display are not implicated in the creation or maintenance of their sense of self, for there is ample evidence that this is indeed the case (Dittmar 1992). But this is most obviously true in a developmental and particularistic sense, as in the case of a child's cuddly toy or comfort blanket, a bride's wedding ring, a teenager's first car, or an old person's family album. Such objects have meaning to their owners because of the part that they have played (or still play) in their life experiences. Such meanings as these, however, are usually invisible to others (or at least they are to strangers). To assume, therefore, that the casual observer can 'read' the consumer goods that an individual possesses in such a way as to reveal the nature of a person's identity is necessarily to override or ignore this dimension. What is typically put in its place is a categorisation which is necessarily both highly general, far from all-embracing, very speculative and (since consumers are not usually subject to interrogation by observers about their consumption habits) not open to falsification. All of this suggests ample ground for scepticism concerning the general claim that the activity of consuming should be viewed as an endeavour by individuals to indicate a chosen 'lifestyle' to others. The central problem here (and it goes back at least as far as Veblen, although it is most apparent in Goffman) is the tendency of sociologists to apply a communication act paradigm to conduct that is essentially instrumental, and consequently 'read backwards' from the presumed (that is imputed by the sociologist) existence of a message to the presumed intention to send one. Consumption is then seen as involving an 'attempt' by the consumer to 'adopt a lifestyle' or 'create an identity' when there are few grounds for any such assumption.

TOURISM: MODERN CONSUMERISM ILLUSTRATED

What is also disturbing about the currently prevailing consumption-as-communication paradigm is the fact that it represents a failure to acknowledge the necessary material basis of consumption. Whilst it is reasonable enough to stress that the sociological approach to consumption seeks to break with that utilitarian focus on the satisfaction of wants which has traditionally characterised economics, to replace it with a paradigm that reduces consumption to merely a process of indication or signification is surely to throw out the baby with the bath-water. For direct encounters with the fundamental materiality of goods must surely underpin every individual's experience of consumption, no matter how much attention is paid to the symbolic or 'meaningful' features of goods (see D. Miller 1987, Part 2, for a critique of the lack of academic analysis of the object). At the same time, these experiences are necessarily private affairs in so far as individuals are required to employ their own senses to judge how far (if at all) a given good 'satisfies' their needs, wants or desires. To this extent the communication paradigm not only neglects the necessarily physical (or perhaps one should say, physiological) dimension of consumption, but it also forces the activity to be viewed as if it necessarily occurred in an other-directed, social context. Both these biases can be compensated for, however, by recognising the extent to which modern consumption practices centre around the pursuit of pleasure, as this necessarily directs attention to the processes through which individuals perceive and interact with the world around them, without however presuming that their actions are necessarily oriented to others.

117

By stressing the extent to which modern consumers are preoccupied with pursuing pleasure rather than obtaining satisfaction, it becomes possible to understand how the physical properties of goods might be implicated in the processes of consumption without however adopting a utilitarian framework or lapsing into a reductionistic materialism. This is because whilst experiencing pleasure is dependent on real physiological processes of arousal and basic proto-typical events of this kind (such as eating, drinking, engaging in sexual activity), and necessarily involves interacting with real objects (including people), such real experiences can quickly become material out of which an individual can construct improved, because imagined, scenarios. What is more, since the stimulation which creates pleasurable arousal can as easily derive from an imagined internal source as a real external one, day-dreaming about possible novel pleasant experiences can become a more than acceptable alternative to repeating already experienced real ones. Indeed, for the modern consumer, well rehearsed in day-dreaming and fantasising, the appeal of the former typically exceeds that of the latter. The implication of this is that individuals should be viewed as less motivated by a concern with any presumed 'satisfaction' which products may yield, or by a concern to communicate messages to others, as by the pleasure which they derive from the self-illusory experiences that they construct out of the images or associations attached to products.[9]

The essential activity of consumption is thus not the actual selection, purchase or use of products, but rather the imaginative pleasure-seeking to which the product image lends itself, real consumption being largely a resultant of this mentalistic hedonism. Using this framework it becomes possible to understand how it is that modern consumption centres upon the consumption of novelty. For modern consumers will desire a novel rather than a familiar product because this enables them to believe that its acquisition and use will supply experiences that they have not encountered to date in reality. It is therefore possible to project on to this product some of that idealised pleasure that has already been experienced in daydreams, and which it is difficult to associate with those familiar products currently being consumed. Actual consumption of a product or service, although it might well provide both satisfaction and pleasure, is nevertheless still likely to be a literally disillusioning experience, since real products cannot possibly supply the same quality of perfected pleasure as that which attends imaginatively enjoyed experiences.[10]

This understanding of the dynamic underlying modern consumerism can be illustrated by reference to tourism. This phenomenon has been the subject of considerable academic interest in recent years (see for example, Turner and Asch 1975; Walvin 1978; MacCannell 1976, 1992; Urry 1990a, 1990b; Pearce and Butler 1992; Corbin 1993). Yet, as John Urry has noted, there is a difficulty in understanding just what it is that tourists consume (Urry 1990b: 33). He attempts to resolve this problem by focusing on the visual character of tourism and hence stresses the importance of the 'tourist gaze', suggesting that what are often short-lived forms of ocular consumption lie at the centre of that complex socio-economic phenomenon which is tourism (Urry 1990a). However, he also notes how tourism constitutes the paradigm case of a consumption practice built around imaginative pleasure-seeking, and that the actual practice of 'gazing' is typically framed by such illusory hedonism. As he observes, this essentially 'leisure' activity focuses on pleasurable experiences, with the critical activity being the tourist's 'anticipation, through day-dreaming and fantasy, of intense pleasure' (ibid.: 3). He also notes that these pleasures are different from those that may be experienced as part and parcel of the normal everyday routine, being set off from these by space and time, with 'the journey' typically marking the process of transition. Or, alternatively, if the activities that tourists engage in are themselves familiar ones (such as eating and drinking, swimming, or shopping), they are rendered 'extraordinary' by being undertaken in an unfamiliar environment. Consequently he stresses how the pleasures of tourism depend on novelty and the necessity of there being ever-new objects to gaze at; consequently demonstrating that, in essence, what tourists actually consume is largely novelty itself. In addition, Urry notes that whilst tourism has a good claim to be the quintessentially modern form of consumption, many other contemporary activities, ones traditionally distinguished from tourism, such as shopping and sport, now increasingly resemble it in form, with a consequent 'universalising of the tourist gaze' (Urry 1990a). The implication to be drawn from this is that if tourism is best understood as a form of imaginative hedonism, then perhaps this might also be the best way to understand modern consumption in general.

NOTES

1 Feminism also contributed significantly to the more 'materialist' strand of consumer studies. See, for example, Pahl 1989.
2 One should also mention that there have been important inputs from other disciplines, especially social anthropology, history, consumer studies and psychology. See the other chapters in this volume.
3 This is far from satisfactory, even as a working definition, since the phrase 'product and service' betrays the continuing influence of economic assumptions.
4 Indeed, it would appear that Veblen's theory has never been subject to the extensive critical evaluation which it deserves. The notable exception in this respect is Mason 1981.
5 The degree to which each of these should be the focus of study may vary over time. Thus in time of recession individuals may expend more effort on the maintenance and repair of goods than in periods of comparative prosperity when purchase may be relatively more important.
6 The perspective adopted in this volume is not by any means an exclusively 'material' one; indeed the title suggests otherwise. Compared with the approach that typifies the culture theorists and postmodernists, however, there is noticeably

more concern with the consumer's resources in general and patterns of debt and spending in particular.

7 The change is from around twenty minutes per day to forty minutes per day. This information comes from Jonathan Gershuny's research as reported in 'Shopping around for salvation', *Independent*, 3 Nov. 1993.

8 See Peter Corrigan's (1989) analysis in 'Gender and the gift: the case of the family clothing economy', *Sociology* 23 (4).

9 In this respect one could say that modern consumers are concerned with the 'meaningfulness' of products. This is not the same as a concern with *the* meaning of a product, nor is there any communicative intent. Meaningfulness relates to the import of a product or service, that is, its significance in relation to an individual's goals, hopes and desires, not to its denotative significance in a code or symbolic system.

10 For a full account of the role of pleasure-seeking in modern consumption, see Campbell 1987.

BIBLIOGRAPHY

Adburgham, Alison (1964) *Shops and Shopping 1800–1914: Where, and in What Manner the Well-dressed Englishwoman Bought her Clothes*, London: George Allen and Unwin.

Appadurai, A. (ed.) (1986) *The Social Life of Things*, Cambridge: Cambridge University Press.

Barber, B. and Lobel, L. (1953) '"Fashion" in women's clothes and the American social system', in R. Bendix and S. Lipset (eds) *Class, Status and Power*, Glencoe, Ill.: Free Press.

Barthes, R. (1968) *The Fashion System*, New York: Hill and Wang.

Baudrillard, Jean (1975) *The Mirror of Production*, St Louis, Mo.: Telos Press.

Baudrillard, Jean (1981) *Towards a Critique of the Political Economy of the Sign*, St Louis, Mo.: Telos Press.

Baudrillard, Jean (1983) *Simulations*, New York: Semiotext.

Baudrillard, Jean (1988) 'Consumer society', in *Jean Baudrillard: Selected Writings*, ed. Mark Poster, Oxford: Polity Press.

Beardsworth, Alan and Keil, Teresa (1990) 'Putting the menu on the agenda', *Sociology* 24, 1.

Beardsworth, Alan and Keil, Teresa (1992) 'The vegetarian option: conversions, motives and careers', *Sociological Review*, 253–264.

Belk, Russell (1991) *Highways and Buyways: Naturalistic Research from the Consumer Behavior Odyssey*, Provo, UT: Consumer Research Association.

Benson, S. P. (1986) *Counter Cultures: Saleswomen, Managers and Customers in American Department Stores, 1890–1940*, Urbana, Ill.: University of Illinois Press.

Blumer, H. (1969) 'Fashion: from class differentiation to collective selection', *Sociological Quarterly* 10, 3.

Boas, F. (1944) *The Mind of Primitive Man*, New York: Columbia University Press.

Bocock, Robert (1993) *Consumption*, London: Routledge.

Bogatyrev, Peter (1971) *The Functions of Folk Costume in Moravian Slovakia*, trans. by Richard G. Crum, The Hague: Mouton.

Bottomore, Tom and Outhwaite, William (eds) (1993) *Blackwell's Dictionary of Twentieth-Century Social Thought*, Oxford: Blackwell.

Bourdieu, P. (1984) *Distinction: A Social Critique of the Judgement of Taste*, trans. by R. Nice, London: Routledge and Kegan Paul.

Bowlby, R. (1985) *Just Looking: Consumer Culture*, London: Methuen.

Branner, Julia and Wilson, Gail (eds) (1987) *Give and Take in Families: Studies in Resource Distribution*, London: Allen and Unwin.

Burke, Peter (1987) *The Historical Anthropology of Early Modern Italy*, Cambridge: Cambridge University Press.

Burrows, R. and Butler, T. (1989) 'Middle mass and the pit: a critical review of Peter Saunders' sociology of consumption', *Sociological Review* 37, 2.

Burrows, Roger and Marsh, Catherine (eds) (1992) *Consumption and Class: Divisions and Change*, Explorations in Sociology 40, British Sociological Association, London: Macmillan.

Campbell, Colin (1987) *The Romantic Ethic and the Spirit of Modern Consumerism*, Oxford: Blackwell.

Campbell, Colin (1991) 'Consumption: the new wave of research in the humanities and social sciences' in F. W. Rudmin (ed.) *To Have Possessions: A Handbook on Ownership and Property* (Special Issue *Journal of Social Behavior and Personality*, 6, 6).

Campbell, Colin (1992) 'The desire for the new: its nature and social location as presented in theories of fashion and modern consumerism', in R. Silverstone and E. Hirsch (eds) *Consuming Technologies: Media and Information in Domestic Spaces*, London: Routledge.

Campbell, Colin (1993a) 'Understanding traditional and modern patterns of consumption in eighteenth century England: a character-action approach', in John Brewer and Roy Porter (eds) *Consumption and The World of Goods*, London: Routledge.

Campbell, Colin (1993b) 'I shop, therefore I am: I love shopping, therefore I am a woman; or shopping, pleasure and the sex war', paper presented at the conference on 'Consumption, Risk, Pleasure and the State in Contemporary Capitalism', Vuoranta, Helsinki.

Campbell, Colin (1994) 'Shopping, pleasure and the context of desire', in *The Global and the Local: Consumption and European Identity*, Gosewijn van Beek and Cora Govers (eds), Amsterdam: Spinhuis Press.

Caplow, T. (1982) 'Christmas gifts and kin networks', *American Sociological Review* 47.

Carter, Erica (1981) 'Alice in the consumer wonderland: West German case studies of gender and consumer culture', in Mica Nava and Angela McRobbie (eds) *Gender and Generation*, London: Macmillan.

Chaney, D. (1983) 'The department store as a cultural form', *Theory, Culture and Society* 1, 3.

Chaney, D. (1990) 'Dystopia in Gateshead: the metrocentre as a cultural form', *Theory, Culture and Society* 7, 4.

Charles, Nickie and Kerr, Marion (1988) *Women, Food and Families*, Manchester: Manchester University Press.

Cheal, D. (1986) 'The social dimensions of gift giving', *Journal of Social and Personal Relationships* 3.

Cheal, D. (1988) *The Gift Economy*, New York: Routledge.

Close, Paul and Collins, Rosemary (eds) (1985) *Family and Economy in Modern Society*, London: Macmillan.

Connor, Steven (1989) *Postmodernist Culture: An Introduction to Theories of the Contemporary*, Oxford: Blackwell.

Corbin, Alain (1993) *The Lure of the Sea: the Discovery of the Seaside in the Western World 1750–1840*, London: Routledge.

Corrigan, Peter (1989) 'Gender and the gift: the case of the family clothing economy', *Sociology* 23, 4.

121

Corrigan, Peter (1993) 'The clothes-horse rodeo; or, how the sociology of clothing and fashion throws its (w)*Reiters*', *Theory, Culture and Society* 10.

Csikszentmihalyi, M. and Rochberg-Halton, E. (1981) *The Meaning of Things: Domestic Symbols and the Self*, Cambridge: Cambridge University Press.

Culler, Jonathan (1981) 'Semiotics of tourism', *American Journal of Semiotics* 1, 1–2. Davies, Ioan (1993) 'Cultural theory in Britain: narrative and episteme', *Theory, Culture and Society* 10, 3.

Davis, Fred (1992) *Fashion, Culture and Identity*, Chicago: University of Chicago Press.

Dittmar, Helga (1992) *The Social Psychology of Material Possessions: To Have is To Be*, Hemel Hempstead: Harvester Wheatsheaf.

Douglas, Mary (1975) 'Deciphering a meal', in *Implicit Meanings: Essays in Anthropology*, London: Routledge and Kegan Paul.

Douglas, Mary (1984) *Food in the Social Order: Studies of Food and Festivities in Three American Communities*, New York: Russell Sage Foundation.

Douglas, Mary (1992) 'In defense of shopping', *Monograph Series Toronto Semiotic Circle* 9.

Driver, Christopher (1983) *The British at Table 1940–1980*, London: Chatto and Windus.

Drury, A. C. and Ferrier, C. W. (1984) *Credit Cards*, London: Butterworth.

Elias, Norbert (1982) *The Civilizing Process*, Oxford: Blackwell.

Elias, Norbert (1983) *The Court Society*, Oxford: Blackwell.

Falk, P. (1994) *The Consuming Body*, London: Sage.

Featherstone, M. (1982) 'The body in consumer culture', *Theory, Culture and Society* 1, 2.

Featherstone, M. (1983) 'Consumer culture: an introduction', *Theory, Culture and Society* 1, 3.

Featherstone, Mike (ed.) (1988) *Postmodernism*, London: Sage.

Featherstone, Mike (1991) *Consumer Culture and Postmodernism*, London: Sage.

Fine, Ben and Leopold, Ellen (1990) 'Consumerism and the Industrial Revolution', *Social History* 15, 2.

Finkelstein, Joanne (1989) *Dining out: A Sociology of Modern Manners*, Oxford: Polity Press.

Finkelstein, Joanne (1991) *The Fashioned Self*, Oxford: Polity Press.

Fischler, Claude (1988) 'Food, self and identity', *Social Science Information* 27, 2.

Fiske, J. (1989) *Understanding Popular Culture*, London: Routledge.

Ford, J. (1988) *The Indebted Society: Credit and Default in the 1980s*, London: Routledge.

Foster, Hal (ed.) (1987) *Postmodern Culture*, London: Pluto Press.

Frisby, D. (1981) *Sociological Impressionism: A Reassessment of Georg Simmel's Social Theory*, London: Heinemann.

Furst, Elisabeth L., Prattala, Ritva, Ekstrom, Marianne, Holm, Lotte and Kjaernes, Unni (eds) (1991) *Palatable Worlds: Sociocultural Food Studies*, Oslo: Solum Forlag.

Gardner, Carl and Sheppard, Julie (1989) *Consuming Passion: The Rise of Retail Culture*, London: Unwin Hyman.

Geist, H. (1983) *Arcades: The History of a Building Type*, Boston: MIT Press.

George, Alison and Murcott, Anne (1992) 'Research note: Monthly strategies for discretion: shopping for sanitary towels and tampons', *Sociological Review* 40, 1.

Gershuny, J. (1982) 'Livelihood IV: household tasks and the use of time', in Sandra Wallman (ed.) *Living in South London*, Aldershot: Gower.

Gershuny, J. and Jones, S. (1987) 'The changing work–leisure balance in Britain,

1961–1984', in J. Horne, D. Jary and A. Tomlinson (eds) *Sport, Leisure and Social Relations*, London: Routledge and Kegan Paul.

Gerth, H. H. and Mills, C. Wright (eds) (1970) *From Max Weber: Essays in Sociology*, New York: Oxford University Press.

Goody, Jack (1982) *Cooking, Cuisine and Class: A Study in Comparative Sociology*, Cambridge: Cambridge University Press.

Goss, Jon (1993) 'The magic of the mall: an analysis of form, function and meaning in the contemporary retail built environment', *Annals of the Association of American Geographers* 83.

Gronmo, Sigmund and Randi, Lavik (1988) 'Shopping behaviour and social interaction: an analysis of Norwegian time budget data', in Per Otnes (ed.), *The Sociology of Consumption: An Anthology*, Oslo: Solum Forlag A/S.

Hall, Stuart and Jefferson, T. (eds) (1976) *Resistance through Rituals: Youth Subcultures in Post-War Britain*, London: Hutchinson.

Hamnett, C. (1989) 'Consumption and class in contemporary Britain', in C. Hamnett, L. McDowell and P. Sarre (eds) *The Changing Social Structure*, London: Sage.

Harris, Marvin (1986) *Good to Eat: Riddles of Food and Culture*, New York: Simon and Schuster.

Harvey, David (1989) *The Condition of Postmodernity*, Oxford: Blackwell.

Hebdige, Dick (1979) *Subculture: The Meaning of Style*, London: Methuen.

Hebdige, Dick (1988) *Hiding in the Light*, London: Routledge.

Jameson, Fredric (1987) 'Postmodernism and consumer society', in Hal Foster (ed.) *Postmodern Culture*, London: Pluto Press.

Jameson, Fredric (1991) *Postmodernism, or the Cultural Logic of Late Capitalism*, London: Verso.

Kaplan, E. A. (1987) *Rocking Around the Clock: Music, TV, Postmodernism and Consumer Culture*, London: Methuen.

Kerr, Marion and Charles, Nickie (1986) 'Servers and providers: the distribution of food within the family', *Sociological Review* 34, 3.

King, Charles W. (1963) 'Fashion adoption: a rebuttal to the "trickle-down" theory', in Stephen A. Greyser (ed.) *Toward Scientific Marketing*, Chicago: American Marketing Association.

Laermans, Rudi (1993) 'Learning to consume: early department stores and the shaping of the modern consumer culture (1860–1914)', *Theory, Culture and Society* 10.

Langman, Lauren (1992) 'Neon cages: shopping for subjectivity', in Rob Shields (ed.) *Lifestyle Shopping: The Subject of Consumption*, London: Routledge.

Lee, Martyn J. (1993) *Consumer Culture Reborn*, London: Routledge.

Levenstein, Harvey (1988) *Revolution at the Table: The Transformation of the American Diet*, Oxford: Oxford University Press.

Lévi-Strauss, Claude (1969) *The Raw and the Cooked*, London: Jonathan Cape.

Lévi-Strauss, Claude (1978) *The Origin of Table Manners*, London: Jonathan Cape.

Linder, S. B. (1970) *The Harried Leisure Class*, New York: Columbia University Press.

Lunt, P. K. and Livingstone, S. M. (1991a) 'Psychological, social and economic determinants of saving: comparing recurrent and total savings', *Journal of Economic Psychology* 12.

Lunt, P. K. and Livingstone, S. M. (1991b) 'Everyday explanations for personal debt', *British Journal of Social Psychology* 30.

Lunt, P. K. and Livingstone, S. M. (1992) *Mass Consumption and Personal Identity*, Milton Keynes: Open University.

Lurie, Alison (1981) *The Language of Clothes*, New York: Random House.

Lyotard, Jean-François (1984) *The Postmodern Condition*, Minneapolis: University of Minnesota Press.

MacCannell, Dean (1976) *The Tourist*, London: Routledge.

MacCannell, Dean (1992) *Empty Meeting Grounds: The Tourist Papers*, London, Routledge.

McCracken, Grant (1985) 'Dress colour at the court of Elizabeth I: an essay in historical anthropology', *Canadian Review of Sociology and Anthropology* 22, 4.

McCracken, Grant (1988) *Culture and Consumption: New Approaches to the Symbolic Character of Consumer Goods and Activities*, Bloomington, Ind.: Indiana University Press.

McKendrick, N., Brewer, J. and Plumb, J. H. (1982) *The Birth of a Consumer Society*, London: Europa.

McRobbie, Angela (ed.) (1989) *Zoot Suits and Second-Hand Dresses: An Anthology of Fashion and Music*, London: Macmillan.

McRobbie, A. and Nava, M. (eds) (1984) *Gender and Generation*, London: Macmillan.

Malinowski, B. (1922) *Argonauts of the Western Pacific*, London: Routledge and Kegan Paul.

Marx, K. (1971) *Capital: Vol. 1. A Critical Analysis of Capitalist Production*, Moscow: Progress Publishers.

Marx, K. (1973) *Grundrisse: Foundations of the Critique of Political Economy*, New York: Vintage Books.

Mason, R. S. (1981) *Conspicuous Consumption: A Study of Exceptional Consumer Behaviour*, Farnborough, Hants: Gower Press.

Mauss, M. (1976) *The Gift*, New York: Norton.

Mayer, Robert (1978) 'Exploring sociological theories by studying consumers', *American Behavioral Scientist* 21, 4.

Mennell, Stephen (1985) *All Manners of Food: Eating and Taste in England and France from the Middle Ages to the Present*, Oxford: Blackwell.

Miller, D. (1987) *Material Culture and Mass Consumption*, New York: Basil Blackwell.

Miller, D. (1992) 'The young and the restless in Trinidad: a case of the local and the global in mass consumption', in R. Silverman and E. Hirsch (eds) *Consuming Technologies: Media and Information in Domestic Spaces*, London: Routledge.

Miller, M. (1981) *The Bon Marché: Bourgeois Culture and the Department Store 1869–1920*, Princeton, NJ: Princeton University Press.

Mintz, Sidney (1985) *Sweetness and Power: The Place of Sugar in Modern History*, New York: Viking.

Moorhouse, H. F. (1983) 'American automobiles and workers' dreams', *Sociological Review* 31.

Moorhouse, H. F. (1991) *Driving Ambitions: A Social Analysis of the Hot-Rod Enthusiasm*, New York: Manchester University Press.

Murcott, Anne (1984) *The Sociology of Food and Eating*, Aldershot: Gower.

Murcott, Anne (1988) 'Sociological and social anthropological approaches to food and eating', *World Review of Nutrition and Diet* 55, 1.

Nava, Mica (1992) 'Consumerism and its contradictions', in *Changing Cultures: Feminism, Youth and Consumerism*, London: Sage.

Oakley, A. (1976) *Housewife*, Harmondsworth: Penguin.

Otnes, P. (1988) 'The sociology of consumption: "Liberate our daily lives"' in P. Otnes (ed.) *The Sociology of Consumption: An Anthology*, Oslo: Solum Forlag A/S.

Pahl, J. (1989) *Money and Marriage*, London: Macmillan.

Pearce, D. G. and Butler, R. W. (1992) *Tourism Research*, London: Routledge.

Prus, Robert and Dawson, Lorne (1991) 'Shop 'til you drop: shopping as recreational and laborious activity', *Canadian Journal of Sociology* 16.

Rudmin, Floyd (ed.) (1991) *To Have Possessions: A Handbook on Ownership and Property* (Special Issue of the *Journal of Social Behavior and Personality* 6, 6).

Saunders, Peter (1986) *Social Theory and the Urban Question*, 2nd edn, London: Hutchinson.

Saunders, Peter (1990) *Social Class and Stratification*, London: Tavistock.

Schwartz, Hillel (1986) *Never Satisfied: A Cultural History of Diets, Fantasies and Fat*, New York: Free Press.

Sekora, John (1985) *Luxury: The Concept in Western Thought, Eden to Smollet*, Baltimore: Johns Hopkins University Press.

Shelton, Beth Ann (1992) *Women, Men and Time: Gender Differences in Paid Work, Housework and Leisure*, Westport, Conn.: Greenwood Press.

Shields, Rob (ed.) (1992) *Lifestyle Shopping: The Subject of Consumption*, London: Routledge.

Sibel, E. (1982) *Lifestyle*, New York: Academic Press.

Silverstone, Roger and Hirsch, Eric (1992) *Consuming Technologies: Media and Information in Domestic Spaces*, London: Routledge.

Simmel, G. (1957) 'Fashion', *American Journal of Sociology* 62.

Simmel, G. (1978) *The Philosophy of Money*, London: Routledge and Kegan Paul.

Sombart, W. (1967) *Luxury and Capitalism*, Ann Arbor, Mich.: University of Michigan Press.

Stone, Gregory P. (1954) 'City and urban identification: observations on the social psychology of city life', *American Journal of Sociology* 60.

Stone, Lawrence (1982) *The Crisis of the Aristocracy 1558–1641*, Oxford: Oxford University Press.

Sullivan, O. (1989) 'Housing tenure as a consumption sector divide: a critical perspective', *International Journal of Urban and Regional Research* 13, 2.

Thompson, Graham F. (1990) '"If you can't stand the heat get off the beach": The United Kingdom holiday business', in A. Tomlinson (ed.) *Consumption, Identity, and Style: Marketing, Meanings, and the Packaging of Pleasure*, London: Routledge.

Tomlinson, Alan and Walker, Helen (1990) 'Holidays for all: popular movements, collective leisure, and the pleasure industry', in A. Tomlinson (ed.) *Consumption, Identity, and Style: Marketing, Meanings, and the Packaging of Pleasure*, London: Routledge.

Turner, Bryan S. (1982) 'The government of the body: medical regimens and the rationalization of diet', *British Journal of Sociology* 33, 2.

Turner, Graeme (1990) *British Cultural Studies: An Introduction*, London: Unwin Hyman.

Turner, L. and Asch, J. (1975) *The Golden Hordes: International Tourism and the Pleasure Periphery*, London: Routledge and Kegan Paul.

Urry, John (1988) 'Cultural change and contemporary holiday-making', *Theory, Culture and Society* 5, 1.

Urry, John (1990a) *The Tourist Gaze*, London: Sage.

Urry, John (1990b) 'The "consumption" of tourism', *Sociology* 24, 1.

Veblen, T. (1925) *The Theory of the Leisure Class*, London: George Allen and Unwin.

Vogler, Carolyn and Pahl, Jan (1993) 'Social and economic change and the organisation of money within marriage', *Work, Employment and Society* 7, 1.

Walvin, J. (1978) *Beside the Seaside: A Social History of the Popular Seaside Holiday*, London: Allen Lane.

Warde, A. (1990a) 'Introduction to the sociology of consumption', *Sociology* 24, 1.

Warde, A. (1990b) 'Production, consumption and social change: reservations regarding Peter Saunders' sociology of consumption', *International Journal of Urban and Regional Research* 14, 2.

Weber, M. (1958) *The Protestant Ethic and the Spirit of Capitalism*, New York: Scribner.

Weber, M. (1978) 'Classes, status groups and parties', in W. G. Runciman (ed.) *Max Weber: Selections in Translation*, Cambridge: Cambridge University Press.

Williams, R. H. (1982) *Dream Worlds: Mass Communication in Late Nineteenth-Century France*, Berkeley, Ca.: California University Press.

Willis, Paul (1978) *Profane Culture*, London: Routledge and Kegan Paul.

Willis, Paul (1990) *Common Culture*, Milton Keynes: Open University Press.

Wilson, Elisabeth (1985) *Adorned in Dreams*, London: Virago.

Wilson, Gail (1987) *Money in the Family: Financial Organisation and Women's Responsibility*, Aldershot: Avebury.

4

FROM POLITICAL ECONOMY TO CONSUMPTION[1]

Ben Fine

INTRODUCTION

Like the others in this volume, this chapter consists of three sections. But it is not able to follow the common pattern entirely because of the weakness of economics' treatment of consumption. In the first section, this is demonstrated, and it is suggested that innovation in the analysis of consumption has mainly been based upon increasingly sophisticated technical and statistical developments but within a continuing conceptual content that is outrageously narrow. In addition, orthodox economics has been isolated from other disciplines so that the scope for interdisciplinary progress has been precluded. Section I concludes by examining the contribution made by political economy. It finds that the social significance of consumption is acknowledged but that it is insufficiently developed in relation to production. Accordingly, whether for orthodox economics or political economy, innovation in the analysis of consumption remains limited.

But political economy does have some potential, and this is explored by looking at a selection of the more recent literature. It is found that the division between production and consumption has been artificially maintained, with greater emphasis either on the supply-side (as in the imperatives of Fordism's mass production in determining what we consume) or on the role of consumption considered independently of how it is provided for other than through purchase. The section concludes by suggesting that a more appropriate way to analyse consumption is in the context of *specific* commodities, treated in terms of the entire chain of activities and relations leading to consumption. In the final section, this approach is illustrated primarily by reference to the role of retailing in modern consumption, with a brief overview of the literature on food systems. But throughout the chapter, mention is made of the way in which various approaches have been employed empirically.

I   The traditions we inherit

THE NEOCLASSICAL ORTHODOXY

Orthodox economics has been remarkably untouched by the explosive interest and innovation in the study of consumption that has been such a prominent feature of the other social sciences. It is worth beginning by exploring why this should be so. Indeed, the conceptual basis for understanding consumption has remained essentially unchanged for over a century, since the marginalist revolution of the 1870s, which witnessed the demise of classical political economy associated with Ricardo and Smith and the establishment of neoclassical economics, organised around supply and demand, which has survived and prospered until the present day.[2] This is all the more remarkable given the disdain with which other social scientists have long perceived the assumptions made by economists.[3]

It will be shown that the theory is impoverished in conceptual content and has counterbalanced this by continuing theoretical developments that have primarily served the requirements of statistical estimation. As a discipline, economics has been extremely isolated from the other social sciences because its methodology is so alien on theoretical and empirical grounds. In practice, simple versions of positivism continue to remain supreme and, to echo the stance of Lady Thatcher, there is no notion of society other than as a set of institutions (of which the market is the most important) and the aggregated behaviour of atomised individuals. Consequently, the iterative process across the social sciences in response to an empirically perceived change in the world of consumption has been of no relevance to the world of orthodox economics.

Thus, consumption is reduced to the theory of the demand for goods. In turn, this is equivalent to the cost-minimising behaviour of the individual in meeting a given level of utility when prices are fixed for the goods involved. There is a formal identity between this analysis and that for the entrepreneur attempting to minimise the cost of producing a given level of output in the light of input prices. For those who have struggled through a first year of economic principles, this ought to be transparent either in the correspondence between the associated optimising conditions – for optimisation, relative marginal utilities (products) or marginal rates of substitution between consumption goods (factor inputs) should equal relative prices – or in the correspondence between indifference (isoquant) curves and the tangential budget lines. Essentially, the consumer is treated as a self-employed firm which seeks to produce utility as cheaply as possible and makes demands for inputs according to their prices.

In addition, economic theory depends upon axiomatic model-building and equilibrium in which many important determinants are taken not only to be exogenous, indeed to be explained on its behalf by other disciplines, but also often to be fixed. This is particularly so of consumer preferences which are pegged to a given utility function, formally $u_i(x_1, x_2, \ldots, x_j, \ldots, x_n)$ where consumer, or often household i, derives utility u from consuming quantities x_j of the n available goods. This assumption concerning the exogeneity and the fixed nature of individual utility, and hence preferences over consumption goods, is so powerful that economic theory often proceeds on the basis of one or other of two extremes – either that all individuals can be treated as if they all have the same preferences which can then be subsumed under a single representative consumer, or that each and every individual is uniquely different with no commonality in underlying preferences. Of course, these assumptions are anathema to other social sciences concerned with the causal origins of preferences and the social processes by which they are either shared or distinct.

Indeed, consumption within economics is almost always treated abstractly without reference to specified items of consumption. It involves pure formalism in which any number of consumption goods are given algebraic symbols to represent them – as in the utility function above. In this light, it is hardly surprising that the nature of consumption goods and of consumption activity cannot be addressed. Even where account is taken of consumption needed to cover the requirements for subsistence, as in the Geary-Stone utility function, this is done abstractly in terms of an unspecified vector of goods. The motivation for this is less to examine, let alone to explain, the physiological or socio-historical basis of subsistence than to provide particular functional or mathematical forms under which econometric methods can be used to specify demand functions statistically.

Further, not only is the economy built up from the atomised behaviour of individuals, but even this methodological reductionism is undertaken within the narrowest analytical scope. For the behavioural assumption underlying the theory of consumption is that the individual is motivated exclusively by the desire to maximise the previously assumed utility. The ability to do this is centrally a function of income available (possibly through work which is seen as a disutility and denial of leisure) and the prices of consumption goods. Again, to other social scientists this approach must appear uninviting because of its extraordinarily narrow analytical boundaries, in terms of both the motivational assumptions (confined to self-satisfaction) and the behavioural assumptions (pursued with ruthless efficiency). In effect, rational economic 'man' combines the basest instincts of a selfish beast with the highest forms of commercial calculation![4]

Perhaps two examples will help to illustrate why these features of the neoclassical orthodoxy hang together and render economics fragile to any innovative incursion around consumption. In the wake of the Keynesian revolution, in which the macro-economy is perceived to depend upon the overall level of demand, it became necessary to specify the overall level of consumer expenditure. This has given rise to the theory of the consumption function to complement other macro-economic aggregates such as the investment function or the demand for money. In exploring the consumption function, an anomaly was discovered. Whilst it was expected that those who were richer would save proportionately more (and hence consume proportionately less) – what Keynes referred to as a psychological law – it was also found that the increase in consumption out of a given increase in income was different in the short run than in the long run. Duesenberry (1967) put forward the relative income hypothesis to explain this. Basically, consumers are stratified and in the short run have a lower propensity to consume because it takes them some time to adapt to being in the higher strata associated with their higher income over time. Obviously, this endogenises consumption[5] since preferences to consume become dependent upon economic stratification and paths of social mobility. Whilst providing a neat explanation for the empirical anomaly around the short- and long-run propensities to consume, the relative income hypothesis was noted for a time but has fallen out of favour, essentially because it would have been associated with multiple equilibria, endogeneity of preferences and social processes. Instead, a preferred explanation has been the permanent income hypothesis, associated with Milton Friedman (1957), in which short-run changes of income are seen as windfalls around a norm and are consumed thinly over the remainder of a lifetime.[6] This approach can be made consistent with the optimising behaviour of individuals with given preferences.

If the fate of Duesenberry's contribution shows how even limited innovation around consumption is threatening to neoclassical theory, a second illustration provided by the work of Becker reveals the paradigm's character when taken to extreme. Becker is best known for his innovative contribution to the new household economics and to the theory of human capital – for which he has been awarded a Nobel prize. Central to his approach is the goal of explaining as many socio-economic phenomena as possible on the basis of the standard assumptions of neoclassical economics, including fixed preferences – although why this should be taken as a goal remains unjustified except as a loyalty oath. In this, considerable ingenuity can be developed. Thus, women going out to work and having fewer children is presumed to reflect their preference for employment given higher wages and the substitution of quality for quantity in offspring. Fewer children give more enjoyment in the less time available since they are consumed in conjunction with the greater material provision that has been made available to, and embodied within, them. Here, then, as a matter of principle, an attempt is made to explain shifting female labour market participation rates and family size on the basis of a representative female consumer who persists from generation to generation holding to the same, exogenously given preferences for work, leisure and children as items of, or the means to, utility-satisfying consumption.[7]

With Stigler, Becker has pursued this approach further, seeking to explain away empirical anomalies associated with neoclassical consumer theory. Thus, an attempt is made to deny the apparent presence of consumption patterns arising out of addiction or habit-forming – which would unacceptably involve the endogeneity of preferences – by suggesting that consumers are in fact merely optimising rationally on the basis of the cumulative experience they have gained from consumption. There is a process of learning by consumption, the gaining of consumption capital, just as workers are deemed to learn-by-doing and to accrue human capital through work experience. This artefact is necessary for otherwise no rational, maximising individual would knowingly enter a consumption path that led to habitual patterns that undermined welfare. The same idea is used to explain what are taken to be the more sophisticated consumption patterns of both wealthier and older consumers. They are just more experienced in the matter of consumption rather than having different, underlying preferences. And advertising is seen not as manipulating consumers but as commanding higher prices for its enhanced products by attaching extra information (consumer-capital) to them.

Thus, whether as an analytical goal taken to extreme, as in the work of Becker, or as an unchanging habit within the discipline, economics has an extremely underdeveloped theory of consumption. Indeed, other than in name alone, its distinctive specification of consumption is analytically limited. And, if a case is to be made for successful development within neoclassical demand theory, it is in the finer specification of the mathematics of the analysis as a means of making empirical estimation more consistent in particular ways.[8] It is worth dwelling on this matter in two revealing aspects. First, essentially the goal is to estimate elasticities – how responsive is demand for consumption goods to price and income changes. The success of the estimates in the statistical terms of 'goodness of fit' can in part be interpreted as a test of whether underlying preferences are fixed and exogenous. For example, the National Food Survey is used to estimate income and price elasticities for particular foods. Where these estimates do not perform well statistically, this is put down to the separate factor of shifting tastes. However, and transparently, from a causal point of view, this is sheer tautology since whatever happens empirically can be interpreted as reflecting an appropriate balance between shifts with given preferences and shifts between preferences. And, because shifts in preferences are taken as the residual explanatory factor if, in accepting this approach, there were shifts in preferences alone, they would be explained as far as possible in terms of elasticities.

Second, the availability of greater, desk-top computing power has enabled large data sets with information on households to be used to estimate demand functions rather than the previously more common practice of treating the aggregate level of demand as if it were the result of a representative individual's chosen consumption patterns. Significantly, such panel data do allow estimation to distinguish between household types by variables such as age, composition, class, etc. It is common, and sensible, to employ such proxies to represent household differences. This again enhances the scope for estimating the demand functions but only by importing the unexamined assumption that the proxy variables give rise to unexplained distinctions and conformities in underlying utility functions. Given the underlying presumption that all (household) preferences are exogenous and fixed, and so potentially equally diverse, why should some groups be treated as sharing tastes as distinct from others? As demonstrated previously, this reflects the imperative of pushing aside the issues of what consumption is and why, other than along well-worn and limited conceptual lines.

Recent developments within consumer theory have been both theoretically and empirically extensive, despite the narrow terrain on which they have been constructed. For, rather than addressing what is consumed (other than in a quantitative sense) and how preferences are formed and exercised, attention has been confined to pushing forward theory as the technical basis on which statistical estimation can be further honed. For example, consumer durables pose particular problems because choice is discrete, and they are considered as capital goods providing a stream of consumer services over time. This has posed the problem of what economists term 'corner solutions'. For, when working with aggregate data or the representative consumer, it can be presumed that some amount of everything will be purchased. This assumption cannot be maintained when working with data at an individual household level, so that models involving frequency of purchase – as well as whether items are purchased or not – have to be developed to fit the data statistically.[9]

The previous paragraph has been primarily concerned with consumer theory at the micro-economic level of demand for particular goods. In estimating aggregate consumer expenditure for macro-economic modelling purposes, the role of the representative consumer has become more sophisticated. Where previously a behavioural assumption was made, such as a fixed proportion of income being spent, the representative consumer in more recent theoretical developments is presumed to optimise over a lifetime, thereby needing to undertake sophisticated intertemporal decisions and to form expectations about the future path of the economy itself. Again, in so far as this has been associated with theoretical innovation, it is entirely in response to the needs of statistical estimation rather than in any deepening of the understanding of consumption itself. Thus, there is a division between the study of consumption from a macro (overall expenditure) and micro perspective, this in spite of 'a common theoretical structure'[10] based on the representative consumer with fixed preferences and motivation as previously outlined.

Economics, then, has always been flush with a wealth of empirical studies, and the development of the study of consumption has even flourished on the continuing basis of a dialogue between the empirical evidence and the theoretical techniques for handling it. There is always room to re-estimate price and income elasticities of individual or aggregate consumption whether because additional data are necessarily generated with the passage of time or because some new theoretical nicety can be incorporated; whether as a result of computer-enhanced statistical capability or through some incremental concession to the realities of consumption as in the recognition of corner solutions. But these advances in techniques and empirical estimation are both prodigious and in extreme disproportion to the conceptual core that has remained both narrow and unchanging. Whatever the validity and use of these studies, in macro-economic forecasting or in designing tax proposals, for example, the persisting weakness of economics in consumption theory is illustrated by the ways in which it has *not* been used. Whilst manufacturers and retailers are well aware of the dependence of demand for their products upon the prices they charge and the income of their potential consumers, they are acutely conscious of other factors and positively seek both to identify them through psychographics, etc. and to manipulate them by changing preferences through advertising. Further, the weakness of consumer theory within economics is demonstrated by the limited space it commands in the *New Palgrave Dictionary of Economics*. This runs to four volumes and over 4,000 pages, but the space devoted to consumption-related topics, depending upon how broadly these are interpreted, is probably less than 100 pages. A topic such as conspicuous consumption warrants an entry of only half of a page![11]

ALTERNATIVES WITHIN POLITICAL ECONOMY

The suggestion that the neoclassical orthodoxy only contains such a limited theory of consumption would come as a surprise and considerable challenge to its practitioners since the school prides itself on moving beyond classical political economy which is presumed to have had a (limited) theory of production (for which read supply) but no theory of consumption (for which read demand). The marginalist revolution is supposed to have remedied the latter with its theory of utility maximisation. But is classical political economy so empty of a theory of consumption or is this simply a void from the viewpoint of the neoclassical perspective?

The answer to the latter is in the affirmative and can especially be seen as such in the light of the poverty of the neoclassical's own theory. Smith and Ricardo, for example, are from a neoclassical perspective quite extraordinarily preoccupied with one consumption good in particular, namely corn. This is because it commands a central position within their theories as symbolic of the working-class means of consumption. In this respect, it is organically linked to a number of central issues – such as the (Malthusian) reproduction of the workforce, the distribution of income, the falling rate of profit and the potential of the capitalist system to sustain continuing accumulation given the trend towards a stationary state (and the potential demise of capitalism as an economically progressive form of social organisation). The point to be made here is less whether Ricardo and Smith or others within classical political economy constructed good or bad theories (and it should be emphasised that there are considerable differences and disputes between them) but more to emphasise that understanding of consumption goods is firmly rooted in the *social properties* that those goods command. This is of no interest to neoclassical economics because, as has been shown, it has no purchase on the significance of particular consumer goods, preferring to consider consumption in the abstract across all goods simultaneously. The latter is a consequence of utility maximisation subject to price and income constraints since all of the individual's consumption decisions have to be made simultaneously, with the proportions in which they are consumed needing to be balanced against their relative prices and ability to satisfy (at the margin).

Thus, the consumption theory to be associated with classical political economy – although not consciously so and extremely underdeveloped – is the mirror image of that putatively provided by neoclassical economics. It deals in particular commodities (such as corn) with definite, socially determined properties rather than in all, unspecified commodities simultaneously in which their properties are purely idiosyncratic to the individual. But where does this leave Marx's political economy? This is germane, particularly as it is argued in much of the recently burgeoning literature on consumption that he had little to say on the matter and was even obstructive in focusing undue attention on production at the expense of consumption.

A careful reading of Marx suggests that matters are otherwise. For his critics have been more concerned to elevate analytically the interpretation of the objects of consumption or consumption relations than they have been to draw out the implications of Marx's political economy for the study of consumption (including their own preoccupations). In one respect, Marx is similar to classical political economy in examining consumption only after it has been assigned a social significance.[12] Indeed, Marx begins *Capital* with consideration of the use and exchange value of the commodity and, far from dropping use value from his subsequent analysis, as many commentators have supposed, it recurs whenever the commodities' properties can be examined socially.[13] Thus, the use values of the following commodities are considered in considerable detail for a number of analytical purposes – money, labour power, means of production and means of consumption, fixed capital, unproductive services, capital functioning in exchange, and land (as a source of rent rather than as a commodity[14]).

134

Of course, along this list, there are few references to consumer goods and most of the use values are concerned with the functioning of the capitalist economy. Within Marxist methodology this is hardly surprising, for an understanding of the distribution of consumption goods, let alone their social significance, would require an economic as well as a social analysis that draws upon but goes far beyond the scope of a work such as *Capital*. Indeed, it could be argued that Marx quite properly curbs what he observes of consumption because it cannot be addressed, other than ideally, within the context of his immediate intentions within *Capital*.[15] Further, his analysis of a generalised commodity-producing society reveals that it does not allow consumption to be read off from other determining economic relations, since quantitative differences in the ability to consume, derived from the distribution of incomes associated with different class positions, have no immediate implications for differentiation in consumption itself. Explicitly, Marx notes:

> [As] worker . . . as consumer and possessor of exchange values, and that in the form of the *possessor of money*, in the form of money he becomes a simple entry of circulation – one of its infinitely many entries, in which his specificity as worker is extinguished.
>
> (Marx 1969: 420–421)

This discussion of Marx highlights a tension within political economy approaches to consumption. Of necessity, there is a need to root analysis in economic forces that give rise to, but are separate from, consumption. As political economy lies within a radical tradition critical of the capitalist economy and/or *laissez-faire* policies, this generally focuses upon the influence of the imperative of profitability, although the role of the power or control of money, whatever its origins, is often prominent. On the other hand, such necessary concerns tend to displace attention away from consumption to more abstract considerations around the chain of activities that are prior to consumption (although, from an analytical point of view, consumption itself – and hence reproduction – is a precondition of these activities). In short, there is a tension between focusing upon the immediate aspects of consumption and their broader, and possibly distant, analytical determinants.

II Recent developments

How this tension might be resolved will be taken up later. In the literature, it has usually been unwittingly avoided by an analytical separation between how commodities are provided (roughly what has been the terrain of political economy) and how they have been received as items of consumption (often the subject matter of other disciplines). Consequently,

135

as the analytical pendulum has currently swung in favour of addressing consumption, political economy has fallen into disrepute for neglecting the ultimate destination of its objects of study, i.e. it has been too concerned with production or supply.

In this light, what follows now is a selective review of some contributions to the political economy of consumption. None of these theories will be pursued in detail as they are often to be found covered in other chapters. This is because there is no systematic political economy of consumption, only a collection of disparate contributions usually originating from and rooted in other disciplines, which have been more open to the incorporation of economic themes than orthodox economics has been to address what it constructs as the non-economic.

POST-FORDISM AND FLEC-SPEC

Consider first the theory of post-Fordism. As a constituent component of the growing preoccupation with postmodernism, post-Fordism is often seen as the economic counterpart and response to the increasingly fluid demands imposed upon consumption by cultural determinants. The economic system is compelled to provide for the pluralism of tastes both through filling market niches and by responding rapidly as these shift frequently and unpredictably. Hence the need for *flexibility* in *products*.

From within political economy, however, the notion of flexibility attached to post-Fordism is both broader in scope and driven from the supply-side. In particular, the term flexible-specialisation (flec-spec for short) has been coined to signify the potential not only to meet shifting market niches but also to do so through a chain of economic organisation which potentially involves cooperative relations between small firms in industrial districts (pooling technology and marketing functions, for example), job enrichment (or, alternatively, intensification) through multiple skilling and task-switching, subcontracting between producers and customers, new forms of work organisation, and 'just-in-time' delivery of inputs to economise on inventories and to conform with the capacity to change product composition and quality.

The theory of post-Fordism, then, from within political economy, is fundamentally based upon the proposition that mass markets for consumption goods have been exhausted so that the producers need to be able to respond to and create market niches for their products. Neither the empirical evidence for these propositions, nor an explanation for them, has ever been satisfactorily offered.[16] Instead, the idea of what must constitute consumption passively follows upon the analytical requirements of the theory of production, and the determinants of differentiation within consumption are left as self-evident even though they have long been the topic of socio-economic analysis. In displacing a stereotyped notion of the

136

past as Fordist by the post-Fordist production of the future, a political economy is employed which is as determinist as the theories of mass production that are heavily criticised as dogmatic. For it is simply presumed that mass markets are satiated and that variety and quality are at the cutting edge of economic competition. Thus, the political economy of post-Fordism is driven by an *unexplored* consumption which is satisfied by flec-spec production. It has the postmodern version of post-Fordism as its inverted counterpart. For this explores the reconstruction of the objects of consumption with a presumption that these are effortlessly provided in material terms by the economic system.[17]

A striking illustration of the poverty of the analysis of consumption in the flec-spec approach is to be found by reference to the evolution of the work of Piore. Previously, he was one of the initiators of the modern version of dual labour market theory. It was developed to explain the problem of black ghettos in US cities in the early 1970s by reference to the secondary or peripheral labour market position occupied by black workers in contrast to the core, primary careered jobs available to whites. Corresponding to this structure within the labour market was posited a parallel duality in the industrial structure between the core of monopolised industries and the periphery comprised of the competitive and vulnerable small-scale sector.[18] This, then, is the theory of advantage and disadvantage under the rule of Fordism.

Now, in terms of consumption, the core industrial sector with its secure and beneficial employment was deemed to satisfy the stable and growing demand for mass-consumption goods, with the periphery providing for the cyclical, and hence insecure, fluctuations around the growth trend. By the 1980s, there has been a reversal in Piore's stance. Remarkably, exactly the same theoretical *structure* is employed in the pioneering contribution to the flec-spec approach by Piore and Sabel (1984), only now the relative merits of the two components in the economy have changed places. Mass production for uniform commodities is viewed as the insecure component of demand (as a part of the crisis of Fordism), and small-scale, flexible production is seen as the basis on which to occupy a more secure commercial position. Where consumption was uniform and supportive of mass production (with limited opportunities for small-scale producers), it is now open to variety and supports the small at the expense of the inflexible large producer. By the same token, the relative merits of employment across the two sectors are also reversed.

Thus, whilst flec-spec places considerable emphasis on the role of demand, both in explaining the crisis of Fordism and the viability of post-Fordism, consumption essentially remains unexamined except along simplistic and generalised notions of variety and satiation. Despite the approach's frequent critique of Marx for his presumed technological (mass production) determinism, the flec-spec analysis is hoist upon its own petard.

Consumption is a passive, if flexible, consequence of production, and it is theoretically constructed in a superficial way by reference to the historically unexplained but dramatic shift from satiation with uniformity to the imperative of variety. Whilst clothing is often taken as the exemplary illustration of the paradigm, it is a sector in which fashion has long been associated with the manufacture of difference, although this is uneven historically and across different segments of the clothing sector, not least between men's and women's wear.[19]

THE GENERATION OF NEEDS

A second approach to consumption within political economy is more long-standing and challenges the virtues rather than the existence or continuing viability of the Fordist regime. It does so by rejecting the orthodox neo-classical view of consumer sovereignty in which supply responds passively to the dictates of consumers whose preferences rule through their purchasing power. Instead, it is argued that monopolies not only distort consumption away from what is ideally required by consumer sovereignty on the basis of given preferences, but that it can also distort the preferences themselves in order to bring them closer to what producers seek to provide.

PRIVATE AFFLUENCE AND PUBLIC SQUALOR

Consequently, consumer preferences are endogenised in a way that manipulates them towards what is required by monopolised capital. The most overt mechanism is through advertising, although the more general portrayal of a desirable lifestyle through the media performs a similar and supportive function. These observations do not, however, explain what is consumed and why – only that it is not what consumers *truly* want or should want. Consequently, as in the work of Galbraith,[20] it involves the incorporation of a theory of false needs, and what is consumed (and an insatiable appetite for consumption) is only understood by reference to what must be an arbitrarily imposed notion of what constitutes true needs. This has been captured by his notion of private affluence and public squalor but, even so, there is only limited analysis of what is consumed, why, and its allocation between the public and the private spheres. What is characteristic of this approach is that supply is driven by the needs of the modern corporation, and that the patterns of consumption are heavily determined by the latter in place of what they would (unspecified) be otherwise.

This involves two closely related weaknesses. The first is the simplistic contrast between the false needs imposed upon consumers and their true needs defined, if at all, by the historically specific morals of the contemporary liberal political economist. This is not to suggest that the notion of false needs must be rejected out of hand. But it must be tied to an understanding of how those needs are generated as well as satisfied (or not). Second, then, the theory does not address the issue of how consumer demand is generated other than as a passive, if generated, response to production. In particular, the mechanisms for creating the necessary preferences and choices – through advertising or the lobbying by vested interests for the predominance of private over public provision, for example – also exclude the active role of consumers and the other ways in which their own lives and preferences are formed.

CONSUMPTION AND STRATIFICATION

Such issues have been addressed in other literature but generally it suffers from the mirror-image deficiency of concentrating on how preferences are generated for consumption without this being linked to how they are satisfied other than through purchase. Thus, patterns of consumption and social stratification have been related to one another. This is more the subject matter of sociology but it finds a place in this chapter in so far as the articulations involved should be understood as incorporating economic processes, since the generation and diffusion of demand across social groups affects the commercial viability of the commodities concerned – what clothing without the fashion system?

Broadly, two different aspects of the issue can be brought to the fore. At one extreme, it can be argued that consumption stratification reflects the stratification that has already been determined by other factors. A suitable example is by reference to class in the classic Marxist sense, by which it could be argued that there is some almost invisible operation of sumptuary laws. As a consequence, working-class and ruling-class consumption are sharply differentiated from each other. The problem here, of course, is in specifying the mechanisms by which these distinctions are both created and maintained, particularly as the willingness and ability to *pay*, not class origin, are the direct determinants of consumption. Whilst quantitative differences in income associated with class will distinguish the levels and composition of consumption, they do not determine them. Further, other determinants of consumption patterns, such as cultural relations, may reinforce the consumption distinctions between classes but they may also moderate them. There is much overlap in consumption patterns, and these have to be identified and explained. Consequently, a more subtle approach is to modify the argument, viewing consumption as an integral part of the process of class structuring, as in the work of Bourdieu (1984).

This is not merely a matter of distinctions in consumption. For classes can pursue their own material interests through establishing their own mode of consumption. This is one way of interpreting the new urban sociology. Starting with the work of Castells, who views the city as a site of collective consumption, this can be seen as an alternative terrain than that of

139

private consumption through the market, and one in which the working class can potentially pursue some command over and levels of consumption other than through the labour market and shopping mall. This raises a number of issues, not least the interaction between public and private provision, at the level of consumption itself (private cars and public roads) as well as through the economic and political processes which privilege or represent the interests of one stratum rather than another – a matter that has often been discussed in the context of the private and social wage.[21] Thus, incorporating ideas such as collective consumption – whether in the context of the city or welfare provision – does not resolve the problem of relating class stratification to consumption patterns, but further (and reasonably) complicates the issues involved. Indeed, the new urban sociology, with its theory of private versus collective consumption, can be seen as an extension of the notion of public versus private affluence, in which the imperatives of the latter, driven by corporations, are less predominant and subject to conflict from below.

As is already implicit, it is by no means essential that the way and extent to which consumption reflects stratification should be tied to any one particular scheme for classification. Indeed, given dependence of consumption upon income, the latter is an obvious means by which to stratify consumption. But the range of potential partitions of the population as the basis upon which distinctions in consumption may be constructed is unlimited. It may be by gender, age, region, ethnic origin, occupation, marital status, education, presence of children, etc. At a certain point, the correspondence between socio-economic classification and consumption stratification becomes the preoccupation of marketing science if not of commercial marketing itself. For both, the goal is to find appropriately defined strata that are more than normally susceptible to the charms of particular products. In other words, to identify lifestyles or whatever through demographics; these can then be associated with particular consumption patterns.

To counterpose social stratification to consumption patterns and to allow either side of the equation to become flexible suggests that the extreme of class determining consumption is open to reversal. Instead of consumption reflecting class position, differentiation or conformity in consumption can itself be used as a means of stratification. This is the path taken in the evolution of Saunders' work – and has its popular counterpart in the cliché of keeping up, or ahead of, the Joneses. Beginning with housing and the presumed pursuit of owner-occupation as the preferred form of housing tenure/consumption, he ultimately constructs an analysis which is unwittingly a parody of the (crudest) Marxist theory of class based upon production, one in which consumers are stratified into class not only to determine their consciousness but also their voting patterns and even the potential to exploit others through their differential advantage in access to consumption (as in greater subsidies and/or returns from capital gains to owner-occupiers than accrue to other forms of tenancy). Significantly, Saunders' analysis has its roots within, and as an extreme form of development of, the new urban sociology discussed earlier. It illustrates how the failure of this to link its theory of consumption to other economic determinants allows the latter to be discarded altogether, and for consumption itself to become the chief characteristic of socio-economic analysis.

Saunders' analysis is undoubtedly a peculiar product of the economic and intellectual climate in the UK, where the drive towards owner-occupation through the privatisation programme of state housing by the Thatcher government gave rise to corresponding theories of the political significance of housing tenure which were then generalised to all consumption.[22] But autonomy in stratification by consumption has a much longer tradition arising out of the various explanations associated with emulation and differentiation, for which Veblen is the classic reference. Leaving aside the moral critiques associated with conspicuous consumption (and the inversion of the laws of economics in so far as something becomes of worth according to how much it costs rather than vice-versa), the major economic significance for such theories lies in their being linked to trickle-down effects.[23] Differentiation and emulation in consumption necessarily imply a hierarchy of tastes. Consequently, those who are wealthier are in a better position to set consumption trends since they have the power to set themselves apart from those who are continually seeking to emulate them. As a corollary, preferences for consumption goods trickle down through the hierarchy, ultimately creating mass markets out of the inno-vation initiated at the top.[24]

For some, such as McKendrick et al. (1982), this is a beneficial process, first coming to fruition in the consumer revolution of the eighteenth century that served as a major factor in the Industrial Revolution. On the other hand, quite apart from being undemocratic in that the wealthier have a bigger vote in what constitutes the path of consumption for all, it can be argued that the role of such innovative consumption is an obstacle to the creation of cheap, mass markets since an impetus is given to fragmen-tation and differentiation at the outset.[25] Indeed, a case can increasingly be made for trickle up rather than trickle down in the diffusion of consumption habits. For clothing, for example, we have the case of common work or leisure items taken up by fashion – as in jeans, sneakers, etc. For food, standardised items of consumption for convenience for working mothers have become the norm, and this has been reinforced by standardised shopping patterns. Models concerning elite, trendsetting consumers – as for electronic goods – are shown to be inappropriate as the video, for example, has been rapidly adopted as a popular form of domestic leisure and child control.[26] And, with welfare or other forms of support in

141

place, even the counterculture to the power of money can be displayed through not spending at all rather than by excessive spending.

Thus, especially today, models of stratification by consumption need to specify more than who consumes and what. From where does the money come, and what makes consumer cultures or chosen objects of consumption persist in their significance, given the other forces with which they compete and interact? It is hardly surprising that such analyses often depend upon specific and socio-economically narrow applications for their purchase – clothing, luxury and the wealthy for example. The arguments may be general but their scope is limited.

FROM HORIZONTAL TO VERTICAL ANALYSIS

This points to a more general feature of theories of consumption. This is that they tend to be what will be termed 'horizontal' – each takes one or more explanatory factors, usually from within a particular academic discipline or motivated by the case of a particular consumption good, and generalises across consumption as a whole. Thus, economics, for example, picks upon utility maximisation and employs it to explain simultaneously the consumption of all goods. Similarly, trickle down seizes upon a particular mechanism for the diffusion of preferences (although it is usually weak on the means by which those preferences are realised).

In contrast, it is proposed here that a 'vertical' approach should be adopted to consumption.[27] First, this implies that explanations around consumption must be specific to particular commodities or groups of commodities. Second, each such commodity should be analysed in the context of the chain of horizontal factors that give rise to it – production, distribution, retailing, consumption and the material culture surrounding it. Each of these separate factors may be common to each consumption good but the way in which they interact with one another will be different. Third, then, each consumption good will be linked to its own differentiated chain of activities which will form an integral unity and will be termed a system of provision. This approach is, in common language and much analysis, already very familiar. For the notion of a clothing system, energy system, housing system, food system, etc., is well established. But it needs to be given explicit theoretical roots to provide a general approach to consumption.

Three corollaries follow immediately from the adoption of an approach based on systems of provision. First, it challenges the general theories of the horizontal factors associated with analyses of consumption. The role of production, retailing, advertising, emulation, etc. will be different from one commodity to the next. Further, the specific role of each of these factors can only be adequately discerned once it is situated in the functioning of the system of provision to which it is attached.

Second, it explains why the goal of interdisciplinary approaches to consumption has proved elusive or limited in scope despite a longstanding recognition of the need for them.[28] With each discipline tending to adopt general, horizontal theories within its own scope, attempts at integration are at best liable to lead to the multidisciplinary stacking of analyses on top of one another, precisely because further progress needs to be commodity-specific.

Third, it becomes possible to make a constructive but critical assessment of the literature on consumption. Any specific contribution can be assessed for the horizontal factors that it addresses, the extent to which these are related to other horizontal factors and hence tied to specific systems of provision even if, as is often the case, claiming a greater generality.[29] The power of this analytical framework for assessing the literature can be gauged by applying it to the theories already covered – an exercise left to the reader but it will confirm the generalisation from particular factors or commodities and the neglect of their functioning within differentiated and integral systems of provision even if insights are obtained for particular components of the latter.

How can this alternative approach be justified? It is tempting to suggest that the proof of the pudding is in the (cooking and the) eating. But it is possible to make a general argument by returning to the commodity as a use and exchange value, for these are the two most basic, general horizontal factors characterising contemporary consumption goods whose interaction is highlighted by the equally universal activity of exchange. At this point, the commodity has been produced and distributed and incorporates certain physical, not necessarily material, properties, although the motive for providing these is governed by the imperative of profitability. As such, the commodity has the potential to satisfy certain use value demands placed upon it, these in turn being open to social (re)construction either through their further physical transformation (as in domestic labour) or through the material culture in which they are interpreted and used. For example, a car has definite physical properties but it offers these within a particular context of the transportation system (availability of roads, parking, public transport as an alternative, etc.) and with particular meanings around masculinity[30] (speed and accessories) or the family (reliability and space), just as chocolate offers sweetness and indulgence.[31]

The creation of the exchange value of the commodity is quite distinct from the social creation of its use value. One has its origins in production and, even though this does give rise to the physical properties of the commodity, it does not determine nor is it identical with the socially determined properties of the use values provided. Chocolate is a physical object made up of definite ingredients but it offers a range of use values, from 'sweetness' to comfort. Of course, adverts are the clearest index of the way in which an attempt is made to endow objects of consumption with a particular content of use value which goes beyond and is distinct from their physical content. But even in the total absence of adverts, the physical properties of commodities cannot be used to read off their social use. Consequently, consumption involves a relationship between the physical and the social properties of the commodity.

This has been sharply demonstrated by Haug (1986) even if within a narrow and over-generalised context. He refers to the relationship as the aesthetic illusion and understands it as a gap between the way in which the commodity is and the way in which it is perceived. Crucially, he sees the gap as widening as a result of the imperatives of cheapening production – with adulteration of ingredients undermining the quality of products. Consequently, in order to guarantee sale, the commodity has to be endowed with other compensating properties or those that conceal what is deficient or transform what is desired. Haug suggests that sexuality is the social property with which commodities become enhanced, and this is promoted through advertising to accommodate the aesthetic illusion.

There is much that is deficient in Haug's construct. It does not seem necessary to conceive of the relationship between the physical and social properties of the commodity as constituting an illusory gap with the slippery connotation of false as opposed to real properties. By analogy with Marx's theory of commodity fetishism, the relationship might be better understood as fetishised – that a car driver's sexuality appears as, in part, what it is, a relationship with a thing. The imperative of profitability renders adulteration neither as the only nor as the most important pressure upon the material properties of the commodity. It can be both enhanced and worsened by mass production and the introduction of new or different materials – home, craft or traditionally made is not a guarantee of a superior product. Nor is sexuality the only dimension that can be used to enhance the social properties of commodities and it does itself have a number of different dimensions.

But the virtue of Haug's approach lies in his method. For, with whatever limitations, he effectively emphasises that consumption is dependent upon a continuing and shifting relationship between the physical and the social properties of commodities. Whilst this might appear to be elementary, two important implications follow. First, it is erroneous to analyse one side of the relationship alone. This has already been seen in the context of criticising those approaches that treat the use values of commodities as given and consumption as the passive consequence of what is produced. But it applies equally to those theories that would construct the social properties of consumption independently of the ways in which they have been delivered. Indeed, the work of Baudrillard (1981, 1988) can be interpreted as having evolved along the lines of releasing itself analytically from the material origins of commodities, treating their physical properties as fixed and focusing on the social construction of their use value alone, through the notion of their symbolic exchange value for example. In other words, the relationship highlighted by Haug becomes extremely one-sided, a gap that only opens on one side.[32]

Second, the transformation around the physical and social properties of the commodity, even at the most general level, will differ from one commodity to the next. Even on the narrow terrain occupied by Haug, different commodities are more or less susceptible to adulteration, have a greater or lesser potential for being endowed with different forms of sexuality and are more or less amenable to advertising campaigns. As soon as it is recognised that the so-called aesthetic illusion is comprised of the whole sequence of activities that connect the creation of the commodity to its consumption, so the case for treating consumption as being based upon differentiated systems of provision is confirmed.

III Systems of provision

There have been many studies of consumption based, usually implicitly, on systems of provision. These, rather than a review of econometric studies of demand or of the consumption function, will be addressed in what follows. In particular, there has been a substantial literature on the political economy of food which is food-system-based. In the work of Goodman and Redclift (1991), for example, the food system is understood as a chain of activities from farm to the household.[33] Emphasis is placed upon the way in which ultimate products, foods, are heavily influenced by the shifting relationship between agriculture and industry. The former is viewed as inflexible because of its dependence upon natural processes. Consequently, capitalist industry is seen as attempting to capture agricultural activity and subordinate it to its own imperatives. It does so through two processes, 'appropriationism' and 'substitutionism'. For appropriationism, agricultural processes are industrialised as in the introduction of mechanisation – the tractor displaces the horse; for substitutionism, industrial inputs displace those provided from within agriculture, as in artificial fertilisers. The impact of these tensions between agriculture and industry are reflected in the nature of the products that are made available for consumption (in terms of foods that have been industrialised through the use of additives, pesticides, uniform crop varieties, etc.).

There are weaknesses in the 'food systems' literature, for it too has tended to place greater emphasis on the supply-side determinants of consumption without addressing what makes products acceptable to consumers. Further, there has been a tendency to caricature all food systems as 'Fordist', geared towards mass production/consumption at a global level and with substantial state support. This has, in turn, left the analysis vulnerable to dramatic changes in outlook in response to the impact of biotechnology (which, for

Goodman and Redclift, substantially releases agriculture from its natural constraints) and the recognition of niche markets that have risen for (no longer) seasonal crops such as cherry tomatoes, avocados, etc. These are made available all year round in part as a result of imperatives on Third World producers to become export-oriented in response to pressures for structural adjustment from international agencies such as the IMF. Commercial agriculture in developing countries serves increasingly exotic markets in the developed world even as domestic sources of staple crops are deficient for many. Indeed, as each country going through structural adjustment becomes export-oriented, so the overall weight on prices is downward, tending to frustrate the intention of raising export earnings.

ON THE RETAILING OF FOOD[34]

One component in these developments has been the fanatical search for product variety to be provided by supermarkets. The supermarket and, most recently, the superstore or hypermarket, has become such a common and regular part of our shopping lives that it is necessary to recall that such forms of retailing are very recent. Whilst department stores and multiples have been around since at least the turn of the century, super-markets date from after the Second World War.[35] Superstores are of an even younger vintage, emerging to considerable prominence over the past twenty years.

In order to illustrate the approach based upon systems of provision, attention will be focused upon these recent developments in retailing, and with particular attention to food. This would not appear to be fertile terrain since common trends in retailing seem to have evolved across many different commodities, suggesting the priority of horizontal over vertical determinants. Even so, it would be necessary to explain why some commodities are amenable to modern forms of shopping while others are not. However, it will be seen that even when the way in which differ-ent commodities are bought and sold is more or less identical, none the less what is consumed and why and with what significance is dependent upon differentiation across systems of provision.

First, why has retailing taken on its present form? Quite apart from the strategies adopted by retail firms themselves, there are crucial historical preconditions that have made those strategies feasible, irrespective of their profitability or desirability. Most obvious is the mass production of commodities, the creation of a system of transportation and communica-tion which has allowed these to be gathered from around the globe, and the generation of sufficient and sufficiently widespread household incomes, with which such goods can be purchased.

But spending power alone has not sufficed to underwrite the evolution of superstores; that power has been exercised in a particular way. Consumers have acquired the facility to shop in ways over and above access to income. They have depended upon their own transport, usually a motor car, in order to travel to and from peri-urban shopping sites, the time or opportunity to make such shopping trips worthwhile, and domestic durables with which to accommodate and make use of the items purchased – microwaves, fridge/freezers, etc. And the location of superstores on the fringes of urban areas has itself been predicated upon an earlier, historical process of urbanisation.

It follows that a wide range of factors has determined the conditions in which retailing has developed – urban restructuring, the rise of mass production/consumption, transportation, globalisation, the shifting division of labour between the household and the formal economy (the presumed commodification of household production), and the availability of 'leisure' time within which to shop. On the latter score, for example, with shopping predominantly the responsibility of women whose access to a car is generally secondary to that of a male partner, the ability to shop at superstores has been dependent upon when men have been free from work (and car use), at weekends and evenings, thereby creating pressure to extend store opening hours over and above those associated with the wish to use the fixed capital embodied in stores as fully as possible.

The processes mentioned in the previous paragraph, and others, are sufficiently general across the Western world that, however unevenly, retailing has been subject to a number of common trends across different countries. There has been an increasing concentration of ownership of retailing, so that it is often perceived to have benefited from a shift in power in its competitive conflict with manufacturers.[36] One index of this has been the growth of own-label products sold in stores alongside, apparently in competition with, branded products.[37] Large retailers have been able to command discounts for bulk purchases, and they have been able to appropriate functions (or not as they choose) from the manufacturer – dealing or dictating in product design, quality control and specification of conditions of delivery (to minimise or shift the burden of warehousing costs).[38]

Retailing has also been subject to 'industrialisation'. It has sought economies of scale and has experienced a series of technological changes that has vastly expanded labour productivity. Most recently, the use of credit cards, EPOS, EFTPOS and electronic scanners has speeded up the pace of store throughput from warehouse to bank,[39] neatly building upon those processes that have already shifted the burden of costs from the retailer to the consumer – the latter comes to the store, collects and chooses the goods (simultaneously when choosing from aisle displays, and without advice or service), waits to be served, and takes away the goods. In short, the historically distant separation of production from sale and, subsequently, of the knowledge of the product from the retailer, has simultaneously deskilled the vast majority of the workforce, reduced the content of

147

shopping itself (to the exchange of goods for money), and has drawn upon the consumer's own time and expense.[40]

Although it cannot be demonstrated by a comparative analysis here, these processes are in many respects more advanced in the UK than elsewhere.[41] Even the US, which long ago gave birth to the supermarket, has been leapfrogged in some respects.[42] During the period 1985 to 1991, the number of out-of-town superstores in the UK rose from 970 to 1,805; over the decade from 1982, the number of stores with scanners installed grew from 10 to 8,179. For food, the number of retail outlets fell from 35.3% to 28% of all outlets from 1980 to 1989, with turnover per outlet increasing by 161.1% compared to 117.5% for retailing in general. From 1985 to 1991, the share of specialist retailers (dairy, butcher, fishmonger, greengrocery, baking and confectionery) fell from 21% to 16%, reflecting their loss of business share to the large, non-specialised retailers.[43]

There has then been an increasing concentration of the grocery business into a very small number of dominant multiples, most notably led by Tesco and Sainsbury. Multiples overall accounted for 78% of the food trade in 1987 compared with 57.1% in 1976 (Gardner and Sheppard 1989: 155). Of this, corporate shares were as follows: Tesco 14.2%, Sainsbury 14.1%, Gateway 11.4%, Argyll 10.2% and Asda 7.7%, so that the five largest retailers accounted for well over half of all sales (ibid.: 163). The growth in concentration has, in part, been the consequence of a rapid and extensive phase of acquisitions; in the 1980s, as much as a quarter of all multiple business in value terms had changed hands, with Argyll in the forefront trading as Presto, Lo-Cost and Safeway. It has also been dependent upon the growth of superstores and significant growth in the selling of their own-label groceries in place of manufacturers' brands. In short, for Lowe (1992), a Marks & Spencer and Sainsbury ethos has been created, 'with its unique blend of quality, service and price performance. It certainly is not the cheapest source of food but its total value for money offer has won over the middle class suburban, car-owning family shopper'.

These developments within UK retailing have given rise to what have been termed 'store wars' rather than 'price wars'. Whilst essentially correct, this view needs further amplification on one point. For price wars can themselves be, and have been, a form of store wars. Under the rubric of loss-leader, supermarkets have long attracted customers by offering a particular, possibly heavily advertised, product at a substantial discount with the aim of selling other products without the discount.

But it has been supplemented, even superseded, by another form of competition based on providing the customer with the widest possible variety of products from which to choose. The point is to be able to offer everything that might be wanted. Apart from explaining the apparent paradox of own-label being marketed alongside branded products, it has also led to mimicry of the high street with provision of in-store bakeries (with artificial baking odours), delicatessens and fishmongers. Neatly providing product range and the fuel for shopping trips, superstores have also become significant sellers of petrol.[44]

Why, however, have these features of retailing become so much more prominent in the UK? It is possible to point to a number of distinctive, interrelated and mutually supportive explanatory factors. A number of these follow from the fact that store wars have primarily been a matter of *site* wars, the ability to obtain and to finance suitable property for superstore development. Why has this been so opportune within the UK? First, Britain has suffered particularly acutely from inner-city decline, partly as a consequence of deindustrialisation, in which jobs, residence and income have shifted in favour of out-of-town shopping. Second, over the period of the Tory governments from 1979, there has been a substantial redistribution of income in favour of the better-off so that, by spending power, consumers have been divided more into two broad if overlapping fractions, made up of those who do and those who do not conform to the once-a-week big shop households (with or without the corresponding money, transport and household durables). Third, the presence of the more affluent households has been dependent upon dual-earners, reflecting the growing participation of women in the workforce, itself affecting when and how shopping occurs.[45]

Within a conventional analysis, these influences would be interpreted as lying on the demand-side of retail services. What of the supply-side? First, as observed, store wars have gone beyond price and variety competition and concern access to sites themselves for which access to finance has been central. Retailers in the UK have had access to capital markets as publicly quoted companies. Second, their ability to raise finance has been closely linked to the evolution of the UK property market. Until recently, spiralling property values and continuing profitability through superstore development sustained access to finance.[46] Whatever the ultimate fragility of this system of accumulation, the raising and use of funds for programmes of superstore expansion is guaranteed by the anticipated profitability and growing asset value of a high proportion of stores still in the process of construction.[47] Third, the financial system in the UK is particularly conducive to property or other forms of speculation by cash-rich corporations in view of the historical absence of financial institutions geared to long-run investment in domestic industry.

Fourth, a totally different factor on the supply-side is the labour market in which superstores have operated.[48] Britain's deindustrialisation has witnessed a decline in manufacturing jobs, a rapid rise in female employment (within services), and an economy characterised by the three lows – low investment, low productivity and low wages.[49] In conjunction with extremely poor levels of labour market support and of childcare, Britain has been particularly dependent upon low-paid, female, part-time labour in which retail services have been most prominent. In 1990, 310,300 female workers in food retailing were part-time compared to 437,900 working full-time.[50]

Fourth, such employment has also conformed to the low skill and training characteristics of the British economy, as exemplified in the mundane and repetitive work associated with its modern form of retailing.[51] This is by way of contrast with the French system and even more so for Germany. As Jarvis and Prais (1988: 34) put it:[52]

> The reason British shop assistants so often know hardly anything about what they are selling is that no one has ever taught them; and those responsible for the main British courses in retailing continue to regard such knowledge as less than essential.

Whatever the reasons for UK retailing being in the vanguard, other than in the skills of its workforce, there have been a number of consequences. First, food retailing has been characterised by very high profit margins, reflecting the high outlays on fixed costs of which funds for property development are an important component.[53] Second, apart from the trend towards one-stop shopping, this has been associated with an increasing variety of products conveniently made available to the superstore shopper, even if that variety might in part be spurious when made up of many different products (including own-label) with minimal differences between them. Thus, current shopping patterns point to an expansion of product choice at the expense of store choice.

Third, and running against such trends, these two features have provided the basis for discount (and other types of) stores competing on the basis of many fewer, often branded products, and products selling at lower prices and in more convenient locations for the customers that they serve.[54] These stores exist in the shadow of the giants but do themselves vary across relatively large-scale multiples,[55] franchises pooling functions such as bulk purchasing and distribution,[56] and the familiar but heavily pressed corner shops. Most notable has been the emerging use of petrol stations as more general outlets for general household goods, and of a widening range of goods delivered with the (almost) daily milk. In short, the standardisation of shopping patterns through the superstores has also facilitated a wide range of outlets to provide for the gaps not served by the weekly shop: 'The High Street trade is becoming more dependent on non-motorist shoppers and distress purchasing' (Key Note 1992b: 29). It has also given rise to the emergence of food manufacturers who, whilst still dwarfed by the retail giants, have prospered by producing a range of products for a variety of customers, covering branded as well as own-label products.[57]

It follows that superstore shopping does not sweep away all before it. It creates differentiation between customers, according to their income and shopping patterns and capabilities (and within the stores themselves – by their very *modus operandi*, there is variation in the shopping baskets purchased); it creates distinctions between goods according to their perishability and regularity of consumption, and according to their being branded or not – with these features influencing the competitive (dis)advantages of a wide variety of alternative forms of shopping.

Thus, despite the general trend towards the dominance of superstore shopping, the impact on what is available and what is purchased is different from product to product. And, to unravel those differences, it is necessary to acknowledge the differences in the way that foods are provided to retailers and consumed by their customers. In many ways, such an approach is surprisingly idiosyncratic when set against the literature concerned with retailing. Theoretical contributions have attempted to formulate general theories,[58] whilst historical approaches have sought to locate the retail function in terms of distinct chronological periods.[59]

A rather different point can be made about the literature on advertising. It tends to fall into two different sorts – one, within economics, sees it as shifting demand curves without specifying how, other than through expenditure incurred for that purpose; the other interprets the meaning of advertising. The latter almost inevitably focuses on the more fanciful advertising associated with branded products. But the fastest-growing form of advertising in the UK is from superstores that have reverted to more blunt (forms of) messages – this is available at these lower prices. Thus, in order to understand who advertises, what and how, it is necessary to go beyond the message and the expenditure to forge a link with developments in retailing and the different position occupied by own-label and branded goods within superstores.[60]

Finally, most of the preceding analysis has not been product-specific even if it has shown how patterns of retailing are differentiated and that these are intimately connected to product manufacture and advertising and how retail services are produced through property and labour markets. Nor has much attention been devoted to the material culture surrounding shopping. As a partial remedy to this neglect, consider the relationship between retailing and the cultural shift towards healthier eating.

The rise of supermarkets has given rise to the availability of a range of health foods in response to, and to promote, consumer concerns. However, the counterpart to greater variety has been a continuing compulsion to consume. Frequently, the purchase of health products is used as a justification for indulging the unhealthy as well – and, of course, cheek-by-jowl or, more exactly, aisle-by-aisle, the superstore encourages such behaviour.[61] Nor are matters so simple. For dairy products, for example, for which high fat cream is considered unhealthy, supermarket retailing has dramatically taken over from doorstep delivery, widely introducing a range of new skimmed and semi-skimmed milks, as well as margarines in place of butter. Without going into detail, this has followed upon a major restructuring of the dairy system, in part a consequence of changes in EC policy.[62] But the production of cream persists and, to a large extent, agricultural policy guarantees levels of output. The result is that agricultural and health policy are mutually inconsistent, but a route must be found for cream to trickle down into the nation's diet. It has done so through the promotion of cheeses and fancy desserts which complement the healthy, skimmed products in the neighbouring cabinets.

A similar story can be told about sugar.[63] Whilst suffering from being dubbed as unhealthy, it has also benefited from EC quota support. The sugar system has been restructured but it has been organised around competing sources of sweetness (whether artificial or from high fructose corn syrup) and of its own supply (beet and cane) which correspond to different geographical origins (EC and tropical) and to different refiners. The fall in demand for domestic consumption has been counterbalanced by the increasing (hidden) use of sugar in manufactured foods, even in those that are paradoxically taken to be healthy, such as breakfast cereals and yoghurt; the growth in the consumption of heavily sugared carbonated drinks has been especially important. Moreover, sugar has even been advertised as healthy in view of its being a 'natural' food; and foods with as much as 25% of their content taken up by sugar are promoted as being healthy in the sense of being (chemical) additive-free.[64]

Thus, despite the apparent and possibly exaggerated trend towards uniformity in retailing, the incidence of such shifting patterns across consumers and products does itself have to be explained along with differences in the way that commodities are produced, advertised and interpreted. This can only be done by reference to the systems of provision to which the products are attached. And the impact of consumer concerns around healthy products is uneven across products according to their forms of provision.

NOTES

1 Research on consumption norms and the female labour market has previously been supported by the Leverhulme Trust, and research on 'What we eat and why: a socioeconomic study of standard items in food consumption' is currently funded by the ESRC under grant X209252016 as part of its Research Programme, 'The Nation's Diet'. Thanks to fellow researchers on these projects. With some refinement and reorienting of the argument, this chapter draws heavily on Fine and Leopold (1993) to which reference will be made for a more detailed account of the topics covered. See also Fine (1993b, 1993c, 1994a) and Fine, Heasman and Wright (1995). Thanks to the editor for ample suggestions for improvements on an earlier draft.

2 See Fine (1982) for an appropriate discussion in this context of the relationship between neoclassical economics and classical political economy.

3 This was most forcibly brought to the notice of anthropologists by Douglas and Isherwood (1980). But for an earlier critical assessment, see Kryk (1923).

4 Consequently, the demand system for animals can be estimated empirically by using reward/punishment as a proxy for prices and income; see Kagel (1981).

5 Economics is highly dependent upon the division between the exogenous (factors taken as given) and the endogenous (those determined within the model).

6 See Green (1979) for a critical assessment.

7 For a critical account of this literature, see Fine (1992).

8 See Deaton and Muellbauer (1980) and Blundell (1988).

9 On these issues, see Keen (1987), Pudney (1989) and Meghir and Robin (1992), for example.

10 See Deaton's entry in the *New Palgrave Dictionary of Economics*, p. 592.

11 Of course, it might be argued that the *New Palgrave* is unrepresentative of the discipline, as is argued by Blaug (1988) who accuses the work of ideological bias. But, whilst he lists 24 omitted topics, none of these essentially involves consumption. So the relative unimportance of consumption to economics is common to widely different conceptions of the field.

12 See the discussion of the relationship between production, consumption and distribution in the *Grundrisse*.

13 See Fine and Leopold (1993, Chapters 18 and 19), and Rosdolsky (1977) and Keen (1991).

14 In Marx's political economy, rent takes the form of a commodity – as the price of the use of land – but is not such as it is not the product of labour. Rather, rent is a form of appropriation of surplus value, following from the historically contingent form assumed by landed property.

15 The subtitle of *Capital* is *A Critique of Political Economy* and, of each of the three volumes individually, *The Process of Production of Capital, The Process of Circulation of Capital*, and *The Process of Capitalist Production as a Whole*, respectively.

16 Hence the approach has been extensively and heavily criticised. See, for example, Curry (1993), Pollert (1991), Brenner and Glick (1991), Mavroudeas (1990), Gibbs (1992), Amin and Robins (1990) and Sayer (1989).

17 For an attempt to provide what might be interpreted as a political economy of postmodernism, see Harvey (1989).

18 See Fine (1987) for a critique of dual labour market theory.

19 See Fine and Leopold (1993, Chapter 9).

20 And, from a more radical perspective, see Baran and Sweezy (1968).

21 See the debate between Fine and Harris (1976, 1979) and Gough (1975, 1979).

22 For debate over the relationship between consumption and class in this context, see Burrows and Butler (1989), Duke and Edgell (1984), Dunleavy (1986), Forrest and Murie (1990), Forrest *et al.* (1990), Hamnett (1989), Harloe (1984), Harrison (1986), Mullins (1991), Pahl (1989, 1991), Pratt (1986), Preteceille and Terrail (1985), Preteceille (1986), Saunders (1984, 1986a 1986b, 1988 and 1990), Saunders and Harris (1990), Savage *et al.* (1990) and Sullivan (1989). See also Fine and Leopold (1993, Chapter 17). For an alternative analysis of the UK housing system, which can be interpreted in terms of the framework for approaching consumption suggested below and serve as an empirical illustration, see Ball (1983).

23 On conspicuous consumption, see Mason (1981, 1984).

24 For a critical assessment of trickle down, see Fine and Leopold (1993, Chapter 11).

25 See Fine and Leopold (1992, 1993, Chapter 10) for a critical assessment of McKendrick *et al.* (1982).

26 See Fine *et al.* (1993) for an account of how the video was initially conceived as being introduced by an elite of electronic consumers, and for an empirical demonstration of how important and how quickly it has become a consumer durable for households with children.

27 See Fine and Leopold (1993, Part I).
28 Hence the chronic crisis of the putative interdisciplinary discipline of consumer behaviour. See Fine and Leopold (1993, Chapter 3).
29 For assessment of food studies by this method, see Fine (1993).
30 See Moorhouse (1988), for example.
31 See Barthel (1989), for example.
32 See Jhally (1987) for a critique of Baudrillard, and Sahlins (1976), for their misinterpretation of Marx's theory of commodity fetishism (as precluding an analysis of the social construction of the use value of commodities) and for their own neglect of the material origins of those use values.
33 For other literature on food systems, see Buttel and Goodman (1989), Friedmann and McMichael (1989), McMichael (1992), McMichael and Myhre (1991), Kenney et al. (1989), Busch et al. (1989), Marsden et al. (1986, 1990, 1992), Lowe et al. (1990), Friedmann (1982, 1987, 1993), Reinhardt and Barlett (1989), Munton (1992), Friedland et al. (1992) and Goodman and Redclift (1989). Marsden and Munton (1991), however, refer to the limited research in this area.
34 See Fine and Leopold (1993, Chapters 16 and 20).
35 For a discussion of department stores, see Benson (1986) and also Williams (1982). For a history of retailing more generally, see Jefferys (1954), Winstanley (1983), Alexander (1970), Mui and Mui (1989) and Adburgham (1981). According to Johnson (1987: 2), the department store has itself been heavily squeezed by the rise of superstores:

> In the 1980s in the UK, traditional department stores suffered. A combination of out-of-town shopping for furniture, furnishings and household goods grew, together with a move by grocery retailers into hypermarket trading with an enlarged consumer durable product range and a rise in propensity of specialist clothing stores, eroded the demand for traditional department store products.

See also Moir (1990), and O'Brien and Harris (1991) for the spatial implications of retailing. Dowling (1993) discusses how this affects the nature of the commodity according to the context within which it is bought and sold.
36 See Grant (1987) and Wrigley (1989).
37 One index of the growth of own-label alongside branded products is shown in the following table, which reveals that proliferation of brands, and hence product choice, has not necessarily been associated with greater market share overall for branded products.

Number of brands and their market share

	PRODUCT				
	Fruit Squash	Baked Beans	Washing-Up Liquid	Instant Coffee	Tea Bags
1976	16	16	13	9	6
	58%	76%	73%	66%	73%
1986	24	20	11	31	27
	52%	66%	74%	73%	66%

Source: Bardus (1987:6)

38 Distribution can account for between 8% and 30% of retail price. It has been estimated that as much as 70% of food product distribution is now centralised through regional distributional centres controlled by retailers even if they do not operate them themselves. See Bardus (1987).

39 See Alter (1989).

40 Bluestone *et al.* (1981) refer to the industrialisation of retailing and see advertising as a way of displacing a sales force.

41 Observing these features, Wrigley (1987: 1285) demands:

> Clearly, if the *distinctive* nature of recent retail restructuring in the United Kingdom is to be understood, then a major research priority is to clarify how the context of restructuring in the United Kingdom differs from that in the other Western economies.

See also Wrigley (1989, 1991, 1992), Mayes and Shipman (1992) and Key Note (1992a, 1992b).

42 The US is often thought of as being a generation ahead of the UK in its food consumption habits, as it may have been in fast food, for example. But concentration of ownership in retailing is much further advanced in the UK, comparable to what has been achieved at a state level in the US, leading to the view that the strength of retailers relative to manufacturers has lagged in the latter, given the high levels of concentration of US food manufacturing. See Wrigley (1989). Lusch (1987) sees the US as exhibiting the same retailing trends as the UK but subject to being 'overstored'.

43 These figures from Key Note (1992b).

44 Foot (1988) finds that a quarter of those shopping at superstores in Reading also purchased petrol. Wrigley (1991) reports that Sainsbury commands 2% of UK petrol sales. However, in 1991, it had 58 petrol stations at superstore locations compared to 120 at Tesco, 94 at Asda, 24 at William Morrison, and 12 at Safeway.

45 For a discussion in the US context, see Dholakia (1987).

46 It has also depended upon the role played by planning permission.

47 Wrigley (1991) suggests that the big five may give way to the big three in the 1990s, given the fragility of ASDA and Gateway, especially in view of dependence upon property values which have led to excessive profitability and expansion in the past. See also Shiret (1991, 1992a, 1992b) on whom Wrigley (1992) draws. Shiret (1992b: 2) notes that:

> In a falling property market the food retailers have continued to bid up the prices of food retail real estate. . . . We have estimated that since 1989 the average capital price of a superstore has increased by around 30% while the capital value of the property market in total has dropped by almost 20%.

Given the limited alternative uses for the associated land banks, a dramatic reversal in such property values is a distinct possibility with devastating implications for the asset value of retailers. For discussion of the different major food retailers see Key Note (1992a, 1992b).

48 See Bowlby (1988), for example, and GLC (1985).

49 See Fine and Harris (1985) on the character of the British economy and Fine (1992) for its implications for the female labour market. Lowe (1992: 69/70) correctly observes:

> The British economy is a low wage economy and UK retailing tends to be part time, low paid and female oriented. Many part time women

155

employees are below the PAYE/National Insurance threshold, so also saving costs for the employer.

50 See Mayes and Shipman (1992). The figures for females in other retailing are 565,800 part-time workers and 1,004,200 full-time, indicating the greater extent of part-time working in food. 237,700 men work full-time in food retailing, 75,500 part-time; for the rest of retailing, the figures are 630,100 and 108,700.

51 Other factors, unique or particularly strong in the UK, include the rapidity with which quality came to be associated with own-label (the Marks and Spencer influence, but also a consequence of a concerted effort on the part of retailers to claim and to promote quality – see Shaw *et al.* (1991)) and the peculiar history of food, drink and tobacco associated with Britain's colonial past (leading to relatively early, large, internationally organised companies with a correspondingly developed system of wholesaling and retailing – consider Home and Colonial Stores, for example). As far as I know, the relationship between Britain's imperial past and the current advanced form taken by its retailing has not been investigated (and is beyond the scope of this study). The role of cooperative societies may also have been of importance.

52 The implications for the general skills and expectations of the workforce are significant since retailing constitutes a tenth of employment as a whole, is subject to high labour turnover and accounts for a disproportionately high number of new entrants and re-entrants to the labour market. Note that there are three times as many part-time retail workers in the UK than in France.

53 Thus, there seem to be limits on the scale economies associated with the retailing function as such – although size may be a way of guaranteeing customers. See Shaw *et al.* (1989).

54 Hence the marginalisation of those who depend upon local access to shopping; see Lewis *et al.* (1985).

55 Key Note (1992b) estimates that leading food discounters took 7.6% of the market in 1992, with Kwik Save in the forefront with 5%. A significant development has been the arrival of foreign retailers such as Netto of Denmark and Aldi of Germany. Netto offers only 650 lines but at prices 15% to 20% below those of the major retailers.

56 On retail alliances, see Lowe (1992) and Dawson and Shaw (1992). Their growth across national boundaries in part reflects the limited but developing internationalisation of retailing.

57 See Grant (1987) for the idea that developments in retailing have not necessarily been to the competitive disadvantage of manufacturers.

58 See Brown (1990) for a review of general theories of retailing (in their wheel, accordion and life-cycle forms according to which different forms come and go or co-exist depending upon the marketing environment and the evolution of competition). See Fine and Leopold (1993, Chapter 20) for a critique of the concept of retail capital, particularly in the light of Ducatel and Blomley (1990).

59 See Gilbert and Bailey (1990) for a review of historical approaches to marketing. Significantly, they find that the literature reveals theoretical and empirical anomalies in general periodisation of retailing (such as the idea of successive eras of cost, sales and marketing competition).

60 See Fine and Leopold (1993, Chapters 14–16).

61 See Heasman (1990).

62 See Heasman (1993b) and Fine *et. al.* (1995).

63 See Heasman (1993a) and Fine *et. al.* (1995).

64 See Roberts (1991) on the pursuit of a 'healthy' label for foods, and Fine and Wright (1991) for an assessment of the food information system more generally.

REFERENCES

Adburgham, A. (1981) *Shops and Shopping, 1800–1914*, London: George Allen and Unwin.

Alexander, D. (1970) *Retailing in England During the Industrial Revolution*, London: Athlone Press.

Alter, M. (1989) 'The UK retail technology market: applications, benefits and future developments in EPoS/EFTPoS systems and software', Special Report no. 2011, London: Economist Intelligence Unit.

Amin, A. and Robins, K. (1990) 'The re-emergence of regional economies? The mythical geography of flexible accumulation', *Environment and Planning D* 8: 7–34.

Ball, M. (1983) *Housing Policy and Economic Power: The Political Economy of Owner Occupation*, London: Methuen.

Baran, P. and Sweezy, P. (1968) *Monopoly Capital*, Harmondsworth: Penguin.

Bardus, A. (1987) 'Competition in the food distribution sector', Conference on Competition Policy in the Food Industries, University of Reading.

Barthel, D. (1989) 'Modernism and marketing: the chocolate box revisited', *Theory, Culture and Society* 6, August: 429–438.

Baudrillard, J. (1981) *For a Critique of the Political Economy of the Sign*, St Louis, Mo.: Telos Press.

Baudrillard, J. (1988) *Selected Writings*, London: Polity.

Benson, S. (1986) *Counter Cultures: Saleswomen, Managers, and Customers in American Department Stores, 1890–1940*, Chicago: University of Illinois Press.

Blaug, M. (1988) *Economics Through the Looking Glass: The Distorted Perspective of the New Palgrave Dictionary of Economics*, Occasional Paper, no. 78, London: Institute of Economic Affairs.

Bluestone, B., Hanna, P., Kuhn, S. and Moore, L. (1981) *The Retail Revolution: Market Transformation, Investment and Labor in the Modern Department Store*, Boston: Auburn House.

Blundell, R. (1988) 'Consumer behaviour: theory and empirical evidence – a survey', *Economic Journal* 98, March: 16–65.

Bourdieu, P. (1984) *Distinction: A Social Critique of the Judgement of Taste*, London: Routledge and Kegan Paul.

Bowlby, S. (1988) 'From corner shop to hypermarket: women and food retailing', in J. Little *et al.* (eds) *Women in Cities: Gender and the Urban Environment*, Basingstoke: Macmillan.

Brenner, R. and Glick, M. (1991) 'The regulation school and the West's economic impasse', *New Left Review* 188, July/Aug.: 45–119.

Brown, S. (1990) 'Innovation and evolution in UK retailing: the retail warehouse', *European Journal of Marketing* 24 (9): 39–54.

Burrows, R. and Butler, T. (1989) 'Review article: Middle mass and the pit: a critical review of Peter Saunders' sociology of consumption', *Sociological Review* 37 (2): 338–64.

Busch, L., Bonnano, A. and Lacey, W. (1989) 'Science, technology, and the restructuring of agriculture', *Sociologia Ruralis* XXIX (2): 118–30.

Buttel, F. and Goodman, D. (1989) 'An introduction to recent trends in the sociology and political economy of agriculture', *Sociologia Ruralis* XXIX (2): 86–92.

Castells, M. (1977) *The Urban Question: A Marxist Approach*, 2nd edn, London: Edward Arnold.

Curry, J. (1993) 'The flexibility fetish: a review essay on flexible specialisation', *Capital and Class* 50, Summer: 99–126.

Dawson, J. and Shaw, S. (1992) 'Inter-firm alliances in the retail sector: evolutionary, strategic and tactical issues in their creation and management', Edinburgh Department of Business Studies, working paper, no. 92/7.

Deaton, A. and Muellbauer, J. (1980) *Economics and Consumer Behaviour*, Cambridge: Cambridge University Press.

Dholakia, R. (1987) 'Feminism and the new home economics: what do they mean for marketing', in A. Firat, N. Dholakia and R. Bagozzi (eds) *Philosophical and Radical Thought in Marketing*, Lexington, Mass.: Lexington Books.

Douglas, M. and Isherwood, Baron (1980) *The World of Goods*, London: Penguin.

Dowling, R. (1993) 'Femininity, place and commodities: a retail case study', *Antipode* 25 (4): 295–319.

Ducatel, K. and Blomley, N. (1990) 'Rethinking retail capital', *International Journal of Urban and Regional Research* 14 (2): 206–227.

Duesenberry, J. (1967) *Income, Saving and the Theory of Consumer Behaviour*, Cambridge, Mass.: Harvard University Press.

Duke, V. and Edgell, S. (1984) 'The political economy of cuts in Britain and consumption sectoral cleavages', *International Journal of Urban and Regional Research* 10: 177–201.

Dunleavy, P. (1986) 'The growth of sectoral cleavages and the stabilisation of state expenditures', *Environment and Planning D* 4: 129–144.

Eatwell, J., Milgate, M. and Newman, P. (eds) (1987) *The New Palgrave: A Dictionary of Economics*, London: Macmillan.

Fine, B. (1982) *Theories of the Capitalist Economy*, London: Edward Arnold.

Fine, B. (1987) 'Segmented labour market theory: a critical assessment', *Birkbeck Discussion Paper in Economics* 87/12.

Fine, B. (1992) *Women's Employment and the Capitalist Family*, London: Routledge.

Fine, B. (1993a) 'Resolving the diet paradox', *Social Science Information* 4, Dec.

Fine, B. (1993b) 'Modernity, urbanism, and modern consumption – a comment', *Environment and Planning D, Society and Space* 11: 599–601.

Fine, B. (1993c) 'Towards a political economy of food', *Review of International Political Economy* 1(3): 519–545.

Fine, B. (1994) 'Consumption in contemporary capitalism: beyond Marx and Veblen – a comment', *Review of Social Economy* LII, Fall(3): 391–396.

Fine, B. and Harris, L. (1976) 'State expenditure in advanced capitalism: a critique', *New Left Review* 98, July/Aug.: 97–112.

Fine, B. and Harris, L. (1979) *Rereading 'Capital'*, London: Macmillan.

Fine, B. and Harris, L. (1985) *The Peculiarities of the British Economy*, London: Lawrence and Wishart.

Fine, B. and Leopold, E. (1990) 'Consumerism and the Industrial Revolution', *Social History* 15 (2): 151–179.

Fine, B. and Leopold, E. (1993) *The World of Consumption*, London: Routledge.

Fine, B. and Wright, J. (1991) 'Digesting the food and information systems', *Birkbeck Discussion Paper* 7/91, Dec.

Fine, B., Heasman, M. and Wright, J. (1995) *Consumption in the Age of Affluence: The World of Food*, London: Routledge.

Fine, B., Foster, N., Simister, J. and Wright, J. (1993) 'Consumption norms, trickle-down and the video/microwave syndrome', *International Review of Applied Economics* 7 (2): 123–143.

Firat, A., Dholakia, N. and Bagozzi, R. (eds) (1987) *Philosophical and Radical Thought in Marketing*, Lexington, Mass.: Lexington Books.

Foot, D. (1988) 'Changes in customer shopping – Savacentre shopping surveys, 1982 and 1987', University of Reading, Geography Papers, no. 103.

Forrest, R. and Murie, A. (1990) 'A dissatisfied state? Consumer preferences and council housing in Britain', *Urban Studies* 27 (5): 617–635.

Forrest, R., Murie, A. and Williams, P. (1990) *Home Ownership: Differentiation and Fragmentation*, London: Unwin Hyman.

Friedland, W., Busch, L., Buttel, F. and Rudy, A. (eds) (1992) *Towards a New Political Economy of Agriculture*, Boulder, Col.: Westview Press.

Friedman, M. (1957) *A Theory of the Consumption Function*, Princeton, Ill.: Princeton University Press.

Friedmann, H. (1982) 'The political economy of food: the rise and fall of the postwar international food order', *American Journal of Sociology* 88 (Supplement): S248–286.

Friedmann, H. (1987) 'The family farm and the international food regimes', in T. Shanin (ed.) *Peasants and Peasant Societies: Selected Readings*, 2nd edn, Oxford: Blackwell.

Friedmann, H. (1993) 'The political economy of food: a global crisis', *New Left Review* 197, Jan./Feb.: 29–57.

Friedmann, H. and McMichael, P. (1989) 'Agriculture and the state system: the rise and decline of national agriculture', *Sociologia Ruralis* XXIX (2): 93–117.

Galbraith, J. (1969) *The New Industrial Estate*, Boston: Houghton Mifflin Co.

Galbraith, J. (1973) *Economics and the Public Purpose*, New York: Basic Books.

Galbraith, J. (1985) *The Affluent Society*, 4th edn, London: Deutsch.

Gardner, C. and Sheppard, J. (1989) *Consuming Passion: The Rise of Retail Culture*, London: Unwin.

Gibbs, D. (1992) '"The main thing today is – shopping": consumption and the flexibility debate', SPA Working Paper, no. 15, School of Geography, University of Manchester.

Gilbert, D. and Bailey, N. (1990) 'The development of marketing – a compendium of historical approaches', *Quarterly Review of Marketing* 15 (2): 6–13.

GLC (1985) *The London Industrial Strategy*, London: GLC.

Goodman, D. and Redclift, M. (eds) (1989) *The International Farm Crisis*, London: Macmillan.

Goodman, D. and Redclift, M. (1991) *Refashioning Nature: Food, Ecology and Culture*, London: Routledge.

Gough, I. (1975) 'State expenditure in advanced capitalism', *New Left Review* 92: 53–92.

Gough, I. (1979) *The Political Economy of the Welfare State*, London: Macmillan.

Grant, R. (1987) 'The retail environment in the UK', in G. Johnson (ed.) *Business Strategy and Retailing*, Chichester: John Wiley.

Green, F. (1979) 'The consumption function: a study of a failure in positive economics', in F. Green and P. Nore (eds) *Issues in Political Economy: A Critical Approach*, London: Macmillan.

Green, F. and Nore, P. (eds) (1977) *Economics: An Anti-Text*, London: Macmillan.

Green, F. and Nore, P. (eds) (1979) *Issues in Political Economy: A Critical Approach*, London: Macmillan.

Hamnett, C. (1989) 'Consumption and class in contemporary Britain', in C. Hamnett, L. McDowell and P. Sarre (eds) *Restructuring Britain: the Changing Social Structure*, London: Sage.

Hamnett, C., McDowell, L. and Sarre, P. (eds) (1989) *Restructuring Britain: The*

Changing Social Structure, London: Sage.

Harloe, M. (1984) 'Sector and class', *International Journal of Urban and Regional Research* 8: 228–237.

Harrison, M. (1986) 'Consumption and urban theory: an alternative approach based on the social division of welfare', *International Journal of Urban and Regional Research* 10: 232–242.

Harvey, D. (1989) *The Condition of Post-Modernity: An Enquiry into the Origins of Cultural Change*, Oxford: Blackwell.

Haug, W. (1986) *Critique of Commodity Aesthetics: Appearance, Sexuality and Advertising in Capitalist Society*, London: Polity Press.

Heasman, M. (1990) 'Nutrition and technology: the development of the market for "Lite" Products', *British Food Journal* 92 (2): 5–13.

Heasman, M. (1993a) 'The persistence of sugar in the British food supply, 1900 to the present day', SOAS Working Paper no. 35.

Heasman, M. (1993b) 'Sacred cows: the end of the current dairy system in England and Wales', mimeo.

Jarvis, V. and Prais, S. (1988) 'Two nations of shopkeepers: training for retailing in France and Britain', Discussion Paper no. 40, London: National Institute of Economic and Social Research.

Jefferys, J. (1954) *Retail Trading in Britain, 1850–1950*, Cambridge: Cambridge University Press.

Jhally, S. (1987) *The Codes of Advertising: Fetishism and the Political Economy of Meaning in the Consumer Society*, London: Frances Pinter.

Johnson, G. (ed.) (1987) *Business Strategy and Retailing*, Chichester: John Wiley.

Kagel, J. (1981) 'Demand curves of animal consumers', *Quarterly Journal of Economics* XCVI (1): 1–15.

Katona, G. (1964) *The Mass Consumption Society*, New York: McGraw-Hill.

Keen, M. (1987) 'Zero expenditures and the estimation of Engel curves', *Journal of Applied Econometrics* 41: 277–86.

Keen, S. (1991) 'Paul Sweezy and the misinterpretation of Marx', *School of Economics Discussion Paper*, no. 91/1, Jan., University of New South Wales.

Kenney, M., Lobao, L., Curry, J. and Goe, W. (1989) 'Midwestern agriculture in US Fordism: from the New Deal to economic restructuring', *Sociologia Ruralis* XXIX (2): 131–148.

Key Note (1992a) *Supermarkets and Superstores*, London.

Key Note (1992b) *Retailing in the UK*, London.

Kryk, H. (1923) *A Theory of Consumption*, Cambridge: Riverside Press, reprinted in 1976, New York: Arnos Press.

Lewis, J., Broadbent, A. and Meegan, K. (1985) *Food Retailing in London: A Pilot Study of the Three Largest Retailers and Londoners' Access to Food*, London: London Food Commission.

Little, J., Peake, L. and Richardson, P. (eds) (1988) *Women in Cities: Gender and the Urban Environment*, Basingstoke: Macmillan.

Lowe, J. (1992) 'European Retail Alliances: Their Impact on the Future of European Retailing', Special Report no. 2207, London: Economist Intelligence Unit.

Lowe, P., Marsden, T. and Whatmore, S. (eds) (1990) *Technological Change and the Rural Environment*, London: David Fulton Publishers.

Lusch, R. (1987) 'A commentary on the US retail environment', in G. Johnson (ed.) *Business Strategy and Retailing*, Chichester: John Wiley.

McKendrick, N., Brewer, J. and Plumb, J. (1982) *The Birth of a Consumer Society: The Commercialization of Eighteenth Century England*, London: Europa Publications.

McMichael, P. (1992) 'Tensions between national and international control of the world food order: contours of a new food regime', *Sociological Perspectives* 35 (2): 343–365.

McMichael, P. and Myhre, D. (1991) 'Global regulation vs the nation-state: agro-food systems and the new politics of capital', *Capital and Class* 43 Spring: 83–105.

Marsden, T. and Munton, R. (1991) 'Global food strategies and environmental change: some preliminary considerations', *Fresh Fruit and Vegetables Globalization Network*, Working Paper no. 7, University of California, Santa Cruz.

Marsden, T., Lowe, P. and Whatmore, S. (eds) (1990) *Rural Restructuring: Global Processes and their Responses*, London: David Fulton Publishers.

Marsden, T., Lowe, P. and Whatmore, S. (eds) (1992) *Labour and Locality: Uneven Development and the Rural Labour Process*, London: David Fulton.

Marsden, T., Whatmore, S., Munton, R. and Little, J. (1986) 'The restructuring process and economic centrality in capitalist agriculture', *Journal of Rural Studies* 2 (4): 271–340.

Marx, K. (1969) *Theories of Surplus Value*, Part II, London: Lawrence and Wishart.

Marx, K. (1973) *Grundrisse*, Harmondsworth: Penguin.

Mason, R. (1981) *Conspicuous Consumption: A Study of Exceptional Consumer Behaviour*, Farnborough: Gower.

Mason, R. (1984) 'Conspicuous consumption: a literature review', *European Journal of Marketing*, 18 (3): 26–39.

Mavroudeas, S. (1990) *Regulation Approach: A Critical Assessment*, PhD Thesis, University of London.

Mayes, D. and Shipman, A. (1992) 'The response of UK retailers to the European Single Market', Discussion Paper no. 6, London: National Institute of Economic and Social Research.

Meghir, C. and Robin, J. (1992) 'Frequency of purchase and the estimation of demand systems', *Journal of Econometrics* 53: 53–85.

Mohun, S. (1977) 'Consumer sovereignty', in F. Green and P. Nore (eds) *Economics: An Anti-Text*, London: Macmillan.

Moir, C. (1990) 'Competition in the UK grocery trades', in C. Moir and J. Dawson (eds) *Competition and Markets: Essays in Honour of Margaret Hall*, London: Macmillan.

Moir, C. and Dawson, J. (eds) (1990) *Competition and Markets: Essays in Honour of Margaret Hall*, London: Macmillan.

Moorhouse, H. (1988) 'American automobiles and workers' dreams', *Sociological Review* 31: 403–426.

Mui, H. and Mui, L. (1989) *Shops and Shopkeeping in Eighteenth Century England*, London: Routledge.

Mullins, P. (1991) 'The identification of social forces in development as a general problem in sociology: a comment on Pahl's remarks on class and consumption relations as forces in urban and regional development', *International Journal of Urban and Regional Research* 15 (1): 119–126.

Munton, R. (1992) 'The uneven development of capitalist agriculture: the repositioning of agriculture within the food system', in K. Hoggart (ed.) *Agricultural Change, Environment and Economy*, London: Macmillan.

O'Brien, L. and Harris, F. (1991) *Retailing, Shopping, Society, Space*, London: David Fulton Publishers.

Otnes, P. (ed.) (1988) *The Sociology of Consumption: An Anthology*, New Jersey: Humanities Press International.

Pahl, R. (1989) 'Is the Emperor naked? Some questions on the adequacy of sociological theory in urban and regional research', *International Journal of Urban and Regional Research* 13 (4): 709–720.

Pahl, R. (1991) 'R. E. Pahl replies', *International Journal of Urban and Regional Research* 15 (1): 127–129.

Piore, M. and Sabel, C. (1984) *The Second Industrial Divide: Possibilities for Prosperity*, New York: Basic Books.

Pollert, A. (ed.) (1991) *Farewell to Flexibility*, Oxford: Blackwell.

Pratt, G. (1986) 'Against reductionism: the relations of consumption as a mode of social structuration', *International Journal of Urban and Regional Research* 10: 377–400.

Preteceille, E. (1986) 'Collective consumption, urban segregation, and social classes', *Environment and Planning D* 4: 145–154.

Preteceille, E. and Terrail, J.-P. (1985) *Capitalism, Consumption and Needs*, Oxford: Blackwell.

Pudney, S. (1989) *Modelling Individual Choice: The Econometrics of Corners, Kinks and Holes*, Oxford: Blackwell.

Reinhardt, N. and Barlett, P. (1989) 'The persistence of family farms in United States agriculture', *Sociologia Ruralis* XXIX (3/4): 201–225.

Roberts, D. (1991) '"Natural": A trading standards viewpoint', *British Food Journal* 93 (1): 17–19.

Rosdolsky, R. (1977) *The Making of Marx's 'Capital'*, London: Pluto.

Sahlins, M. (1976) *Culture and Practical Reason*, Chicago: University of Chicago Press.

Saunders, P. (1984) 'Beyond housing classes: the sociological significance of private property rights in means of consumption', *International Journal of Urban and Regional Research* 8: 202–225.

Saunders, P. (1986a) *Social Theory and the Urban Question*, 2nd edn, London: Hutchinson.

Saunders, P. (1986b) 'Comment on Dunleavy and Preteceille', *Environment and Planning D* 4: 155–163.

Saunders, P. (1988) 'The sociology of consumption: a new research agenda', in P. Otnes (ed.) *The Sociology of Consumption: An Anthology*, New Jersey: Humanities Press.

Saunders, P. (1990) *A Nation of Home Owners*, London: Unwin Hyman.

Saunders, P. and Harris, C. (1990) 'Privatisation and the consumer', *Sociology* 24 (1): 57–75.

Savage, M., Watt, D. and Arber, S. (1990) 'The consumption sector debate and social mobility', *Sociology* 24 (1): 97–117.

Sayer, A. (1989) 'Postfordism in question', *International Journal of Urban and Regional Research* 13 (4): 666–695.

Shanin, T. (ed.) (1987) *Peasants and Peasant Societies: Selected Readings*, 2nd edn, Oxford: Blackwell.

Shaw, S., Dawson, L. and Blair, L. (1991) 'The sourcing of retailer brand food products', Edinburgh University Department of Business Studies, Discussion Paper no. 91/17.

Shaw, S., Nisbet, D. and Dawson, J. (1989) 'Economies of scale in UK supermarkets: some preliminary findings', *International Journal of Retailing* 4 (5): 13–26.

Shiret, T. (1991) 'Tesco PLC: a company capitalising too much interest?', London: Crédit Lyonnais Laing.

Shiret, T. (1992a) 'How much hot air do you like in your accounts?', London: Crédit Lyonnais Laing.

Shiret, T. (1992b) 'Property again', London: Crédit Lyonnais Laing.

Stigler, G. and Becker, G. (1977) 'De gustibus non est disputandum', *American Economic Review* 67 (2): 76–90.

Sullivan, O. (1989) 'Housing tenure as a consumption-sector divide: a critical perspective', *International Journal of Urban and Regional Research* 13 (2): 183–200.

Veblen, T. (1924) *The Theory of the Leisure Class: An Economic Study of Institutions*, London: Allen and Unwin.

Williams, Rosalind (1982) *Dream Worlds: Mass Consumption in Late Nineteenth Century France*, London: University of California Press.

Winstanley, M. (1983) *The Shopkeeper's World, 1830–1914*, Manchester: Manchester University Press.

Wrigley, N. (1987) 'The concentration of capital in UK grocery retailing', *Environment and Planning A* 19: 1283–1288.

Wrigley, N. (1989) 'The lure of the USA: further reflections on the internationalisation of British grocery retailing capital', *Environment and Planning A* 21: 283–288.

Wrigley, N. (1991) 'Is the "Golden Age" of British grocery retailing at a watershed?', *Environment and Planning A* 23: 1537–1544.

Wrigley, N. (1992) 'Sunk capital, the property crisis, and the restructuring of British food retailing', *Environment and Planning A*, vol. 24, 1521–1530.

5

CONSUMPTION WITHIN HISTORICAL STUDIES

Paul Glennie

I The significance of consumption for history

INTRODUCTION AND BACKGROUND

Earlier this century, industrial and agricultural revolutions were being discovered almost everywhere that historians looked. Recently it has been consumer revolutions, at least among European and American historians (little literature has hitherto addressed other histories of consumption, though see Clunas 1991). Phrases like the birth of consumer society, emergent modern consumption, the rise of mass consumption, and the rise of mass market culture have been applied to the sixteenth and early seventeenth centuries (Thirsk 1978); Restoration England (Earle 1989: Shammas 1990; Weatherill 1988); the early eighteenth century (Eversley 1967); the Georgian period (Campbell 1987; McKendrick, Brewer and Plumb 1982; Williams 1987); the late nineteenth century (Fox and Lears 1983; Fraser 1981; Lee 1981); and between the two World Wars (Miller 1991). And, of course, each account raises questions about defining 'consumer society', and about consumption's connections to wider economic and cultural changes.

This proliferation reflects both continuous growth in Western consumption, and historians' various definitions of 'consumer society'. In addition, work on consumption is characterised by fragmentation, with very many local case-studies. Most general treatments of consumption either cover short periods and a single country, or take a long-run comparative view only for certain goods. The sheer variety of available sources (artefactual, documentary, visual, literary), and the divergent agendas of specialised research fields in different countries, exacerbate diversity and fragmentation. Different histories inform, and are informed by, highly divergent general analyses on consumption, and many historians distrust explicit theorising as a comparative and synthesising device.

All in all, then, the upsurge in historical work on consumption has been a general, but not a coherent, phenomenon. It falls far short of a fundamental metamorphosis of the discipline, even of economic and social history alone. Few historians would claim that the key to all modern history is emergent consumer society. On the other hand, it is hard to see consumption becoming dislodged from a position centre-stage, or that future books on *The Culture of Capitalism* (Macfarlane 1987) could ignore consumption altogether. At many different times, consumption contributed prominently to new modes of culture, especially but not exclusively among middle-rank society.

Despite differences in chronology and emphasis, most accounts incorporate three common features. First, most historians agree on certain attributes of consumer societies: growing per capita consumption of commodities; intensifying production and reorganised distribution systems; increasing social divisions of labour and increasing social mobility (both symbolised by consumer goods); growing individualism in social life; and consumer acquisitiveness tied to fashion and, increasingly, advertising. Second, most accounts stress key transformatory periods, using metaphors of transition and revolution. Modern consumption (however defined) is juxtaposed to a dichotomous phenomenon called pre-modern consumption, in which people were 'users of things', engaged in a natural activity oriented to use values, rather than 'consumers of commodities' (even if most would acknowledge that any such task-oriented society is hard to find). However, transition metaphors inevitably diminish the significance of changing consumption patterns and practices at other times. From this follows a third common feature: the conflation of *mass consumption* (the size of the market), *modern consumption* (usually defined in terms of consumption practices), and *mass culture* (systematic manipulation by capital of consumer knowledges through mass media and advertising images). Emphasising a single period of transformation presumes that these three dimensions co-vary.

It must be appreciated that historians' preoccupations have differed from those of many social scientists interested in histories of consumption. The emphases – and the silences – in historians' writings reflect those preoccupations. Much political, social and cultural history has marginalised consumption patterns and processes. First, such history commonly dichotomises elite culture and popular culture, patricians and plebeians, the respectable and the rude (Thompson 1974). The rise of 'bottom-up' social history (Burke 1991; Sharpe 1987), renewed stress on the enduring power of political-religious elites and their sustained aristocratic cultural and political hegemony over the middling orders (Clark 1985), and the waning of 'bourgeois revolution' interpretations of the English Civil War, all focused attention away from 'the middling sort of people' (Earle 1989; Wrightson 1982). Second, for many historians, politics and religion lie at the core of cultural history. Party and denomination are central to identities and power while consumption is a by-product of (at best) marginal significance in understanding social change (Clark 1985, 1986, 1992).

For economic historians two debates relating to consumption have been particularly and perennially important. The first concerns long-run trends in living standards (especially during industrialisation), examining real income, wealth distribution, and broader measures of quality of life, including life expectancy and deteriorating environments (Cole 1981; Lindert 1986; Williamson 1984). The second considers whether industrialisation depended on prior shifts in the scale and structure of demand (Eversley 1967; Gilboy 1932; Mokyr 1977). Both debates consider consumption shifts mainly through their connections with changes in production, the 'core' concern of economic history, well illustrated by their fixation with wage-rates (i.e. employers' labour costs), rather than households' total income and spending (Woodward 1984).

Much North American work on consumption lies within lively, and political, debates on the extent and intensity of early capitalism and capitalist mentalities (Appleby 1993). Virtuous images of frontier, pioneering and agrarian simplicity were central to post-1776 national identity (Breen 1993). Many historians worked within contemporary accounts of early Americans' non-market ethos (Clark 1990; Henretta 1978; Merrill 1977). This image has become increasingly qualified (Lemon 1972, 1980; Pruitt 1984; Rothenberg 1988). Recent discussions emphasise that local systems of mutuality and exchange coexisted with capitalist commodity markets (Kulikoff 1989, 1993; Vickers 1990). Increasing attention to consumption also derives from work on the rising nineteenth-century middle classes (Blumin 1989; Bushman 1992; Vinovskis 1991), and on the focus of material culture studies on everyday life as well as connoisseurship (Deetz 1977; Larkin 1988; Martin 1993; Schlereth 1989a).

Although definitions of 'consumer society' involve both material environments and mentalities, and linking the two is a common aim among historians whose specific interpretations differ considerably, in practice most writers prioritise one element over the others. The literature exhibits a persistent separation between that defining consumer culture through material objects (substantial populations with disposable income involved in markets for commodities), and that concerned with cultural representations (changes in cultural representations of goods, activities and social identities; consumption practices as skills in use). Historians stressing the early-modern period generally employ the former definition and attempt to identify what people have and how much is accessible to them, while scholars of the nineteenth century have been more concerned with the changing meaning of things, and the promotion of 'drives to consume'.

The persistence of different approaches is reflected in the organisation of this chapter. Section II consists of two parts dealing with (a) involvement in consumption of goods and services, through evidence on ownership and spending, given constraints of availability and wealth; and (b) the meanings of consumer objects, their relationship to more abstract cultural discourses, and connections between social change and discourses of consumption (by which I mean sets of ideas that define relationships between objects' meanings and people's identities). Obviously this separation is artificial: these topics are not merely intimately connected, but mutually constitutive. Section III then discusses work on retailing and consumer cultures, much of which has made an explicit attempt to articulate the accessibility of goods with experiences of desiring and obtaining goods.

HISTORIOGRAPHICAL CHANGE

In the recent historiography of consumption, a central place is occupied by Neil McKendrick (McKendrick 1974; McKendrick, Brewer and Plumb 1982). Much recent work on consumption forms a succession of reactions to McKendrick's ideas. For McKendrick, modern consumption emerges in late-eighteenth-century England as new commercial and industrial wealth accelerated social mobility and, with it, an explosion of competitive and emulative consumption. The upwardly mobile consumed emulatively, whereas existing elites sought novel or differentiating behaviour, thereby fuelling further emulation. An emulative consumer culture eventually diffused from middle-class to working-class consumers when wages rose. Thus, both consumption of particular items and the ideas informing consumption decisions diffused down the social hierarchy. The rapidity of these emulative diffusions distinguished modern consumer societies from earlier instances of fashion mania.

Yet McKendrick's account was largely researched from sources relating to producers and traders, from which it is difficult to identify the new consumers, and how and why their demand changed. As a reviewer observed: 'it would be even more interesting to know . . . how [consumers] perceived and regulated their contribution to the much vaunted home demand. The eighteenth-century home market remains an elusively vague concept' (Earle 1983: 454). McKendrick's account now stands in substantially revised form, consequent upon clarification of the *growth*, *size*, *social depth* and the *range of commodities* involved in the Anglo-American market for consumer goods, and about the mechanisms of cultural change.

On both sides of the Atlantic, McKendrick's late-eighteenth-century birth of consumer society has been replaced by earlier expansion, irregular but incremental, of consumer cultures associated with commercial capitalism (Mukerji 1983; Spufford 1984; Thirsk 1978). Newer, less-Anglocentric approaches exploiting demand-side sources make mass consumption less dependent on factory mass production, and replace emulation with different models of consumer knowledges and practices.

Since the debates described above have directed empirical work and formed a prism through which it has been interpreted, both have changed radically in recent years. At risk of marginalising some pioneering pieces of work, a

167

schematic outline of historiographic change may be summarised quite briefly. For many years, understandings of consumption depended on inferences from sources such as contemporary social commentary (including debates among the educated about the debilitating effects of luxury on the poor, and about sumptuary legislation); from trade statistics (including the volume of tea, sugar or cotton imports); from studies of production and distribution (for example, of publishing, pottery and luxury furniture trades); from material culture (including vernacular housing and museum-based artefactual studies, much dominated by connoisseurship rather than social history).

The 1980s saw a decisive acceleration in the exploitation of demand-side sources, and the study of consumption shifted sharply towards cultural topics. Both quantitative and qualitative research addressed social, geographical and gender patterns in the usage of, and spending on, consumer goods, especially new groceries and durable goods. Processes and spaces of selling received similarly intense attention, particularly through analyses of the impacts of advertising, and of department stores, especially on women. Treatments of material culture and of household function moved beyond connoisseurship to the social history of artefacts. Middling sort and plebeian attitudes to consumer goods received new attention, eclipsing portrayals of consumer attitudes based on social commentary.

In Europe and America, feminist history has been crucial in work on consumption, stressing the functioning of families as economic units, and showing the power of eighteenth-century bourgeois 'separate spheres' discourses, with their consignment of women (and women's consumption) to domesticity (Davidoff and Hall 1987). Later work analysed women's changing positions and powers; clarified how women were both agents and objects of nineteenth-century consumer culture (Hall 1992; Richards 1991); and pioneered the theorising of consumption as pleasure, not mere leisure, and as political, not simply escapist. Connections between the expanding eighteenth-century material world and changes in women's roles clearly involved rather more than the emergence of 'separate spheres'.

For those advocating broader definitions of social history, consumption appears centre-stage amid a more complex process in which political stability was sought and manufactured by an increasingly broad constituency seeking to repair divisive crises in social, intellectual and religious life during the Civil War and Commonwealth (Holmes 1993; Innes 1987; Langford 1989; Plumb 1967; Porter 1992; Speck 1992). On Charles II's Restoration (1660), this broad constituency promoted a culture of order and stability which was decisively consolidated under the Hanoverian kings after 1715. The new polite culture shared by diverse social groups emphasised three themes: security of property; personal propriety; and distancing from 'the lower sort of people'. Gentility in everyday personal conduct established trustworthiness and fitness for social authority. Plumb's 'pursuit of stability' involved aristocratic and gentry sociability in towns, where commercialised elite leisure activities diffused to the urban middling sort. Many writers link the 'pursuit of stability' and commercialised leisure, Borsay speaking of an 'urban renaissance' of newly widespread activities, conducted in a new public world of walks, streets, shopping parades, assembly rooms and other amusement centres, spaces intended for the enjoyment and cultivation of new heterosocial manners (Borsay 1977, 1989; Clark 1984; Holmes and Szechi 1993). Concern with elite pursuit of political stability invites the assumption that emulation dominated consumption behaviour (Borsay 1989; Plumb 1982). But not all historians see the urban middling sort as merely the new culture's salespeople and consumers, passively following upper-class practices. On these accounts, they were adapters not mere adopters, and are to be counted among the creators of consensual cultures, including consumption cultures (Barry 1991; Earle 1989), with obvious implications for McKendrick's chronology. The key point for historians of consumption is the centrality of consumption to lifestyles embodying consensus polite culture: *the forms of culture now seen as dominating town life were essentially there to be purchased by consumers* (Barry 1991: 208).

II A review of the historical literature

THE EXISTENCE AND EXTENT OF MASS MARKETS

The social depth of the market, the range of commodities involved, and the chronology and geography of changing consumption patterns are all fundamental issues in discussing mass consumption, and all are characterised by a wide range of interpretations. However, different aspects of consumption have received uneven attention. More work exists on consumption of durable household goods, new groceries, luxuries, and a growing array of service and leisure activities, than on housing and everyday food and clothing (though see Harte 1991; Mennell 1985; Roche 1989; Shammas 1990). This reflects both the available sources and the prevailing definitions of consumer society. Moreover, some changes are much more visible and dramatic than others in common sources, and impressions of a booming consumer market are undoubtedly enhanced by the many studies of new commodities and the relative scarcity of studies of items whose use was declining.

Use of probate inventories

Prior to the modern era of household expenditure surveys, information on people's involvement with consumer goods, and consumption patterns by gender, age, wealth, status and location, comes mainly from documentation of consumers' possessions, information on purchasing patterns (given the availability of different consumer goods), and from contemporary commentary.

Information on consumers' possessions, especially in England and North America, has been mainly drawn from probate inventories. These were valuations of a deceased's movable property, that is excluding real estate, compiled by administrators of their estate (Moore 1980; Overton 1984). Inventories' potential to illuminate consumption from the consumer side is considerable, at least for durable goods and groceries. Similar documents were compiled in many European countries and in North America, enabling some international comparisons. Inventories are scarce in England before c.1540 and after c.1730, whereas in many European countries and in North America, large numbers of nineteenth- and even twentieth-century probate inventories survive, although many await their historians (Moore 1980; Schuurman 1980; Walsh forthcoming).

However, inventory analyses face technical and interpretative problems. First, coverage of spending is incomplete because inventories exclude real estate, perishable items such as food and drink, and non-material items such as entertainment. Second, inventories record net accumulation – at best an indirect measure of demand, requiring data or models of purchase and depreciation rates for different commodities (de Vries 1993; Glennie forthcoming; Shammas 1993). Third, appraising practices, inventory formats and the detail of recording varied over space and time, which inhibits the interpretation of comparative material (Erickson 1990; Spufford 1990). Fourth, those dying do not represent the whole living population because of life-cycle variations in wealth and property ownership. Life-cycle effects have been explored mainly in North America, reflecting favourable conditions for nominal linkage and the availability of ancillary information (J. T. Main 1985; Main and Main 1988). Fifth, inventories, although surviving in very large numbers, were not compiled for everyone. Their coverage is socially biased (the poor are under-represented everywhere, but unevenly so) and temporally uneven. Patriarchal property laws meant that probate involved mostly men, but only some men, biased towards higher-status groups (Ambler et al. 1987; Horn 1988). In North America where more men were inventoried, the problem is less acute but still present (G. Main 1982). Thus, interpreting ownership patterns requires consideration of how inventoried persons represent the population at large. Since the degree of social bias varies over space and time, casual comparisons of different studies are hazardous.

Two complementary systematic approaches to inventoried consumer goods dominate the literature, respectively addressing total household wealth and its composition, and the spread of new consumer items. The former reflects analysts' interest in wealth accumulation and distribution (Hanson-Jones 1980; Schuurman 1980). The latter focuses on social and cultural differentiation in domestic comfort and amenity. Much work of both types is 'quantitative descriptive' (Carr and Walsh 1988; Main and Main 1988; Pardailhé-Galabrun 1988; Walsh *et al.* 1988; Walsh 1993; Weatherill 1988) or qualitative (Roche 1981; Spufford 1984; Larkin 1988), with comparatively few sophisticated statistical studies (Shammas 1990).

That many analyses of inventories tabulate the changing ownership of consumer goods has led some commentators to deride inventories as incapable of revealing anything of goods' meanings and uses. Whilst inventories certainly need to be integrated with other types of material, such derision ignores the contextual information that inventories provide. First, they show the material combinations in which items appeared: the same item possessed alone, or in conjunction with others, might have radically different meanings. Second, the positions of items within houses hint at the conduct of everyday domestic activities. Third, the ways in which items are described may themselves be revealing about how both owners and appraisers viewed them.

Work on England

The most important overview of British material remains Weatherill's depiction of social and geographical patterns in new consumer goods ownership, 1675–1725, using about 3,000 inventories from eight areas of England (Weatherill 1986a, 1986b, 1988, 1993). Weatherill found a rapid uptake of a block of entirely new household goods among the middling ranks who comprised half the English population in *c.*1675, and two-thirds by mid-eighteenth century in *c.*1750, with sharp social and geographical variations. Many goods were involved: joined furniture (framed beds, chairs and tables, as opposed to trestles and boards); new furniture finishes and upholstery, new fabrics, bed and window curtains, windowglass, ceramics, carpets, pictures, looking glasses, knives and forks, teapots, coffee pots, cups and saucers, drinking glasses, clocks, books, globes, maps, prints, musical instruments, and more. English spending focused on clothing, textiles, metalware, furniture and other cheap consumer goods, rather than luxuries.

Both architectural historians and documentary sources point to changes in structures of domestic space, and the place of material objects therein (Barley 1990; Garrard 1980). In England changing house-plans and room layouts, especially in towns, involved a growing distinction between public and private rooms (Brown 1986; Cruickshank and Burton 1990; Dyer 1981; Priestley *et al.* 1982). Parlours were crucial as specialised spaces for sociability and as locations for novel furnishings and ornaments (Williams 1987).

However, patterns of possessions reflected more than consumer preferences. Geographical variations also reflected the supply networks that made goods available, changing prices, and income constraints among potential consumers. Households' market involvement was strongly shaped by changes in landholding and proletarianisation (de Vries 1993; Hudson 1992; Rule 1992). Only residual variations not explicable in these terms, suggests Weatherill, should be interpreted as differential demand. Nevertheless, consumer goods ownership departed from wealth and status hierarchies: traders owned more than equivalently wealthy (and higher status) gentry and professionals; yeomen farmers were out-consumed by artisans. This prompted Weatherill to suggest that some groups possessed a stronger 'consumption ethic' than others.

Shammas (1990) compared long-run trends in spending patterns, and household wealth and its composition, in England and North America. Shammas' work is important in considering new groceries, such as tobacco, tea, coffee and sugar, as well as durable goods, and in exploring consumption patterns prior to the spread of novel goods. She identifies sharply rising real values of English household possessions during the seventeenth century, and stability thereafter despite the increased accumulation of consumer goods (Shammas 1993). This apparent paradox is explained by the cheapness of many novel goods; by generally falling prices because of increasingly efficient production and distribution; and by cheaper substitutes for established goods. In combination, these trends enabled substantial growth in the volume of possessions, without higher total valuations. Shammas emphasises long-run stability in overall spending patterns: early-modern demand shifts were *within* traditional consumption categories of food, groceries and consumer durables, rather than between them.

Macro-economic indicators also point to a considerable expansion in consumption. Work on trade figures, domestic output, occupational structure, and retailing and services growth, have all indicated persistent growth in many consumer goods sectors of the industrial economy during the sixteenth and seventeenth centuries (Berg 1985). Tobacco, sugar, rum, tea, coffee and chocolate, joined spices, raisins and currants as widely consumed imported groceries, especially where prices fell, with tobacco and sugar 'a constant presence in the lives of a significant number of Englishmen and women before 1700', and tea after 1720 (Goodman 1994; Schivelbusch 1980; Shammas 1993: 182).

In a welcome innovation, given the many factors identified as influences on consumption patterns, Shammas applies multivariate statistical analysis to wealth and consumer durables ownership, finding no significant urban, market or education effects on English domestic possessions once variations in wealth and household size were allowed for (Shammas 1977, 1982, 1990, 1993). However, the empirical base for these explorations is narrow, especially for England, and the comparability of her results uncertain.

Studies of booming consumption of novel consumer goods 1660–1730 urgently require a long-run context, but demand-side early-modernists have largely ignored work on medieval consumption. Neither archaeological evidence for medieval peasant houses (Dyer 1989), nor the earliest probate inventories (before 1550) bear out assertions about earlier material poverty. Weatherill uses no inventories from before 1650, and Shammas only one small sample from Elizabethan Oxfordshire. There is also an awkward gap, explicable only for some countries by lost sources, between work on early-modern and nineteenth-century consumer goods, the latter approached mainly thematically (Briggs 1988).

A particularly controversial issue for English historians has been the social depth of consumer goods markets. Pioneering work envisaged a mass market for modest consumer goods such as clothing accessories, hosiery, chapbooks and knives among 'wage labourers, cottagers and smallholders' from the seventeenth century, partly resulting from economic 'projects' (Spufford 1984; Thirsk 1978). Weatherill (1988) argued that a mass market for durable consumer goods did not extend so far, at least until after 1700. She was sceptical towards claims 'that there was a "mass" market for these kinds of goods, or a humble "consumer society", in the late-seventeenth or early-eighteenth century. There were limits, and those limits were reached at some point between the craftsmen and the small farmers' (Weatherill 1988: 193).

However, Weatherill's database contained just twenty-eight labourers, and much was inferred from wider patterns of ownership and wealth. More broadly-based analyses of labouring households show similarities in the composition of household wealth and house-size for labourers and other men with similar wealth (Glennie forthcoming). Labourers were spending on apparel, linens, pewter, brass and other traditional items. But in terms of new consumer durables, men styled 'labourers' were coming adrift at the bottom of the consumption hierarchy. They differed markedly from the poorest craftsmen and husbandmen in their low possession of even the cheapest novel items: a potential source of social distinction between labourers and many of their neighbours. Possibly, labourers' spending focused disproportionately on non-durable consumption, on tobacco, alcohol and betting at this time: certainly, the situation changed. The goods of John Harpham, labourer of Askham (Nottinghamshire), were valued on 27 April 1782 at a meagre £2. 13s. 6d., which included not only his bedstead and bedding, four joined tables and eight chairs, but also six 'delf' plates, a set of knives and forks and a looking glass, together worth less than two shillings (Glennie forthcoming). While claims that plebeian versions of glassware, tea sets and cutlery were familiar in 'nearly everyone's daily life' from the 1730s seem exaggerated, various durables and groceries were bought by poor households whose income fell short of meeting basic food, clothing and housing needs (Shammas 1990).

In any case, some of the poor could experience new commodities without spending. William and Thomas Cox, farmers at Stanborough

173

(Hertfordshire) in the 1750s, provided meals for labourers harvesting, hay-making, or hoeing turnips. Although including traditional elements like mutton, carrots and beer, over half of the cost went on tea, sugar, coffee, chocolate, sago, biscuits and rum (Glennie forthcoming). Some recipients were employed throughout the year (with annual family wages of about £25), but others were casual seasonal workers.

The sheer irregularity of labouring lives could have a counter-intuitive effect on consumption, depending on the form of wages (Smith 1991). Workers receiving irregular amounts were more likely to purchase consumer goods, including expensive items, than workers receiving the same total annual pay might in frequent small sums. Thus, pocket watches, a key symbol of late-eighteenth-century working men's status (Thompson 1967), frequently attracted those with large wage packets following payment of peak season wages after the harvest, sea voyages, fishing or whaling trips (Styles forthcoming). Court deposition evidence about how stolen money or other cash windfalls were spent also provide revealing catalogues of plebeian consumer longing (Styles 1994).

The considerable second-hand trades (especially for clothes) were crucial for poorer consumers, who bought from specialised second-hand dealers and pawnbrokers, from fences of stolen goods, and in routine, everyday petty dealing amongst themselves (Lemire 1988, 1990, 1991a, 1991b; Styles 1994). There is much evidence that urban labouring people patronised large drapers' shops and similar establishments: these were not exclusive preserves of the well-to-do. Depositions in court cases for theft indicate that the presence in shops of labouring people asking to look at cotton prints or hand-kerchiefs was not considered unusual, nor to demand special vigilance as self-evidently a cover for theft (Abelson 1980; Styles 1994).

Important recent work has reiterated the size and significance of small farming households, who sought to minimise their contact with land and labour markets (Howkins 1994; Neeson 1992). To a degree, some such households also sought to minimise contact with markets for consumer goods, through household provisioning and barter with neighbours (Reed 1991), which qualifies some more sweeping claims about the extent of con-sumer goods markets. On the other hand, goods like tobacco and tea had long since penetrated these worlds. Perhaps the interesting questions to be asked here are about how household strategies involved both barter and elements of consumerism, moving beyond presumptions that one element necessarily excluded the other.

Work on Continental Europe

Among the first systematic uses of inventories to discuss consumption was de Vries' elegant demonstration of substantial changes in 'peasant' demand patterns in Friesland between 1600 and 1800. In the booming Dutch economy, prosperous commercial farmers and tradesmen concentrated their growing expenditure on luxury goods such as gold, silver, books, clocks and paintings (de Vries 1974, 1975).

> Dutch rural demand patterns failed to provide markets for important industrial products. But this failure cannot be accounted for by a stubborn peasant traditionalism. Dutch consumption habits underwent profound changes but not in the 'right' direction for economic development.
>
> (de Vries 1975: 244–245)

While there are few comparable studies for seventeenth-century France, there are indications that French consumption was closer to Dutch than to English experience (Baulant, Schuurman and Servais 1988; Muchembled 1988, 1990). By the mid-eighteenth century, perhaps fifty years later than in England, Parisian markets for a range of new goods were expanding rapidly (Fairchilds 1993a; Roche 1989), but evidence beyond the capital is sketchy at present.

Scope for wider comparisons is presently limited. There is valuable work exploring material culture and consumption in late eighteenth- and nineteenth-century Austria, particularly lower-class consumption of new foods (sugar), consumer durables (watches), clothing and housing (Sandgruber 1982). Much German and Italian work revolves around debates on middle-classes versus aristocratic consumption, and on consumption and fascism (analyses of which entwine with mass culture debates through their emphases on uncritical consumers) (*Risorgimento* 1991; Tierstein 1993).

Work on North America

Colonial North American markets clearly expanded very rapidly owing to a combination of rapid population growth and consumption changes. They were heavily dependent on mother countries for consumer goods, with important consequences for commodity production there (Zahedieh 1994). Although assemblages of consumer goods varied in different areas, several reviewers build on similarities between consumption in New England and the Chesapeake region to postulate a general American consumption history (Carson forthcoming; Shammas 1990; Walsh forthcoming).

Initially, North American consumption was socially undifferentiated, except in scale. Before 1700, even elite households focused their consumption on traditional categories of goods. Aside from precious metals, and better quality furniture, the daily material world of the rich resembled that of the poor. Socially, seventeenth-century material culture was remarkable for its sameness (Bushman 1992; Martin 1993; Walsh 1993). Social differentiation became much more obvious after 1700. Elites adopted distinctive luxury lifestyles, following English models, with material props, including japanned furniture, teaware, elaborate looking-glasses, and formal dining equipment, whose character was nicely caught by the common descriptive term, 'elegancies'. American elite houses underwent changes of scale and plan, being increasingly organised for formal entertainment. 'Practical everyday functions gave way to relatively infrequent occurrences of primarily symbolic significance ... the occasions of formal entertainment when the gentry achieved its climactic expression' (Bushman 1992: 121; Kasson 1990).

Simultaneously, middling American consumers expanded their consumption but in another direction, by increasing spending on traditional consumption goods. A sea-change in middling consumption, with a proliferation of the new items, was delayed until after 1730, and middling Americans lagged well behind their English counterparts. Thereafter change was swift. 'Even on the rude frontier of eighteenth-century Kentucky, a remarkably sophisticated, international pattern of consumption laid a cultural basis for American life' (Perkins 1991: 499). The late-eighteenth-century Philadelphia poor spent on rum, burials, smallpox vaccinations and other items, despite shortfalls in daily necessities, as they 'dined like prisoners, dressed in the same fashion as almshouse inmates', crowded into cramped quarters, and went without essential clothing and fuel (Smith 1991). Store ledgers testify that some of the most meagrely inventoried consumers bought tea, sugar and haberdashery. American frontier consumers included black slaves. At a Louisville Kentucky store in 1794–1795 one 'Jack' bought goods including tea, buckles, velvet, thread, shoes and a hat (Perkins 1991).

A single consumer revolution?

North American commentators commonly consider English and colonial consumption changes as a single process, occurring at different speeds in different places. (Note Shammas' singular *Pre-Industrial Consumer in England and America*.) They portray England and colonial America as at different stages of similar journeys, beginning with expansion in traditional areas of consumption, followed by growing consumption of novel items, and the social and geographical diffusion of new consumption habits. They stress similarities among North American, British and some European literatures, with variations only in scope and timing (Bushman 1992; Carson 1994; Martin 1993; Walsh forthcoming). A similar point has been made about France and New France (Dechêne 1992). Acceptance of such claims is premature without more detailed discussion of both patterns of material possessions (are the patterns as similar as has been asserted?), and whether differing patterns of possessions resulted simply from variations in chronology and population composition, or from differing consumption processes.

Consumer goods, consumer knowledges and aspirations

All the literatures surveyed examine relationships between possessions and consumer culture for aristocratic and middle-class consumers rather than poorer consumers, and typically treat the development of consumption discourses as subsequent to the experience of goods. Thus Fine and Leopold (1990) properly criticise McKendrick's argument, that domestic servants' imitation of employers was at the forefront of mass consumption, since servants' pay was insufficient. But they simply assume that servants' lack of means precluded them from holding sophisticated ideas about various consumer goods. Likewise, Richards (1991) argues that poorer nineteenth-century consumers responded to advertising and emulated middle-class consumer culture because of their limited prior experience with consumer goods.

It seems clear however that, notwithstanding the importance of ability to purchase goods, feelings for consumer goods co-existed with minimum material comfort and social standing (Tierstein 1993). The comparative economic insignificance of labouring-class consumption conceals the existence and development of strong working-class discourses about consumption and social interaction. Moreover there were qualitative differences among the consumption discourses of different classes (Johnson 1988; Thrift and Glennie 1993; Williams 1987). Possibly, material sparsity intensified the personal meanings of particular items compared with richer consumers. Clothing was highly nuanced, central to self-identity, for the poor, notwithstanding their limited wardrobes. Clothing was central to eighteenth-century newspaper advertisements' descriptions of runaway slaves, labourers, servants and criminals (Prude 1991; Styles 1989, forthcoming). Through clothes, labourers 'purposefully and self-consciously shaped their appearance . . . visually asserted their own intentions and identities. . . . to announce their own priorities and purposes . . . common folk knew fashion . . . palpable evidence that laborers had their own needs and desires' (Prude 1991: 126, 154, 155).

When incomes rose, working-class consumption decisions stemmed from consumption cultures formed within low-income contexts, and middle-class incomprehension of impoverished families' spending reflects their insensitivity regarding the social dimensions of working-class consumption behaviour, and its differing consumption discourses (Johnson 1988). That middling Americans read odd blendings of clothes (such as stylish hats with old jackets) as flippant and as mocking the co-ordinated apparel of gentility indicates their ignorance of syncretist and hybrid discourses of smartness, also exemplified in the use of elements of African dress traditions by freed slaves (Prude 1991).

The suggestion here is that widespread cultures of consumption very nearly always preceded mass markets for consumer goods rather than the other way about. This possibility obviously raises several issues about interpreting patterns of ownership and consumption of various goods. It also, equally obviously, increases the importance of explorations of the meanings of consumer goods for their users in the past, not least in avoiding assumptions that consumption was motivated by emulation, and it is to this that I now turn.

THE MEANINGS, SIGNIFICANCE AND IMPERATIVES OF CONSUMPTION

Cultural meanings and social functions of goods

Consumer goods' meanings could be shaped over a potentially long life, not merely the moment of purchase, raising questions of motivation and the qualitative aspects of desirability. Obviously, qualitative shifts or variations in meanings need not be tied to quantitative shifts or variations in ownership. For example, gender differences in inventoried consumer durables may have been small (Weatherill 1986b), but the critical questions involve what goods *meant* to women compared to men.

Attempts to understand objects' symbolic meanings for their users constantly encounter tensions between goods' cultural meanings and their social functions. In practice, most studies prioritise one or other dimension. Consumption discourses were powerfully constitutive of social structures, through both consensus and division. Material culture invested with new meanings linked social characterisation to everyday cultural practices, through consumer goods' ability to express wealth (through accumulation of goods); social standing (through differentiation in possessions); and cultural position (where particular possessions 'flagged' certain cultural discourses).

Where changing consumption patterns and consumer mentalities are discussed together, historians often draw on single general treatments. For example, Weatherill (1988) uses Goffman's distinction between public 'front' and private 'back' behaviour in concluding that, since new purchases were concentrated in 'front region' parlours and main chambers, the dominant motive for increased consumption was display. Several studies of particular consumption sectors draw on Elias' *The Civilising Process* (Mennell 1985, 1989), and studies of nineteenth-century consumption draw particularly on Simmel and Marx. However, much of this work tends to reduce goods' symbolic meanings to their social functions.

Others emphasise consumption as pleasure-seeking rather than emulation, and a means of shaping self-image for oneself rather than to impress others (Campbell 1987; Earle 1989). Most recently, Campbell (1993) develops the notion of 'character confirming conduct', in which people monitored and evaluated their own consumption and conduct using character ideals such as the aristocrat, the dandy and the romantic. Whether people did draw on a common stock of images (or whether this assumption simply allows images to be taken from literature and social commentary rather than primary research), and whether their monitoring was as intellectual as Campbell claims, are currently under debate (Glennie and Thrift 1995b). Not least, ideas about 'the individual' were changing, and there are parallels between some discussions of consumer identities, and Abercrombie, Hill and Turner's (1986) distinction between individual*ism* (the autonomy of individuals in relation to society) and individual*ity* (the cultivation of consciousness, will and personal identity, and its recognition in other people).

Studies of meanings and discourses of consumption

Given that accounts of cultural mentalities based on contemporary commentary reflect pervasive social–political discourses (Campbell 1993; Sekora 1977; Styles 1994), several studies of how specific objects and activities were perceived, utilised and projected have used diaries, correspondence and similar materials. They aim to uncover how objects' meanings were produced in different cultural settings and over time; how meanings invested in consumer goods compared with those of heirlooms, home-produced artefacts, and gifts; and how goods were used as props in public life and in intra-household actions, especially where these practices were not explicitly discussed.

The lessons and implications emerging from such studies are complex. Consumption did not depend on unthinking emulation. Goods usually had multiple meanings, frequently combining utilitarian, ornamental and private associations, and these meanings connected to notions of identity and social ideology. Divisions between private use and public display were far from clear-cut. There were many different vocabularies of luxury and longing through which objects were imbued with sentimental associations by their history, or their incorporation in ethics of collecting or curatorship. Meanings and uses were ascribed to objects as they were incorporated into practices, which might be ritualised or spontaneous, and whose character changed over time. Interpretations of conduct were inconsistent, and depended on existing personal and social relationships with the people involved (Vickery 1993; Whitbread 1988).

Women, in particular, used consumer goods both to establish their families' abstract attributes (status, lineage), much as men used land, and to recognise and negotiate personal qualities of taste, sociability and worth (Vickery 1993; Whitbread 1988). Their wills consistently reveal a self-conscious, emotional involvement in household goods, clothing and personal effects. Such intensity of meaning appears only occasionally among men, and is largely restricted to guns and animals.

179

The meanings of consumer objects were grasped through language deriving from many cultural discourses, addressing behaviour through abstract concepts such as luxury, comfort, self-sufficiency, prudence, restraint, hospitality, novelty, elegance, lineage, gentility, refinement, solidity, respectability, sociability and cleanliness. These discourses varied in their explicit concern with accumulation or differentiating consumption, and their association with particular 'marker' commodities. Discourses of domestic comfort and sufficiency were long-standing and widespread, as were newer discourses of novelty and accumulation. Differentiation-focused discourses were more restricted, but spreading. Discourses had diverse origins, diverse implications for consumption, and were themselves partly constituted by consumption behaviour. They became combined into broader complexes, varying socially and regionally.

The same goods might have very different meanings for different consumers. Consumer goods were acquired piecemeal, in a long series of *ad hoc* spending decisions, and mere ownership, especially in small numbers, did not imply adherence to associated discourses (Martin 1993). Initially, middling people's occasional amenities were small tokens, not symptoms of an incipient refined lifestyle: 'gentility flecked lives without coloring them' (Bushman 1992: xii). When tea spread to working-class diets, the practice of tea-drinking changed, dropping most ceremonial and mannered aspects for more utilitarian considerations of caffeine and sugar stimulation (Mintz 1985, 1993).

Several new consumer items, including tobacco and new beverages, were associated with new social practices, of varying formality (Schivelbusch 1980). *All* novel goods by virtue of their unfamiliarity offered consumers a lot of interpretative scope, and novelty became an important end in itself. Developing consumption discourses prized novelty as itself a source of pleasure: 'the kind of receptiveness to visual novelty and differentiation usually associated with the Victorian middle classes was already present at relatively humble levels of the domestic market from the late-seventeenth century' (Styles 1993: 540). Even as they developed, discourses about novelty were extended from exotic items to familiar materials and non-luxury goods, including textiles, leather goods, wooden furniture and metalwares (Kusamitsu 1991). That goods offered novelty became a prime consideration for merchants, producers and shopkeepers, who stressed novelty in motifs, design or manufacturing techniques, as well as in a good's materials and function (Styles 1988). Similar decoration or design principles could span several physical media, exemplified by Orientalism (Mukerji 1983).

Inevitably, various consumption discourses interacted and changed over time in relation to commodities or consumption practices. As goods became familiar, discourses of novelty became less relevant: goods' meanings depended more on other consumption discourses, and became more rigid.

In turn, maintaining sensations of novelty through consumption necessitated the pursuit of new unfamiliar commodities (Campbell 1987). Thus, novelty-prioritising consumption discourses impelled fashion, and promoted diffusions of new goods, giving an illusion of emulative behaviour. McKendrick's argument that novelty depended on fashion as a differentiating response to emulation, is inverted. As consumption discourses became more rigid, notions of behaviour became more normative to class and gender positions, with increasingly formal instruction on behaviour in nineteenth-century etiquette and behavioural manuals (Kasson 1990).

Similarly, consumption of elegancies by middling Americans in the 1740s cannot be seen as emulation-driven. Middling American consumers acquired only some types of available elegancies in a deliberate, selective fashion (Main 1989, Walsh *et al.* 1988). But neither can it be seen as novelty-driven: by 1750 elegancies had long been in shops and were an established part of middling consumer knowledges. Elegancies and novel experience were by now much less closely entwined than they had been for middling English consumers or elite Americans before 1700. Moreover, the *language* of elegancies had changed. Consumption that connoted novelty and adventurousness in 1690 was by 1750 remarkable chiefly for its conservative respectability, and such goods' meanings centred on social standing and solidity.

It is debatable, therefore, whether English, European and North American consumer societies were at different stages of a common journey. There were dissimilarities not just in chronologies of consumption, but in the dominant meanings of consumption processes. American middling consumption in 1750 was not simply a lagged version of English middling consumption in 1700, but drew on particular North American consumer discourses, mainly stressing comfort, surplus and accumulation, rather than novelty differentiation and informed taste (Walsh forthcoming), reinforced by socially selective migration from Europe, and by features of American industrial organisation (Fischer 1989; Styles 1993; Zahedieh 1994).

Accommodating consumption

Nevertheless, all nascent capitalisms in the early-modern West did experience increasing tensions between increasing commodification, and discourses about consumption's destructive moral and corrosive social effects. Consumption contended with several other cultural systems in ascribing meanings to actions and objects. Dilemmas about consumption and social stability characterised middling-sort society in England, France, the Netherlands, Germany and Austria, and North America. In each case, consumption was made morally legitimate through notions of responsible consumption, which defined socially appropriate styles, timings and settings for consumption, and were inflected particularly through moralising about women's roles.

Consumption discourses absorbed and neutralised a series of critiques of consumption as an activity. Thus critiques of *luxury* were turned into critiques of waste, and an accommodation of consumption disciplined by taste (Sekora 1977). Discourses of Republican *equality*, central to independent national identity in the United States after the Colonial War (Breen 1988, 1993), were also (ironically) accommodated by ideologies of 'refined' behaviour (Bushman 1992). Evangelical doubts about *materialism* were largely neutralised through the linking of consumption to discourses of the family, domesticity and godliness (drawing heavily on developing discourses of female purity), and to discourses of self-help in which the poor's willingness and ability to work hard earned them rights to consume, thus mutually enhancing consumption and capitalist production (Schama 1987, 1989). All in all, the adaptation and interweaving of discourses of consumption and morality ensured that society 'could have its material cake and eat it morally too' (Barker-Benfield 1992: xviii), to be <u>Polite *and* Commercial People</u> (Langford 1989).

The profusion of new consumer goods was intimately associated with new sensibilities and new social taxonomies, with consumption providing cultural orientation. For example, Bushman (1992) discusses *refinement* as a system of gentility, bodily restraint, and regard for feelings, involving beautification, self-fashioning, social behaviour, and built and cultural environments. Barker-Benfield (1992) defines sensibility as a psycho-perceptual scheme in which individual consciousness possessed an acute sensual receptiveness to inner feelings and the outside environment. Refinement and sensibility depended on a cultivated capacity for spiritual and moral self-fashioning: neither simply reflected social class.

The middle classes' deliverance from the suffering of those whom Defoe thought 'fare hard' and 'really pinch and suffer want', was essential for refinement and sensibility (Barker-Benfield 1992; Earle 1989; Bushman 1992). A sharply increased awareness of how one's appearance, speech, deportment and property appeared to others was central to refinement, with the corollary of increasingly judgemental views about others' appearances. The same features that enabled association provided standards for exclusion (and such boundary markers and their meanings could change over time). Both concepts were highly gendered. Women's domestic roles gave them authority over the relations of new objects to human activities in the home, creating discourses of domesticity highly susceptible to marketing of durables (Strasser 1982; Miller 1991). 'Cultural change was generated privately as well as in . . . public institutions' (Barker-Benfield 1992: xxv).

Moreover, the accelerating social extension of genteel culture after 1790 transmuted into a diffuse and fragmentary form of refinement rather than a coherent lifestyle, that Bushman terms 'vernacular gentility'. This was not unthinking mimicry. When components were detached from one system of refinement, their meanings became more open for incorporation into new consumers' own interpretations. For example, the characteristic Victorian desire for large numbers of refined objects constituted 'tasteful' room decoration very differently from gentry refinement. Likewise, new sensibilities among poorer eighteenth-century Parisians were not complete replacements of older views, but evolving hybrids in which 'dull custom and archaism, novelty and modernity were combined' (Roche 1981, 1987: 126).

Overall, contemporaries experienced refinement as a complex and internally contradictory process. This ambivalence, and the mutual exchanges and compromises among discourses of consumption and anti-consumption, gave such discourses their dynamic and shifting character. The flexibility of cultural-social discursive terms like 'refinement', 'taste' and 'sensibility' enabled a continuous struggle over their meanings. Flexibility and improvisation in consumers' adaptations of emblems of refinement explain why some regard the spread of parlour culture as a democratic movement: refined 'taste' could empower bourgeois groups as a source of everyday cultural authority (Bushman 1992).

Similar tensions existed beyond the Anglo-American empire, most clearly described in *The Embarrassment of Riches* between Dutch commercial prosperity and material abundance, and Calvinist discipline against extravagance and avarice (Schama 1987; Schuurman 1989; Sutton 1984). Here too, definitions of extravagance were reworked. Dutch culture endorsed accumulation and display within the private home, but avoided ostentatious display in publicly visible architecture and clothing. Schama also notes the centrality of sensibility and women in creating new domestic environments. Similar themes emerge from writing on eighteenth-century Paris: bourgeois tension between consumption and sensibility (Roche 1981; Schama 1987); growing emphasis on appearances, clothing, manners and hygiene as indicative of moral standing (Roche 1981, 1989; Vigarello 1989).

In Germany and Austria, too, middle-class ambivalence about commercial culture and consumerism sustained debates on luxury (Breckman 1991); consumption discourses were intertwined with changing ideals of domestic femininity (Tierstein 1993); and, later, distinctive patterns of consumption were central to white-collar households' construction of a sense of their distinct class identity (Coyner 1977).

International differences in relations among sensibilities, social taxonomies and consumer cultures, remain an important research area. Differences there certainly were, for example the English association of sentimentality with piety, compared with French sentimentality's association with secularism (Langford 1989; Barker-Benfield 1992; Schama 1989). Contrasting mentalities have been described for readers of early popular fiction, pamphlets and almanacs, with English society less subservient, more aware of the possibilities of upward social movement, and more liable to ridicule its 'betters' than the French (Capp 1979; Spufford 1981).

Much remains to be done on international and regional differences in relations between consumption and moralities, not least in evaluating whether international similarities reflect the diffusion of ideas, or several independent developments. Schematic international comparisons inevitably homogenise regional differences, and some stress that both gentry refinement and vernacular refinement took many very different forms in North America (Jaffee 1993: 398). The fragmentary and locally constructed nature of vernacular gentility must have made regional variations almost inevitable (Bushman 1986).

Migration and consumption

Most case-studies of consumption are place-based, although many accounts of changing consumer cultures emphasise the movement of commodities, ideas and people. Several studies of migration to North America have discussed migrants' motives (Anderson 1991; Cressy 1987), and have suggested longstanding regional variations in 'consumption folkways' which can be traced directly to specific migration periods and sources (Fischer 1989, but see Greene *et al.* 1991). However, only Horn (1988) explicitly compares possessions and spending of migrants' home and destination areas. From a very early date, migration to North America was associated with scope for material abundance as well as with religious liberty. In the nineteenth century, this vision of consumer abundance became ever stronger, and has generated the most substantial study of migrants and consumption.

Late-nineteenth- and early-twentieth-century Jewish migrants from Eastern Europe to the United States moved from a world of scarcity to one of abundance. Ordinary Americans possessed items restricted to small affluent minorities in many East European countries. Indeed, migrants to America 'could gain a sense of social membership more quickly as consumers than as workers' (Heinze 1990: 219), and mass consumption was a component of Jewish acculturation there. Heinze argues for a distinctive response among Jews compared with other European immigrants.

However, their goal of establishment in American society clashed with the preservation of a respectful relationship to God, hitherto achieved partly through the highly selective use of luxuries on religious holidays (especially significant in the poorest communities). With luxuries becoming everyday items, luxury objects lost this spiritual specificity, and Jewish attitudes towards luxuries changed. In constructing a distinctively American-Jewish identity, abundance was selectively focused on the important holidays of Succoth, Chanukah and Passover, within a more general incorporation of abundance into everyday life. The new secular luxury revolved around summer family holidays and equipment for domestic leisure (such as parlour pianos), reinforced traditional ideals of family life, and conveyed a version of North American refinement. Creating elements of a new cultural identity with consumer goods, Jews showed great resourcefulness in using consumer goods as emblems of secular adjustment and progress. By 1890, national advertisers viewed Jewish communities as a distinct market, susceptible to specific campaigns that integrated Jewish values, claims for American product superiority, and the importance of purposeful leisure.

The specific responses of groups other than the Jews remains to be studied, but presumably varied with their motivations to assimilate; their comprehension of American culture; the domesticity of their social life; the extent to which they migrated as families; and their specific attitudes to luxury and abundance as such.

III   Case study

DEPARTMENT STORES AND CONSUMER CULTURE

Diagnoses of fundamental transformations in consumers' experiences of objects after about 1850 identify department stores and mass advertising as central to an 'epochal . . . reorganisation of cultural meaning' (Lears 1989), establishing consumer durables and cultural creation of demand at the heart of twentieth-century Western culture. Department stores were pivotal sites of cultural appropriation and identity construction, through their ability to create the meanings of commodities and consumers.

Department stores naturalised everyday encounters with consumer goods through three intertwined processes. First, by making selling more efficient and controlled for retailers, who instilled knowledge and skills among consumers through demonstrations and specialist shopstaff (Fraser 1981; Laermans 1993; Miller 1981). Second, by innovatively displaying commodities as spectacle, with goods and promotional images used to construct fantasy milieux or even paradisaical character (Williams 1982). Contemporary novelists, including Dreiser (*Sister Carrie*) and Zola (*Le Bon Marché*), perceived an astonishing and powerful transformation as consumers were seduced by big city urban department stores (Blomley 1995; Bowlby 1985; Miller 1981; Schudson 1984; Williams 1982). The spectacular representation of commodities defined marketing as image-making, and connected with other spectacular representations of commodities such as exhibitions (Breckenridge 1989; Mitchell 1989). Consumption was increasingly *the* sphere in which national, class and gender identities were negotiated and articulated among the middle classes (Richards 1991).

Finally, department stores were gendered spaces. They constituted a new public sphere for women, in which bourgeois women could function as consumers (Laermans 1993; Leach 1984; Miller 1981; Williams 1982). Sensitivity to gendered spaces was highly significant because of the power of bourgeois discourses dividing the social world into 'separate spheres': a masculine public-political sphere; and a feminine (though still patriarchal) domestic-private sphere. Separate spheres discourses intensified in the eighteenth and nineteenth centuries, influenced by political economy and Christianity, to become a central component of Western middle-class identity (Davidoff and Hall 1987), and to influence plebeian culture (Hall 1992). The price of women's domestic respectability was a denial of women's competence in negotiating public space, in which women were cast as unknowledgeable and unskilled. As spaces designed specifically for women, department stores brought order to the potential chaos of women customers, and stores became a safe public arena. Like the promenade (Scobey 1992), stores opened 'the public' safely to women without threatening men's public power.

The extent of a sea-change in historians' attitudes, in under twenty years, may be gauged from Willan's comment that 'the big department store . . . is only the village store writ large' (Willan 1976: 63) is nigh on unthinkable today! However, it is striking that early department stores (around 1850) were mainly in France and North America, only appearing in England, the most prosperous consumer society in the early-modern world, considerably later (Fraser 1981). Why was this, if department stores were so integral to modern consumption? How did goods of distant origin or novel character reach early-modern consumers? That accounts treating department stores as central to transformations in consumption require qualification is suggested by at least six lines of work.

First, take work on earlier retailing and consumption, topics treated very sketchily by most writers on department stores. Important literatures are developing on the sheer numbers and variety of shops in pre-modern and early-modern times (Fairchilds 1993a, 1993b; Mui and Mui 1989; Shammas 1990; Styles 1993). Scores of thousands of retail shops were very widely distributed throughout the eighteenth-century English countryside, with specialist shopkeepers in even the smallest towns. The association of shopping locales and leisure activities was very widespread, certainly not confined to London and resorts such as Bath, and was patronised by a wide social range (Borsay 1989, 1990; McInnes 1990; Willan 1976). Village shopkeepers' accounts testify to the social depth of the market, and their small customer hinterland is indicative of the dense geographical distribution of shops. Local studies show the proliferation of shops as a long drawn-out process (Buck 1991; Mitchell 1981, 1984; Pennington and Sleights 1991).

The proliferation of small shops reflects growing consumption of exotic groceries, such as sugar, tea, tobacco, currants, raisins, spices, some new fabrics and clothing accessories, which were specific to shops. However, shops' viability depended on their also selling familiar commodities such as cloth and candles. Shops increasingly dominated open markets in supplying household goods. The density of English markets never approached its medieval level (Britnell 1993; Chartres 1990). Even village shops drew on a huge geographical range of import, wholesale and producer suppliers (Willan 1970; Braudel 1981, vol. 2). Similar observations have been made for North America, notwithstanding a less dense distribution of shops there (Larkin 1988; Martin 1993; Perkins 1991; Schlereth 1989b). Outside the towns, country stores and taverns played a key role (Farmer 1988; Thorp 1991).

Moreover, earlier shops were far from small, drab, unchanging places. Like department stores, early-modern shops experienced tensions between customer service and efficiency, and reshapings of shop spaces anticipated some features of department stores. Topographical and architectural sources indicate that, although shops varied enormously in specialism, stock and layout, the broad chronology of changing shop exteriors seems common to most large towns, reflecting glass-making technology, falling taxes on sheet glass, and general ideas about display (Fawcett 1990; Girouard 1990). Even small town shops in seventeenth-century England (and on the eighteenth-century American frontier), were commonly fitted out with display windows, display shelves, glass cupboards, counters and shopboards, candles and mirrors for internal lighting, and seating for customers (Buck 1991; Glennie and Whyte forthcoming; Glennie and Thrift 1995b; Pennington and Sleights 1991; Perkins 1991).

Second, the concentration on department stores and shops marginalises other channels through which goods were acquired. Consumers of most social strata acquired goods from vendors in open markets and fairs, directly from artisan producers, or from hawkers, chapmen and peddlers, not to mention through non-market exchange. Very many poorer consumers drew on the huge second-hand trades in clothing, household, farm and trade items (Cox and Cox 1985–86; Lemire 1988, 1991a, 1991b; Styles 1994; Woodward 1985). Although historians of each particular channel of goods tend to downplay the significance of others, it is clear that none of these channels was entirely conservative and residual.

For some new consumer goods, chapmen and peddlers were important distribution channels, more dynamic than storekeepers, geographically in advance of the spatial frontier of shopkeeping, and the agents of artisan entrepreneurs producing much more standardised products (Jaffee 1991; Spufford 1984).

> Peddlers and consumers could both share in the self-fashioning of new identities through the exchange of goods that facilitated the democratization of gentility and the fluidity of social identities that

marked this era. . . . [Peddlers] brought the message as well as the means of personal mobility.

(Jaffee 1991: 513, 523)

It is especially noteworthy that door-to-door peddlers interacted particularly with women since women were pivotal consumers within the household. Thus habituation to consumer goods did not necessarily depend on shops, never mind department stores.

Third, much work stresses early-modern shopping's interactive and social nature, drawing on business records; personal and household accounts; criminal court depositions; topographies, journeys, poems, plays and letters. In the absence of advertising, popular knowledge derived heavily from seeing goods, both in shops and in everyday use, and through conversation with shopstaff and with other potential consumers. Shopkeepers and others provided information about goods and their use in 'polite' commodity culture. This information was not disinterested, and consumers were neither uncritical nor passive in receiving it. Consumers developed their own senses of what things meant, commonly going into shops to look at, touch and talk about goods. Shops were just one of several everyday social spaces in which people learned about commodities, styles and their uses and meanings, and where people deployed their understanding. Diaries and shopmen's manuals suggest that the nature of goods, and their appropriateness for particular people or purposes, were not exclusively intellectual considerations, but were at least partly intuitive based on practical experience of people's conduct. Women were prominent in these processes: their involvement in shopping, consuming and actively discussing consumption did not await the first stores.

Similar points have been made for North America as well as England, and with respect to mail order catalogues as well as shops. Shopping was a form of entertainment, offering frontier settlers 'an exciting glimpse of the outside world . . . consumer goods from around the world titillated the senses and fired the imagination' (Perkins 1991: 503). American rural consumers read and interpreted catalogues in their own ways (Purser 1992). Other historical work similarly views 'consumers' as active participants, in the visual characterisation of objects and people (Corfield 1990); and in studies of popular participation in urban pageantry (Klein 1992) and coronation celebrations (Tresidder 1992). Since department store narratives understate the social nature of shopping and consumption practices, and posit consumers for whom the meanings of objects are constituted individually and intellectually, consumers' sociality and their capacities to engage in self-reflection and to develop their own interpretations of goods are all downplayed (Glennie and Thrift 1992, 1995a, 1995b). And in the nineteenth and twentieth centuries, there were other important ideas about the social dimensions of consumption, including consumer cooperation (Furlough 1991; Purvis 1990).

Fourth, if one generation of feminist historians highlighted the power of separate spheres arguments in bourgeois social thought, their successors have pointed to the limitations of separate spheres as an analytical framework (Vickery 1993b; Willen 1992). Universalising middle-class experience obscures class specificities in the gendering of consumption, marginalises working women's other activities outside the home, and obscures intermediate, liminal spaces (Hall 1992; Stansell 1987). Not least, women played important roles in early-modern shops, although this narrowed after about 1750, with intensifying 'separate spheres' discourses, and the rise of professional shopmen in larger establishments (Buck 1991; Styles forthcoming; Weatherill 1988).

Fifth, much work on semiotics of advertising and spectacle has not considered signs and symbols beyond advertising itself. Thus Richards (1991) avoids the issue of the creation outside the advertising of signs and symbols used in advertising, and their rooting in private and public social relationships among people and goods in use, beyond instants of purchase and representation in advertisements. Yet both printed images and popular cultures surrounding mass printed images had changed much in the century before 1851. For example, P. Anderson (1991) traces the growth of sensation in the emergent culture of 'mass' pictorial magazines. Such studies militate against Richards' treatment of consumers of the popular as inert and inexperienced in dealing with visual images.

Finally, department stores themselves were very varied in their locations, layouts, sales force organisation, and interaction among managers, store workers and customers, all of which had implications for the shopping practices of different clienteles (Benson 1986; Lawrence 1992; Miller 1991; Reekie 1992; Strasser 1989). Recent commentators emphasise that, in seeking to shape everyday discourses of consumption, department stores often adapted older practices to new commercial settings (Tierstein 1993). M. B. Miller's (1981) and R. H. Williams' (1982) stresses on continuities in paternalist work organisation, in selling, and on the diversity of French middle-class consumer cultures, were neglected compared with their discussions of stores' dynamic and innovative features.

Taken together, recognition of the dynamism of earlier retail environments; the extent of consumers' pre-existing skills, in both shopping and encountering visual images; and the sophistication of earlier consumption cultures blurs distinctions between department stores and earlier shops. Consequently, this literature may enable a closer specification of exactly which aspects of experiences of acquisition changed for which consumers. Department stores may have been most important where consumer cultures were comparatively narrow and shallow by the mid-nineteenth century, both directly and through their impact on other shops (Nord 1986).

189

More broadly, these books draw attention to consumers' own practices and knowledge at the expense of advertising images, as sources of the meanings of objects. They qualify hyperbolic accounts of the marketplace as the determinant site for constructing the meanings of consumer goods, and the identities of consumers. This is not to propose a solely demand-focused approach, but it is to emphasise that producers and consumers collaborated in creating meaning systems to make sense of new objects. Linked to accounts of how the meanings of commodities were formed throughout periods of use, rather than in moments of buying, they move the debate towards greater integration of manipulationist and voluntarist accounts of consumer culture.

CONCLUDING COMMENTS

Defined through the presence of socially extensive markets for consumer durables, widespread consumer responsiveness to new products, and active discourses about meanings of consumption, mass consumption neither emerged during industrialisation nor depended on 'mass culture' consumption processes. Neither Whiggish assumptions of progressive, unidirectional change nor accounts of one-off transformations from 'primitive' to 'modern' consumption can be sustained. Even so, much about consumption patterns and consumption processes in the past, especially before the nineteenth century, remains obscure.

Several specific issues are prominent in a research agenda. We know too little about why particular things became desirable whereas others did not. On this topic, we require closer integration of documentary evidence and interpretation of the forms and materials of artefacts. We need to know more about the sources, other than advertising, of consumer knowledge and practices, and about how consumer goods entered people's lives. When Brewer and Porter argue that 'remove knowledge, publicity and advertising, and the itch to consume does not merely subside; as a *mentalité*, it becomes unthinkable' (1993: 6), they highlight lacunae in our apprehension of early consumer knowledge. More generally, work is required, at all levels of the market, on links between changes in overall spending patterns and in the possession of particular items. Both need to be linked to the history of prices, in order to distinguish novel attitudes from simple changes in economic circumstances (de Vries 1993; Shammas 1993). Finally, overall understanding of consumption choices requires serious studies of consumer goods that were going out of use, or being used more narrowly: studies of expanding consumption sectors alone cannot provide an overall picture.

Four more general conclusions may also be offered. First, the changing historiography of consumption shows the disabling effect of binary divisions between supply *or* demand in explaining consumption patterns; between material *or* attitudinal approaches to consumer culture; between public (social) *or* private (cultural) spheres in consumer identities; between 'vertical' (systems of provision) *or* 'horizontal' (identity) approaches to analysing commodity meanings. Second, while certain themes appear ubiquitous (including the existence of tensions between middle-class and aristocratic consumption; the importance of consumption for middling-sort identities; debates on luxury and the masses; and the impact of mass production and advertising), these parallels have thus far swamped perceptions of more nuanced contrasts. Yet practices among producers, distributors, retailers and consumers varied geographically, as did the meanings attaching to particular goods. We need work addressing consumer cultures in various political, economic and cultural settings, comparable to recent reassessments of once axiomatic cultural and religious dimensions to literacy patterns (Goody 1987; Spufford forthcoming). Third, there is the danger of detaching consumption behaviour from everyday life, and of attributing too much autonomy to culture from economic, political and social contexts. Explicitly comparative studies are also required to clarify 'consumers' in relation to other senses of identity, such as family, land, community and custom, party, spiritual faith and nationality (Brewer and Porter 1993; Tierstein 1993). Fourth, the argument that Western cultural processes have been distinctive, and constitute a unique consumption history is currently an act of faith. We cannot point to much work on other societies before the late-nineteenth century. Where we can, as in Clunas' account of Wen Zhenheng's late-Ming *Superfluous Things* (*c.* 1620), there appear both striking contrasts and striking parallels in discussions of material culture, market relations, and social status and relationships (Clunas 1991).

Finally, and for a wider constituency, there is a sense in which histories of consumption themselves become consumer objects, as books, exhibitions, television, radio and video productions, and as historical and heritage sites. As consumer objects, histories of consumption play a part in the constitution of identity through images of tradition, everyday life, family and nationality. So does the heritage marketing of very many commodities including food, clothing, furniture, textiles, household decorations, ornaments and games. Here, histories of consumption matter for more than an academic audience. For a popular audience, histories of consumption and the consumption of history have become closely intertwined.

REFERENCES

Abelson, E. S. (1980) *When Ladies Go A-Thieving: Middle-Class Shoplifters in the Victorian Department Store*, New York: Oxford University Press.

Abercombie, N., Hill, S. and Turner, B. S. (1986) *Sovereign Individuals of Capitalism*, London: Allen and Unwin.

Ambler, R. W., Watkinson, B. and Watkinson, L. (eds) (1987) *Farmers and Fishermen: The Probate Inventories of Clee, South Humberside 1536–1742*, Hull: University of Hull.

Anderson, P. (1991) *The Printed Image and the Transformation of Popular Culture 1790–1860*, Oxford: Clarendon Press.

Anderson, V. D. (1991) *New England's Generation: The Great Migration and the Formation of Society and Culture in the Seventeenth Century*, Cambridge: Cambridge University Press.

Appleby, J. (1993) 'A different kind of independence: the post-war restructuring of the historical study of early America', *William and Mary Quarterly*, 3rd series 50: 245–267.

Barker-Benfield, G. J. (1992) *The Culture of Sensibility: Sex and Society in Eighteenth-Century England*, Chicago: Chicago University Press.

Barley, M. (1990) *The Buildings of the Countryside 1500–1750*, Cambridge: Cambridge University Press.

Barry, J. (1985) 'Popular culture in seventeenth-century Bristol', in B. Reay (ed.) *Popular Culture in Seventeenth Century England*, Beckenham: Croom Helm, pp. 59–90.

Barry, J. (1991) 'Provincial town culture, 1640–1780: urbane or civic?', in J. Pittock and A. Webb (eds) *Interpretation and Cultural History*, Basingstoke: Macmillan, pp. 198–234.

Baulant, M., Schuurman, A. J. and Servais, P. (eds) (1988) *Inventaires Après-Décès et Vente de Meubles: Apports à une histoire de la vie économique et quotidienne (XIVe–XIXe siècle)*, Actes du séminaire tenu dans le cadre du 9ème Congrès International d'Histoire Economique de Berne (1986), Louvain-la-Neuve: Academia.

Benson, S. P. (1986) *Counter Cultures: Saleswomen, Managers and Customers in American Department Stores, 1890–1940*, Urbana, Ill.: University of Illinois Press.

Berg, M. (1985) *The Age of Manufactures: Industry, Innovation and Work in Britain 1700–1820*, London: Fontana.

Blomley, N. (1995) '"I'd like to dress her all over": commodities and consumers in Zola's *Le Bon Marché*, in N. Wrigley and M. Lowe (eds) *Retailing, Consumption and Capital: Towards the New Economic Geography of Retailing*, Harlow: Longman.

Blumin, S. M. (1989) *The Emergence of the Middle Class: Social Experience in the American City, 1760–1900*, Cambridge: Cambridge University Press.

Borsay, P. (1977) 'The English urban renaissance: the development of provincial culture, c.1680–c.1760', *Social History* 5: 81–603.

Borsay, P. (1989) *The English Urban Renaissance: Culture and Society in the Provincial Town, 1660–1770*, Oxford: Clarendon Press.

Borsay, P. (1990) 'The emergence of a leisure town or an urban renaissance?' *Past and Present* 126: 189–196.

Bowlby, R. (1985) *Just Looking: Consumer Culture in Dreiser, Gissing and Zola*, London: Methuen.

Braudel, F. (1981–1984) *Civilisation and Capitalism 15th–18th Century*: vol. 1, *The Structures of Everyday Life – The Limits of the Possible*; vol. 2, *The Wheels of Commerce*; vol. 3, *The Perspective of the World*, London: Collins.

Breckenridge, C. A. (1989) 'The aesthetics and politics of colonial collecting: India at world fairs', *Comparative Studies in Society and History* 31: 195–216.

Breckman, W. G. (1991) 'Disciplining consumption: the debate on luxury in Wilhelmine Germany, 1890–1914', *Journal of Social History* 24: 485–505.

Breen, T. H. (1986) 'An empire of goods: the anglicization of colonial America, 1690–1776', *Journal of British Studies* 25: 467–499.

Breen, T. H. (1988) '"Baubles of Britain": the American and consumer revolutions of the eighteenth century', *Past and Present* 119: 73–104.

Breen, T. H. (1993) 'Narrative of commercial life: consumption, ideology, and community on the eve of the American revolution', *William and Mary Quarterly* 50: 471–501.

Brewer, J. and Porter, R. (eds) (1993) *Consumption and the World of Goods*, London: Routledge.

Briggs, A. (1988) *Victorian Things*, London: Batsford.

Britnell, R. (1993) *The Commercialisation of English Society 1000–1500*, Cambridge: Cambridge University Press.

Brown, F. E. (1986) 'Continuity and change in the urban house: developments in domestic space organisation in seventeenth-century London', *Comparative Studies in Society and History* 28: 558–590.

Buck, A. (1991) 'Buying clothes in Bedfordshire: customers and tradesmen 1700–1800' *Textile History* 22: 211–238.

Burke, P. (1991) 'Overture: the new history, its past and future', in P. Burke (ed.) *New Perspectives in Historical Writing*, Oxford: Polity Press, pp. 1–23.

Bushman, R. L. (1986) 'Regional material culture: a review of "The Great River: Art and Society of the Connecticut Valley, 1635–1820"', *William and Mary Quarterly*, 3rd series 43: 245–251.

Bushman, R. L. (1992) *The Refinement of America: People, Houses, Cities*, New York: Knopf.

Campbell, C. (1987) *The Romantic Ethic and the Spirit of Modern Consumerism*, Oxford: Blackwell.

Campbell, C. (1993) 'Understanding traditional and modern patterns of consumption in eighteenth-century England: a character-action approach', in J. Brewer and R. Porter (eds) *Consumption and the World of Goods*, London: Routledge.

Capp, B. (1979) *Astrology and the Popular Press 1500–1800*, London: Faber.

Carr, L. G. and Walsh, L. S. (1988) 'The standard of living in the Colonial Chesapeake', *William and Mary Quarterly* 45: 136–159.

Carson, C. (forthcoming) 'The consumer revolution in colonial British America: why demand?' in C. Carson *et al.* (eds) *Of Consuming Interests: The Style of Life in Eighteenth-century America*, Virginia: University Press of Virginia.

Chartres, J. (ed.) (1990) *Agricultural Markets and Trade, 1500–1750*, Cambridge: Cambridge University Press.

Clark, C. (1990) *The Roots of Rural Capitalism: Western Massachusetts, 1780–1860*, Ithaca, NY: Cornell University Press.

Clark, J. C. D. (1985) *English Society, 1688–1832: Ideology, Social Structure and Political Practice during the Ancien Regime*, Cambridge: Cambridge University Press.

Clark, J. C. D. (1986) *Revolution and Rebellion: State and Society in England in the Seventeenth and Eighteenth Centuries*, Cambridge: Cambridge University Press.

Clark, J. C. D. (1992) 'Reconceptualizing eighteenth-century England', *British Journal for Eighteenth Century Studies* 15: 135–139.

Clark, P. (ed.) (1981) *Country Towns in Pre-Industrial England 1500–1800*, Leicester: Leicester University Press.

Clark, P. (ed.) (1984) *The Transformation of English Provincial Towns*, London: Hutchinson.

Clunas, C. (1991) *Superfluous Things: Material Culture and Social Status in Early Modern China*, Oxford: Polity Press.

Cole, W. A. (1981) 'Factors in demand 1700–1780', in R. Floud and D. McCloskey (eds) *The Economic History of Britain since 1700*, Cambridge: Cambridge University Press, pp. 36–65.

Colley, L. (1986) 'Whose nation? Class and national consciousness in Britain 1750–1830', *Past and Present* 113: 97–117.

Corfield, P. J. (1987) 'Small towns, large implications: social and cultural roles of small towns in eighteenth century England and Wales', *British Journal for Eighteenth Century Studies* 10: 125–138.

Corfield, P. J. (1990) 'Walking the city streets: social role and social identification in the towns of eighteenth-century England', *Journal of Urban History* 16: 132–174.

Cox, N. and Cox, J. (1984) 'Probate inventories: the legal background' (in two parts), *Local Historian* 16: 133–145 and 16: 217–227.

Cox, N. and Cox, J. (1985–86) 'Valuations in probate inventories', *Local Historian* 16: 467–477 and 17: 85–100.

Coyner, S. (1977) 'Class consciousness and consumption: the new middle class during the Weimar republic', *Journal of Social History* 10: 310–331.

Cressy, D. (1987) *Coming Over: Migration and Communications Between England and New England in the Seventeenth Century*, Cambridge: Cambridge University Press.

Cruickshank, D. and Burton, N. (1990) *Living in the Georgian City*, London: Viking.

Davidoff, L. and Hall, C. (1987) *Family Fortunes: Men and Women of the English Middle Class*, London: Hutchinson.

Dechêne, L. (1992) *Habitants and Merchants in Seventeenth Century Montreal*, Montreal: McGill-Queen's University Press.

Deetz, J. (1977) *In Small Things Forgotten: The Archaeology of Early American Life*, Garden City, New York: Anchor-Doubleday.

Defoe, D. (1721) *The Fortunes and Misfortunes of Moll Flanders*, London.

Defoe, D. (1726) *The Complete English Tradesman*, London.

De Vries, J. (1974) *The Dutch Rural Economy in the Golden Age*, Berkeley, Ca.: Berkeley University Press.

De Vries, J. (1975), 'Peasant demand patterns and economic development: Friesland 1550–1750' , in W. N. Parker and E. L. Jones (eds) *European Peasants and Their Markets*, Princeton, NJ: Princeton University Press.

De Vries, J. (1993) 'Between purchasing power and the world of goods: understanding the household economy in early modern Europe', in J. Brewer and R. Porter (eds) *Consumption and the World of Goods*, London: Routledge, pp. 85–132.

De Vries, J. (1994) 'The industrial revolution and the industrious revolution', *Journal of Economic History* 59: 249–270.

Dyer, A. (1981) 'Urban housing: a documentary study of four Midland towns 1530–1700', *Post-Medieval Archaeology* 15: 207–218.

Dyer, C. (1989) *Standards of Living in Medieval England, 1200–1500*, Cambridge: Cambridge University Press.

Earle, P. (1983) review of McKendrick, Brewer and Plumb (1982), *Economic History Review*, 2nd series 36: 453–455.

Earle, P. (1989) *The Making of the English Middle Class: Business, Society and Family Life in London, 1660–1730*, London: Methuen.

Elias, N. (1978, 1982) *The Civilising Process*, (2 volumes), Oxford: Blackwell.

Erickson, A. L. (1990) 'An introduction to probate accounts', in G. H. Martin and P. Spufford (eds) *The Records of the Nation*, London: HMSO.

Eversley, D. E. C. (1967) 'The home market and economic growth in England', in E. L. Jones and G. E. Mingay (eds) *Land, Labour and Population in the Industrial Revolution*, London: Edward Arnold, pp. 209–252.

Ewen, E. and Ewen, S. (1982) *Channels of Desire: Mass Images and the Shaping of American Consciousness*, New York: McGraw-Hill.

Fairchilds, C. (1993a) 'The production and marketing of populuxe goods in eighteenth-century Paris', in J. Brewer and R. Porter (eds) *Consumption and the World of Goods*, London: Routledge, pp. 228–248.

Fairchilds, C. (1993b) 'Consumption in early modern Europe. A review article', *Comparative Studies in Society and History* 35: 850–858.

Farmer, C. J. (1988) 'Persistence of country trade: the failure of towns to develop in Southside Virginia during the eighteenth century', *Journal of Historical Geography* 14: 331–341.

Fawcett, T. (1990) Eighteenth-century shops and the luxury trade', *Bath History* 3: 49–75.

Fine, B. and Leopold, E. (1990) 'Consumerism and the industrial revolution', *Social History* 15: 151–179.

Fine, B. and Leopold, E. (1993) *The World of Consumption*, London: Routledge.

Fischer, D. (1989) *Albion's Seed: Four British Folkways in America*, Oxford: Oxford University Press.

Forty, A. (1986) *Objects of Desire: Design and Society from Wedgwood to IBM*, London: Thames and Hudson.

Fox, R. W. and Lears, T. J. J. (eds) (1983) *The Culture of Consumption: Critical Essays in American History*, New York: Pantheon Books.

Foy, J. H. and Schlereth, T. J. (1989) *American Home Life, 1880–1930: A Social History of Spaces and Services*, Knoxville: University of Tennessee Press.

Fraser, W. (1981) *The Coming of the Mass Market, 1850–1914*, London: Hamish Hamilton.

Furlough, E. (1991) *Consumer Co-operation in France: The Politics of Consumption*, Ithaca, NY: Cornell University Press.

Garrard, R. (1980) 'English probate inventories and their use in studying the significance of the domestic interior, 1570–1700', *A. A. G. Bijdragen* 23: 55–81.

Gay, J. (1716) *Trivia: Or the Art of Walking the Streets of London*, London.

Gilboy, E. (1932) 'Demand as a factor in the industrial revolution' in A. Cole *et al.* (eds) *Facts and Factors in Economic History*, Cambridge, Mass.: Harvard University Press, pp. 620–639.

Girouard, M. (1990) *The English Town*, London: Yale University Press.

Glennie, P. D. (forthcoming) 'Early-modern English farm labourers: work, income, consumption'.

Glennie, P. D. and Thrift, N. J. (1992) 'Modernity, urbanism and modern consumption', *Environment and Planning D: Society and Space* 10: 423–443.

Glennie, P. D. and Thrift, N. J. (1993) 'Modern consumption: theorising commodities *and* consumers', *Environment and Planning D: Society and Space* 11: 603–606.

Glennie, P. D. and Thrift, N. J. (1995a) 'Consumption, shopping and gender' in N. Wrigley and M. Lowe (eds) *Retailing, Consumption and Capital: Towards the New Economic Geography of Retailing*, Harlow: Longman.

Glennie, P. D. and Thrift, N. J. (1995b) 'Consumers, identities, and consumption spaces in early modern England', *Environment and Planning A* 27.

Glennie P. D. and Whyte, I. (forthcoming) 'Towns in an agrarian economy 1540–1700' in P. Clark (ed.) *The Cambridge Urban History of Britain, volume 2: 1540–1700*. Cambridge: Cambridge University Press.

Goodman, J. (1994) *Tobacco in History: The Culture of Dependency*, London: Routledge.

Goody, J. (1987) *The Interface Between the Written and the Oral*, Cambridge:

Cambridge University Press.

Greene, J., Anderson, V. P., Horn, J., Levy, B., and Landsman, N. C. (1991) 'Albion's seed: four British folkways in America: a symposium', *William and Mary Quarterly* 48: 223–308.

Greer, A. (1985) *Peasant, Lord and Merchant: Rural Society in Three Quebec Parishes 1740–1840*, Toronto: University of Toronto Press.

Hall, C. (1992) *White, Male and Middle-Class: Essays in Feminism and History*, Oxford: Polity Press.

Hanson-Jones, A. (1970) *The Wealth of a Nation-To-Be: The American Colonies on the Eve of the Revolution*, New York: Columbia University Press.

Harte, N. B. (1991) 'The economics of clothing in the seventeenth century', *Textile History* 22: 277–296.

Heinze, A. R. (1990) *Adapting to Abundance: Jewish Immigrants, Mass Consumption and the Search for American Identity*, New York; Columbia University Press.

Henretta, J. (1978) 'Families and farms: mentalité in pre-industrial America', *William and Mary Quarterly*, 3rd series 46: 120–144.

Holmes, G. (1993) *The Making of a Great Power: Late-Stuart and Early-Georgian Britain*, London: Longman.

Holmes, G. and Szechi, D. (1993) *The Age of Oligarchy: Pre-Industrial Britain 1722–1783*, London: Longman.

Horn, J. (1988) 'Adapting to a New World: a comparative study of local society in England and Maryland, 1650–1700', in L. S. Walsh, P. D. Morgan and J. B. Russo (eds) *Colonial Chesapeake Society*, Chapel Hill: University of North Carolina Press, pp. 133–175.

Horowitz, D. (1985) *The Morality of Spending: Attitudes Towards the Consumer Society in America 1875–1940*, Baltimore: Johns Hopkins University Press.

Horowitz, H. (1987) 'The mess of the middle class revisited: the case of the "big bourgeoisie" of Augustan London', *Continuity and Change* 2: 263–296.

Howkins, A. (1994) 'Peasants, servants and labourers: the marginal workforce in British agriculture, c. 1870–1940', *Agricultural History Review* 42: 49–62.

Hudson, P. (1992) *The Industrial Revolution*, London: Edward Arnold.

Innes, J. (1987) 'Jonathan Clark, social history and England's "Ancien Regime"', *Past and Present* 115: 65–200.

Jaffee, D. (1991) 'Peddlers of progress and the transformation of the rural North', *Journal of American History* 78: 511–535.

Jaffee, D. (1993) 'The beautiful and the respectable: the search for gentility in early America', *Reviews in American History* 21: 394–399.

Johnson, P. (1988) 'Conspicuous consumption amongst working class consumers in Victorian England', *Transactions of the Royal Historical Society*, 5th series 38: 27–42.

Kasson, J. E. (1990) *Rudeness and Civility: Manners in Nineteenth-Century America*, New York: Hill and Wang.

Klein, B. (1992) '"Between the bums and the bellies of the multitude": civic pageantry and the problem of the audience in late-Stuart London', *London Journal* 17: 18–26.

Kulikoff, A. (1986) *Tobacco and Slaves: The Development of Southern Culture in the Chesapeake, 1680–1800*, Chapel Hill: University of North Carolina Press.

Kulikoff, A. (1989) 'The transition to capitalism in rural America', *William and Mary Quarterly*, 3rd series 46: 122–132.

Kulikoff, A. (1993) 'Households and markets: toward a new synthesis of American agrarian history', *William and Mary Quarterly*, 3rd series 50: 342–355.

Kusamitsu, T. (1991) 'Novelty, give us novelty: London agents and northern manufacturers', in M. Berg (ed.) *Markets and Manufacture in Early Industrial Europe*, London: Routledge, pp. 114–137.

Laermans, R. (1993) 'Learning to consume: early department stores and the shaping of modern consumer culture 1860–1914', *Theory, Culture and Society* 10: 79–102.

Langford, P. (1989) *A Polite and Commercial People: England 1727–1783*, Oxford: Clarendon Press.

Larkin, J. (1988) *The Reshaping of Everyday Life 1790–1840*, New York: Harper and Row.

Lawrence, J. C. (1992) 'Geographical space, social space, and the realm of the department store', *Urban History* 19: 64–83.

Leach, W. R. (1984) 'Transformations in a culture of consumption: women and department stores, 1890–1925', *Journal of American History* 71: 319–342.

Lears, J. (1989) 'Beyond Veblen: rethinking consumer culture in America', in S. J. Bronner (ed.) *Consuming Visions: Accumulation and Display of Goods in America, 1880–1920*, New York: Norton, pp. 73–97.

Lee, C. (1981) 'Regional growth and structural change in Victorian Britain', *Economic History Review*, 2nd series 34: 438–452.

Lemire, B. (1988) 'Consumerism in pre-industrial and early industrial Britain: the trade in secondhand clothes', *Journal of British Studies* 27: 1–24.

Lemire, B. (1990) 'The theft of clothes and popular consumerism in early modern England', *Journal of Social History* 24: 255–275.

Lemire, B. (1991a) *Fashion's Favourite: the Cotton Trade and the Consumer in Britain, 1660–1800*, Oxford: Clarendon Press.

Lemire, B. (1991b) 'Peddling fashion: salesmen, pawnbrokers, taylors, thieves and the second-hand clothes trade in England, c. 1700–1800', *Textile History* 22: 67–82.

Lemon, J. T. (1972) *'The Best Poor Man's Country in the World': A Geographical Study of Early Southeastern Pennsylvania*, Baltimore: Johns Hopkins University Press.

Lemon, J. T. (1980) 'Comment on James A. Henretta's "Families and farms: mentalité in pre-industrial America" [and reply], *William and Mary Quarterly*, 3rd series 37: 688–700.

Lenman, B. P. (1990) 'The English and Dutch East India Companies and the birth of consumerism in the Augustan world', *Eighteenth-Century Life* 14: 47–65.

Levine, D. (1991) 'Consumer goods and capitalist modernisation', *Journal of Interdisciplinary History* 22: 67–77.

Lindert, P. (1986) 'Unequal English wealth since 1670', *Journal of Political Economy* 94: 1127–1162.

Lindert, P. (1988) 'Probates, prices and preindustrial living standards', in M. Baulant *et al.* (eds) *Inventaires*, pp. 171–180.

Lindert, P. and Williamson, J. G. (1983) 'English workers' living standards during the industrial revolution: a new look', *Economic History Review*, 2nd series 36: 1–25.

Macfarlane, A. (1987) *The Culture of Capitalism*, Oxford: Blackwell.

McInnes, A. (1988) 'The emergence of a leisure town: Shrewsbury 1660–1760', *Past and Present* 120: 53–87.

McInnes, A. (1990) 'The emergence of a leisure town or an urban renaissance?', *Past and Present* 126: 196–202.

McKendrick, N. (1974) 'Home demand and economic growth: a new view of the role of women and children in the industrial revolution', in N. McKendrick (ed.) *Historical Perspectives: Studies in English Thought and Society in Honour of*

J. H. *Plumb*, London: Hutchinson.

McKendrick, N., Brewer, J. and Plumb, J. H., (1982) *The Birth of a Consumer Society: The Commercialization of Eighteenth-Century England*, London: Hutchinson.

Main, G. (1982) *Tobacco Colony: Life in Early Maryland, 1650–1720*, Princeton, NJ: Princeton University Press.

Main, G. (1989) 'The distribution of consumer goods in colonial New England: a sub-regional approach', in P. Benes (ed.) *Early American Probate Inventories*, Dublin Seminar for New England Folk Life, Annual Proceedings 12: 153–168.

Main, G. and Main, J. T. (1988) 'Economic growth and the standard of living in southern New England, 1640–1774', *Journal of Economic History* 48: 27–46.

Main, J. T. (1985) *Society and Economy in Colonial Connecticut*, Princeton, NJ: Princeton University Press.

Marchand, R. (1985) *Advertising the American Dream: Making Way for Modernity, 1920–1940*, Berkeley: University of California Press.

Martin, A. S. (1993) 'Makers, buyers and users: consumerism as a material culture framework', *Winterthur Portfolio: A Journal of American Material Culture* 28: 141–157.

Mennell, S. (1985) *All Manners of Food: Eating and Taste in England and France from the Middle Ages to the Present*, Oxford: Blackwell.

Mennell, S. (1989) *Norbert Elias: Civilisation and the Human Self-Image*, Oxford: Blackwell

Mennell, S., Murcott, A. and van Otterloo, A. H. (1992) *The Sociology of Food*, London: Sage.

Merrill, M. (1977) '"Cash is good to eat": self-sufficiency and early exchange in the rural economy of the United States', *Radical History Review* 4: 42–71.

Miller, D. (1987) *Material Culture and Mass Consumption*, Oxford: Blackwell.

Miller, M. B. (1981) *The Bon Marché: Bourgeois Culture and the Department Store, 1869–1920*, Princeton, NJ: Allen and Unwin.

Miller, R. (1991) '"Selling Mrs. Consumer": advertising and the creation of suburban socio-spatial relations, 1910–1930', *Antipode* 23: 263–301.

Mintz, S. W. (1985) *Sweetness and Power: The Place of Sugar in Modern Life*, New York: Viking.

Mintz, S. W. (1993) 'The changing roles of food in the study of consumption', in J. Brewer and R. Porter (eds) *Consumption and the World of Goods*, London: Routledge, pp. 261–273.

Mitchell, S. I. (1981) 'Retailing in eighteenth- and early nineteenth-century Cheshire', *Transactions of the Historic Society of Lancashire and Cheshire* 130: 37–60.

Mitchell, S. I. (1984) 'The development of urban retailing 1700–1815' in P. Clark (ed.) *The Transformation of English Provincial Towns*, London: Hutchinson, pp. 259–283.

Mitchell, T. (1989) 'The world as exhibition', *Comparative Studies in Society and History* 31: 217–236.

Mokyr, J. (1977) 'Supply vs. demand in the industrial revolution', *Journal of Economic History* 37: 981–1008.

Moore, J. S. (1980) 'Probate inventories: problems and prospects', in P. Riden (ed.) *Probate Records and the Local Community*, Gloucester: Alan Sutton, pp. 11–28.

Muchembled, R. (1988) *L'Invention de l'homme moderne: Sensibilités, moeurs et comportements collectifs sous l'Ancien Régime*, Paris: Fayard.

Muchembled, R. (1990) *Société et mentalités dans la France moderne XVIe–XVIIIe siècle*, Paris: Armand Colin.

Mui, H.-C. and Mui, L. H. (1989) *Shops and Shopkeeping in Eighteenth-Century England*, London: Routledge.

Mukerji, C. (1983) *From Graven Images: Patterns of Modern Materialism*, New York: Columbia University Press.

Neeson, J. (1992) *Commoners*, Cambridge: Cambridge University Press.

Nord, P. (1986) *Paris Shopkeepers and the Politics of Resentment*, Princeton, NJ: Princeton University Press.

O'Brien, P. (1985) 'Agriculture and the home market for English industry, 1660–1820', *English Historical Review* 100: 773–800.

Overton, M. (1984) 'Probate inventories and the reconstruction of agricultural landscapes', in M. Reed (ed.) *Reconstructing Past Landscapes*, London: Croom Helm, pp. 70–96.

Pardailhé-Galabrun, A. (1988) *La Naissance de l'Intime. 3,000 Foyers Parisiens, XVIIe-XVIIIe siècles*, Paris: PUF.

Pennington, J. and Sleights, J. (1991) 'Steyning towns and trades 1559–1787', *Sussex Archaeological Collections* 130: 164–188.

Perkins, E. (1991) 'The consumer frontier: household consumption in early Kentucky', *Journal of American History* 78: 486–510.

Plumb, J. (1967) *The Growth of Political Stability in England, 1675–1725*, London: Macmillan.

Plumb, J. H. (1982) 'The commercialization of leisure in eighteenth-century England', in N. McKendrick *et al.*, *Birth of a Consumer Society*, pp. 265–285.

Porter, R. (1992) 'Georgian Britain: an ancien regime?', *British Journal for Eighteenth Century Studies* 15: 140–144.

Poster, M. (1992) 'The question of agency: Michel de Certeau and the history of consumerism', *Diacritics*, Summer: 94–107.

Pounds, N. J. G. (1989) *Hearth and Home: A History of Material Culture*, Bloomington, Ind.: Indiana University Press.

Pred, A. (1991) 'Spectacular articulations of modernity: the Stockholm exhibition of 1897', *Geografiska Annaler B* 73: 45–84.

Priestley, U., Corfield, P. J. and Sutermeister, H. (1982) 'Rooms and room-use in Norwich housing, 1580–1730', *Post-Medieval Archaeology* 16: 93–123.

Prude, J. (1991) 'To look upon the "lower sort": runaway ads and the appearance of unfree labourers in America, 1750–1800', *Journal of American History* 78: 124–158 (see also 78: 1192).

Pruitt, B. H. (1984) 'Self-sufficiency and the agricultural economy of eighteenth-century Massachusetts', *William and Mary Quarterly*, 3rd series 41: 333–364.

Purser, M. (1992) 'Consumption as communication in nineteenth-century Paradise Valley, Nevada', *Historical Archaeology* 26: 106–116.

Purvis, M. (1990) 'The development of co-operative retailing in England and Wales 1851–1901: a geographical study', *Journal of Historical Geography* 16: 314–331.

Reed, M. (1991) '"Gnawing it out": a new look at economic relations in nineteenth-century England', *Rural History* 1: 83–94.

Reekie, G. (1992) 'Changes in the Adamless Eden: the sexual and spatial transformation of a Brisbane department store 1930–90', in R. Shields (ed.) *Lifestyle Shopping*, London: Routledge, pp. 170–193.

Richards, T. S. (1991) *The Commodity Culture of Victorian England: Advertising and Spectacle, 1851–1914*, London: Verso.

Risorgimento (1991) Special journal issue on consumption in fascist Italy.

Roberts, M. (1985) '"Words they are Women, and Deeds they are Men": Images of work and gender in early modern England', in L. Charles and L. Duffin (eds) *Women and Work in Pre-industrial England*, London: Croom Helm, pp.

122–180.

Roche, D. (1981) *Le Peuple de Paris: Essai sur la culture populaire au XVIIIe siè-cle*, Paris: Aubier Montaigne. Translated as *The People of Paris: An Essay in Popular Culture in the 18th Century,* Leamington Spa: Berg (1987).

Roche, D. (1989) *La Culture des Apparences: Une Histoire du Vêtement (XVIIe–XVIIIe Siècle)*, Paris: Fayard.

Rothenberg, W. (1988) 'The emergence of farm labour markets and the transformation of the rural economy: Massachusetts, 1750–1855', *William and Mary Quarterly*, 3rd series 48: 537–566.

Rule, J. (1992a) *Albion's People: English Society, 1714–1815*, London: Longman.

Rule, J. (1992b) *The Vital Century: England's Developing Economy, 1714–1815*, London: Longman.

Sandgruber, R. (1982) *Die Anfänge der Konsumgesellschaft, Konsumgüterverbrauch, Lebensstandard und Alltagskultur in Östereich im 18. und 19. Jahrhundert*, Munich: Oldenberg Verlag.

Schama, S. (1987) *The Embarrassment of Riches: An Interpretation of Dutch Culture in the Golden Age*, London: Collins.

Schama, S. (1989) *Citizens: A Chronicle of the French Revolution*, New York: Knopf.

Schivelbusch, W. (1980) *Das Paradies, der Geschmack und die Vernunft*, Munich: Carl Hanser. Translated as *Tastes of Paradise: A Social History of Spices, Stimulants and Intoxicants*, New York: Pantheon Books (1992).

Schlereth, T. J. (1989a) *Victorian America, 1876–1915*, New York: Harper and Row.

Schlereth, T. J. (1989b) 'Country stores, country fairs, and mail-order catalogues: consumption in rural America', in S. J. Bronner (ed.) *Consuming Visions: Accumulation and Display of Goods in America, 1880–1920*, New York: Norton, pp. 339–375.

Schmidt, L. E. (1991) 'The commercialization of the calendar: American holidays and the culture of consumption, 1870–1930', *Journal of American History* 78: 887–916.

Schudson, M. (1984) *Advertising, the Uneasy Persuasion: Its Dubious Impact on American Society*, New York: Basic Books.

Schuurman, A. (1980) 'Probate inventories: research issues, problems and results', *A.A.G. Bijdragen* 23: 19–31.

Schuurman, A. (1989) *Materiële Cultuur en Levenstijl: Een Onderzoek naar de taal der dingen op het Nederlandse Platteland in de Negentiende Eeuw: de Zaanstreek, Ooost-Groningen, Oost Brabant*, Wageningen, Netherlands: A.A.G. Bijdragen 30.

Scobey, D. (1992) 'Anatomy of the promenade: the rise of bourgeois sociability in nineteenth-century New York', *Social History* 17: 203–227.

Sekora, J. (1977) *Luxury: The Concept in Western Thought from Eden to Smollett*, Baltimore: Johns Hopkins University Press.

Shammas, C. (1977) 'The determinants of personal wealth in seventeenth-century England and America', *Journal of Economic History* 37: 513–531.

Shammas, C. (1982) 'Consumer behavior in colonial America', *Social Science History* 6: 67–86.

Shammas, C. (1990) *The Pre-Industrial Consumer in England and America*, Oxford: Clarendon Press.

Shammas, C. (1993) 'Changes in English and Anglo-American consumption from 1550–1800', in J. Brewer and R. Porter (eds) *Consumption and the World of Goods*, London: Routledge, pp. 177–205.

Sharpe, J. A. (1987) *Early Modern England: A Social History 1550–1760*, London: Edward Arnold.

Smith, B. G. (1991) *The "Lower Sort": Philadelphia's Labouring People, 1750–1800*, London: Cornell University Press.

Snell, K. D. M. (1985) 'The family', in his *Annals of the Labouring Poor: Social Change and Agrarian England 1660–1900*, Cambridge: Cambridge University Press, pp. 320–373.

Speck, W. A. (1992) 'Will the real eighteenth century please stand up?' *Historical Journal* 32: 203–206.

Spufford, M. (1981) *Small Books and Pleasant Histories: Popular Fiction and its Readership in Seventeenth-Century England*, Cambridge: Cambridge University Press.

Spufford, M. (1984) *The Great Reclothing of Rural England: Petty Chapmen and their Wares in the Seventeenth Century*, Cambridge: Cambridge University Press.

Spufford, M. (1990) 'The limitations of the probate inventory', in J. Chartres and D. Hey (eds) *English Rural Society, 1500–1800: Essays in Honour of Joan Thirsk*, Cambridge: Cambridge University Press, pp. 139–174.

Spufford, M. (forthcoming) 'Literacy, trade and religion in the commercial centres of Europe'.

Stansell, C. (1987) *City of Women: Sex and Class in New York, 1789–1860*, Chicago: University of Illinois Press.

Stigler, G. J. (1954) 'The early history of empirical studies of consumer behaviour', *Journal of Political Economy* 62: 95–113.

Strasser, S. (1982) *Never Done: A History of American Housework*, New York: Pantheon Books.

Strasser, S. (1989) *Satisfaction Guaranteed: The Making of the American Mass Market*, New York: Pantheon Books.

Styles, J. (1988) 'Design for large-scale production in eighteenth-century Britain', *Oxford Art Journal* 11: 10–16.

Styles J. (1989) 'Print and policing: crime advertising in early-modern England', in D. Hay and F. Snyder (eds) *Policing and Prosecution in Britain 1750–1850*, Oxford: Clarendon Press, pp. 55–111.

Styles, J. (1993) 'Manufacture, consumption and design in eighteenth-century England', in J. Brewer and R. Porter (eds) *Consumption and the World of Goods*, London: Routledge, pp. 527–554.

Styles, J. (1994) 'Clothing the north of England, 1660–1800', *Textile History* 25: 139–166.

Styles, J. (forthcoming) *Clothing and Consumption in Eighteenth-century England*.

Sutton, P. C. (1984) *Masters of Seventeenth Century Dutch Genre Painting*, London: Royal Academy of Art.

Thirsk, J. (1978) *Economic Policy and Projects: The Development of a Consumer Society in Early Modern England*, Oxford: Clarendon Press.

Thompson, E. P. (1967) 'Time, work-discipline and industrial capitalism', *Past and Present* 37: 56–97.

Thompson, E. P. (1974) 'Patrican society, plebeian culture', *Journal of Social History* 7: 382–405.

Thornton, P. J. (1978) *Seventeenth-Century Interior Decoration in England, France and Holland*, London: Yale University Press.

Thorp, D. B. (1991) 'Doing business in the Backcountry: retail trade in colonial Rowan county, North Carolina', *William and Mary Quarterly*, 3rd series 48: 387–408.

Thrift, N. J. and Glennie, P. D. (1993) 'Historical geographies of urban life and modern consumption', in G. Kearns and C. Philo (eds) *Selling Places: the City as Cultural Capital, Past and Present*, London: Pergamon, pp. 33–48.

Tierstein, L. (1993) 'Redefining consumer culture: recent literature on consumption and the bourgeoisie in western Europe', *Radical History Review* 57: 116–159.

Tresidder, G. A. (1992) 'Coronation day celebrations in English towns 1685–1821: Elite hegemony and local relations on a ceremonial occasion', *British Journal for Eighteenth Century Studies* 15: 1–16.

van der Woude, A. and Schuurman, A. (eds) (1980) *Probate Inventories: A New Source for the Historical Study of Wealth, Material Culture, and Agricultural Development*, Wageningen, Netherlands: *A. A. G. Bijdragen* 23.

Vickers, D. (1990) 'Competency and competition: economic culture in early America', *William and Mary Quarterly*, 3rd series 47: 3–29.

Vickery, A. (1993a) 'Golden age to separate spheres: a review of the categories and chronology of English women's history', *Historical Journal* 36: 383–414.

Vickery, A. (1993b) 'Women and the world of goods: a Lancashire consumer and her possessions, 1751–81', in J. Brewer and R. Porter (eds) *Consumption and the World of Goods*, London: Routledge, pp. 274–301.

Vigarello, R. (1989) *The Concept of Cleanliness*, Cambridge: Cambridge University Press.

Vinovskis, M. (1991) 'Stalking the elusive middle class in nineteenth-century America', *Comparative Studies in Society and History* 33: 582–587.

Walsh, L. S. (1983) 'Urban amenities and rural self-sufficiency: living standards and consumer behaviour in the Colonial Chesapeake, 1643–1777', *Journal of Economic History* 43: 109–117.

Walsh, L. S. (1993) 'Consumer behaviour, diet, and the standard of living in late-colonial and early-Antebellum America 1770–1840', in R. E. Gallman and J. J. Wallis (eds) *American Economic Growth and Standards of Living Before the Civil War*, Chicago: University of Chicago Press, pp. 217–261.

Walsh, L. S. (forthcoming) 'Living standards and consumption patterns in the United States as revealed by probate inventories, 1640–1830', in C. Carson *et al.* (eds) *Of Consuming Interests: The Style of Life in Eighteenth-century America*, Virginia: University Press of Virginia.

Walsh, L. S., Carr, L. S., Main, G. and Main, J. (1988) 'Toward a history of the standard of living in British North America', *William and Mary Quarterly*, 3rd series 45: 116–170.

Weatherill, L. (1986a) 'Consumer behaviour and social status in England, 1660–1750', *Continuity and Change* 1: 191–216.

Weatherill, L. (1986b) 'A possession of one's own: women and consumer behaviour in England, 1660–1740', *Journal of British Studies* 25: 131–56.

Weatherill, L. (1988) *Consumer Behaviour and Material Culture in Britain 1660–1760*, London: Routledge.

Weatherill, L. (1993) 'The meaning of consumer behaviour in late-seventeenth and early-eighteenth century England', in J. Brewer and R. Porter (eds) *Consumption and the World of Goods*, London: Routledge, pp. 206–227.

Whitbread, H. (1988) *"I Know My Own Heart": the Diaries of Anne Lister 1791–1840*, London: Virago.

Willan, T. S. (1970) *An Eighteenth-Century Shopkeeper: Abraham Dent of Kirkby Stephen*, Manchester: Manchester University Press.

Willan, T. S. (1976) *The Inland Trade: Studies in English Internal Trade in the Sixteenth and Seventeenth Centuries*, Manchester: Manchester University Press.

Willen, D. (1992) 'Women in the public sphere in early modern England: the case of the urban working poor', in D. O. Helleby and S. M. Reverby (eds) *Gendered Domains: Rethinking Public and Private in Women's History*, Ithaca, NY: Cornell University Press, pp. 183–198.

Williams, P. (1987) 'A social history of the home, 1700–1900', in N. Thrift and P. Williams (eds) *Class and Space*, London: Routledge and Kegan Paul, pp. 154–204.

Williams, R. H. (1982) *Dream Worlds: Mass Consumption in Late Nineteenth-Century France*, Berkeley: University of California Press.

Williamson, J. G. (1984) 'British mortality and the value of life, 1781–1931', *Population Studies* 38: 157–173.

Wilson, E. (1992) 'The invisible flâneur', *New Left Review* 191: 90–110.

Woodward, D. (1984) 'Wage rates and living standards in pre-industrial England', *Past and Present* 91: 28–46.

Woodward, D. (1985) '"Swords into ploughshares": recycling in pre-industrial England', *Economic History Review,* 2nd series 38: 175–191.

Wrightson, K. (1982) *English Society 1580–1680*, London: Hutchinson.

Zahedieh, N. (1994) 'London and the colonial consumer in the late seventeenth century', *Economic History Review* 47: 239–261.

6

GEOGRAPHIES OF
CONSUMPTION

Peter Jackson and Nigel Thrift

INTRODUCTION

Geographical research on consumption has expanded dramatically in the last decade, transcending traditional divisions in the subject between the economic and the cultural and coming to occupy something of a vanguard position. Traditionally, economic geographers have concentrated on the location of economic activity and, more recently, on the transition from Fordist to more flexible modes of production, charting the shift from manufacturing to service industries and tracing out the evolution of an increasingly global economy. In contrast, social and cultural geographers have traditionally been more concerned with the distribution of goods and services (particularly items of collective consumption such as education and public housing), focusing on inequalities of gender, race and class. But, like economic geographers, they, too, tended to ignore many areas of everyday consumption such as shopping, advertising and the media. Today, an understanding of the processes of consumption is central to debates about the relationship between society and space. Geographical perspectives on consumption – and on the dialectics of globalisation and localisation, and the shifting boundaries of the public and the private – have begun to command attention across the social sciences as part of a growing interdisciplinary concern with 'mapping the futures' (Bird *et al.* 1993).

Geographies of consumption have progressed beyond generally descriptive analyses of retailing and supermarket location most especially to embrace theoretically informed research on restructuring and deregulation (Bromley and Thomas 1993; Clarke 1991, 1995; Crewe and Davenport 1992; Crewe and Forster 1993; Ducatel and Blomley 1990; Marsden and Wrigley 1994; O'Brien and Harris 1991; Wrigley 1988; Wrigley and Lowe 1995). Geographical interest in consumption is also manifested in numerous studies of shopping malls (Butler 1991; Chaney 1990; Goss 1992, 1993; Hopkins 1990, 1991, 1992; Shields 1989, 1991; Winchester 1992) and spectacular sites of consumption such as world fairs and expositions

(Ley and Olds 1988; Pred 1991). There is also a growing interest in a range of other consumption spaces from tele-shopping to car boot sales (Davies and Llewelyn 1988; Gregson and Crewe 1994) and evidence of an increasing historical depth to geographical understandings of contemporary consumption (Clarke and Purvis 1994; Domosh 1990; Glennie and Thrift 1992, 1994; Miller 1983, 1991). While shopping malls and world exhibitions may have become, in Benjamin's terms, 'sites of pilgrimage to the commodity fetish' (Benjamin 1978: 151), geographers have done more than simply map their changing locational dynamics. Pred's work, part of a large-scale comparative project, exemplifies this trend, examining various consumption sites in Stockholm (from the Art and Industrial Exhibition of 1897, through the city's early twentieth-century shopping arcades, to the contemporary mixed-use, retail-entertainment complex of the Globen) (Pred 1991). Following his earlier work on everyday language as a form of 'consumer resistance' to the universalising tendencies of modernity (Pred 1990), his recent work on consumption theorises such resistances in terms of 'symbolic discontent', articulated in complex ways with historically and geographically specific capitalist modes of production (Pred and Watts 1992).

These examples show that geographers are increasingly conceiving of consumption as a process that goes on before and after individual, isolated and momentary acts of purchase (Miller 1987). Accordingly, they have begun to trace the process of consumption back into the social relations of production and forward into cycles of use and re-use, according to what Richard Johnson (1986) describes as a virtually endless 'circuit of consumption' (see Figure 6.1).

The recent 'cultural turn' in human geography came at the end of a period that had been dominated theoretically by various strands of Marxist political economy (Peet and Thrift 1989). Throughout this period, consumption studies tended to be left to the relatively untheorised field of retail geography. When Marxist geographers, such as David Harvey, started to become interested in 'the condition of postmodernity', their work still emphasised production. There are many individual references to consumption in Harvey's work, including discussions of advertising and the cultural-encoding of urban reinvestment (see Harvey 1985a, 1985b). In much of this work, consumption is treated as part of 'the politics of distraction' (Harvey 1989: 61) rather than as a substantive topic on its own account. The culture of consumption is reduced to the economic imperative of sustaining sufficiently buoyant levels of demand to keep capitalist production profitable. Consumption is about 'the cultivation of imaginary appetites' (ibid.: 106); it is part of the 'surface froth and evanescence, the fragmentations and disruptions, so characteristic of present political economy' (ibid.: 179). Even Sharon Zukin's recent work on *Landscapes of Power* (1991) says more about the production of these landscapes than

205

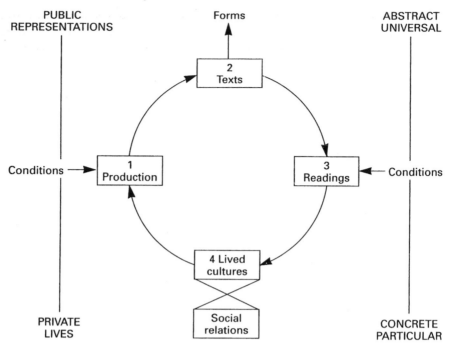

Figure 6.1: Richard Johnson's 'circuit of culture'

about the way they are consumed. Her discussion of downtown reinvestment (Zukin 1991: 202–215), for example, makes a number of tantalising points about the relationship between gentrification and cuisine, but her analysis of the cultural significance of gourmet food and the rise of the 'reflexive consumer' lacks the depth and rigour that characterise her earlier work on the transformation of New York's art-market and the creation of a real-estate market for luxury 'loft-living' in SoHo (Zukin 1982).

SURVEY

Having made these introductory remarks, we have divided our survey of the literature into three sections concerned with reviewing geographical work on the changing *sites* of consumption; the *chains* that link consumption's multiple locations; and the *spaces and places* of contemporary consumerism. Included in this review are studies by those who identify themselves as geographers and studies that emphasise questions of space and place, irrespective of their authors' disciplinary affiliations. After a consideration of two case-studies from our own research, we conclude with some reservations about the field as currently constituted which are, at the same time, an indication of some possible future directions for geographical research on consumption. Whereas ten years ago geographies of consumption hardly existed, new social geographies are beginning to form. These geographies have both increased in number and become more subtle. In particular, like other workers in the social sciences and humanities, geographers have begun to understand the importance of studying consumption as practice (de Certeau 1984). In other words, a trajectory of interest has now been established in geography which cannot be quashed. Transported into the border countries of consumption by this trajectory, it is now possible to see the outline of other places.

Sites

Not surprisingly, geographers have devoted much of their attention to the spatial patterning of consumption. In particular, the literature has been concerned with how social relations of consumption are constructed through a tissue of sites. The message that the sites of consumption are important has usually been articulated by deploying a standard 'postmodern' narrative. That is, particular sites of consumption are chosen as representative, and as representations, of a new stage of postmodern commodification. There is a symbiotic relationship between this new stage of commodification and particular social groups. Specifically, members of the new middle classes are usually revealed in the narrative as the cheerleaders for new forms of consumerism as they follow lifestyles that convert symbolic capital into economic capital and vice versa.

A perfect example of these tenets in operation can be found in the work of Paul Knox (1991). For Knox, Western societies are being transformed into a landscape that is like a supermarket writ large. The whole of the landscape is geared towards consumption. Thus Knox identifies several processes of economic restructuring which have been responsible for constructing a new landscape of consumption. The most important of these is the move from a Fordist regime of mass production and mass consumption to more international and flexible forms of capitalism, in which production is ever more closely intertwined with the demands of consumers. The chief impetus for this restructuring is located in the rise of a new class fraction, Bourdieu's 'new bourgeoisie' which acts as 'an R and D lab for commodity aesthetics, the promoter of a new (intensified) consumption ethic, a new model of consumption in which there is a heavy emphasis on taste and aesthetics, and a new (postmodern) sensibility' (Knox 1991: 184).

Mediated by a new, more intense and flexible development industry, the result is a consumer landscape based around the aesthetic values of historic preservation and postmodern architecture, which is gradually 'overwriting' the older urban landscapes and, at the edge of cities, is able to forge its own distinctive landscape forms. The new consumer landscape consists of four main types of site. The first of these is the gentrified areas of the inner city, reliant on the values of historic preservation. The second is private, comprehensively planned, suburban and exurban communities, typically working to exploit 'cluster zoning' or to provide:

> comprehensively designed environments in which the amenities (tennis, golf, swimming, etc.), architectural styles (colonial revival, Tudor, larger than life Cotswold, etc.), landscaping (lavish, meticulously trimmed, and brimming with special features like cast iron and brass sign work), layout (maximising rustic views and amenity footage) and security (symbolised by gatehouses or imposing gateways and operationalised by card key systems) are carefully targeted to appeal to the lifestyles and status identities of particular fractions of the middle class income group.
>
> (Knox 1991: 199–200)

By our accoutrements shall you know us, so to speak. The third type is what Knox calls 'festival settings', large-scale redevelopments intended to create focal settings for an integrated package of upscale offices, transit shops, impulse retailers, restaurants, hotels, offices, concert halls and art galleries. The mix has now become something of a cliché, since practically every North American city has at least one such development intended to act as a motor to boost consumption. Finally, Knox points to high-tech corridors, new commercial landscapes that include large amounts of office space but also, again, opportunities to consume in the shape of jogging tracks, fitness centres, cycle trails, coffee shops, flower shops, and so on.

Knox's new urban landscape is hardly confined to North America. Much the same kinds of development can be found in countries like Britain, fuelled especially by the growth of the so-called 'service class' of managers and professionals (Thrift 1987, 1989). Gentrification abounds in many urban areas and is the subject of numerous studies (e.g. Smith and Williams 1986). Planned suburban and exurban communities have become common, albeit usually on a smaller scale than in North America. Festival settings have become commonplace in most British cities, fostered by the growth of the heritage industry and local authority 'cultural strategies' aimed at mixing culture and shopping (Bassett 1993). There are even some embryonic high-tech corridors (Morgan and Sayer 1988; Massey, Quintas and Wield 1992). In other words, across much of the Western world, the same elements of a consumption landscape recur – the privileged housing estates, the shopping malls, the retail parks, and so on (Zukin 1991). In some senses, there undoubtedly is a new world of consumption.

But this kind of broad-brush approach is not without its problems. Most particularly, it can seem as though what is being constructed is a packaged landscape devoid of any local detail, except for a few design flourishes. Detailed studies of particular sites of consumption give the lie to this idea of a homogeneous set of processes producing only homogeneity. The two sites most commonly considered by geographers have been gentrifying inner-city areas and shopping malls. It is to these two sites that we now turn.

There is a large literature on gentrification within geography, a literature which has become increasingly concerned with the way in which houses are refurbished as consumer objects by members of the new middle classes in line with prevailing notions of taste. This literature ranges from 'postmodern' inner-city waterfront redevelopment like False Creek, Vancouver (Ley 1986; Mills 1988) to areas of the inner city increasingly subject to historic preservation such as Spitalfields in London (Jacobs 1992). Often drawing on the work of Bourdieu (1984), such studies usually interpret gentrification as involving the use of various marks of distinction in a ceaseless attempt by the new middle classes to convert economic capital into cultural capital and vice versa. As Michael Jager argues in his study of the aesthetics of gentrification in Melbourne: 'in a generalised consumption society, where class distinctions no longer appear so rigid and where consumption habits are not so rigidly dictated by class position, there is a constant jockeying for class position, played out in the sphere of consumption' (Jager 1986: 90).[1]

For some considerable time, the literature on gentrification has appeared to be sterile, with a limited number of authors endlessly critiquing each other to no great end (e.g. Hamnett 1991; Smith 1992). However, the recent addition of a gender dimension into gentrification research has given it a real fillip. Specifically, it has destabilised the idea that all gentrification can be seen as a war of class position fought out with consumer objects. Thus, some areas of gentrification are perhaps better interpreted as concerned with the construction of different forms of masculinity and femininity than marks of class; while others seem to be simply the preserves of women with moderate incomes who, juggling the demands of childcare and paid employment, can often only afford to buy into inner-city neighbourhoods (Rose 1989; Bondi 1991).

What is perhaps surprising is that in all the geographical literature on gentrification there is remarkably little work that tries to deal with gentrification in terms of specific commodities. Most of the literature remains highly generalised, often based on aggregate surveys and statistics. As a consequence it is prone to rather heroic assertions about consumption. There is, as yet, no geographical equivalent of Miller's (1988) work on kitchen furnishings as revelations of lifestyle 'choice'.

The second site most commonly considered by geographers has been the shopping mall. Until recently much of this work centred on one particular mall, the West Edmonton Mall in Canada, which seems to have drawn geographers like moths to a flame (see the special issue no. 35 of the *Canadian Geographer*, 1991). More recently, other malls have become the object of geographical scrutiny. Yet, with few exceptions, geographers have revealed the residual influence of Marxian political economy in the subject by clinging to the idea of the shopping mall as either a frothy piece of spectacle or an essentially threatening presence, able to bend consumers to its will, or both. Goss (1993), for example, describes the mall as a symbolic landscape designed by the 'captains of consciousness' to persuade, even to bully, consumers into consuming. The tale is, in other words, of glitzy appearance masking a grimmer, more instrumental reality:

> The shopping center apparently caters to all, with circuses for the masses and fine art for the elite, consciously providing those 'in the know' with the means to mark their distinction. More seriously, this optimistic assessment underestimates the capacity of the organisational intelligence behind the spatial strategies of control. A sophisticated apparatus researches consumers' personal profiles, their insecurities and desires, and produces a space that comfortably satisfies both individual and mass consumers and manipulates the behavior of both to not-so-different degrees.
>
> (Goss 1993: 40–41)

The current geographical literature on malls displays two related problems. First, there is, to use de Certeau's (1984) terms, too much emphasis on strategies of control and too little emphasis on tactics, on the reappropriation of space by consumers for purposes that exceed those of the designers. As Goss himself points out, 25 per cent of consumers in one survey of mall users had no intention of making a purchase. Second, the literature is too often constructed in a historical vacuum. Yet any acquaintance with the history of streets, arcades, department stores and the like constantly demonstrates the ways in which new forms of sociality are invented which endlessly produce uses of consumer spaces that are other than those intended (Glennie and Thrift 1992, 1993, 1995).

How, then, can we summarise the state of the current geographical literature on sites of consumption? The literature can, perhaps, best be described as suffering still from too great a degree of determinism. Relations of class, gender, sexuality and race are too often seen as unbending lines of force manifested in consumption spaces rather than as actively negotiated constructions of what count as consumption spaces (Frow and Morris 1993). This conclusion can be justified by pointing to four main omissions in the current geographical literature.

First, as noted above, geographers have tended to ignore the active roles of consumers in shaping contemporary consumer cultures. Consumers rarely feature in geographical accounts as living, breathing complexes of subject positions with myriad concerns, concerns which spread outside consumption narrowly defined. Part of the reason for this, which forms the second omission, is that most geographers have concentrated on a very limited range of sites which have tended to be the more formalised ones like malls. Other sites, less formal gathering places like high streets or car-boot sales have received much less attention (but see Glennie and Thrift 1992; Gregson and Crewe 1994). Part of the reason for this state of affairs, and this forms the third omission, is that too many geographers do not conceive of social relations as dynamic practices, constantly being forged anew by creative *bricoleurs* using spaces creatively. As McRobbie (1993: 407–408) puts it in her discussion of youth cultures:

> it's not so much that . . . meanings can now be recognised as including questions of gender, sexuality, race and identity but rather that what is significant is how in different youth cultural 'venues' there are different permutations of class, gender and racial meanings being explored.

According to McRobbie, gender, sexuality, race and identity have to different degrees become 'unfixed' over the last fifteen years, making both for more fluid permutations and the more creative use of these permutations. But these fluidities and usages still often come together in fixed sites:

> The [rave] subculture far outstrips other forms of youth entertainment because of *where* it takes place. Outside the regulatory space of the home or the school, the more autonomous space of the subculture contributes directly to the weakening of these other institutional ties.
>
> (McRobbie 1983: 424, our emphasis)

Finally, geographers have found it difficult to get away from the tyranny of the single site. Yet, this is clearly a necessary move. This is partly because studies of sites like shopping malls show that they are highly diverse, catering to different clienteles, being used in different ways, producing different experiences and memories, as Morris (1988, 1989) has shown in her studies of contrasting malls and motels. Partly, too, it is because consumption is the result of a series of acts that are located in different sites. And, in any case, actual purchase is often only a small part of these acts (Shields 1992b). Thus, there can be 'no studies of exemplary sites of production of either "modernity" or "everyday life"; no studies of *the* shopping mall form, *the* motel form, *the* tower form, *the* theme park, *the* beach, *the* pub . . .' (Morris 1993: 394). Clearly, it is necessary for geographers to move towards the analysis of multiple sites or consumption chains, as we do in the next section.

Chains

How have the few geographers who have attempted to consider multiple sites gone about the task? Two main approaches have been taken. The first of these has been concerned with the problem of relating human time-allocation to commodity use. In other parts of the social sciences, this is a problem that has been ceded to economics and economists (e.g. Becker 1965; Ghez and Becker 1975). In Becker's basic time allocation model, households are seen as microscopic firms which combine time with market goods and services to produce more basic 'commodities', essentially consumption events (which also require time to play out) that generate utility. In this model, time is a scarce resource. The use of time includes a cost that has to be balanced against the costs of the use of the 'capital equipment' that has to be used, leading to a 'harried leisure class' (Linder 1970) dedicated to consuming quality at maximum expense.

This kind of economic approach is not without flaws (Carlstein and Thrift 1978). In particular, it tends to produce highly individual accounts, in which each household is assumed to consume independently of others. It is also highly abstract, in that acts of consumption are wrenched out of their context as spatially and temporally specific events. At the same time, the approach does point to the need to consider opportunity costs as a vital aspect of consumption. The economic account does at least highlight the fact that the choice of certain kinds of consumption makes other kinds of consumption impossible.

Time-geography (see Carlstein, Parkes and Thrift 1978; Parkes and Thrift 1980; Carlstein 1982) can be seen as, in part, an attempt to avoid the difficulties of the economic account of time allocation and commodity use whilst retaining an emphasis on the importance of opportunity costs. Time-geography was developed by the Swedish geographer, Torsten Hägerstrand, as a way of describing the space–time structure of social events and at the same time analysing the interdependence of these events, precisely because they have a space–time structure. The familiar time-geographic diagrams are 'maps' of situated activities. The diagrams demonstrate the essential reciprocity of the social use of space and time in that once certain activities are chosen, other activities become impossible:

> It is obvious that the enormous number of situations which constitute the life of society are mutually regulated by its components: people and objects that leave one situation and enter new ones in the same or a different place. These situations are chained to one another in a complicated web.
>
> (Hägerstrand 1979, cited in Carlstein and Thrift 1978: 238)

In other words, time-geography is the study of possibilities. Most particularly, what the approach shows is that consumption must always involve the consumption of time and space. At the same time, it also problematises what is meant by consumption by focusing on what Carlstein calls 'interaction effects':

> Conventional wisdom has it that consumption is the use (or acquisition through purchase) of goods or services for want satisfaction, but we consume many other things which do not fit very neatly into the crude categories of 'goods and services', such as various composite socio-environmental situations. We not only consume the food at dinner but in many respects we also consume the whole dining situation by participating in it, just as we may consume a situation such as a forest hike without eating the trees. In all these different situations we consume space (space–time) and we also consume time the instant it is generated, as it were, since we cannot consume human time . . . .
>
> Irrespective of all this . . . neither 'consumption' nor 'production' activities can occur unless they are associated with transport or movements of some form. People in urban-industrial societies do not get all commodities delivered to them at the instant that they are wanted, but spend a considerable amount of time travelling and shopping. So which movement and transport possibility boundaries can be identified and why are we never told of them? Or why is there so little discussion of consumption possibility boundaries in economics? And why are there factors of production but seldom if ever factors of consumption, distribution or transport?
>
> But suppose we accept 'consumption' as a fruitful category: time-geographically and in its concrete manifestations, consumption then becomes a process of resource utilisation in which human individuals must be in physical contact and proximity to various inputs used in different time–space situations. The human individual is a localised input–output entity who requires and desires inputs such as food, water, air, information, equipment, shelter, settlement space and human time. . . . All these inputs and the situations which they constitute, potentially compete with or displace other situations involving other participants. Much of the innate logic of consumption . . . disappears when abstracted from the time–space context, as when consumption is regarded as a propensity of households to purchase commodities. Even when the volume of input and output time per period is specified, as is generally the case in economics, the underlying logistic aspects of assembly, disassembly, processing and transport still deserve attention. When these interaction aspects of consumption are taken into account, it is obvious that there are numerous constraints that impinge on how consumption situations can be generated.

(Carlstein 1982: 52–54)

Time-geography has been extensively criticised in geography. For example, it has been criticised as being inherently masculinist by those who have concentrated on its description of individual paths without recognising the importance of situated interdependence which is time-geography's *raison d'être* (e.g. Rose 1993). It has been criticised as being a *danse macabre*, bereft of most of what makes us human, by those who see only technology without spirit. But, in the study of consumption, it has three uses which together begin to support Gell's (1992: 321) judgement that the (time-) geographers' maps 'have profound but unexplored implications for the processes of human cognition'. The first is that it stresses social situatedness. Space, time and consumption are seen to be intimately linked together, in a long chain of sites. Second, time-geographic modes of description allow for the possibility of a democracy of things (Latour 1993). People, animals, plants and all kinds of commodities are all described in the same way: as paths in time and space. Rather than an anthropocentric vision, time-geography offers a vision in which all things influence each other. Most particularly, the biographies of commodities (Kopytoff 1986) can be easily depicted (see Hägerstrand 1994). Third, time-geography provides the elements of a graphical 'language' which is able to capture the simultaneities and conjunctures of the interaction of people and commodities in ways that ordinary language finds difficult. Pred's (1990) account of late-nineteenth-century Stockholm provides perhaps the best example of this kind of usage. In this account, time-geographic diagrams not only figure as reconstructions of the lives of particular people at a particular place in history, they also act as an allegory for the process of commodity accumulation itself. Lives and goods intermesh in ways that are continually evolving.

With its emphasis on a web of time–space paths, time-geography lays particular emphasis on movement. In turn, this can be seen to have further important consequences. First, it provides a means of depicting the different forms of movement and the different visualisations of the world that they prompt, with direct consequences for consumption. For example, walking provides a very different mode of visualising objects from the 'panoramic' mode of visualisation that is obtained by driving in a car (Schivelbusch 1986) – with direct consequences for the way we relate to objects. It is probably no coincidence that the rise of the panoramic mode of perception in the early nineteenth century, most especially as a result of railway travel, should cross with the rise of 'recreational' walking which values walking as a means of 'getting back' to primordial modes of visualising and, in general, of relating to objects (Wallace 1993).

Second, time-geography's emphasis on movement draws attention to modes of social interaction which are co-present but not necessarily intimate. These kinds of co-presence often take place in sites intended to promote movement – the street, the supermarket, the market square, the carnival. This is the art of the encounter rather than the planned meeting, of the fleeting gaze rather than the completed study. It often goes under the tag of 'sociality' and it appears to be increasingly crucial to the maintenance of modern commodity cultures since it provides a new, unstable but still effective form of group ethics which is often bound up with particular commodities used in particular ways to articulate particular identities (Shields 1992a; Maffesoli 1992; Glennie and Thrift 1992, 1993).

Time-geography is a method that has generally been used to describe interaction at the relatively small time–space scale of everyday life: for example, as a means of considering the ways in which activities are lived out in particular, relatively localised chains of sites, often known as activity spaces. But, increasingly, interaction cannot be framed in this way. Sites are connected up across the whole world in ways that are increasingly common. These global webs are usually grasped by paying attention to what Fine and Leopold (1990, 1993) call 'systems of provision': commodity-specific chains which connect up production, marketing, distribution, consumption and the material culture surrounding these different elements. Such chains have, of course, been a longstanding feature of many different kinds of economy as Mintz's (1993) study of Caribbean sugar production clearly shows. But over recent years these claims have changed their character in three ways. First, the *length* of these chains has tended to increase markedly. Many commodities are now produced on a world-wide scale, to the point where this may well be becoming the norm. Second, the *pace* of activity in these chains has increased. Production, marketing, distribution and consumption all tend to be more rapid, because of technological changes and because of the associated cultural adjustments to these changes – increasingly we live in a culture that expects rapid gratification. Third, chains have become more complex. They have more *depth* in so far as they are likely to involve more places.

In geography, perhaps the most graphic examples of research on these commodity chains come from work on the internationalisation of the food industry (Friedland, Barton and Thomas 1981; FitzSimmons 1986; Whatmore 1994; LeHeron 1994). The internationalisation of the food industry has continued apace, especially since the 1960s, predicated on three main changes (Marsden and Little 1990). The first of these changes is the application of agrochemical and mechanical technologies, together with genetic engineering, to the production of animals and plants. This has led to the gradual evolution of biological commodities which are more and more standardised. Thus there is the evolution of the 'world steer' (Sanderson 1986), contingent upon new forms of insemination, feed technologies and transportation technologies. Again, there is the expansion of hybrid tomatoes which require genetic knowledge and specialised growing technologies (Busch, Lacy, Burkhardt and Lacy 1991). The second change has been the increasing dependence on state intervention in national food

215

systems and the concomitant need for new forms of international regulation. Much of the competition in international food markets has in fact taken place in the interstate realm, in particular over levels of food price support. The final change has been the increasing importance of the strategies of a few multinational corporations. In particular, these multinational corporations are moving upstream and downstream in the food commodity chain. Thus, agro-industrial corporations have tended to move upstream from agricultural production and processing into marketing and distribution. Meanwhile retailers have increasingly moved downstream in so far as they have become more concerned to fix a web of subcontractor relationships so as to be able to guarantee supplies and prices. Again, multinational corporations have become involved in more and more commodities. For example, British food retailers have been slowly moving into the United States (Wrigley 1992).

This burst of internationalisation has meant that food commodity chains are increasingly spread across the world. One illustrative example is the organisation of beef production via forward contracts between calf producers in northern Mexico and feedlots in Texas and California. In this case, 'there is an authentic international division of labour, in that the final product comes from sequential production in "parts", "components" or "inputs" in two countries with very different productive specialisation' (Goodman and Redclift 1991: 159). Other recent examples of transnational agro-industrial integration include exports of Mexican winter vegetables to the United States, Chilean fruit to Europe, Central American meat packing for US hamburgers, oilseeds and feed grains for European livestock from Argentina, Brazil and Thailand, and Brazilian exports of chicken and frozen orange juice concentrate.

The literature on food commodity chains is still hesitant in two areas. First, there is a paucity of work on final consumption and its effects on the commodity chain as a whole. Yet, because of internationalisation, Western consumer tastes have come to dominate much of the world. Goodman and Redclift (1991) document some of the shifts in Western food preferences, towards convenience foods, 'healthier' foods, organic foods and towards 'different' foods that possess the patina of otherness. The pressure from retailers to develop new products that can cope with these shifts in taste resonates back through commodity chains, sometimes with adverse effects:

> In countries like Brazil and Thailand increased monocultivation of land is linked, albeit indirectly, to changes in food consumption practices in the United Kingdom and other industrial countries. Monocultivation is an element in the ecological crisis affecting developed and developing countries alike.
>
> (Goodman and Redclift 1991: 29)

216

The second area in which the literature on food commodity chains still stutters is concerned with method. Food commodity chains have mainly been treated in a limited way. In particular, few authors have tried to treat the whole of a commodity chain – from production, through distribution and marketing to consumption, and including the whole material culture of the commodity (but see Fine and Leopold 1993). Similarly, the range of methods used has been limited. For example, there have been few attempts to carry out so-called 'bifocal' or multi-focal ethnographies (Marcus 1992) that take in all the sites in the commodity chain. An exception is the work of Ian Cook (1994) who has been able to integrate political economy and ethnography in an exemplary fashion. Cook considered the commodity chain associated with exotic tropical fruits. These are new and different foods for which a market has only recently been constructed in the West. Cook carried out ethnographic work on a plantation in Jamaica and with supermarket executives who were introducing the fruit into Britain. In particular, it was clear that the executives had very specific demands about the look of the fruit, and this had immediate consequences for how they were grown in Jamaica.

As well as concerning themselves with the material processes that link together various *sites* in the construction of complex consumption *chains*, geographers have also been concerned with the ideological construction of different consumption *spaces*, a process that is often most clearly revealed through the metaphors with which contemporary consumption cultures are described. These metaphorical spaces and places and their relation to material geographies 'on the ground' form the subject of our next section.

Space and place

Studies of consumption are littered with spatial metaphors from centres and margins to boundaries and transgressions, distinctions between public and private places, and the geographies of visibility and invisibility. Mort provides a classic example in his study of the changing consumption spaces of young men in the contemporary city:

> Urban geographers have been telling us for a long time that space is not just a backdrop to real cultural relations. Space is material, not just in physical terms. It carries social meanings which shape identities and the sense we have of ourselves. For young men (and young women) it is the spaces and places of the urban landscape which are throwing up new cultural personas – on the high street, in the clubs, bars, brasseries, even on the terraces. It seems as if young men are now living out quite fractured identities, representing themselves differently, feeling different in different spatial situations.
>
> (Mort 1988: 218–219)

Long familiar with such a spatialised vocabulary, geographers have been keen to draw out the material implications of these territorial allusions, to 'ground' metaphor in hopefully not too literal a way (Smith and Katz 1993). A particularly fruitful use of spatial metaphor is Lefebvre's distinction in *The Production of Space* (1991), between 'spaces of representation' (such as shopping malls and department stores) and 'representations of space' (in advertising and other media). Sometimes, the distinction between these two kinds of space has become blurred as art imitates life in media representations of shopping spaces, such as Woody Allen's *Scenes from a Mall* (1991) or as life imitates art in the symbolic evocation of other places and times that are characteristic of many contemporary shopping environments, blurring the boundaries between work and leisure, drudgery and pleasure (Prus and Dawson 1991).

Shopping malls and department stores are designed as spaces for the representation of goods. They are the consumption industry's shop window and, not surprisingly, have attracted the geographer's critical gaze. Dowling's discussion of Woodward's department store in Vancouver highlights the contemporary significance accorded to the display of goods. In the words of Woodward's President, quoted in 1935:

> Window displays not only tell and show the public what we have to sell, but by their cleanliness, neatness and constant change, bring to the customer's mind the fact that, as a store, we are on our toes, so to speak. WINDOWS REFLECT THE VERY CHARACTER OF THE WHOLE ORGANIZATION.
>
> (Quoted in Dowling 1993: 306)

Metaphors of visibility, reflection and the gaze have played a central part in recent discussions of the transition from modernity to postmodernity. Consumption is regularly examined in terms of urban spectacle, and the 'dialectics of seeing' have been identified as central to the cultural politics of shopping (Buck-Morss 1989). Until recently, however, much of this literature has tended to overlook the practices and values of consumers and to privilege the analyst's own reading of the signs and symbols of contemporary consumption. This tendency is now being redressed as studies of the semiotics of advertising and the symbolic geographies of consumption (e.g. Gottdiener 1986; Sack 1988; Shields 1992b) are being joined by other studies that seek out the voices of actual consumers, respecting their active role as creative agents before, during and after the moment of purchase (e.g. Goss 1993; Jackson 1993; Winchester 1992; Jackson and Holbrook 1995). Rather than continue to focus on highly spectacular mega-malls, we should recall that what Goss (1993) calls the 'magic of the mall' extends well beyond these relatively unusual and spectacular sites to include more mundane and everyday spaces. Cosgrove has attempted to describe the cultural and symbolic experience of such everyday environments in the following passage, which is worth quoting at length:

On Saturday mornings I am not, consciously, a geographer. I am, like so many other people of my age and lifestyle, to be found shopping with my family in my local town-centre precinct. It is not a very special place, artificially illuminated under the multi-storey car park, containing an entirely predictable collection of chain stores . . . fairly crowded with well-dressed, comfortable family consumers. . . . Geographers might take an interest in the place because it occupies the peak rent location of the town, they might study the frontage widths or goods on offer as part of a retail study, or they might assess its impact on the pre-existing urban morphology. But I'm shopping.

Then I realise other things are happening: I'm asked to contribute to a cause I don't approve of; I turn a corner and there is an ageing, evangelical Christian distributing tracts. The main open space is occupied by a display of window panels to improve house insulation – or rather, in my opinion, to destroy the visual harmony of the street. Around the concrete base of the precinct's decorative tree a group of teenagers with vividly coloured Mohican haircuts and studded armbands cast the occasional scornful glance at middle-aged consumers. I realise that, unemployed as they almost certainly are and of an age when home is the least comfortable environment, they will 'hang around' here until this space is closed off by the steel barriers that enclose it at night.

The precinct, then, is a highly textured place, with multiple layers of meaning. Designed for the consumer, to be sure, and thus easily amenable to my retail geography study, nevertheless its geography stretches way beyond that narrow and restrictive perspective. The precinct is a symbolic place where a number of cultures meet and perhaps clash.

(Cosgrove 1989: 118–119)

Harvey makes a similar point about the enormous range of meanings that may lie dormant within the apparently mundane world of contemporary consumption:

I often ask beginning geography students to consider where their last meal came from. Tracing back all the items used in the production of that meal reveals a relation of dependence upon a whole world of social labor conducted in many different places under very different social relations and conditions of production. That dependency expands even further when we consider the materials and goods used in the production of goods we directly consume. Yet we can in practice consume our meal without the slightest knowledge of the intricate geography of production and the myriad social relationships embedded in the system that puts it upon our table.

(Harvey 1990: 422)

219

Harvey is not alone in emphasising the 'hidden geographies' of production that lay masked ('embedded') within the social relations of contemporary consumption until they are uncovered ('traced back' and 'revealed') by the expert observer. Other critics also remark on the 'masking' of specific social relations of production in contemporary consumer capitalism. Thus, Shields describes 'consumption sites' as places where media images can be purchased as ready-to-wear 'masks' (Shields 1992: 1), while Sack talks of the (backstage) history of extraction, manufacture, and distribution being 'virtually obliterated' when the finished product is presented to the public (Sack 1992: 118). Lee asks why, when a commodity arrives in our shops, it should show 'no manifest trace at all of the labour that was invested in it during its production' (Lee 1993: xii). Lee goes on to show how surplus value, 'revealed' in the exploitation of labour, is 'concealed' in the fetishism of commodities and how the commodity form is 'the mask hiding the expropriation of value by one class at the expense of another' (ibid.: 25).

Such metaphors betray the problems that consumption raises for many on the left, a feeling that any study of consumption risks glorifying the market and abandoning longstanding commitments to those who are engaged in more 'productive' forms of employment. The danger of such a stance is that it risks abandoning the field altogether to a triumphant right-wing obsession with consumer choice and an uncritical celebration of 'enterprise culture'. Rather than engaging with consumption cultures, as Mort recommends, 'at the point where the market meets popular experience and lifestyles on the ground' (Mort 1988: 215), critical studies of consumption have all too often degenerated into a kind of vacuous moralising, substituting indignation and denunciation for genuine analysis. As well as failing to engage with the pleasures of consumption, such studies also tend to ignore the very ironies and ambiguities that give contemporary consumer culture so much of its power and dynamism. Fortunately, things are beginning to change and studies have emerged that engage with the complexities of, for example, home-ownership, as simultaneously a source of stored value, of existential security and conspicuous display (Saunders 1984, 1989; Warde 1990, 1991). Similarly, there have been important studies of the contradictory roles of domestic technology, as simultaneously a source of female emancipation and of 'more work for mother' (Cockburn 1993; Cowan 1983; Hayden 1981, 1984; Miller 1983, 1991).

Zukin provides a particularly telling extension of the 'masking' metaphor, arguing that shopping malls give material form to a symbolic landscape of consumption, their imagery 'seduc[ing] men and women to believe in the landscape of a homogeneous mass consumption by masking centralised economic power in individual choice' (Zukin 1991: 142). The language of seduction is hardly accidental. Many studies of consumption refer to department stores and shopping malls as places of temptation, desire and consummation. Fiske (1989), for example, writes of 'shopping for pleasure' (though, ironically, the activities he describes take place in the hallowed setting of 'cathedrals of consumption'). Fiske also highlights the gendered nature of contemporary consumerism, illustrating some of its complexities and contradictions. On the one hand, he cites the (patriarchal) idea that 'a woman's place is in the mall', that women are 'born to shop', while, on the other hand, he shows how the mall provides a space in which women can be public, empowered and free (Fiske 1989: 19–20). It is just such contradictions between exploitation and empowerment that retailers and advertisers try to exploit in appealing to women as consumers (cf. Bowlby 1985; Blomley 1993; Leslie 1994). Moreover, as Wilson has demonstrated in *The Sphinx in the City* (1991) and as Walkowitz explores in her historical study of the *City of Dreadful Delight* (1992), the dialectics of desire and dread can be mapped on to the social geography of the city, historically and in the present day. For example, Wilson shows how, in the nineteenth century, cities like Paris and Chicago came to symbolise pleasure, excitement and consumption, a set of meanings that were inextricably tied up with the sexualisation of the city. Department stores, such as those explored in Emile Zola's *Au Bonheur des dames* (1883) and in Theodore Dreiser's *Sister Carrie* (1900), encouraged a transgression of the conventional bourgeois boundaries between a private, feminine space of domestic interiors and the public, masculine world of the streets. In such liminal spaces, Wilson argues, money threatened to replace morality as consumption became a substitute for virtue (Wilson 1991: 59). Walkowitz makes a similar point, arguing that shopping emerged as a newly elaborated female activity at the end of the nineteenth century: 'Many women go to the shops for no reason beyond the desire of looking round and generally surveying things, they are possibly tempted and succumb before leaving' (*Fortnightly Review*, 1895, quoted in Walkowitz 1992: 49). Entering the ambiguous spaces of the street and the store was not a source of unalloyed pleasure for nineteenth-century women, placing shopgirls and 'shopping ladies', regardless of class, in a vulnerable position (Walkowitz 1992: 46–47). Significantly, in such ambiguous circumstances, some women devised 'personal maps and proscribed zones to organise their walks around the West End' (ibid.: 51).

Metaphors of seduction and temptation are central to Reekie's (1993) historical analysis of sex and selling in the Australian department store. In place of the benevolent paternalism implied in most official histories of the department store, she shows how such stores were implicated with the development of new codes of heterosexuality, new formulations of sexual identity, and new bodily regimes: 'the department store created a sexual culture which formulated and reinforced men's power over women' (Reekie 1993: xiii). The 'culture of selling' that evolved during the nineteenth century drew on 'scientific' principles but also tapped into existing conventions of (heterosexual) romantic love.[2] According to Reekie's research, department store culture, like the modern office environment whose gender politics have been investigated by Pringle (1988), was 'saturated with the dynamics of sex' (Reekie 1993: xiv). Faced with the 'shimmering seductiveness' of tables strewn with delicate dress materials and snow-white damasks, patriarchal values were threatened by the new pleasures and opportunities being made available to women by the rise of the commodity fetish. These new cultures of consumption drew forth a stream of misogynistic commentary such as this from the *Australian Worker* in 1906:

> Women sweating, struggling, swarming round the damaged gloves; snarling, gesticulating over the eighteen-penny muslins. Scratch a bargain-hunter and you get a Tartar every time. . . . Their fat, bulging, gloating eyes are twinkling with greed. Their hands lovingly fondle the prizes they are losing their self-respect to win. Never once do they pause to realise that someone must go short that their insatiable greed may be satisfied.
>
> (Reekie 1993: 16–17)

The moral indignation of the final sentence does little to disguise the disgust and horror that characterise the rest of this passage, linking women's apparently promiscuous desire for luxury goods with their allegedly voracious and insatiable sexual appetites. In such circumstances, as Pringle (1983: 90) has pointed out, Marx's argument about consumption as the *consummation* of production takes on a range of emotional and sexual connotations that were scarcely noticed in Marx's original insight. Nowadays, Pringle argues (1983: 98), 'consumption is directly sexual, for we are offered back a "complete" masculine or feminine identity through consumption patterns. We are under pressure to constantly "produce" ourselves through consuming commodities.' Geographers have shown how particular images are appropriate to the marketing of particular commodities, drawing on place-specific representations of masculinity and 'race' (e.g. Jackson 1994). Clammer (1992) makes a similar point about national identities, arguing that shopping can be likened to the 'buying of identity' and that contemporary Japanese consumption represents a kind of trying on of different models of society.

The ambiguities and inconsistencies of the links between consumption and identity should not be underestimated and have been the subject of investigation by social psychologists such as Lunt and Livingstone (1992). For example, while women still purchase the majority of men's clothing (Moore 1991), advertisers have not been slow to exploit the additional marketing opportunities provided by changing masculinities. Indeed, it has frequently been argued that the 'new man' amounts to little more than the creation of a new niche market (Chapman 1988; Jackson 1991).

Returning to more traditional geographical territory, it is also noticeable how sexual motifs are incorporated into the design of shopping spaces such as the mega-mall at West Edmonton, both in the larger-than-life statue of police officers arresting prostitutes on Bourbon Street in New Orleans and in the elaborate decor of some of the themed hotel bedrooms. Janice Williamson argues that such environments help 'to construct guilty pleasures as tantalisingly sinful' (Williamson 1992: 110). While for some men and women shopping malls have become the latest cruising grounds, indulging in what Mort calls 'the hyper-eroticisation of a visit to the shops' (Mort 1989: 162), the geography of consumption also involves a range of much less obviously sexualised meanings. For example, Judith Williamson writes about the everyday pleasures of shopping, the movies, the streets and the classroom as the diverse contexts for many of our contemporary 'consuming passions' (Williamson 1986),[3] while for Moore (1991: 210), shopping centres have become our twentieth-century 'gardens of earthly delights'. It is even reported that 'many Americans prefer shopping to sex' (*Forbes* magazine, quoted in Goss 1993: 18).[4]

Department stores and tea shops provided nineteenth-century women with a 'dream world' (Williams 1982) in which they could safely imagine themselves sharing the privileges of the masculine *flâneur*. The other 'dream world' of contemporary consumption is, of course, advertising, with its evocation of other places and lifestyles, designed to enthral and attract the potential purchaser. Geographers have investigated the conceptions and uses of space by advertising agencies (Clarke and Bradford 1989), arguing that spatiality is part of the very nature of the 'consumer society' (Clarke 1991). According to Sack (1992: 25), advertising is the idealised form of consumption, playing a constitutive role in the creation of the contemporary 'consumer's world'. But, as with Miller's (1983, 1991) work on the relations between advertising and the creation of American suburbs in the early years of the twentieth century – highly gendered as well as class-specific environments – we still know too little about how such advertisements were (and are) actually read by consumers. While one can infer the intended class and gender address of such advertisements with reasonable degrees of confidence, inferences about the effects of advertising on gender identities, roles and relations are much more hazardous. The same text or image can be read quite differently from different subject positions and we need to know much more about who buys particular goods and services, and how they are incorporated in people's lives, as well as more on the production and distribution of particular advertising campaigns. Burgess and Wood's (1988) analysis of the London Dockland Development Corporation's television and billboard campaigns is still exceptional in its analysis of the impact of advertising on the locational decisions of small firms.

Others have argued that consumption is a place-creating and place-altering act, arguing that places of consumption can be treated as three-dimensional advertisements (Sack 1992: 133). Often, such analyses engage in a critical deconstruction of advertising material with too little attention to the diverse circumstances of its actual consumption. Despite these criticisms, there has been a burgeoning literature on local authorities' and development agencies' attempts at 'selling places' since Burgess's (1982) pioneering work. There have been studies of the role of the arts and heritage in urban redevelopment (Zukin 1982, 1987; Jacobs 1992) and of campaigns to revitalise cities through sporting and cultural events (Boyle and Hughes 1991; Foley 1991; Whitt 1987). In each case, the coining of a witty slogan ('Glasgow's Miles Better') and appropriate evocations of landscape and place ('Why move to the middle of nowhere when you can move to the middle of London?') have been vital ingredients in 'selling places' (Kearns and Philo 1993; Gold and Ward 1993). As with many studies of the 'heritage industry', however, it is often implied that such forms of regeneration are only skin deep, 'gilding the smokestacks' in Watson's (1991) telling phrase, rather than providing a more substantial basis to civic renewal.

Geographers have been slow to appreciate the ambiguities of contemporary advertising which demand the active participation of their audiences, providing advertisers with an opportunity for increased engagement with the consumer but also opening up a space for alternative readings and consumer resistance (see Figure 6.2). They have been better attuned to the transformations of nature and environment implied in contemporary

Figure 6.2 Consumer resistance to advertising
Photo © Jill Posener, 1979 (Acme cards, 0171–284 3306)

advertisements (e.g. Burgess 1990). But here too the optimism of some observers seems misplaced. Mass consumption may 'empower us in our daily lives to change our culture, to transform nature, and to create place' (Sack 1992: 102) but rarely under circumstances of our own choosing. As with consumption in general, therefore, it is possible to entertain both optimistic and pessimistic readings of the significance of contemporary advertising. Sack's reading is resolutely upbeat:

> Mass consumption . . . is among the most important means by which we become powerful geographical agents in our day-to-day lives. . . . As consumers, we are capable of altering these [natural, social and intellectual] environments simply by being links in the production–consumption chain.
>
> (Sack 1992: 3)

Others (e.g. David Clarke 1991) provide a more negative reading of the 'hyper-reality' of advertising, offering pleasure but denying satisfaction in a cynical strategy of consumer exploitation. But, as John Clarke (1991) has argued, such simple oppositions between optimistic and pessimistic readings offer little potential for understanding the complex worlds of contemporary consumption. Similarly, Moore parodies such simplistic dichotomies in her witty essay on shopping malls:

> There are two ways to look at it. . . . You can denounce it all completely, drone on about the lack of civic space, bemoan the eroding of genuine cultural amenities in favour of numbing commerciality. . . . Or you can denounce the fuddy-duddy, puritans of the old left and the new left and become Next Left.
>
> (Moore 1991: 213)

In place of these sterile oppositions, we need to trace the contours of specific geographies of consumption and to join others in the (sometimes desperate) search for the 'audiences' of contemporary consumption (Ang 1991). Only by engaging directly with consumers will we be able to gain any purchase on the potential discrepancies between advertisers' encoded messages and their diverse decodings and to examine the effectiveness of advertising and the possibilities of its subversion.

CASE-STUDIES

Some of the key issues in the geography of consumption can be illustrated by reference to our own work. Thrift and Leyshon (1992) are concerned to link together economic and cultural change via studies of the consumption of particular high-status commodities. In contrast, Jackson is concerned with aspects of popular culture and everyday life (advertising, the media and shopping) and with exploring the links between consumption and identity. Yet this research also has common threads in its appeal to notions of national identity and to the gendered nature of representations.

Thrift and Leyshon's main concern was the study of the boom period in the City of London in the mid-1980s and its effects on consumption patterns in the Southeast of England (see also Thrift 1990). They begin by tracing out the way in which the economic boom of the mid-1980s generated a substantial increase in the salaries and bonuses of not only the partners and directors of City firms but also many other senior managers and professionals, as a result of factors like skills shortages, the internationalisation of the City's labour market, an increasingly complex institutional structure, and a general rise in salary and career expectations. These salaries and bonuses were rapidly converted into actual wealth as a result of a number of processes, including substantial asset price inflation. Thus:

> until 1987, at least, the market in stocks and shares boomed (and well-off people are more likely to keep this in money and shares). Then, after 1987, a period of high real interest rates meant that those who had switched their assets into bank or building society deposits still gained. Even more strikingly, through the 1980s markets in housing, antiques, fine art and other social assets all ran enthusiastically onwards and upwards.
>
> (Thrift and Leyshon 1992: 294)

In this account, salary and bonus inflation provided the means by which City workers could pursue high-consumption lifestyles with particularly dramatic impacts on the Southeast of England, where most of these city workers lived. Using Bourdieu's (1984) by now familiar model of the various forms of capital accumulation, Thrift and Leyshon argue that City workers strove to convert their new-found economic capital into social and cultural capital. In particular, this meant that City workers fixed on 'positional goods' (Hirsch 1977) which could most effectively demonstrate their powers of judgement. In turn, the markets for these goods boomed, since they became more sought after precisely as they became relatively more scarce.

Thrift and Leyshon illustrate these contentions through the study of one particular example of a positional good, namely the country house. Before the 1980s, the market in country houses was generally moribund. During the 1980s it boomed, even ahead of the general housing market boom. To begin with, this was the result of the injection of wealth from City workers who pursued country houses because of cultural resonances, which gave them value beyond their function. In particular, the country house proved to be the conductor of a whole series of discourses about English national identity, including nature and the countryside, heritage, and a heavily gendered idea of domesticity. These discourses were often drawn on in

226

knowing and ironic ways, yet this did not lessen their attractiveness, at least so far as the buyers of country houses were concerned.

Thrift and Leyshon also show how the initial boost to the country house market provided by City workers in the Southeast of England subsequently spread nationwide. In other words, in the 1980s the commodity was able to articulate economic capital (as an economic asset) with social capital (as a site of meeting and display) and cultural capital (as a representation of Englishness).

Our second case-study concerns the relationship between consumption and identity. Just as we have argued for the need to reconceptualise 'consumption' as a process that extends well beyond the point of sale, so too are we concerned to rethink conventional approaches to 'identity', emphasising its fluid and dynamic nature rather than assuming identities to be in any way fixed or singular. The literatures of sociology and cultural studies are helpful here in conceptualising identity as a reflexive process of self-actualisation (Giddens 1991; Lash and Friedman 1992) and arguing that hybridity and creolisation (cultural mixing) are characteristic of most if not all modern identities (Rutherford 1990). Within consumption studies, a useful starting-point is the suggestion that our identities are affirmed and contested through specific acts of consumption: we define ourselves by what we buy and by the meaning that we give to the goods and services that we acquire. But there is no essential, one-to-one, correspondence between particular commodities and particular identities: the same commodity can have radically different meanings for different individuals and for the same individual over time. Advertising and marketing campaigns have begun to realise this in targeting their products to specific niches. But rather than targeting particular market segments by associating their product uniquely and unambiguously with a particular lifestyle, they are increasingly trying to position their products in order to take advantage of the ambiguous and shifting boundaries of people's identities. As the industry's paper *Campaign* put it: 'Lifestyle advertising is about differentiating oneself from the Joneses, not as in previous decades, keeping up with them' (quoted in Mort 1988: 209). So, for example, the English National Opera's 'Known for the Company we Keep' campaign, which featured the semi-naked torso of stage technician Karl Phillips would have been read differently by different audiences according to their different subject positions. As has been argued elsewhere (Jackson 1993), the success of the campaign depended on the ambiguities of its address in terms of the audience's variable gender, class, racial and sexual positions.

Other recent campaigns have also attempted to capitalise on current debates about the shifting nature of racial and gender identities. A good example is Ogilvy and Mather's relaunch of Lucozade as an 'in-health' soft drink, shorn of its earlier associations with the sick room ('Lucozade Aids Recovery') (Jackson 1994). The highly successful repositioning of the

227

original brand and a range of associated products depended on Lucozade's endorsement by a number of black sports personalities (Daley Thompson, John Barnes and Linford Christie). These men were depicted in television and billboard advertisements in a variety of active roles, literally embodying the alleged virtues of the product. The advertisements tapped into the audience's culturally constructed assumptions about race, class and gender. But the success of the campaign depended on the choice of these particular black men and on the consumer's assumed knowledge of their particular personalities. This knowledge helped Lucozade avoid some of the more negative stereotypical associations of an anonymous and rapacious black male sexuality while making subtle allusions to the links between sporting and sexual performance. The choice of different black sportsmen, such as Frank Bruno, Mike Tyson or Justin Fashanu, would have evoked very different images of black masculinity from those intended here. Such constructions of race, class and gender are, we argue, historically and geographically specific (Jackson and Penrose 1993), a point that is frequently overlooked in studies of 'mass' consumption which, until recently, have also tended to assume a socially undifferentiated audience.

CONCLUSIONS

Over the last ten years, as this chapter has documented, geographers have begun to build up a considerable record of research into consumption. However, like all such records, it is still stronger in some areas than others. Geographers have been in the vanguard of studies of the design and use of shopping malls, contributing vigorously to the literature on 'selling places' and increasing our appreciation of the contemporary significance of world fairs and expositions. They have injected a serious concern for space, place and landscape into studies of advertising and the media and have been at the forefront of research on the production and consumption of environmental meanings, acknowledging our increasingly mediated understanding of the natural world. However, in other areas, geographical research still lacks momentum. Here, we highlight five such areas which also form an agenda for future research.

Geographers now routinely transcend the boundaries between the economic and the cultural. But this is not to say that these boundaries have completely broken down. Thus, it is still too often assumed that cultural approaches to the economic are confined to the field of consumption (rather than extending to all areas of economic life). Conversely there is still a tendency for studies of consumption to be exclusively 'cultural', paying insufficient attention to other parts of the 'circuit of culture', such as the social relations of production. Economic research could benefit from a more thorough acknowledgement of the cultural construction of some of its basic terms such as work, skill or money, while cultural studies should pay more heed to changing modes of production and to their relationship with the development of niche markets and 'lifestyle' advertising.

There have been several recent calls in geography for a more historical approach to consumption (e.g. Glennie and Thrift 1992, 1993). Although examples of the approach exist (e.g. Miller 1983, 1991), the fact remains that such calls are generally honoured in the breach. It is not so much that more studies of the historical geography of consumption are needed – although they undoubtedly are – as that most current geographical studies of contemporary consumption have too little historical sensitivity or depth. This state of affairs must surely change and a start might be made by further clarifying the vexed relationship between consumption and (an often poorly specified) 'modernity'.

As well as paying insufficient attention to the historical specificity of much current research on consumption, geographers have also been surprisingly lax in acknowledging its geographical particularity. Most geographical research on consumption has been resolutely occidental in character. There is a remarkable paucity of work which extends beyond Anglo-American frames of meaning, such as that of Chua (1992) on women shopping for fashion in Singapore, or Clammer (1992) on shopping in Japan. Given the pace of cultural and economic change in the Pacific Rim and the Far East, and the rapid development of various forms of market economy in Eastern Europe and the former Soviet Union, the scope for research in these areas is vast and largely unexplored.

Further studies are also needed more generally not only to examine the ways in which processes of consumption become part of the place-based constitution of social identities but also to recognise that these identities are not unitary or fixed but hybrid and dynamic (Hall 1994; Keith and Pile 1993). The shade of an absolutist Cartesianism, which regards consumption cultures as founded only in representation, still stalks too much contemporary geographical work. Rather than thinking of consumption cleavages working along various separate 'dimensions' of social stratification (by gender and ethnicity, for example) which then combine in various ways in particular places and at specific times, we need to explore their mutual constitution in place and time, such that our gendered identities are already racialised and our class identities are simultaneously gendered, and so on. Vron Ware (1992) gives an excellent example of such an approach in her recent work on white women, racism and history.

Finally, perhaps it is at last possible to herald the coming of the 'ethnographic moment' in geographies of consumption. There have been numerous theoretical calls in the discipline for the wider use of ethnographic studies of consumption, yet actual examples are still few and far between. That moment is now overdue if geographical studies of consumption are to become rooted in particular places, are to take sufficient account of historical and cultural specificity, and are to pay more than just cursory attention to the voices of consumers 'on the ground'.

ACKNOWLEDGEMENTS

This paper was written under the auspices of ESRC grant no. R000234443. Thanks to Sarah Whatmore who was instrumental in introducing us to the literature on international food chains.

NOTES

1 For a critique of Bourdieu's argument in relation to changing British lifestyles and consumer cultures, see Savage *et al.* (1992, Chapter 6).
2 That these conventions are still powerfully at work today is suggested by one of the respondents in Valentine's survey of lesbian perceptions and experiences of everyday space: 'There's nothing like a Saturday morning in the town centre to make you feel unconventional' (1993: 395).
3 Gardner and Sheppard (1989) use a similar title in their study of the rise of retail culture.
4 The Canadian evidence is, characteristically, more subdued: 'Time spent in shopping centres ranks third after that spent at home and work or school by the average Canadian' (Hopkins 1992: 11).

REFERENCES

Ang, I. (1991) *Desperately Seeking the Audience*, London: Routledge.
Bassett, K. (1993) 'Urban cultural strategies and urban regeneration: a critique, *Environment and Planning A* 25: 1773–89.
Becker, G. S. (1965) 'A theory of the allocation of time', *Economic Journal* 75: 493–517.
Benjamin, W. (1978) 'Paris, the capital of the nineteenth century', in *Reflections: Essays, Aphorisms, Autobiographical Writings* trans. E. Jephcott, New York: Schocken Books, pp. 146–162.
Bird, J., Curtis, B., Putnam, T., Robertson, G. and Tickner, L. (eds) (1993) *Mapping the Futures: Local Cultures, Global Change*, London: Routledge.
Blomley, N. (1993) '"I'd like to dress her all over": masculinity, power and retail space', paper presented to the IBG conference, Royal Holloway, University of London.
Bondi, L. (1991) 'Gender divisions and gentrification: a critique', *Transactions, Institute of British Geographers* 16: 190–198.
Bourdieu, P. (1984) *Distinction: a Social Critique of the Judgement of Taste*, trans. R. Nice, London: Routledge and Kegan Paul.
Bowlby, R. (1985) *Just Looking: Consumer Culture in Dreiser, Gissing and Zola*, New York: Methuen.
Boyle, M. and Hughes, G. (1991) 'The politics of the representation of the "real": discourses from the Left on Glasgow's role as European City of Culture, 1990', *Area* 23: 217–228.
Bromley, R. and Thomas, C. (eds) (1993) *Retail Change: Contemporary Issues*, London: UCL Press.
Buck-Morss, S. (1989) *The Dialectics of Seeing: Walter Benjamin and the Arcades*

Project, Cambridge, Mass.: MIT Press.

Burgess, J. (1982) 'Selling places: environmental images for the executive', *Regional Studies* 16: 1–17.

Burgess, J. (1990) 'The production and consumption of environmental meanings in the mass media: a research agenda for the 1990s', *Transactions, Institute of British Geographers* 15: 139–161.

Burgess, J. and Wood, P. (1988) 'Decoding Docklands: place advertising and the decision-making strategies of the small firm', in J. D. Eyles and D. M. Smith (eds) *Qualitative Methods in Human Geography*, Cambridge: Polity Press, pp. 94–117.

Busch, L., Lacy, W. B., Burkhardt, J. and Lacy, L. R. (1991) *Plants, Power and Profit: Social, Economic and Ethical Consequences of the New Biotechnologies*, Oxford: Basil Blackwell.

Butler, R. W. (1991) 'West Edmonton Mall as a tourist attraction', *Canadian Geographer* 35: 287–295.

Carlstein, T. (1982) *Time Resources, Society and Ecology*, London: Allen and Unwin.

Carlstein, T. and Thrift, N. J. (1978) 'Afterword: towards a time–space structured approach to society and environment', in T. Carlstein, D. N. Parkes and N. J. Thrift (eds) *Timing Space and Spacing Time, vol. 2: Human Activity and Time Geography*, London: Edward Arnold, pp. 225–263.

Carlstein, T., Parkes, D. N. and Thrift, N. J. (eds) (1978) *Timing Space and Spacing Time, vol. 2: Human Activity and Time Geography*, London: Edward Arnold.

Chaney, D. (1990) 'Subtopia in Gateshead: the MetroCentre as a cultural form', *Theory, Culture and Society* 7: 49–68.

Chapman, R. (1988) 'The great pretender: variations on the new man theme', in R. Chapman and J. Rutherford (eds) *Male Order: Unwrapping Masculinity*, London: Lawrence and Wishart, pp. 225–248.

Chua, B. H. (1992) 'Shopping for women's fashion in Singapore', in R. Shields (ed.) *Lifestyle Shopping: the Subject of Consumption*, London: Routledge, pp. 114–135.

Clammer, J. (1992) 'Aesthetics of the self: shopping and social being in contemporary urban Japan', in R. Shields (ed.) *Lifestyle Shopping: the Subject of Consumption*, London: Routledge, pp. 195–215.

Clarke, D. B. (1991) 'Towards a geography of the consumer society', *Working Paper* 91/3, School of Geography, University of Leeds.

Clarke, D. B. (1995) 'The limits to retail capital', in N. Wrigley and M. Lowe (eds) *Retailing, Consumption and Capital: Towards the Economic Geography of Retailing*, London: Longman.

Clarke, D. B. and Bradford, M. G. (1989) 'The uses of space by advertising agencies within the United Kingdom', *Geografiska Annaler* 71B: 139–151.

Clarke, D. B. and Purvis, M. (1994) 'Dialectics, difference and the geographies of consumption', *Environment and Planning A* 26: 1091–1109.

Clarke, J. (1991) '"Mine eyes dazzle": cultures of consumption', in *New Times and Old Enemies: Essays on Cultural Studies and America*, London: Harper Collins, pp. 73–112.

Cockburn, C. (1993) 'Gender and technology in the making', Lecture at the Gender Research Institute, London School of Economics.

Cook, I. (1994) 'New fruits and vanity: the role of symbolic production in the global food economy', in L. Busch, (ed.) *From Columbus to Conagra: the Global Station of Agriculture and Food Order*, Lawrence, Kansas: University of Kansas Press.

Cosgrove, D. (1989) 'Geography is everywhere: culture and symbolism in human

231

landscapes', in D. Gregory and R. Walford (eds) *Horizons of Human Geography*, London: Macmillan, pp. 118–135.

Cowan, R. S. (1983) *More Work for Mother: the Ironies of Household Technology from the Open Hearth to the Microwave*, Oxford: Basil Blackwell.

Crewe, L. and Davenport, E. (1992) 'The puppet show: changing buyer–supplier relationships within clothing retailing', *Transactions, Institute of British Geographers* 17: 183–197.

Crewe, L. and Forster, Z. (1993) 'Markets, design, and local agglomeration: the role of the small independent retailer in the workings of the fashion system', *Environment and Planning D: Society and Space* 11: 213–229.

Davies, R. L. and Llewelyn, R. (1988) *The Development of Teleshopping and Teleservices*, Oxford Reports on Retailing, Harlow: Longman.

de Certeau, M. (1984) *The Practice of Everyday Life*, Berkeley: University of California Press.

Domosh, M. (1990) 'Shaping the commercial city: retail districts in nineteenth-century Boston', *Annals, Association of American Geographers* 80: 268–304.

Dowling, R. (1993) 'Femininity, place and commodities: a retail case study', *Antipode* 25: 295–319.

Ducatel, K. and Blomley, N. (1990) 'Rethinking retail capital', *International Journal of Urban and Regional Research* 14: 207–227.

Fine, B. and Leopold, E. (1990) 'Consumerism and the industrial revolution', *Social History* 15: 151–179.

Fine, B. and Leopold, E. (1993) *The World of Consumption*, London: Routledge.

Fiske, J. (1989) 'Shopping for pleasure', in *Reading the Popular*, London: Unwin Hyman, pp. 13–42.

FitzSimmons, M. (1986) 'The new industrial agriculture: the regional integration of speciality crop production', *Economic Geography*, 62: 334–353.

Foley, P. (1991) 'The impact of major events: a case study of the World Student Games and Sheffield', *Environment and Planning C: Government and Policy* 9: 65–79.

Friedland, W. H., Barton, A. E. and Thomas, R. J. (1981) *Manufacturing Green Gold: Capital, Labour and Technology in the Lettuce Industry*, Cambridge: Cambridge University Press.

Frow, J. and Morris, M. (eds) (1993) *Australian Cultural Studies: a Reader*, Sydney: Allen and Unwin.

Gardner, C. and Sheppard, J. (1989) *Consuming Passion: the Rise of Retail Culture*, London: Unwin Hyman.

Gell, A. (1992) *The Anthropology of Time: Cultural Construction of Temporal Maps and Images*, London: Berg.

Ghez, G. R. and Becker, G. S. (1975) *The Allocation of Time and Goods over the Life-cycle*, New York: Columbia University Press.

Giddens, A. (1991) *Modernity and Self-identity: Self and Society in the Late Modern Age*, Cambridge: Polity Press.

Glennie, P. D. and Thrift, N. J. (1992) 'Modernity, urbanism and modern consumption', *Environment and Planning D: Society and Space* 10: 423–443.

Glennie, P. D. and Thrift, N. J. (1993) 'Modern consumption: theorising commodities and consumers', *Environment and Planning D: Society and Space* 11: 603–606.

Glennie, P. D. and Thrift, N. J. (1995) 'Consumption, shopping and gender', in N. Wrigley and M. Lowe (eds) *Retailing, Consumption and Capital: Towards the New Economic Geography of Retailing*, London: Longman.

Gold, J. and Ward, S. (eds) (1993) *Place Promotion: the Uses of Publicity and Public*

Relations to Sell Towns and Regions, London: Belhaven.

Goodman, D. and Redclift, M. (1991) *Refashioning Nature: Food, Ecology and Culture*, London: Routledge.

Goss, J. (1992) 'Modernity and post-modernity in the retail landscape', in K. Anderson and F. Gale (eds) *Inventing Places: Studies in Cultural Geography*, Melbourne: Longman Cheshire, pp. 159–177.

Goss, J. (1993) 'The "magic of the mall": an analysis of form, function, and meaning in the contemporary retail built environment', *Annals, Association of American Geographers* 83: 18–47.

Gottdiener, M. (1986) 'Recapturing the centre: a semiotic analysis of shopping malls', in M. Gottdiener and A. Ph. Lagopoulos (eds) *The City and the Sign: an Introduction to Urban Semiotics*, New York: Columbia University Press, pp. 288–302.

Gregson, N. and Crewe, L. (1994) 'Beyond the high street and the mall: car boot fairs and the new geographies of consumption in the 1990s', *Area* 26: 261–267.

Hägerstrand, T. (1994) 'Action in the everyday physical world', in A. D. Cliff, P. Gould, A. G. Hoare and N. J. Thrift (eds) *Diffusing Geography. Essays for Peter Haggett*, Oxford: Basil Blackwell.

Hall, S. (1994) 'New cultures for old', in D. Massey and P. Jess (eds) *The Shape of the World*, Oxford: Oxford University Press.

Hamnett, C. (1991) 'The blind men and the elephant: the explanation of gentrification', *Transactions, Institute of British Geographers* 16: 173–189.

Harvey, D. (1985a) *Consciousness and the Urban Experience*, Oxford: Basil Blackwell.

Harvey, D. (1985b) *The Urbanization of Capital*, Oxford: Basil Blackwell.

Harvey, D. (1989) *The Condition of Postmodernity*, Oxford: Basil Blackwell.

Harvey, D. (1990) 'Between time and space: reflections on the geographical imagination', *Annals, Association of American Geographers* 80: 418–434.

Hayden, D. (1981) *The Grand Domestic Revolution: a History of Feminist Designs for American Homes, Neighborhoods and Cities*, Cambridge, Mass.: MIT Press.

Hayden, D. (1984) *Redesigning the American Dream: the Future of Housing, Work, and Family Life*, New York: W. W. Norton.

Hirsch, F. (1977) *Social Limits to Growth*, London: Routledge and Kegan Paul.

Hopkins, J. S. P. (1990) 'West Edmonton Mall: landscape of myths and elsewhereness', *Canadian Geographer* 34: 2–17.

Hopkins, J. S. P. (1991) 'West Edmonton Mall as a centre for social interaction', *Canadian Geographer* 35: 268–279.

Hopkins, J. S. P. (1992) 'Landscape of myths and elsewhereness: West Edmonton mall', unpublished PhD dissertation, McGill University, Montreal.

Jackson, P. (1991) 'The cultural politics of masculinity: towards a social geography', *Transactions, Institute of British Geographers* 16: 199–213.

Jackson, P. (1993) 'Towards a cultural politics of consumption', in J. Bird *et al.* (eds) *Mapping the Futures: Local Cultures, Global Change*, London: Routledge, pp. 207–228.

Jackson, P. (1994) 'Black male: advertising and the cultural politics of masculinity', *Gender, Place and Culture* 1: 49–59.

Jackson, P. and Holbrook, B. (1995) 'Multiple meanings: shopping and the cultural politics of identity', *Environment and Planning A*.

Jackson, P. and Penrose, J. (eds) (1993) *Constructions of Race, Place and Nation*, London: UCL Press.

Jacobs, J. M. (1992) 'Cultures of the past and urban transformation: the Spitalfields market redevelopment in East London', in K. Anderson and F. Gale (eds) *Inventing Places: Studies in Cultural Geography*, Melbourne: Longman Cheshire, pp. 194–211.

Jager, M. (1986) 'Class definition and the aesthetics of gentrification', in N. Smith and P. Williams (eds) *Gentrification of the City*, London: Unwin Hyman, pp. 78–91.

Johnson, R. (1986) 'The story so far: and further transformations', in D. Punter (ed.) *Introduction to Contemporary Cultural Studies*, London: Longman, pp. 277–313.

Kearns, G. and Philo, C. (eds) (1993) *Selling Places*, Oxford: Pergamon.

Keith, M. and Pile, S. (eds) (1993) *Place and the Politics of Identity*, London: Routledge.

Knox, P. L. (1991) 'The restless urban landscape: economic and socio-cultural change and the transformation of metropolitan Washington, DC', *Annals, Association of American Geographers* 81: 181–209.

Kopytoff, I. (1986) 'The cultural biography of things: commodification as a process', in A. Appadurai (ed.) *The Social Life of Things*, Cambridge: Cambridge University Press, pp. 64–94.

Lash, S. and Friedman, J. (eds) (1992) *Modernity and Identity*, Oxford: Basil Blackwell.

Latour, B. (1993) *We Have Never Been Modern*, Brighton: Harvester Wheatsheaf.

Lee, M. J. (1993) *Consumer Culture Reborn: the Cultural Politics of Consumption*, London: Routledge.

Lefebvre, H. (1991) *The Production of Space*, trans. D. Nicholson-Smith, Oxford: Basil Blackwell.

LeHeron, R. (1994) *Globalised Agriculture: Political Choice*, Oxford: Pergamon.

Leslie, D. A. (1994) 'Disciplining women: femininity, post-Fordism and the "new traditionalism"', *Environment and Planning D: Society and Space* 11: 689–708.

Ley, D. (1986) 'Alternative explanations for inner city gentrification: a Canadian assessment', *Annals, Association of American Geographers* 76: 521–535.

Ley, D. and Olds, K. (1988) 'Landscape as spectacle: world's fairs and the culture of heroic consumption', *Environment and Planning D: Society and Space* 6: 191–212.

Linder, S. B. (1970) *The Harried Leisure Class*, New York: Columbia University Press.

Lunt, P. and Livingstone, S. (1992) *Mass Consumption and Personal Identity: Everyday Economic Experience*, Milton Keynes: Open University Press.

McRobbie, A. (1993) 'Shut up and dance: youth culture and changing modes of femininity', *Cultural Studies* 7: 406–426.

Maffesoli, M. (1992) *The Time of Tribes*, London: Sage.

Marcus, G. (1992) 'Past, present and emergent identities: requirements for ethnographies of late twentieth-century modernity worldwide', in S. Lash and J. Freidman (eds) *Modernity and Identity*, Oxford: Basil Blackwell, pp. 309–330.

Marsden, T. and Little, J. (eds) (1990) *Political, Social and Economic Perspectives on the International Food System*, Aldershot: Avebury.

Marsden, T. and Wrigley, N. (1994) 'Regulation, retailing and consumption'. Paper presented at the AAG conference, San Francisco.

Massey, D., Quintas, P. and Wield, D. (1992) *High-tech Fantasies: Science Parks in Society, Science and Space*, London: Routledge.

Miller, D. (1987) *Material Culture and Mass Consumption*, Oxford: Basil Blackwell.

Miller, D. (1988) 'Appropriating the state on the council estate', *Man* 23: 353–372.

Miller, R. (1983) 'The Hoover(R) in the garden: middle-class women and suburbanization, 1850–1920', *Environment and Planning D: Society and Space* 6: 191–212.

Miller, R. (1991) '"Selling Mrs Consumer": advertising and the creation of suburban socio-spatial relations, 1910–1930', *Antipode* 23: 263–301.

Mills, C. (1988) 'Life on the upslope: the postmodern landscape of gentrification', *Environment and Planning D: Society and Space* 6: 169–189.

Mintz, S. W. (1993) 'The changing roles of food in the study of consumption', in R. Brewer and R. Porter (eds) *Consumption and the World of Goods*, London: Routledge, pp. 261–273.

Moore, S. (1991) *Looking for Trouble: on Shopping, Gender and the Cinema*, London: Serpent's Tail.

Morgan, K. and Sayer, K. (1988) *Microcircuits of Capital: 'Sunrise' Industries and Uneven Development*, Cambridge: Polity Press.

Morris, M. (1988) 'At Henry Parkes Motel', *Cultural Studies* 2: 1–47.

Morris, M. (1989) 'Things to do with shopping centres', in S. Sheridan (ed.) *Grafts*, London: Verso, pp. 193–225.

Morris, M. (1993) 'Metamorphoses at Sydney Tower', in E. Carter, J. Donald and J. Squires (eds) *Space and Place: Theories of Identity and Location*, London: Lawrence and Wishart, pp. 379–396.

Mort, F. (1988) 'Boys own? masculinity, style and popular culture', in R. Chapman and J. Rutherford (eds) *Male Order: Unwrapping Masculinity*, London: Lawrence and Wishart, pp. 193–225.

Mort, F. (1989) 'The politics of consumption', in S. Hall and M. Jacques (eds) *New Times: the Changing Face of Politics in the 1990s*, London: Lawrence and Wishart, pp. 160–172.

O'Brien, L. and Harris, F. (1991) *Retailing: Shopping, Space and Society*, London: David Fulton.

Parkes, D. N. and Thrift, N. J. (1980) *Times, Spaces and Places: a Chronogeographic Approach*, Chichester: John Wiley.

Peet, R. and Thrift, N. J. (eds) (1989) *New Models in Geography: the Political-Economy Perspective* (2 vols) London: Unwin Hyman.

Pred, A. (1990) *Lost Words and Lost Worlds: Modernity and the Language of Everyday Life in Late Nineteenth Century Stockholm*, Cambridge: Cambridge University Press.

Pred, A. (1991) 'Spectacular articulations of modernity: the Stockholm Exhibition of 1897', *Geografiska Annaler* 73B: 45–84.

Pred, A. and Watts, M. J. (1992) *Reworking Modernity: Capitalisms and Symbolic Discontent*, New Brunswick: Rutgers University Press.

Pringle, R. (1983) 'Women and Consumer Capitalism', in C. V. Baldock and B. Cass (eds) *Women, Social Welfare and the State*, Sydney: Allen and Unwin, pp. 85–103.

Pringle, R. (1988) *Secretaries Talk: Sexuality, Power and Work*, London: Verso.

Prus, R. and Dawson, L. (1991) 'Shop till you drop: shopping as recreational and laborious activity', *Candian Journal of Sociology* 16: 145–164.

Reekie, G. (1993) *Temptations: Sex, Selling and the Department Store*, Sydney: Allen and Unwin.

Rose, D. (1989) 'A feminist perspective of employment restructuring and gentrification: the case of Montreal', in J. Wolch and M. J. Dear (eds) *The Power of Geography*, London: Unwin Hyman, pp. 118–138.

Rose, G. (1993) *Geography and Feminism*, Cambridge: Polity Press.

Rutherford, J. (1990) *Identity: Community, Culture, Difference*, London: Lawrence and Wishart.

Sack, R. D. (1988) 'The consumer's world: place as context', *Annals, Association of American Geographers* 78: 642–664.

Sack, R. D. (1992) *Place, Modernity, and the Consumer's World: a Relational*

Framework for Geographical Analysis, Baltimore and London: Johns Hopkins University Press.

Sanderson, S. F. (1986) 'The emergence of the "world steer": internationalisation and foreign domination in Latin American food production', in F. Jullis and W. Hollis (eds) *Food, State and International Political Economy*, Lincoln: University of Nebraska Press.

Saunders, P. (1984) 'Beyond housing classes: the sociological significance of private property rights in means of consumption', *International Journal of Urban and Regional Research* 8: 202–225.

Saunders, P. (1989) 'The sociology of consumption: a new research agenda', in P. Otnes (ed.) *The Sociology of Consumption*, Atlantic Highlands, NJ: Humanities Press.

Savage, M., Barlow, J., Dickens, P. and Fielding, T. (1993) *Property, Bureaucracy and Culture: Middle-Class Formation in Contemporary Britain*, London: Routledge.

Schivelbusch, W. (1986) *The Railway Journey: the Industrialisation of Time and Space in the Nineteenth Century*, Berkeley: University of California Press.

Sharp, C. (1981) *The Economics of Time*, Oxford: Martin Robertson.

Shields, R. (1989) 'Social spatialization and the built environment: West Edmonton Mall', *Environment and Planning D: Society and Space* 7: 147–164.

Shields, R. (1991) *Places on the Margin: Alternative Geographies of Modernity*, London: Routledge.

Shields, R. (1992) 'The individual, consumption cultures and the fate of community', in R. Shields (ed.) *Lifestyle Shopping: the Subject of Consumption*, London: Routledge, pp. 99–113.

Shields, R. (ed.) (1992) *Lifestyle Shopping. the Subject of Consumption*, London: Routledge.

Smith, N. (1992) 'Blind man's buff, or Hamnett's philosophical individualism in search of gentrification', *Transactions, Institute of British Geographers* 17: 110–115.

Smith, N. and Katz, C. (1993) 'Grounding metaphor: towards a spatialised politics', in M. Keith and S. Pile (eds) *Place and the Politics of Identity*, London: Routledge, pp. 67–83.

Smith, N. and Williams, P. (eds) (1986) *Gentrification of the City*, London: Unwin Hyman.

Thrift, N. J. (1987) 'The geography of late twentieth century class formation', in N. Thrift and P. Williams (eds) *Class and Space*, London: Routledge and Kegan Paul, pp. 207–253.

Thrift, N. J. (1989) 'Images of social change', in L. McDowell, P. Sarre and C. Hamnett (eds) *The Changing Social Structure*, London: Sage, pp. 12–42.

Thrift, N. J. (1990) 'Doing global regional geography', in R. J. Johnston, J. Haver and G. A. Hoekveld (eds) *Regional Geography*, London: Routledge, pp. 180–207.

Thrift, N. J. and Leyshon, A. (1992) 'In the wake of money: the City of London and the accumulation of value', in L. Budd and S. Whimster (eds) *Global Finance and Urban Living*, London: Routledge, pp. 282–311.

Valentine, G. (1993) '(Hetero)sexing space: lesbian perceptions and experiences of everyday spaces', *Environment and Planning D: Society and Space* 11: 395–413.

Walkowitz, J. (1992) *City of Dreadful Delight: Narratives of Sexual Danger in Late-Victorian London*, London: Virago.

Wallace, A. (1993) *Walking, Literature and English Culture: the Origins and Uses of the Peripatetic in the Nineteenth Century*, Oxford: Clarendon Press.

Warde, A. (1990) 'Production, consumption and social change: reservations regarding Peter Saunders' sociology of consumption', *International Journal of Urban* and *Regional Research* 14: 228–248.

Warde, A. (1991) 'Gentrification as consumption: issues of class and gender', *Environment and Planning D: Society and Space* 9: 223–232.

Ware, V. (1992) *Beyond the Pale: White Women, Racism and History*, London: Verso.

Watson, S. (1991) 'Gilding the smokestacks: the new symbolic representations of deindustrialised regions', *Environment and Planning D: Society and Space* 9: 59–70.

Whatmore, S. (1993) 'Sustainable rural geographies?', *Progress in Human Geography* 7: 538–547.

Whatmore, S. (1994) 'Global agro-food complexes and the refashioning of rural Europe', in A. Amin and N. J. Thrift (eds) *Globalisation, Institutions and Regional Development in Europe*, Oxford: Oxford University Press, pp. 46–67.

Whitt, A. (1987) 'Mozart in the metropolis: the arts coalition and the urban growth machine', *Urban Affairs Quarterly* 23: 15–36.

Williams, R. (1982) *Dream Worlds: Mass Consumption in Late Nineteenth Century France*, Berkeley: University of California Press.

Williamson, J. (1986) *Consuming Passions: the Dynamics of Popular Culture*, London: Marion Boyars.

Williamson, J. (1992) 'I-less and Gaga in the West Edmonton Mall: towards a pedestrian feminist reading', in D. H. Currie and V. Raoul (eds) *The Anatomy of Gender: Women's Struggle for the Body*, Ottawa: University of Carleton Press, pp. 97–115.

Wilson, E. (1991) *The Sphinx in the City: Urban Life, the Control of Disorder, and Women*, London: Virago.

Winchester, H. P. M. (1992) 'The construction and deconstruction of women's roles in the urban landscape', in K. Anderson and F. Gales (eds) *Inventing Places: Studies in Cultural Geography*, Melbourne: Longman Cheshire, pp. 139–156.

Wrigley, N. (ed.) (1988) *Store Choice, Store Location and Market Analysis*, London: Routledge and Kegan Paul.

Wrigley, N. (1992) 'Antitrust regulation and the restructuring of grocery retailing in Britain and the USA', *Environment and Planning A* 24: 727–750.

Wrigley, N. and Lowe, M. (eds) (1995) *Retailing, Consumption and Capital: Towards the New Economic Geography of Retailing*, London: Longman.

Zukin, S. (1982) *Loft Living: Culture and Capital in Urban Change*, Baltimore: Johns Hopkins University Press.

Zukin, S. (1987) 'Gentrification: culture and capital in the urban core', *Annual Review of Sociology* 13: 129–147.

Zukin, S. (1991) *Landscapes of Power: from Detroit to Disney World*, Berkeley: University of California Press.

237

7

PSYCHOLOGICAL APPROACHES TO CONSUMPTION

Varieties of Research – Past, Present and Future

Peter Lunt

Locating the problem of consumption within psychology

PSYCHOLOGY AND CONSUMPTION: DISCIPLINARY ISSUES

The study of economic psychology, or psychological economics, is a growing field of research. Economic psychologists are interested in a variety of topics, for example, everyday understandings of the economy, the psychological factors underlying household economic decisions, and the relations between personal identity and mass consumption. There is a *Journal of Economic Psychology* and an *International Association for Research in Economic Psychology*, which holds an annual conference and produces a newsletter. Currently there is an initiative by the Economic and Social Research Council entitled *Economic Beliefs and Behaviour*. Research in economic psychology is conducted by social psychologists, cognitive psychologists (focusing on economic decision-making) and developmental psychologists (focusing on children's developing understanding of economic processes).

However, those of us interested in economic psychology could not claim that our concerns lie at the heart of our discipline, as do several contributors to the present volume. Cognitive, computational and neurological approaches dominate the contemporary academic discipline of psychology. In research resources, professorial positions, journal editorships and other indicators of institutional power, social psychology is a poor relation. Even within social psychology, interest in economic psychology is, at best, an emerging field. Moreover, very few of the social psychologists who study economic beliefs and behaviour have an awareness of and interest in consumption as understood and discussed in this volume. My focus in this chapter, therefore, concerns the potential of what is a point on the periphery, at the margins of the discipline.

238

Psychology has traditionally been concerned with abstraction rather than an analysis embedded in the material conditions of everyday life. In contemporary psychological theory, there is little or no explicit examination of such assumptions, and despite some critique (Parker 1989), the hegemony of laboratory-based methods using experimental manipulation to test hypotheses from tentatively held theories still exists. In contrast, the approaches to consumption represented in this book presuppose the philosophical critique of positivism, the privileging of ethnographic modes of investigation, and the analysis of behaviour as dependent upon its cultural context.

Regarding the subject matter of this chapter, the field of economic psychology, one can identify two approaches. The first approach is largely ignorant of cultural approaches to consumption and is mainly concerned with developing the relationship between economics and psychology. The second engages with cultural approaches, offering a social psychological approach to mass consumption as part of a broader interdisciplinary enterprise, and so finds itself adopting a critical attitude towards psychological economics. Since the present position is that both views co-exist side by side in research on psychological approaches to consumption, I will review both positions in this paper. Both these approaches are a reaction to the initial formulation of economic psychology by Katona (1951). I will outline his position and then describe the recent attempts to elaborate his approach as decision theory and in experimental economics. I will then outline the reaction to Katona that attempts to incorporate research from other social science disciplines. A review of recent psychological research in consumption will be followed by two case-studies one (by Livingstone) illustrating the cultural approach to the psychology of consumption, the other (by Ostmann) illustrating recent developments in experimental economics.

THE ORIGINS AND DEVELOPMENT OF ECONOMIC PSYCHOLOGY

In its early days, economic psychology focused primarily on the relationship between psychology and economics. As George Katona stated at the beginning of his seminal book, *Psychological Analysis of Economic Behaviour* (1951):

> In this book we shall cut through the time-honoured boundaries of two scientific disciplines, economics and psychology. We shall look at economic processes as manifestations of human behaviour and analyse them from the point of view of modern psychology.
>
> (Katona 1951: 3)

Katona established the initial agenda for the empirical study of psychological aspects of economic behaviour. As part of that agenda he established a way of conceiving of the relations between the disciplines of psychology and economics. Katona glossed over the within-discipline differences among approaches to psychology: 'There are . . . among all present-day scientific psychologists fundamental agreements which are of great import to economic psychology' (ibid.: 28).

Katona asserts that psychology is an empirical discipline committed to the hypothetico-deductive method with two conceptions of behaviour, molar and molecular: that behaviour is characterised by plasticity within broad limits, and that psychological analysis makes use of intervening variables. Broadly, Katona offered a version of linguistic behaviourism, itself common in psychology, which commits research to the inference of mediating psychological variables based on the controlled observation of behaviour.

Despite his influential position as 'the father of economic psychology', Katona's work has received little critical attention. I will concentrate here on the implications of his principles for the interdisciplinary relationship between economics and psychology. Katona asserts a positivist account of a neat fit between the two disciplines. Under this view, there exist 'objective' economic conditions whose impact on individuals' behaviour is mediated by subjective beliefs about the economy. He argues that at any given time there is no consensus on future developments in the economy. There are always competing accounts as to whether the economy will improve or decline in the short or long term. Under such conditions people need to make up their minds about these uncertainties to decide whether to consume or to save. These aspects of public opinion become significant to the economy if, under changing economic conditions, a large group of people all change their consumption behaviour at once. In particular, if they change their propensity to save or consume as a group they can influence macro-economic phenomena such as the money available for investment. Such effects can exaggerate the business cycle if a perceived upturn in the economy encourages optimism and spending or if a perceived downturn produces pessimism and saving.

Through these concerns Katona established an agenda for economic psychology that is still highly influential. This includes making a clear distinction between the economic and the social psychological variables in any theoretical or methodological position, and consequently, between objective and subjective views of the economy. Much work following Katona has therefore focused on investigating social perception of economic indicators. For Katona social psychological processes work at the level of the individual as opposed to the group or the public. Economic behaviour is understood as the aggregated perceptions and behaviours of individuals, thus representing the public as a mass. This has resulted in an emphasis in substantive research on decision-making in consumption.

ELABORATING ATTITUDE THEORY IN RELATION TO DECISION-MAKING

Within social psychology, attitude theorists have been concerned to characterise the various influences on attitudes in the development of an intention. This work has influenced the contemporary reception of Katona's agenda for economic psychology. The most influential approach of this kind is the Theory of Reasoned Action proposed by Fishbein and Ajzen (Ajzen and Fishbein 1980). Fishbein and Ajzen argue that the intention to behave in a particular way weighs attitudinal elements against normative beliefs. People are supposed to perform a cost benefit analysis of the barriers and benefits of behaving in a particular a way multiplied by an evaluation of each cost and each benefit that determines their attitude. Normative beliefs are the perception of the views of significant others towards the behaviour multiplied by evaluations of those views.

More recent formulations of the theory have incorporated habitual decision-making and aspects of control, both of which constrain the application of the decision-making process. The value of this approach is that it has the potential to explain apparent inconsistencies in attitudes and behaviour as the result of normative and contextual influences. A person may behave in a way that is inconsistent with their attitudes if they either suspect the costs of the behaviour outweigh its advantages or they feel that disapproval from significant others will result. In the theory of reasoned action the intention to buy is determined by a weighted combination of the perceived costs and benefits of buying the item and perceptions of how others will evaluate the behaviour. People's habits and their perceived control over events surrounding the decision and its consequences can modify the influence of subjective norm and attitude.

The theory of reasoned action is a general approach to voluntary decision-making which has demonstrated psychological validity that can accommodate a variety of attitudinal, economic and social influences on economic decision-making. The main value of such an approach is in isolating the factors that influence the choice between preferences. This was the application pioneered by Fishbein and Ajzen themselves in their studies of consumer behaviour. They argue that the interpretation of preferences in consumer behaviour should be approached 'as if' it were just another kind of decision-making: 'there is really nothing particularly unusual about consumer behaviour. It is human action involving a choice among various alternatives, and there is little reason to assume that novel and unique processes will have to be invoked in order to account for such action' (Ajzen and Fishbein 1980: 149).

Fishbein and Ajzen used this approach to predict the intention to choose particular brand names of beer or motor cars. They were arguing against the notion that choice can be understood exclusively as a function of qualities of the brands (including price). They could predict intention to buy from attitudes and subjective norms and found several context effects, such as whether one is buying for own use or for others, which also influence the decision. Research on decision-making in economic psychology rarely systematically applies the model of reasoned action. However, with Katona's agenda for the subject, the study of consumption decisions is the dominant approach to economic psychological research.

EXPERIMENTAL ECONOMICS

I have argued that the combination of the agenda set by Katona in combination with the elaboration of attitude theory has led to the dominance of decision-making models in economic psychology. However, people make decisions in a state of uncertainty. People often (maybe typically) do not have all the information available to make a cost-benefit analysis and evaluation of constraints. People make decisions under uncertainty and thus they rely on a variety of heuristics that do not require the level of information that would be necessary for a full rational analysis.

The work of Tversky and Kahneman (1981) has been influential in establishing that, in handling statistical information, people rely on a variety of heuristics such as analogy or representativeness to make their decisions. This approach has become very influential in economic psychology in recent years. Both economists and psychologists have elaborated a critique of the rationality assumptions of economic theory that people base their decisions on principles of self-interest and knowledge of a variety of economic constraints and utilities such as future income. Experimental economics adopts Simon's (1957) notion of bounded rationality as a model for judgements under uncertainty. This principle asserts that people adopt particular, specified modes of reasoning which operate reasonably rather than optimally. If a way of thinking about an idea has worked well in the past or for a similar decision, then people will satisfice and adopt that solution rather than check to see if there is a more optimal one.

Guth *et al.* (1992) argue that there are two approaches to experimental economics which offer quite different notions of the relationship between economics and psychology. Experimental economics encompasses a variety of techniques that simulate in some controlled way aspects of economic (usually financial) decision-making. An advantage of this method is that there is a set of methods in game theory already applied to a wide range of psychological processes such as conflict, bargaining and negotiation, altruism, intergroup relations, and personal relationships.

Experimental economists set up 'games' that have clearly specified parameters. Rules constrain the behaviour of players and the utilities that can be maximised are controlled. Researchers then invite people to play the game. Deviations from maximum utility can be explained as a function of changes in constraints and utilities. There is no need for a radical shift in economic modelling if this approach is used to obtain subjective values for utilities and constraints under different conditions. However, a match has to be found between the specification of the game and some real-world set of constraints and utilities under which personal financial decisions operate. This turns out to be less a question of external validity and more one of matching against what is known about the distribution of a particular economic behaviour.

An alternative approach to experimental economics has also developed which aims to incorporate some psychological theory into an experimental economics approach. Informed by theories of bounded rationality, this approach suggests that decision-making is best understood not as the ineffectual application of standard, logical reasoning but of a variety of heuristics. The heuristics are common modes of reasoning which lead to a variety of biases in both the processing of information and the making of inferences. This challenges the economist's assumptions concerning rationality in economic decision-making and replaces them with a psychological account of rationality assumptions. This would place psychological experimentation in a position of challenging the assumptions of economic models and offering 'psychologically real' alternative assumptions rather than filling out the values for constraints and utilities.

CULTURALIST APPROACHES TO ECONOMIC PSYCHOLOGY

I have identified three approaches to economic psychology that attempt to build on Katona's initial agenda for the subject. As part of 'social cognition' they all reduce the process of consumption to the choice between preferences. They are all, broadly speaking, based on experimental (at least quasi-experimental) methods. Crucially, they all concern the exclusive relation between psychology and economics as disciplines and are constructed in a way that preserves the distinction between the disciplines.

In other recent work in economic psychology there have been the beginnings of the development of alternative connections with other social sciences. This move is prefigured in the conclusions of Lea, Tarpy and Webley's (1987) book *The Individual in the Economy*. They argue for what they call 'double causation'. That is that any 'economic behaviour' always takes place within a material context and that the economy is in part a consequence of aggregated economic behaviours. There is no reference in these works to social theory concerned with the structure agency problem (say Giddens, Bourdieu or Habermas) but there is reference to particular work by sociologists (e.g. Geshuny) and anthropologists (e.g. Douglas).

More recently there has been an opening out of the subject to include relations with other disciplines. For example, Lunt and Livingstone (1992) are influenced by anthropology, cultural studies and social theory in their book *Mass Consumption and Personal Identity*. Furnham and Lewis (1986) in *The Economic Mind* draw on anthropology and sociology. Dittmar (1992) cites sociology and the new consumer studies (see Belk in this volume). Finally, Livingstone (1992) draws on media theory and feminist critique (see Morley in this volume). In these works in economic psychology there has been an opening out of methods, and a movement of the subject towards consumption as reflected in other contributions in this book. This is a move away from decision theory and an embracing of cultural approaches to consumption.

These approaches, influenced by other social sciences, however, tend to adopt an agenda and definitions from economics. They take economic phenomena and treat them 'as if' they were social psychological phenomena. Economics is regarded as reductive and as ignoring significant social-psychological aspects of economic beliefs and behaviour. This psychologically driven approach has had notable success but there are problems. Sometimes researchers adopt psychological theories piecemeal, such as Dittmar's (1992) use of social identity theory or Furnham's use of personality theory. Alternatively they use a variety of psychological theories to inform exploration in some area of consumption (e.g. Lunt and Livingstone's 1991 work on savings and debt). In the former case the problem is that the topic (for example, ownership in Dittmar's work) is defined by economics in the first instance and in practice does not map neatly on to social identity theory developed to provide a cognitive account of prejudice. Similarly, Furnham uses locus of control to explain a variety of economic beliefs with some success. However, this must be a partial approach. Clearly, economic phenomena do not come packaged up into domains that map neatly on to social psychological explanations.

These approaches also tend to use broader social science literature as a means to critique economic approaches but ignore the substantive contributions from other disciplines. An example would be the wide citing of Douglas and Isherwood by all these researchers for their critique of economists' conceptions of possessions. Douglas and Isherwood (1978) are seen as useful allies in the critique of economics. However, work of Dittmar (1992) and Lunt and Livingstone (1992) on ownership do not make substantive use of Douglas and Isherwood. This trend is also reflected in textbooks that adopt a topic-based approach with an agenda set by economics (Furnham and Lewis 1986) or an agenda set by a variety of psychological theories applied to economic questions (Lea, Tarpy and Webley 1987). The question of exploring a more substantive interdisciplinarity remains.

APPLYING ECONOMIC PSYCHOLOGY

Economic psychology has always concerned itself with social problems and this provides an impetus to interdisciplinary work because social problems attract many social science disciplines. For example, in the 1930s there were several social psychological studies of poverty and unemployment (Jahoda *et al.* 1972). This theme was taken up again in the 1980s (Kelvin 1980). Similarly, a variety of highly publicised social problems around the economy – for example, debt and household budgeting, tax evasion, consumer sentiment (business confidence) – have all attracted research. These issues have all provided an impetus to economic psychology because they have clear policy relevance. Also the debates over some political issues have identified clear roles for the consumer in recent years. For example, the environmental or green movement and economic boycotts combine high-level political concerns with low-level commercial concerns. The consumer is political. These processes appear to researchers (and did so in the 1930s) to escape formulation as individual decisions and require an account concerning psychological, social and cultural processes. Such problems inevitably attract the attention of different disciplines in the social sciences and the promotion of interdisciplinary work.

LOOKING TO THE FUTURE

I have argued that there are two views (embedded in two traditions) about the present and future of economic psychology, both of which turn on arguments about interdisciplinarity. One approach urges a severing of the special relationship between economics and psychology to embrace theories and methods from a broader range of social science disciplines. The other seeks to elaborate Katona's agenda through the development of methods to study economic decision-making as reasoned action or as part of game theory. The question remains as to whether any connection can be made between these very different approaches to the future of economic psychology. The danger of the two strands developing separately is that interdisciplinary approaches to consumption can end up saying nothing to and about economics and vice versa, while experimental economics lacks validity in relation to real-world accounts of consumption. The split is a profound one reflecting a broad division in the social sciences and indeed within contemporary social psychology.

Research traditions in economic psychology: a literature review

There is an enormous literature on economic psychology (see Furnham and Lewis 1986; Lea, Tarpy and Webley 1987; and Lunt and Livingstone 1992, for overviews). What follows is a selective review covering some of the works most relevant to consumption. Because of the influence of applied research, economic psychology is most readily organised as approaches to economic problems, in other words as substantive research issues rather than, say, theoretical positions.

SAVINGS AND DEBT

The study of consumers' decisions about the relative distribution of household income is an important area of research in economic psychology. Economic theories of saving are mainly concerned with saving as a mechanism that consumers use to distribute their income over the life course (Modigliani 1970). Warneryd (1989) points out that all economic theories other than monetary theories assign some role to psychological variables. These approaches either argue for the influence of personality-like traits (thrift or self-control) or suggest that the psychological mechanisms are idiosyncratic and therefore reduce to error variance by analogy to the multiple sources of error underlying a normal distribution. The income approach is designed to predict macro-economic processes but may be a blunt instrument for designing policy or predicting trends in consumer behaviour, both of which interest the economic psychologist (Lea, Tarpy and Webley 1987).

Most studies adopt an interview or questionnaire method to collect detailed information about household or individual income and expenditure along with a profile of social and psychological characteristics. Analytically they then look for correlations among the financial, social and psychological variables as predictors of saving (Lindqvist 1981; Lunt and Livingstone 1992). There has been little predictive success with this approach, although Lunt and Livingstone (1992) did find a cluster of variables that discriminated savers from non-savers. After partialling out economic and social variables (which explained negligible amounts of variance in their data), they found a number of social-psychological predictors of saving. Fom these predictors a profile emerges for savers compared to non-savers of an internal attributional style (accepting personal responsibility), use of social support (talking to friends and relations about money), and using fixed rather than flexible financial management. These results are suggestive but these early studies, showing which economic, social and psychological variables are correlated with saving, need to be enhanced with more reliable and extensive surveys and more detailed qualitative work into the practical details of financial management.

The study of indebtedness is comparatively recent and underdeveloped (Lea *et al.* 1993) but was boosted by the increase in personal debt during the 1980s in the United Kingdom (Curwen 1990; Hartropp *et al.* 1987; Leigh-Pemberton 1989; Parker 1988). These papers reflect the introduction of flexible forms of payment which went hand in hand with the development of a flexible accumulation economy (Harvey 1989). Galbraith (1970) made a similar suggestion about the way that hire purchase had been developed to support the mass production economy in the prewar years. Only recently have systematic approaches to the social psychology of debt emerged (Berthoud and Kempson 1990; Ford 1988; Livingstone and Lunt 1992). Lea *et al.* (1993) argue that such studies offer an analysis of either crisis debt or the use (and misuse) of credit. Lea *et al.* attempt to summarise this first stage of social psychological research into debt. They suggest that the definition of debt needs working on to distinguish credit (voluntary or manageable debt) from unmanageable debt that is not necessarily crisis debt. Researchers need to work on the distinction between different sources of debt (Livingstone and Lunt 1992) and definitions based on the causes of debt to distinguish the effects of poverty from psychological variables (Lea *et al.* 1993). The increasing variety of methods of obtaining credit and debt, and changing social attitudes towards credit, suggest that the definition of debt will need constant revision and elaboration. This diversity in consumption also shows that straightforward economic criteria are unlikely to provide an adequate basis for definition and that a closer study of the practical circumstances of debt is required.

Livingstone and Lunt (1993) conducted survey and interview studies that showed that the traditional distinction between savings and debts was not adequate to deal with contemporary financial arrangements. In a survey they found many combinations of different kinds of saving and debt. People ranged in their consumption strategies from those who had neither savings nor debts to those who had various forms of both savings and debts. This challenges traditional definitions of saving and debt as a simple monetary opposition that most socio-economic theories have adopted to date. The trend towards diversity in forms of credit and debt is likely to continue in the future. The consumer will be offered an increasing variety of savings and 'credit' schemes over different terms and with widely different conditions. There is little research on the consumer's involvement in these more elaborated resources for personal financial management.

POSSESSIONS AND OWNERSHIP

There has been considerable interest in possessions in the psychological literature and various attempts to understand the processes through which personal and social identities are bound up with objects. Kamptner (1989) discusses a range of categories of object meanings based on personal interviews with people at different stages of the life course. Drawing on Csikszentmihalyi and Rochberg-Halton (1981), Kamptner produces a typology of symbolic functions for objects. The symbolic functions are concerned with maintaining personal identity. They include encoding of

247

personal history, ideal self, significant others and self-expression. There are also objects that symbolise transcendent aspects of identity. Besides these symbolic functions, goods may affect one's mood, providing pleasure, escape or security. Objects can be valued for their intrinsic qualities, such as being useful, irreplaceable, part of a collection, or handmade. A single object may carry a variety of functions. For example, a teddy bear may remind one of childhood, seen as a time of security and innocence, or of the grandmother, now dead, who gave it as a gift. The teddy may be the only object that has 'always' been there. It may encode self-identity being short and dumpy and rather battered. Some objects lend themselves more readily to certain meanings, such as photographs that encode memories or mark personal history. Generally, however, objects are open to different meanings and to different categories of meanings.

Csikszentmihalyi and Rochberg-Halton account for the symbolic meanings of objects as a balance between two dynamic forces: differentiation, 'separating the owner from the social context, emphasizing his or her individuality' (Csikszentmihalyi and Rochberg-Halton 1981: 38), and similarity, where 'the object symbolically expresses the integration of the owner with his or her social context' (ibid.: 39). Different cultures emphasise the balance between the two forces differently. For example, in Western material culture the individualising force is dominant. An account of gender differences in identity and ownership can also be formulated in those dimensions with femininity giving more emphasis to integration. Csikszentmihalyi and Rochberg-Halton found that men and younger people expressed a more differentiated and action-oriented sense of self. Also, women and older people tended more towards contemplation and other-orientation. Similar findings have been shown for men versus women (Dittmar 1989; Kamptner 1989).

The role of material objects as part of the imaginary has been shown in the ethnographic work of Caughey (1984). The imaginary functions of goods are developed in psychodynamic accounts of involvement with goods. Turkle (1984) uses a Kleinian approach to examine relations with objects such as computers. Turkle argues that objects can be symbolically powerful because of the interaction of cultural myths in which an object is imbued with the psychic anxieties, emotions or dilemmas faced by particular individuals.

A useful distinction was introduced by Prentice (1987) between instrumental and symbolic functions of possessions. Instrumental functions allow people to manipulate or control the environment to meet a need. Furby (1978) presents an elaboration of control dimensions of objects that suggests that control is complex and symbolically defined in relations with objects. Her analysis shows that the apparent instrumental (e.g. a vase) often has symbolic functions.

The above work focuses on the individual in relation to objects. Lunt and Livingstone (1992) suggest that this approach needs to be extended to include the way that objects are part of the dynamic of family relations. They use concepts from family therapy (Byng-Hall 1978; Olson *et al.* 1983; Reiss 1981) which attempts to characterise family relations using communication concepts. The dimensions of family communication include the way the family establishes boundaries and roles, the locus or domain of relations, how close or separated members of the family are, agreements about definitions of appropriate behaviours and sanctions, expression of affect and control, expressions of family identities, and problem-solving techniques (Cohler and Grunebaum 1981). In interviews with family members, Lunt and Livingstone found objects frequently mentioned as the markers of these dimensions of family relations. Goods are used to mark boundaries and role identities, provide sites of contestation and control, and to punish and reward. Communication technologies are also used to create the boundaries between the family and the outside world. Gender relations were particularly marked by ownership and rights of use over goods.

There has been a shift of emphasis in recent research on ownership and possessions away from the notion that goods provide symbolic utility and act as signs of status, towards an exploration of the way that goods provide opportunities for self-expression and personal development. The impetus for this change in emphasis has come partly from rapid changes in the domestic environment in recent times. The range of domestic objects has changed dramatically (Forty 1986; Madigan and Munro 1990) over the last few decades and this is likely to continue into the future (Putnam 1993). Underlying this concern over the changing domestic landscape is a debate over technological determinism. If material environments condition identities, then changes in material conditions will produce threats to identity. What happens when the diversity of goods becomes the most salient feature of consumption? Here there has to be a move away from classic Marxist notions and two trends are discernible. Most theorists accept the notion that this proliferation leads to a breakdown in goods functioning as markers of social status. There is then a divergence of opinion concerning the social psychological implications. One reading suggests that this diversification leads to fragmentation and loss of identity, such that power structures are no longer mirrored in personal identity and are therefore no longer visible in the everyday. Consequently, people lose awareness of their political place and become immersed in a hedonistic self-serving life. The other approach suggests that these changes in consumption break down the system of exchange and identity by highlighting choice, allowing for the formation of locally bound identities that escape control.

ECONOMIC BELIEFS

There has been considerable interest in the understanding that ordinary people have about the economy. This has partly been as an extension of the economic socialisation literature to the adult domain. This literature accepts what is said in economic textbooks as 'economic fact' and then goes on to show how shockingly ignorant most people are. However, there has also been considerable effort to map the broader understanding that people have of the economy. One approach has been part of social cognition. It aims to characterise people's knowledge about the economy using a variety of semantic representation methods. The areas of the economy that have been studied using this approach have been unemployment (Furnham 1982a, 1982b; Furnham and Lewis 1986; Lunt 1989) and poverty (Furnham 1982b; Lunt and Livingstone 1991). From this approach several dimensions of people's understanding have emerged (internal/external; controllable/uncontrollable) and an understanding has been gained of the implicit causal models people construct of economic processes. These findings challenge the view that economic decisions are taken from a narrow perspective and suggest that people build mental models of the economy which influence their economic judgements.

Another approach taken has been to examine the accounts people give of economic processes during focus group discussions (Lunt and Livingstone 1992). This approach shows that people have a complex view of the relation between economic change and personal financial decisions. There was much concern over the social and psychological consequences of the recent shifts in the consumer economy. People used a variety of oppositions to characterise these changes: cash/credit; simplicity/complexity; budgeting/borrowing, control/loss of control; institutional control/individual responsibility; necessities/luxuries; being careful/having pleasure; second-hand/new.

ECONOMIC SOCIALISATION

There was recently a special issue of the *Journal of Economic Psychology* that dealt with economic socialisation. The present review will focus on those articles and a recent review article by Webley and Lea (1993). Three stages of research can be distinguished (Webley and Lea 1993). There have been initial demonstrations of children's involvement with and understanding of economic matters. After this initial work the application of Piagetian stage theory to developing conceptions of exchange has been explored. Following this there has been the turn to the social in the examination of social influences on economic socialisation.

Initial work focused on describing economic aspects of the child's world (see Berti and Bombi 1988 for a review). The Piagetian approach to cognitive development is a stage theory which suggests that the child's understanding of the economy depends on their stage of cognitive development. The economy is a complex multivariate system that is beyond the cognitive resources of young children. Children, therefore, construct various working models of the economy according to their ability to

250

represent processes at different developmental stages. This approach received a systematic application to the development of economic understanding in the work of Berti and Bombi (1988). There have subsequently been several studies exploring the stages in the development of economic understanding. Various problems with the stage approach surfaced in the literature during the 1970s and 1980s. Differences have emerged over studies concerning the number and type of stages in the development of economic understanding. There are also concerns that an abstract cognitive approach would miss out crucial social factors (Emler and Dickinson 1985). Also, alternative notions of cognitive development have emerged such as that of Leiser (Leiser *et al.* 1990). He suggests that children first gain an understanding of components of the economy which are then built up into an understanding of more complex economic processes (Leiser *et al.* 1990).

Researchers have also provided an analysis of the influence of social factors on economic socialisation. There are several approaches. Lassarre and Roland-Levy (1989) emphasise practical demonstration in everyday life as the means of socialisation through activities such as shopping. Also, schools do not provide a formal education in economic matters. Similarly, Webley *et al.* (1991) emphasise the influence of informal play activities, such as swapping marbles. Emler and Dickinson (1985) study the different knowledge available to different social classes and the influence this has on economic socialisation. For them social knowledge is unevenly distributed in society and these substantial differences are part of the mechanism for reproducing the inequalities in the economy.

There have been several studies of cross-cultural differences in economic socialisation. Leiser and his collaborators organised a study of ten countries using the same questionnaire (Leiser *et al.* 1990; Roland-Levy 1990a). The countries surveyed were: Austria (Kirchler and Praher 1990), Germany (Leiser *et al.* 1990), the United States (Harrah and Friedman 1990), Poland (Wosinski and Pietras 1990), Yugoslavia (Zabukovec and Polic 1990), Norway (Brusdal 1990), Israel (Leiser and Zaltsman 1990), Algeria and France (Roland-Levy 1990b), and Denmark (Lyck 1990). Middle-class, mainstream children were interviewed in each country in three age groups: 8, 11 and 14 years old. The interviews were concerned with understanding, reasoning and attitudes in the economic sphere. The data were aggregated across countries and a variety of common trends in development was observed. Young children think that shops fix the price of goods at a level that reflects the inherent value of the commodity. As they get older, children attribute prices to the market and government policies, although they still believe that there is a component of the price fixed by the inherent value of the goods. It appears that children do not understand the nature of profit until the age of 11. Leiser *et al.* (1990) also report a dissociation in young children's minds between the exchange of money for

251

goods and the exchange of money for work. This reflects previous work in the area, which found that before 11 years, children understand the economy as several autonomous processes. Only after 11 do children start to see the relation between different aspects of the economy and to develop some idea of the economy as a system (Berti and Bombi 1988; Burris 1983; Danziger 1958; Furth 1980; Jahoda 1979). Similar patterns were found for reasoning and attitudes (Leiser, Sevon and Roland-Levy 1990).

Leiser, Sevon and Roland-Levy (1990) suggest that in the development of economic understanding there is a shift from the use of an explanatory model based on perceptible social relations to one based on underlying, often 'invisible' economic relations. These general trends appear robust to the authors though it was difficult to make sense of the many differences between cultures. For example, there were some differences attributable to the different institutional conditions in countries. There were also differences between specific pairs of cultures that appeared idiosyncratic and difficult to explain using broad cultural comparisons.

EVERYDAY ECONOMIC DECISION-MAKING

Decision-making is a basic orientation to economic psychology rather than a topic area. It therefore covers a huge amount of diverse literature. I will concentrate here on recent papers that explicitly use a decision-making paradigm. There has been revival of interest in the relation between personality and economic decision-making. Weak but discernible relations have been found between locus of control and consumption preferences (Lunt and Livingstone 1991); preferences for different types of resources correlate with a personality dimension from idealistic to materialistic (Stangl 1993); innovation–adaptation is weakly associated with innovative food choice mediated by involvement (Foxall and Bhate 1993). There are also general personality styles that correlate with approach to consumption (Dittmar 1989; Prince 1993). Bandstatter (1993) suggests that personality should become the dominant mediating variable studied by economic psychologists in relation to economic decision-making. He reviews literature which shows that a range of personality variables is involved in economic decision-making, including national characteristics, self-monitoring, sex role schema and need for cognition. Bandstatter suggests that future research should concentrate on the 'big five' dimensions of personality (emotional stability, extroversion, conscientiousness, agreeableness, openness).

Most research into economic decision-making adopts a cognitive decision-making paradigm similar to that of Ajzen and Fishbein (1980) rather than a personality approach. East (1993) used Ajzen's theory of planned behaviour to predict application for shares in the privatisation of public utilities in the UK. Intention was a strong predictor of application for shares and was in turn predicable from attitude, subjective norm, perceived control and past behaviour. In particular, friends' and relatives' evaluations, the financial resources to make the investment, and the perceived profits and security of the investment were all important. East's paper is exemplary in applying the full model from Ajzen's recent work whereas many papers measure only a partial set of predictors.

Livingstone and Lunt (1993), in a study that combines prediction of saving and debt, found that a combination of social perception and personality variables was required to discriminate different strategies of personal financial management. Further research needs to explore the combined effects of personality, social-cognitive variables, economic and demographic variables. It is also important to begin the process of modelling the interaction between such variables by developing and testing causal models of such sets of variables.

EXPERIMENTAL ECONOMICS

The following reviews the special issue on experimental economics in the *Journal of Economic Psychology*, vol. 13, no. 2 (1992). Oppewal and Tougareva (1992) study an extension of the two-person ultimatum game (Thaler 1988) in which a third person is included along with information about the needs of the players. The results from this game challenge economic rationality assumptions. Players attempt to produce equitable outcomes rather than the player who is holding the money taking nearly all of it. Meyer (1992) makes a similar argument about the impact of norms and self-interest in ultimatum bargaining. Meyer outlines two theoretical accounts of the bounded rationality of behaviour in ultimatum bargaining. One line follows Elster (1989) in arguing that the behaviour of subjects in these games is best understood as an attempt to maintain consistency between their behaviour and their beliefs and perceptions of norms rather than in maximising their return. An alternative account can be given concerning a Machiavellian use of norms to rationalise self-interested behaviour. This debate is at the heart of two emerging traditions in experimental economics that treats nonmaximising behaviour either as an example of the operation of social sources of rational decision-making (bounded rationality) or as a rationalisation of self-interest.

Ostmann (1992) studies the impact of social perception on experimental bargaining. Ortona and Scaciati (1992) report experiments on the endowment effect where possessed goods are given a high value. Ortona and Scaciati suggest that their results are interpretable using either economic rationality assumptions or psychological assumptions. This conclusion illustrates a problem in this literature, namely the belief that the data will (ultimately) decide between explanations which make full rationality assumptions and those that do not. The history of science suggests that theories usually have enough flexibility to cope with apparent anomalies and that data underdetermine theory. One problem is that the experimental methods adopted in this area already constrain subjects towards rational behaviour, with psychological effects defined as generating patterns of behaviour that cannot be accounted for using rationality assumptions. The specification or theorising of psychological influences on decisions needs clarification if specifiable alternative hypotheses are to be generated.

Tietz (1992) tries to clarify the decision theories based on bounded rationality. The bounded rationality concept originates in Simon's (1957) theorising and a variety of experimental approaches to decision-making. There is a wealth of criticism of the rationality assumptions of *Homo Economicus* but as yet there is no consensus on alternatives. Tietz suggests that one reason for this is the predominance of the one-shot experiment in the area (this could be a general criticism of experimental psychology). He proposes repeated experiments and the use of cognitive conflicts to increase subjects' involvement. There is a developing consensus that the experiment is the unique and appropriate method to answer these questions; that the field of possible alternative bases for a bounded rationality have been identified; and that experimental economists have already exhausted the possibilities of alternatives in considering information biases, normative assumptions and consistency theory. The challenge to develop alternative methods, and to reconsider other approaches to rationality remains.

Emerging research traditions: two case-studies

I have chosen to look at two areas of work that illustrate the split in directions in contemporary economic psychology. The paper by Livingstone illustrates work that has its roots in cultural theory; it uses qualitative methods in a field setting, and it offers the potential for collaboration with broader movements in social science reflected in this volume. The second example from experimental economics illustrates a more formal treatment of the relation between psychology and economics.

CASE-STUDY I   THE MEANING OF DOMESTIC TECHNOLOGIES, BY SONIA LIVINGSTONE

Livingstone (1992) conducted personal construct analysis interviews with several families concerning their understanding of domestic technologies. The idea behind the work is that the way that people construct domestic technologies can be understood as part of family relations. Domestic goods are not construed in terms of their inherent and functional qualities alone but as part of the way that family members interact with one another.

Personal construct theory suggests that people's understanding of their phenomenal world is built up out of key terms or constructs that are rich in meaning for the particular person.

Livingstone aims to develop an understanding of the constructs used by people to understand their domestic technologies as part of their conception of the domestic environment and personal relations. Livingstone interviewed husbands and wives separately in their own homes. She asked them to name the domestic technologies they had in their homes. People were then asked to group the objects into categories based on similarity. Livingstone then used the 'triadic method' to examine discriminating concepts for the technologies. People picked the odd technology out from the triads and then gave the reasons for their choice. The analysis consists of ordering and interpreting these reasons. In the analysis Livingstone observed several gender differences in the constructs used to make sense of domestic technologies. She suggests that gender differences are most marked in the use of the constructs of necessity, control, functionality and sociality.

Women talk of domestic technologies as necessary in their lives. They use a variety of constructs to represent the necessity of various technologies in their everyday lives: 'lifeline', 'important', 'use a lot', 'essential' and so on. Non-domestic technologies are represented in opposition to necessity, using concepts such as 'luxury' and 'rarely use'. These objects are represented through their usefulness and convenience. The spectre of domestic life without such objects is very salient to the women in Livingstone's sample. Both men and women used the construct 'control' to describe domestic technologies. However, men and women construed 'control' differently. Women talked of being in control of objects or using objects to gain control over things and processes in the domestic sphere. In contrast, men see control as mastery. Men see control as a means to gain achievements and rewards. For example, a man who ironed (a necessary activity for women) could construe it as an achievement, talking of the skills accomplishment involved. This links with a distinction that Livingstone offers of the home being a site that offers work to women and leisure to men (see also Morley in this volume). In contrast, men characterised objects in functional terms more than did women. They used the tool analogy to characterise the role of domestic technologies in their lives. This was often achieved by presenting a technical description of objects and evaluative comparisons as how much one could get out of particular objects.

Livingstone also reports differences in terms of sociality/privacy. Men talked more of the objects as substitutes for social interaction whereas women talked more of the domestic technologies as facilitators of social interaction. This is compatible with Csikszentmihalyi and Rochberg-Halton's distinction between the use of objects to differentiate or integrate the self. These functions also operate within the family conceived as a communication system. Women act to support and sustain the domestic functions of the family and its social relations. Men act to construct a leisure space for their personal gratification. This is a potential site of contestation around domestic technologies.

Livingstone also notes two general tendencies in people's descriptions of domestic technologies. They tend to use passive constructions with agent deletion thereby reducing their role in the construction of the object. Also, women seemed more aware of the revealing nature of ownership, compared to men who thought that ownership depended on the qualities of the objects! For example, the gendered use of the telephone illustrates the different ways this apparently simple object gets coded with meanings due to its perceived place in gendered domestic activity. A man describes the telephone in the following terms:

That's functional [the telephone]. . . . For example, I ring my brother if I want to ask if I can borrow his sledgehammer. . . . I don't really want to know what he did yesterday and I don't tell him what I did yesterday. . . . As I say, it's purely functional.

(Livingstone 1992: 120)

In contrast a woman describes it as:

It's [telephone] a connection to other people, other worlds, prevents me from being isolated. And if you can't get to see people, you can chat to them. So I enjoy the fact that it's there, to be in contact with people.

(Livingstone 1992: 121)

Livingstone then shows the application of this personal construct analysis of the role of domestic technologies in family interaction. She focuses on the dimension from cohesion to dispersal. Livingstone shows how the gender differences she observes in her interviews interact with family dynamics. The cohesive family partly constructs itself as such by sharing constructs for their domestic technology. In contrast an extremely dispersed or disengaged family do not share constructs for their domestic technologies. Livingstone concludes:

Domestic space, leisure time, financial resources, and ownership all combine to permit different arrangements of family life. . . . Further research should ask whether technologies are used to facilitate family cohesion and unity or family dispersal and diversity, how families negotiate their choices and what implications their understandings and decisions have for family life, technology use and gender relations.

(Livingstone 1992: 128)

CASE-STUDY II EXPERIMENTAL ECONOMICS

The example of experimental economics I have chosen to look at in detail is a paper by Axel Ostmann (1992). Ostmann studies bargaining in an experimental context. He starts by stating a basic assumption of the experimental economics approach:

> Imagine a group of mutually interdependent agents striving for a solution in a conflict of interest. They communicate, compromise, come to an agreement with all or some of their partners. If we abstract sufficiently from social, personal and other concrete components of situations we can find abstract game-theoretical representations of many (different) situations by identifying and specifying the conflict and the structure for communication and cooperation.
>
> (Ostmann 1992: 233)

Ostmann argues that many aspects of conflict are unobservable in real-life contexts, which makes systematic observation impossible. Ostmann proposes that controlled experimentation will reveal stronger data than observation in the sense of making fewer assumptions concerning the unobservable influences on overt behaviour. The assumption is that this process of abstraction and control over variables leads to an analysis of *fundamental* processes. In particular, the means of communication in experimental games and the system of contingencies for payment outcomes is controlled by the experimenter. The only remaining assumptions are that the players will follow the rules of the role play and that they will (rationally) attempt to gain the best outcome from the game.

This last assumption is the critical one for distinguishing the two approaches to experimental economics. Do we make full rationality assumptions concerning the subject or a bounded rationality approach? Ostmann ties this distinction to that of normative versus descriptive models. According to Ostmann, full rationality assumptions are more appropriate to the study of macro-level or aggregate data. To examine the real processes of, for example, bargaining, quite different rationality assumptions informed by psychological theory have to be made. He argues that the game-theoretic approach coupled with bounded rationality assumptions can be used to model 'real', complex behaviour. The formal properties of models do not have to be abandoned to examine everyday economic behaviour. This stands in direct contrast to the approach adopted by Livingstone, which moves closer to sociological and anthropological approaches.

The key development in experimental economics is to allow a psychological account of rule-governed decision procedures to replace the notion of maximum value of choice between preferences. As Ostmann suggests:

> A fundamental idea of the bounded rationality approach is that in most situations agents do not form preferences. Instead they are

assumed to use relatively simple rules and procedures for handling the situation according to their current knowledge.

(Ostmann 1992: 236)

Ostmann describes a series of experiments using bargaining games. His initial aim in this research is to isolate social effects caused by the presence of other players from the way in which individuals process the information available in the game (procedural rationality) to model the interaction between information processing and social influence processes. The bargaining games invite players with given resources to engage in bargaining to produce coalitions with other players according to certain rules to win over any other potential coalition formed by other members. Obviously, if everyone simply formed an overarching coalition they would all win, so an added constraint is the instruction to form the minimal winning coalition. For example, in a four-person game where there is one strong and three weak players the following coalitions can win: {1,2}, {1,3}, {1,4} and {2,3,4} (from Ostmann 1992).

Using variations in utilities, the 'roles' of the players can be varied (which means the coalitions that are winning will change) and players can have symmetric (substitutable) or asymmetric roles. Ostmann gives these 'roles' qualitative descriptions such as strong, protector, bourgeois. Communication is also limited in these games so that the participant is restricted to a set of experimenter-defined acts: proposals, offers, demands, agreements. These are not to be confused with their everyday counterparts because every attempt is made to strip them of argumentation and emotion. The sequence of acts is also controlled using either randomisation procedures or a prearranged sequence.

All these controls reduce the game and distance its relation to real-life bargaining. In effect, the games are attempts to rule out hot cognition and see how people act when all distractions from a cold rational decision are removed. According to Ostmann, the only motivation operating in such games is personal aspiration. The games are played out and the interactions among participants recorded. These are then content-analysed using a scheme derived from Bales' interactional analysis. Each turn is coded as exercising or resisting influence; friendly or unfriendly; and purposeful controlled or emotionally expressive. This coding is translated into two scores, the fight score (degree of conflict) and the initiation score (amount of involvement/withdrawal in the bargaining process). Ostmann found that fighters who do not initiate are often rejected from coalitions whereas those with low initiation scores are never rejected. Symmetrical players are usually treated equally (they resist attempts to play them off). Larger than optimal coalitions tended to be formed. Because of the control of the procedure Ostmann feels confident in asserting that these features of bargaining are qualitative consequences of the cognitive (rather than emotional or normative) constraints of bargaining in a group.

CONCLUSIONS

Robben and Groenland (1993) suggest that the future of economic psychology lies in confronting the greater complexity and reality of economic beliefs and behaviour. They also suggest a move from a narrow but deep analysis of a few economic decision-making processes to a broader and more superficial treatment. Robben and Groenland also argue that the progress of economic psychology until now has partly been based on attempts by researchers to maintain a distinction between psychological and sociological and economic approaches to consumption. The present chapter has argued that it may be inconsistent to both hope for a broadening of the topics covered by economic psychology and retain the existing disciplinary boundaries. In particular it will become increasingly difficult to maintain an exclusive relationship with economics. Sociology and anthropology have provided and continue to provide complex accounts of the detail of consumption processes.

I have argued that there is a broad consensus that the approach propounded by Katona, by which principles from psychology are used to supplement economic models, is questioned by both advocates of experimental economics and by those researchers who study the culture of consumption. There has been little or no dialogue between these different approaches to consumption. A potential problem is that this polarisation may result in social 'variables' being treated as part of the design of game theory experiments and the 'economic' disappearing from the study of the meanings of consumption.

Such issues are not simply methodological but reflect disagreement concerning how to deal with complexity in real social situations. The experimentalist gets parameters of variation under control in experimental design whereas the more interpretative approaches offer embedded observation of the variety of consumption processes. Social psychology is attracted by both approaches because of its connection with rational decision-making theory and its connection with microsociology.

I have argued that a key element of these different approaches to the development of economic psychology is interdisciplinarity. The experimental economics approach seeks to integrate psychology and economics more closely, whereas the cultural approach seeks to relate psychological work to a broader cross-section of the social sciences. However, for researchers in both these traditions there has been a move away from viewing economic psychology as an applied area. Researchers now expect the interdisciplinary enterprise to affect their core discipline, whether that be economics or psychology. This is also a historical problem for social psychology. The case of economic psychology is just one example.

Finally both the experimental economics and the cultural approach are responding to growing feelings among researchers that social science analysis has to become more complex and more grounded in everyday life. These developments are reflected in consumption practices becoming more complex at the level of the involvement of the individual in the economy. These changes are part of the move towards postmodern conditions or flexible accumulation. These very different views of recent changes in capitalist societies agree that at the level of the life of the consumer there has been a remarkable diversification and change in recent years. The increasing importance of the consumer in Western economies provides the impetus to more grounded and more complex analyses of everyday economic beliefs and behaviour.

ACKNOWLEDGEMENTS

Thanks to Sonia Livingstone and Danny Miller for comments on an earlier version of this paper.

REFERENCES

Ajzen, I. and Fishbein, M. (1980) *Understanding Attitudes and Predicting Social Behaviour*, Englewood Cliffs, NJ: Prentice-Hall.

Bandstatter, H. (1993) 'Should economic psychology care about personality structure?', *Journal of Economic Psychology* 14 (3): 473–494.

Berthoud, R. and Kempson, E. (1990) *Credit and Debt in Britain*, Report of first findings from the PSI survey, London: Policy Studies Institute.

Berti, A. E. and Bornbi, A. S. (1988) *The Child's Construction of Economics*, Cambridge: Cambridge University Press.

Brusdal, R. (1990) 'Norwegian children's descriptions of the consequences of poverty and wealth', *Journal of Economic Psychology* 11 (4): 545–556.

Burris, V. (1983) 'Stages in the development of economic concepts', *Human Relations* 36: 791–812.

Byng-Hall, J. (1978) 'Family myths used as defence in conjoint family therapy', *British Journal of Medical Psychology* 40: 239–250.

Caughey, J. L. (1984) *Imaginary Social Worlds: a Cultural Approach*, Lincoln, Nebraska: University of Nebraska Press.

Cohler, B. J. and Grunebaum, H. U. (1981) *Mothers, Grandmothers and Daughters*, New York: Wiley.

Csikszentmihalyi, M. and Rochberg-Halton, E. (1981) *The Meaning of Things: Domestic Symbols and the Self*, Cambridge: Cambridge University Press.

Curwen, P. (1990) *Understanding the UK Economy*, London: Macmillan.

Danziger, K. (1958) 'Children's earliest conceptions of economic relationships', *Journal of Social Psychology* 47: 231–240.

Dittmar, H. (1989) 'Gender identity-related meanings of personal possessions', *British Journal of Social Psychology* 28: 159–171.

Dittmar, H. (1992) *The Social Psychology of Material Possessions: To Have is To Be*, Hemel Hempstead: Harvester.

Douglas, M. and Isherwood, B. (1978) *The World of Goods: Towards an Anthropology of Consumption*, Harmondsworth: Penguin.

East, R. (1993), 'Investment decisions and the theory of planned behaviour', *Journal of Economic Psychology* 14 (2): 337–376.

Eiser, J. R. (1986) *Social Psychology: Attitudes, Cognition and Social Behaviour*, Cambridge: Cambridge University Press.

Elster, J. (1989) *The Cement of Society: A Study of Social Order*, Cambridge: Cambridge University Press.

Emler, N. and Dickinson, J. (1985) 'Children's representation of economic inequalities', *British Journal of Developmental Psychology* 3 (2): 191–198.

Ford, J. (1988) *The Indebted Society: Credit and Default in the 1980s*, London: Routledge.

Forty, A. (1986) *Objects of Desire: Design and Society, 1750–1980*, London: Thames and Hudson.

Foxall, G. R. and Bhate, S. (1993) 'Cognitive styles and personal involvement of market initiators for "healthy" food brands: Implications for adoption theory', *Journal of Economic Psychology* 14 (1): 1–16.

Furby, L. (1978) 'Possessions: towards a theory of their meaning and function throughout the life cycle', in P. B. Baltes (ed.) *Life-span Development and Behavior*, New York: Academic Press.

Furnham, A. (1982a) 'Explanations for unemployment in Britain', *European Journal of Social Psychology* 12: 335–352.

Furnham, A. (1982b) 'Why are the poor always with us? Explanations for poverty in Britain', *British Journal of Social Psychology* 21: 311–322.

Furnham, A. and Lewis, A. (1986) *The Economic Mind: The Social Psychology of Economic Behaviour*, Brighton: Wheatsheaf.

Furth, H. (1980) *The World of Grown-ups*, New York: Elsevier.

Galbraith, J. K. (1970) *The Affluent Society*, 2nd edition, London: Pelican Books.

Guth, W., Warneryd, K.-E., and Lea, S. E. G. (1992) 'Editorial: economic psychology and experimental economics', *Journal of Economic Psychology* 13 (2): 199–201.

Harrah, J. and Friedman, M. (1990) 'Economic socialisation in children in a midwestern American community', *Journal of Economic Psychology* 11 (4): 495–514.

Hartropp, A., Hanna, R., Jones, S., Lang, R., Mills, P. and Schluter, M. (1987) *Families in Debt: The Nature, Causes and Effects of Debt Problems and Policy Proposals for Their Alleviation*, Jubilee Centre Research Paper No. 7, Cambridge: Jubilee Centre Publications.

Harvey, D. (1989) *The Condition of Postmodernity*, Oxford: Blackwell.

Jahoda, G. (1979) 'The construction of economic reality by some Glaswegian children', *European Journal of Social Psychology* 9: 115–127.

Jahoda, M., Lazarsfeld, P. and Zeisel, H. (1972) *Marienthal: The Sociography of an Unemployed Community*, London: Tavistock.

Kamptner, N. L. (1989) 'Personal possessions and their meanings in old age', in S. Spacapan and S. Oskamp (eds) *The Social Psychology of Aging*, Newbury Park: Sage.

Katona, G. (1951) *Psychological Analysis of Economic Behaviour*, New York: McGraw-Hill.

Kelvin, P. (1980) 'Social psychology 2001: The social psychological bases and implications of structural unemployment', in R. Gilmour and S. Duck (eds) *The Development of Social Psychology*, London: Academic Press.

Kirchler, E. and Praher, D. (1990) 'Austrian children's economic socialization', *Journal of Economic Psychology* 11 (4): 483–494.

Lassarre, D. and Roland-Levy, Ch. (1989) 'Understanding children's economic socialization', in K. Grunert and F. Olander (eds) *Understanding Economic Behavior*, Dordrecht, Boston, London: Kluwer Academic Publishers, pp. 347–368.

Lea, S. E. G., Tarpy, R. M. and Webley, P. (1987) *The Individual in the Economy: A Survey of Economic Psychology*, Cambridge: Cambridge University Press.

Lea, S. E. G., Webley, P. and Levine, R. M. (1993) 'The economic psychology of consumer debt', *Journal of Economic Psychology* 14 (1): 85–120.

Leigh-Pemberton, R. (1989) 'Personal credit problems', *Bank of England Quarterly Bulletin* 29 (2): 243–245.

Leiser, D., Sevon, G. and Roland-Levy, Ch. (1990) 'Children's economic socialization: Summarizing the cross-cultural comparison of ten countries', *Journal of Economic Psychology* 11 (4): 467–468.

Leiser, D. and Zaltsman, J. (1990) 'Economic socialization in the kibbutz and the town in Israel', *Journal of Economic Psychology* 11 (4): 557–566.

Lindqvist, A. (1981) 'A note on determinants of household saving behaviour', *Journal of Economic Psychology* 1: 39–57.

Livingstone, S. M. (1992) 'The meanings of domestic technologies: A personal construct analysis of familial gender relations', in R. Silverstone and E. Hirsch (eds) *Consuming Technologies: Media and Information in Domestic Spaces*, London: Routledge.

Livingstone, S. and Lunt, P. (1993) 'Savers and borrowers: strategies of personal financial management', *Human Relations* 46 (8): 963–985.

Lunt, P. K. (1989) 'The perceived causal structure of unemployment', in K. Grunert and F. Olander (eds) *Understanding Economic Behaviour*, Amsterdam: Kluwer.

Lunt, P. K. and Livingstone, S. M. (1991) 'Psychological, social and economic determinants of saving: comparing recurrent and total savings', *Journal of Economic Psychology* 30: 309–323.

Lunt, P. and Livingstone, S. (1992) *Mass Consumption and Personal Identity*, Milton Keynes: Open University Press.

Lyck, L. (1990) 'Danish children's and their parents' economic understanding, reasoning and attitudes', *Journal of Economic Psychology* 11 (4): 583–590.

Madigan, R. and Munro, M. (1990) 'Ideal homes: gender and domestic architecture', in T. Putnam and C. Newton (eds) *Household Choices*, London: Futures Publications.

Meyer, H.-D. (1992) 'Norms and self-interest in ultimatum bargaining: the prince's prudence', *Journal of Economic Psychology* 13 (2): 215–232.

Modigliani, F. (1970) 'The life-cycle hypothesis and inter-country differences', in W. Eltis (ed.) *Inflation, Growth and Trade*, Oxford: Clarendon.

Olson, D. H., McCubbin, H. I., Barnes, H. L., Larsen, A. S., Muxen, M. J. and Wilson, M. A. (1983) *Families: What Makes Them Work*, Beverley Hills: Sage.

Oppewal, H. and Tougareva, E. (1992) 'A three-person ultimatum game to investigate effects of differences in need, sharing rules and observability on bargaining behaviour', *Journal of Economic Psychology* 13 (2): 1–16.

Ortona, G. and Scaciati, F. (1992) 'New experiments on the endowment effect', *Journal of Economic Psychology* 13 (2): 277–296.

Ostmann, A. (1992) 'The interaction of aspiration levels and the social field in experimental bargaining', *Journal of Economic Psychology* 13 (2): 233–262.

Parker, G. (1988) 'Credit', in R. Walker and G. Parker (eds) *Money Matters: Income, Wealth and Financial Welfare*, London: Sage.

Prentice, D. A. (1987) 'Psychological correspondence of possessions, attitudes and values', *Journal of Personality and Social Psychology* 53: 993–1003.

Prince, M. (1993) 'Women, men and money styles', *Journal of Economic Psychology* 14 (1): 175–182.

Putnam, T. (1993) 'Beyond the modern home: shifting the parameters of residence', in J. Bird, B. Curtis, T. Putnam, G. Robertson and L. Tickner (eds) *Mapping the Futures: Local Cultures, Global Change*, London: Routledge.

Reiss, D. (1981) *The Family's Construction of Reality*, Cambridge, Mass.: Harvard University Press.

Robben, H. S. J. and Groenland, E. A. G. (1993) 'Editorial: The future of economic psychology', *Journal of Economic Psychology* 14 (3): 455–460.

Roland-Levy, Ch. (1990a) 'Economic socialisation: basis for international comparisons', *Journal of Economic Psychology* 11 (4): 469–482.

Roland-Levy, Ch. (1990b) 'A cross-national comparison of Algerian and French children's economic socialization', *Journal of Economic Psychology* 11 (4): 567–582.

Simon, H. A. (1957) *Models of Man*, New York: Wiley.

Stangl, W. (1993) 'Personality and the structure of resource preferences', *Journal of Economic Psychology* 14 (1), 1–16.

Thaler, R. H. (1988) 'Anomalies: the ultimatum game', *Journal of Economic Perspectives* 2 (4): 195–206.

Tietz, R. (1992) 'Semi-normative theories based on bounded rationality', *Journal of Economic Psychology* 13 (2): 297–314.

Turkle, S. (1984) *The Second Self: Computers and the Human Spirit*, New York: Simon and Schuster.

Tversky, A. and Kahneman, D. (1981) 'The psychology of choice and the framing of decisions', *Science* 211: 4353–4358.

Warneryd, K. (1989) 'On the psychology of saving: An essay on economic behavior', *Journal of Economic Psychology* 10: 515–541.

Webley, P. and Lea, S. E. G. (1993) 'Towards a more realistic psychology of economic socialization', *Journal of Economic Psychology* 14: 461–472.

Webley, P., Levine, R. M. and Lewis, A. (1991) 'A study in economic psychology: children's saving in a play economy', *Human Relations* 44: 127–146.

Wosinski, M. and Pietras, M. (1990) 'Economic socialization of Polish children in different macro-economic conditions', *Journal of Economic Psychology* 11 (4): 515–528.

Zabukovec, V. and Polic, M. (1990) 'Yugoslavian children in a situation of rapid economic changes', *Journal of Economic Psychology* 11 (4): 529–544.

8

CONSUMPTION STUDIES AS THE TRANSFORMATION OF ANTHROPOLOGY

Daniel Miller

I The significance of consumption for anthropology

THE DEVELOPMENT OF AN ANTHROPOLOGY OF CONSUMPTION

It is not hard to find references to studies of consumption at almost any period of modern anthropology. These are most often found within works that were primarily concerned with other topics prominent at the time, such as spheres of exchange (Bohannon 1955), gifting (Gregory 1982), the study of prestige goods (Friedman and Rowlands 1977), sumptuary laws, cargo cults (Worsley 1957), boundary maintenance (Hodder 1982) and so forth. Sometimes they are linked through the category of 'material culture' with archaeological concerns. None of this, however, amounted to a recognised category of consumption studies. They were largely isolated instances of concern with consumption that had no accretive result. More sustained has been a continual movement of anthropologists into commerce. This included several figures who appear in Belk's chapter because, although trained in anthropology, they moved into business and consumption studies.

Arnould and Wilk (1984) noted that on the whole such early works emphasised the manner in which consumption was, in practice, subordinated to larger concerns and therefore did not threaten the overall concept of culture which was used to valorise most studies in American anthropology in particular. This is suggested also by studies in the 1940s and 1950s where anthropologists often ended their ethnographic works with a chapter on social change, which increasingly became premised on the arrival of Western goods in the particular region. In general 'Western' consumption goods were viewed as a loss of culture and threat to the anthropological object of study.

The arrival of mass consumption is often identified with the coming of the market as noted in the earlier debates between formalists who espoused the relevance of economist's models and substantivists such as Polanyi who romanticised the resistance to disembedded forms of transaction. Yet as Dilley (1992: 12–13) has recently noted, even the latter nevertheless failed to critique the assumptions that follow from the use of the term 'market'. This implies a clear, logical and impersonal system which would finally lead to the destruction of inalienable relations with objects and those transactions still embedded in community.

This historical trajectory implies that as long as there was an explicit or even implicit culture concept as a definitional premise of anthropology, then consumption not only did not, but in a profound sense could not, arise within the discipline. It lay too close to the usually unstated core justification for the project of anthropology as the establishment of an 'other' constituted by holistic and unfragmented culture against which modernity – that is the form of society from which the anthropologist had come, could be judged as loss. The point is made directly in cartoons that may be found from time to time in journals such as *Punch* and the *New Yorker* which showed archetypal 'natives' with bones through their noses exhorting each other to put away the radios (later televisions, or some other conspicuous commodity) because 'the anthropologists are coming'.

Of course, there has always been an anthropology of modernity, and works that dispute such crass generalisations about anthropological predilections for 'unadulterated' otherness. Nevertheless, these cartoons give a valid indication of why people are drawn to the study of anthropology and of the great attraction among a non-professional audience of anthropological films, books and TV programmes. Within the discipline this stance has been constantly upheld by vulgarised versions of Mauss's distinction of gift and commodity or Tonnies of Gemeinschaft and Gesellschaft (there are a number of alternatives). These are used to create a standard dichotomy which again could most easily be symbolised by the presence of absence of mass commodities.

It follows that the rise of an anthropology of consumption in the last two decades has more than parochial implications. It constitutes a transformation in the nature of the discipline as a whole. Perhaps for anthropology more than for any other discipline (though see Fine, Chapter 4, for an alternative candidate), the study of consumption represents first the threat of dissolution and the end to its historical project, but ultimately, quite the opposite, it opens up the promise of a significant future.

In practice the development of a more self-conscious study of consumption by anthropologists arose from quite different trajectories than those studies which might have been expected to represent its precursors. Anthropology on the whole is a small discipline and it is only quite recently that the academic output has not been overwhelmingly concerned with substantive ethnographic accounts of peoples as remote from metropolitan areas as possible. It is perhaps surprising then that its influence on the social sciences and humanities has perhaps been second only to philosophy. Probably the single most significant eruption of anthropological thought on to other disciplines occurred during the late 1960s and early 1970s with the influence of Lévi-Strauss's particular brand of structuralism and the associated studies of semiotics. These were first prised from linguistics and their subsequent anthropological appropriation emulated by most other social studies.

Although Lévi-Strauss himself has been largely concerned with 'tribal' societies, there are some lines of descent between his work and the establishment within anthropology of a new study of consumption. One of these derives from the writings of a number of other French intellectuals. These included Jean Baudrillard, who in three books between 1969 and 1972 established the study of systems of objects, but then also transcended this with a critique of the idea of objects as a representational system (see especially 1981). There was also the influential book *Mythologies* by Barthes (1973), which also focused on the critique of the commodity as sign. In contrast the work of de Certeau (1984) suggested a more positive role for consumption as a form of resistance. French structuralism and post-structuralism began to influence anthropology partly through writings on the semiotics of material culture. These included the final chapter of Sahlins' *Culture and Practical Reason* (1976), but also the work of several archaeologists such as Hodder (1982) and Shanks and Tilley (1986: 172–240).

What was missing in these works was a sense that a quite new perspective was required on the process of consumption itself or its significance in the modern world. The birth of the new anthropology of consumption may therefore unambiguously be dated to 1978–1979 with the publication of *The World of Goods* by Mary Douglas and Baron Isherwood (1978) in Britain and *La Distinction. Critique sociale du jugement* by Pierre Bourdieu (1979) in France. The contribution of these works to theories of consumption will be discussed in the following section but here my concern is to appreciate why they were pivotal in establishing a new sense of consumption and why this should take place in anthropology.

In the British case it is not surprising that it was Mary Douglas who ensured that these issues were raised sooner rather than later. This is consistent with Douglas's particular contribution to British social anthropology. This was only one of a whole string of publications that demonstrated a willingness to take anthropological ideas out of their normative disciplinary concerns and apply them to other domains such as biblical narratives, the study of organisations or risk.

The World of Goods was directed not primarily at anthropologists, but at the discipline which up to that point would have seemed synonymous with the concept of an academic study of consumption, that is economics. This may account in large measure for the importance of the book, since by pointing out (rather gently on the whole) the quite ludicrous assumptions that the discipline of economics made with respect to consumption, the sense that there simply did not exist an adequate alternative perspective on that topic became palpable.

In the case of Pierre Bourdieu it was equally evident that this rise to perspicacity was wholly appropriate for an individual who was again never definable as an anthropologist in the narrow sense of that term, but had always spanned a wide range of disciplinary concerns from educational studies to the arts. Nevertheless while Douglas remained closer to a dominant anthropological lineage from Durkheim through Lévi-Strauss that was concerned with principles of order *per se*, Bourdieu achieved his enormous importance through that other core strand of anthropological concerns, namely the formation of methodologies for the study of social relations. Bourdieu argued simultaneously that the structure of consumption was the key to the reproduction of class relations, but also that it thereby provided a novel mechanism by which analysts could study social relations in some objectified form – here as a pattern of taste.

Building upon these earlier works the study of consumption became more concretely established through a series of books in the latter half of the 1980s. These included *The Social Life of Things* by Appadurai in 1986, *Material Culture and Mass Consumption* by Miller in 1987, *Culture and Consumption* by McCracken in 1988 and *The Social Economy of Consumption* edited by Rutz and Orlove in 1989. In addition there appeared a number of monographs which did not necessarily position themselves within this topic but provided important scholarly work to exemplify the new theoretical trend. These included the work of Mintz (1985), Tambiah (1984), Thomas (1991) and Weiner and Schneider (eds, 1989).

THE CONSEQUENCES OF AN ANTHROPOLOGY OF CONSUMPTION

I have suggested that for anthropology more than any other discipline (except perhaps economics) the study of consumption may represent a fundamental transformation. It was the consumption of 'Western' goods that the discipline was largely defined against in an act of what Carrier (1992) has called Occidentalism. But simply to inject a new consideration of consumption would not constitute such a shift. There were two gambits open to anthropology which would preserve the status quo. In an article called 'Drinking cash', Toren (1989) examines the Kava ceremony in Fiji as a means by which money can be introduced but then subsumed within traditional cosmologies, its potential for the articulation of separate spheres partially neutered by ritual which detaches it from market exchange and engages it as an object of ceremonial exchange. This has been a common theme in relation to both money and commodities. Anthropologists have stressed the ability of traditional systems of meaning and exchange to incorporate that which might have been expected to threaten them. The second possibility was to regard mass consumption of commodities as simply an erosion of culture. As societies enter into the world economy, they are assumed to give up their historical 'birthright' for a mess of homogenising consumption porridge, which results in an almost measurable loss of 'culture' understood as those attributes of difference which made them originally of interest to anthropological study. It is probably the case that until recently anthropological studies of consumption were dominated by these two perspectives, neither of which represented a challenge to the implicit presuppositions of at least the public face of anthropology.

It is only when mass consumption is regarded as diversity *a posteriori* – that is, a source of difference which emerges from trajectories that are not merely reliant upon past historical diversity – that the significance of this new area of concern becomes evident. This requires that the particular forms of consumption in a region are no longer viewed as part continuity of cultural difference and part loss. Instead they must be regarded as an authentic variant of the mass consumer societies that make modernity a comparative and heterogeneous presence rather than an assumed global homogenisation. Otherwise the subject of anthropology as a discipline seems destined to shrink into a largely historical concern. Societies can be lauded for their spirit of 'resistance' to capitalism or elegies composed for lost specificity, but there is almost a fatalism with respect to the unsentimental march of history towards mass consumption, with poverty almost coming to play the part of a remission of grace for the unchanged.

In the 1980s a new attitude arose with the celebration of creolised and syncretic movements (e.g. Gilroy 1993). This was paralleled by the emergence of the terms 'local' and 'global', which in as much as they replaced the term 'Westernisation', allowed for a greater contribution from a diversity of regions to new forms of homogeneity but also recognised the new heterogeneity of metropolitan regions. Reluctantly the prejudices of a search for authenticity implied in arguments about the 'invention of tradition' are abandoned. Anthropologists grant that apples can be as much a nostalgic element in a Caribbean national cuisine as raisins can be part of a traditional ritual dish in a temperate zone. Different roads to modernity are recognised, first as Sahlins (1988) argues as 'cosmologies of capitalism' with structural continuities recognised between before- and post-capitalist periods. Later new differences are seen to emerge from often unprecedented sources, utilising the possibilities of consumption goods to produce significant rather than merely superficial distinctions.

Through the study of consumption anthropology recasts its subject matter as diversity, which is expanding in the contemporary world rather than contracting. New Age Californians and Singaporean puritanism are accepted as authentic modernities of consumption. Clichés about narcissism and individualism as the inevitable outcome of the encounter with mass consumption are contradicted by evidence for new, highly egalitarian and normative forms of domestic consumption. Overall there is a new equality between the 'bizarre' uses made of consumption forms by 'Western' peoples and all other societies. A generic West or America no longer provides the benchmark of normative use against which other people's consumption would be regarded as distinct or derivative.

I believe this has a positive effect upon the moralities of anthropology, since it should spell the end of that romantic nostalgia which had the effect of allowing only 'Western' peoples to be the true inheritors of the industrial revolution. It means that West Africans in suits playing video games are no longer seen as somehow unnatural or lacking authenticity, and we can have ethnographies of the consumption of personal computers in Africa (e.g. Jules-Rosette 1990) that do not patronise. It also means that poverty is regarded as just that – a relative lack of resources. This does not mean that all peoples should either desire mass consumption or that this be seen as a positive achievement. Desire for goods is not some natural attribute of humanity, and anthropology should continue to document the many varied responses to the possibilities of consumption, which are as likely to be as diverse in the future as in the past. We should always be prepared for the society that sees shopping as a variant of hunting rather than a variant of exchange (Overing 1992). There have been asceticisms and conservatisms of many kinds throughout history and today there is a powerful green movement which eschews the waste and immorality of many aspects of mass consumption. But it is important that green ideology is regarded as the conscious understanding of novel forms of responsibility, rather than Amazonian Indians being fostered as other people's projection of primitive affluence.

To conclude, I suggest that the acceptance of consumption as an equal arena of anthropological enquiry is regarded as a fundamental coming to maturity of anthropology – a final expunging of latent primitivism. The discipline may support resistance of peoples to the encroachments of the market where this is a locally expressed goal, but should not promote their exclusion from the products of industrial society otherwise. As such, culture itself will no longer be regarded as an attribute to be lost or gained, but rather as a process or struggle by which all peoples of the world attempt to make sense of the world and make claims to social and material forms and institutions integral to the process by which we make ourselves.

II A review of the anthropological literature

DEFERRED AND LIMITED CONSUMPTION

Given the radical nature of these changes it is not surprising that the major contribution of anthropology until recently was less a study of consumption than a challenge to assumptions about any natural propensity to desire goods. Probably the single most influential article was 'The original affluent society' (1974) where Sahlins destroyed the earlier evolutionary hypothesis that saw human history as a move towards leisure through successive modes of production that gradually freed us from the demands of subsistence. Sahlins showed that societies that live by hunting and gathering often not only had available, but also indulged in, more leisure time than societies that live by other means. Especially in lush tropical regimes, people may have had few possessions but they were not poor, because perceived needs were few and easily attainable.

Equally important were examples of societies where there was a clear injunction against immediate consumption. One of the clearest cases derives from the study by Munn (1986) of Gawa island within the famed 'Kula' ring off the coast of Papua New Guinea. Witches and other malevolent spirits provide a powerful sanction against those who would wish to eat what they themselves produce. Such consumption is regarded as wasteful because the products have not been used to expand culture or what locally is regarded as the feats of islanders and the fame of the island. Only when products are part of complex exchange cycles do they provide the instruments for cultural skill and reputation, after which they may be properly consumed. Also working in Melanesia, Strathern (1988) argues against the assumption of Western philosophy that people have a 'natural' right to the products of their labour. For a people more interested in exchange than production, the foods and objects produced are understood as having a natural relation to their intended destination rather than to those who happen to grow or make them. Other goods, according to Weiner (1985), embody the lineage or history of a group. They are thereby regarded as inalienable, essential to the integument of the society as objectified presence.

In such studies cosmology provides a kind of pre-emptive resistance to the imperatives of what was to become, with the introduction of commodities, mass consumption. Rather different in tone are those studies of the initial encounter with goods which suggest rituals or acts of resistance to the increasing encroachment of consumption goods. Although much disputed, this represents one of the most influential interpretations of Melanesian cargo cults. In these, people constructed complex rites, including the building of airstrips, in order to accomplish what was often seen as a wresting back of the magic power to conjure goods that seemed

270

to have been appropriated by whites. Worsley (1957), in particular, represented these millenarian movements as precisely a coming-to-consciousness of the disinherited; comparable to militant millenarianism amongst the historical poor of Western Europe. A clearer example of myth as rejection comes in Guss's (1986) analysis of myths constructed by the Yekuana of southern Venezuela, which sees the local culture hero as the producer of goods who also deceived the Spanish into thinking they had invented them.

One of the most explicit developments of a concept of resistance has been offered by Comeroff (1990). As is common in the response of many anthropologists to mass consumption, she juxtaposes the deep symbolic and material integration of particular classes of goods, in this case cattle, with the threat of the dissolution of such linkages to a totalising social system. This occurred through modern developments which resulted in what she describes as the reduction of 'goodly beasts' to merely 'beastly goods'. A contrast may be drawn with cases such as that of the Amish documented by Umble (1992). Here a community constructs itself around a self-conscious refusal to accept most of the possibilities of consumption utilised by those who surround them, and accepts some (such as the telephone) only with very clear constraints on their social use. Without such religious resources resistance is more difficult, as Weismantel (1989) reveals by documenting the considerable pressures on groups without such a holistic cosmology to adopt the customs of those around them. In this case the children of impoverished Indians of highland Ecuador attempt to force their parents to adopt expensive white bread in a battle of stigma against sentiment. They thereby repeat a pattern which historically has in many regions replaced the local equivalent of boiled cereal (a gruel or porridge) with bread.

The notion of resistance is clearly heavily permeated by more general premises in the writings of political economy which have influenced anthropologists. This sometimes includes a generalised puritanism which assumes that the desire for goods is based on an irrational materialism. Other critiques may lurch between a notion of utilitarian value (mainly in sociological accounts) and a functionalism which asserts a symbolic value (mainly in anthropological accounts) essential to traditional social reproduction. These approaches are bolstered by an approach to commodities that sees them as inevitably fetishistic vehicles of false consciousness. The frame of reference partially inverts in development anthropology, where poverty is conceptualised as a lack of access to goods, but retains a notion of 'basic needs'. This flies in the face of virtually all anthropological work on pre-industrial material culture which suggests that it is utilitarianism itself, as an abstract principle, which is the primary sign of encroaching modernity. Such approaches represent the 'other' to an emergent celebration of consumption in cultural studies and popular culture studies, which

271

project romantic ideas of consumption as resistance to capitalism amongst the working classes of industrial societies. Of course there are also more sophisticated treatments of this issue, as for example Abu-Lughod's (1990) discussion of the use of lingerie amongst young Bedouin women.

Resistance cannot be an assumed perspective on the encounter with goods. By contrast, Hugh-Jones (1992) notes how some groups, such as the Amazonian Indians, have been utilised in Western debates as a model for the 'natural' or 'green' refusal of materialism. This is in marked contrast to actual experience which, he suggests, often takes the form of an avaricious greed for goods well beyond that previously experienced by visitors, and therefore coming as something of a shock. The problem has tended to be precisely this utilisation of other peoples as exemplifications of ideal states rather than a consideration of the local conditions which accounts for the wide variety of different attitudes to the consumption of particular forms of goods. This may equally pre-empt an expansive materialism and its expressive possibilities, as they may reflect that Western ideology which sees this as the destruction of the most cherished local values.

CONSUMPTION AND ECONOMIC ANTHROPOLOGY

Anthropological approaches to the economy have tended to rest upon dualistic foundations such as that between 'formalist' and 'substantivist' economic principles (Polanyi 1957). Recently the older distinction of gifts and commodities theorised by Mauss has come to prominence and is clearly defined by Gregory (1982). In general, the concern has been to differentiate societies typically studied by anthropologists, which are characterised by the embedded nature of economic acts, as against societies where the economy is relatively unfettered by the social consequences of exchange. In some cases the two economies are juxtaposed as a contemporary dualism (e.g. Brookfield and Hart 1971). Anthropologists have therefore tended to emphasise restrictions on exchangeability. For example, discussions of 'spheres of exchange', such as Douglas (1958) on Raffia cloth amongst the Lele, suggested that what might have been taken as currencies were actually only exchangeable for a limited range of goods, or for goods from outside the region. A particularly fine example of this point comes from Price's (1984) study of the Saramaka Maroons of the Surinam rain forest. She analyses the aesthetics of women's embroidery in terms of their exchange with the trade goods men bring back from work on the coast. Goods that represent the alienation of monetary exchange are thereby reincorporated back into the reproduction of social systems.

This tendency to dualism has been challenged in a number of recent works. In a recent edited collection on barter, Humphrey and Hugh-Jones (1992) show how barter systems do not fit the expectations of gift-commodity distinctions. They suggest barter may emerge from a variety of sources including the rejection of monetarised regimes (as in Barcelona during the Spanish Civil War), but also may provide an alternative to gifting in requiring the independent establishment of systems of trust and evaluation between exchange partners. Appadurai (1986) provides the most concerted attempt to derive an approach to commodities through the established trajectory of anthropological studies of exchange, by concentrating precisely on the degrees of exchangeability. He criticises earlier anthropological studies which too easily defined 'traditional' exchange as pure constraint and commodity exchange as pure freedom of exchangeability. Goods purchased from shops subsequently may pass in and out of situations of inalienability, as may goods in less monetarised societies. Recent work has included a new emphasis on the conditions of inalienability (Weiner 1985) and an emphasis on how these differences act as a cultural biography of things themselves (Kopytoff 1986).

Probably the most subversive article in recent years with respect to this tradition is a study by Gell (1992) of Melanesia. Gell starts with the astonishing claim that the classic form of gift exchange (that used in social reproduction) is best understood as derived from, and therefore secondary to, commodity barter. In order to make this claim he has to show that commodity-like exchange, so far from being a recent result of colonial presence, was a key characteristic of pre-colonial trade in this region. The article should be read in full, but briefly the suggestion is that males, in particular, utilised the freedom of intertribal exchange with its elements of fame and danger to contrast with the relative constraint on intragroup exchange roles. In certain circumstances they were able to make reproductive exchange, such as marriage payments, dependent upon models developed in the sphere of external trade.

The critique of evolutionary and dualistic models of exchange has opened the ground for an acceptance of more diverse and contingent models, first of exchange, and then in turn for the emergence of forms of consumption. An example in Pacific studies is the work of Thomas (1991), who shows how the considerable diversity of exchange systems led to quite different points of encounter with trading and commodities in the early contact period. As noted by Sahlins with respect to Hawaii (1992), this could equally be cast in terms of the emergence of diverse regimes of consumption. This recent work in the Pacific represents a more mature phase in the study of the colonial encounter, allowing for a wide variety of responses and consequences rather than merely projecting an assumption as to its likely outcome.

A very different approach to consumption arises out of another branch of economic anthropology than that concerned with gifting. This is a long-standing interest in the evaluation of wealth and poverty and the abilities of households to cope with different forms of demand. Work in Latin American slum households at a time of high inflation and falling income (or growing commoditisation e.g. Heyman 1990) may make consumption decisions highly salient but also expose the processes by which priorities are established (e.g. Selby *et al.* 1990). This may include actual consumption priorities, as in studies by Jelin (1991) within Buenos Aires, but also the significance of family relations and economic support, as Fonesca (1991) argues with respect to the importance of male siblings in a Brazilian slum. As in the case of sociologists studying in more affluent areas such as Britain (e.g. Pahl 1984), anthropologists have tended to focus upon household relations with respect to their place in production rather than consumption. In this respect it is interesting to compare the earlier work of Sharma (1980) on gender in India, which focuses exclusively on production, with her later ethnography (1986), which demonstrates the importance of women's consumption skills in the move to an urban environment.

While some anthropologists contribute to larger macro studies of household expenditure, most such work falls into the domain of economics. More often anthropologists have been concerned to challenge the assumptions of economics itself with regard to motivation. In particular, they contrast the use of more individualistic models to their own focus upon the social foundations of demand. Rutz and Orlove (1989) talk in terms of a 'social economy' approach which addresses similar concerns to economists but with an emphasis on social structure and social values. Rutz's own work in Fiji (1989) is concerned with time expenditure, both in relation to Becker's models but also *vis à vis* the importance of social status in explaining choices made in food consumption. New foods are often assimilated within the established connotations of traditional foods: such as root crops with egalitarianism, or beef as a kind of 'super-pig' for ceremonial occasions. The foundation for this critique of economists' views about the sources of the desire for goods was provided by Douglas and Isherwood (1978). But the more general impact of that book has been a move away from such concerns and instead a concentration of anthropological research on the symbolic and expressive dimensions of consumption acts, which is the concern of the next section. Meanwhile the anthropological critique of economics has passed beyond the old formalist/substantivist debate to a more radical questioning of basic economic terminology and the presentation of growing empirical support for the idea that the pure market relations presupposed as foundational to modern consumption may simply not exist, even within highly developed consumer markets (e.g. Alexander 1992; Carrier 1994).

CONSUMPTION IN THE CONSTITUTION OF THINGS AND PERSONS

Douglas and Isherwood contrasted economists' approaches to consumption with a structuralist concern with the use of objects to create order in the world as a system of categories. They then used these ideas to return back to economic concerns such as definitions of relative impoverishment. In later work Douglas has concentrated on the implications of her more general culture theory based on grid/group analysis, for the study of consumption and material culture more generally (Douglas 1992). Douglas's earlier semiotic approach was akin to that employed by Sahlins (1976), who drew up classificatory 'trees' to map the choices, made by American workers, of appropriate clothing.

Such work gave rise to important debates about the relationship between the order that was present in the classification of things and the prevalent social order. Barthes (1973) stressed the importance of commodities as myths cementing ideological positions, typically that of the most powerful interests of the time. As noted above, Baudrillard went further in reducing people to mannequins who merely legitimate arrays of goods through embodying the 'lifestyles' that are used to justify their purchase.

Anthropological interventions in such debates have been more prosaic but also more carefully observed. A key distinction is brought out in two papers in a book on the consumption of drink edited by Douglas (1987). On the one hand drinks may construct the world as it is. So, for example, Mars (1987) documents the pattern of drinking by which the longshoremen of Newfoundland determine who is part of their social world and their relative reputation within it. By contrast, some of the papers in the same book reflect not a given world so much as an ideal world. Bott's (1987) study of Kava drinking in Tonga emphasises the ceremonial and symbolic quality by which an idealised set of hierarchical relations is established in a formal state.

One of the points that emerges from anthropological concerns with goods as classificatory is that ideology is by no means a new phenomenon and many of the consequences that are glibly projected on to capitalism also applied in non-capitalist contexts. Perhaps the strongest evidence for this continuity of analysis is provided by the work of Bourdieu (1984) who himself applies similar methodological and interpretive schemata to both contexts. His enormously important study of taste in France clearly demonstrates how the vast array of distinctions in people's consumption preferences reflect key social distinctions. These are mainly between class fractions but they also reproduce other distinctions of gender, and different forms of prestige such as business capital as against aesthetic capital. On the other hand, as with Barthes, he sees these uses of taste as ideological in the sense that they provide the naturalised foundations for the reproduction of social inequalities. The artificial source of such inequalities is made to appear natural by the alliance between educational pretensions to meritocracy and the belief that differences in taste reflect mere individual idiosyncrasy.

As such this study of contemporary French mass consumption remains true to Bourdieu's earlier (1977) study based on North African peasant communities. Here too the practical taxonomies found in the order and the sense of appropriate use of a wide range of objects such as house form and calendars are seen to naturalise social differences and inequalities, in particular, between men and women. In this case, however, objects have if anything still greater importance than in capitalist societies because they, and not formal pedagogic systems, provide the basis for socialisation into distinct social roles.

The work of Bourdieu provides a link between those anthropologists who are primarily concerned with social relations and view goods as merely a means for uncovering these, and those who give more serious attention to material culture itself, and the specific means by which culture is constructed as both social and material worlds. Hendry (1989), for example, by focusing upon the art of wrapping presents, is able to demonstrate a link between the etiquette of exchange and consumption on the one hand and an aesthetic principle which so pervades Japanese life as to be much more than merely the 'form' of relationships. As in Mars's study of drinking patterns, when so much of one's life is devoted to the reproduction of accepted cultural forms, it is problematic to see this as the mere surface to some true anthropological goal conceived of as abstract social relations. This is also why Baudrillard's formula cannot be accepted. Ironically it is often in non-capitalist societies that it would be more true to say the individual is merely the stand upon which cultural forms are hung, while it was with the emergence of capitalism itself that there developed some of the strongest liberal ideologies which projected humanity as the only acceptable goal of life.

The case of Hindu South Asia provides an instance where the senselessness of trying to privilege either social or material order becomes evident. Established Hindu cosmology long recognised a close association between consumption and social and personal constitution. In much of the traditional law (Dharmasastra) the sense that 'you are what you eat' is taken quite literally and this is reflected in the beliefs and daily practices of most Hindus with respect to ingestion. Thus, for example, certain foods are thought to make a person hot, given to violence and intemperance. These foods are therefore mainly proscribed for higher castes such as the Brahmin, who are expected to retain a cool intellectual manner, but are permitted to those high castes such as the Rajput, who are renowned for their military abilities and bearing. The logic of ingestion as consumption may lead to complex practices such as those of the ascetic funerary priests of Benares, documented by Parry (1982), who carefully invert normal rules of ingestion in order to become appropriate for their particular ritual roles. Similar concerns are addressed to the processes by which aspects of the ingested substances are refined into bodily forms such as blood and semen or are excreted as waste, and there is considerable concern for the proper evacuation of body orifices.

This concern with the specificity of acts of consumption is not restricted to food. Most goods are carefully chosen as being appropriate, often to a precise sub-caste, such that virtually all goods and raw materials can be classified according to their relative purity and thus acceptability to high castes. The effect is to create a parallel to the hierarchies of goods documented by Bourdieu but in this case the relationship of social and material worlds is explicit and one does not meet the denials often found in France. In the field of clothing, for example, Bayly (1986) and Cohen (1989) document the historical developments by which the way in which the person is enveloped in cloth was used to create images of hierarchical encompassment between kings and subjects as part of larger tributary systems based around the exchange of cloth. These were in turn exploited by the British in attempts to place themselves at the apex of hierarchical orders through the development of their own rituals and through often only partially understood adaptations of rules about head coverings or the appropriate times for shoes to be discarded, etc. The dynamics of such systems are also revealed by Bean's (1989) study of the development of the characteristic clothing associated with Gandhi and the Congress movement he founded. In parallel to the explicit experimentation of marketing agencies in trying to sell new styles, Gandhi experimented with a number of sartorial forms before the final development of the 'Mahatma' garb in 1921, which was adopted by hundreds of millions of followers thereafter.

Following from these debates as to the proper relation between the pattern of goods documented in consumption and the constitution of social order, several theorists have attempted to develop a more comprehensive approach. They regard culture as a dynamic process through which both persons and things equally can be understood as part of this process of societal self-construction. There is a strong complementarity in this ambition between the ideas published by Strathern (1988) with respect to Melanesia and by Miller (1987) attempting a more general theory of culture. Miller uses the concept of objectification in order to transcend theories of symbolism. He argues that the Hegelian notion of the dialectic is more appropriate for studying the continual process by which culture develops, in as much as values and social relations are not prior to the cultural form they take, and therefore not reflected by them, but are created in the act by which cultural forms come into being. Miller focuses on the place of material culture in this process of objectification, ending with a specific emphasis upon goods within contemporary mass consumption. This is justified by the argument that there has been a historical shift in the relative importance of consumption as against production and distribution in the constitution of society and culture. Consumption has become the main arena in which and through which people have to struggle towards control over the definition of themselves and their values. This struggle is often posed against larger institutions such as capitalism and the state, which would impose these upon them. The final plea is for research into the circumstances within which these struggles take place and how they are perceived by those engaged upon them.

In many respects the emphasis on objects in Miller could be substituted by the emphasis on subjects by Strathern. Strathern also takes as her point of departure a revision of certain ideas in Marxist anthropology. In her case it is the assumption that there is a given relationship between goods and those whose labour produces them. More radically Strathern challenges the humanism which underlies not only Marxist but also liberal positions in the West based around assumptions about integral individuals and their rights. Instead she argues that in Melanesia it has been both persons and especially aspects of persons that are the objects used in exchange. The constitution of social being therefore is again contingent upon a dialectical process by which persons are conceived of as sometimes integuments, but sometimes merely repositories for a combination of aspects of other persons who are in relation of exchange with them. Thus gender itself is often a mere state of divisibility, necessitating a distinction being made, so that these two different forms can be united in productive labour or reproduction. At other times the person is better understood as androgynous – merely the evidence for the productive capacity of others. Consumption as well as identity is here the sign not of one's own agency but of the agency of others.

Although these two books are distinguished in their respective emphasis upon things or persons as objects, later work combines their approach. MacKenzie (1991), for example, exemplifies many of Strathern's points through an exemplary study of New Guinea net bags and the complementarity of male and female labour and ritual use, such that the bags themselves help objectify the sense of gender prevalent in this area. Miller (1988), in an application of his theoretical ideas to the study of the consumption of state-given kitchens by tenants of a North London council estate, in turn takes a 'Melanesian' perspective. He shows how the development of 'do-it-yourself' as a form of male labour appropriate to the home environment provides the complement to female control over the aesthetics of the home to create a dynamic to the conceptualisation of gender itself within this British class fraction.

In such work the acts of consumption (as also previously acts of production and acts of exchange) become less a separate arena of economic life and instead become studied as the primary cultural sphere in which any number of value-creating human processes may be observed. As such, as is typical in anthropology, one aspect of social life may be primarily studied as an idiom for another. For example, Hirsch (1993) recently studied (alongside several colleagues) North Londoner's discussions of the possibilities of New Reproductive Technologies. On the one hand couples were worried about the new possibilities of social engineering; on the other hand there were stories of concern about people, in effect, renting the wombs of surrogate mothers. What emerges from the interviews is that couples are working out their attitude to commodities and consumption as a sense of the proper relationship between the state and the market. A balance was being sought which prevented the kind of individualism with respect to 'choosing' one's progeny that would make childbirth too akin with shopping, and which also prevented such strong state control over these technologies as would deprive people of that degree of choice they felt would be reasonable for them to assume.

To conclude this section: the debate over the implications of consumption reflects a longstanding concern with the role of material objects in society. This has moved very quickly from the foundations established by Douglas and Isherwood and Bourdieu. In many respects it leads to areas that are hardly specific to consumption itself, such as new ways of understanding society, culture and gender. On the other hand there has arisen, as noted in the introduction, an increasing realisation that, irrespective of the particular interests of the anthropologists, it is increasingly consumption as an activity which has become the arena of practice within which such topics must be studied. Even in Melanesia there are numerous voices arguing for a move away from an emphasis upon gifting, as reconstructed in pre-colonial situations, to a world in which it is the consumption of beer, betel-nut, coffee and similar resources which provide the forms through which such societies are now developing (Carrier and Carrier 1991; Foster forthcoming; Hirsch 1990; Strathern 1984). In short, almost irrespective of the specific domain of enquiry, consumption is increasingly the world of practice with which the anthropologist must engage.

CONSUMPTION, CAPITALISM AND MODERNITY

To engage with consumption means also engaging in the larger context for consumption which today is usually (though not always) the world of capitalism. Here two main tendencies may be noted in anthropology. The dominant concern has been with a generalised approach to capitalism which renders it as almost synonymous with Western expansion and colonialism, usually with the anthropologist taking the perspective of the 'local' defined as the people studied. A less pronounced tendency has been a more relativistic perspective which focuses upon the diversity within capitalism and capitalist society. The advantage of the latter is that it has the effect of putting Western societies on a more equal footing with all other societies. It is no longer the case that American forms of shopping or status competition become viewed as the 'natural' form of consumption and those of all other regions aberrant variations upon this.

With regard to consumption, one implication of the first approach has been the consequences of Western consumption for production in the developing world. A clear example of such a linkage is provided by Mintz (1985), who traces the development of sugar consumption, mainly in Europe, and the major transformation of diet that it represented during the period of industrialisation where it provided a quick form of available energy. He then documents the corresponding development of early agro-industry in the sugar plantations in the Caribbean and elsewhere which supplied the sugar to satisfy this new demand. Historians such as Goodman (1993) are now undertaking similar work with regard to items such as tea, coffee and tobacco. One need only add spices in the early period and opium in the later period to appreciate how fundamental the evolution of new consumption tastes were to the development of colonialism. Swallow (1982) provides another poignant case showing how contemporary fashions in Britain (in this case for cheesecloth) could have devastating effects on South Asian weavers as demand rises and falls for reasons that are unknown to, and unpredictable for, the producers.

The second inference has been drawn from the link between changes in demand and consumption in the regions that produce goods according to First World specifications. A relevant case-study is documented by Spooner (1986) with regard to the ironies of authenticity. This is a criterion that does not concern the Iranian Turkeman with respect to the carpets they produce, but increasingly will become their concern with regard to the Western goods, such as blue jeans, which they import in exchange for carpets. Most commonly, anthropologists have been concerned for the loss of self-sufficiency in the regions they have tended to research (e.g. Gewertz and Errington 1991), and have documented the means by which imported goods and cash incomes have been 'tamed' by being incorporated within traditional structures of use (see p. 268).

The desire of anthropologists to 'protect' their subjects of study from being transformed by outside forces has been challenged by a more general relativism with respect to both capitalism and consumption. One of the main challenges to a focus on mass consumption as 'Westernisation' has been to note the relative neglect of the historical importance of areas such as India and China, which dominated Old World trade and production for much of recorded history. Sahlins in an important paper (1988) has argued for continuities between pre-capitalist and capitalist China (see also Hamilton and Lai 1989), and that the same point can also be made for the transformation of early capitalism in areas such as Hawaii and the Northwest coast of America. This was partly because there were powerful imperatives towards very particular modes of consumption in both areas. The use of the terms 'local' and 'global' have allowed for greater consideration of the contribution all regions make to what is locally perceived of as 'global' homogenising forms. As a corollary of this, Miller (1992) notes a case where imported images (in this case American soap opera) may be more empowering of local concerns than locally produced images. Often this happens when, as Wilk (1990) argues for television more generally, new communications and other media may undermine local elites. Drakulic (1992) makes a similar point with regard to the imperatives to consumption as undermining communist regimes, which increasingly became characterised as a culture of 'shortages'. In each case, however, consumption as local emancipation may become merely the vehicle for greater loss of autonomy and greater subservience to larger economic powers, a point discussed in more detail in the introductory chapter.

The early anthropological work on consumption was passionate about how this arena had been neglected because of the overwhelming interest in production and exchange relations. This 'point' is increasingly being seen as having been established. Today more anthropologists are trying to examine the relationship between these three domains. Miller (in preparation) is currently researching the different ways a small region (Trinidad) conceptualises itself through the whole gamut of production, marketing, advertising, retail and consumption. Several researchers have also examined the manner by which advertising, marketing and retailing may pre-empt the concerns of consumers to appropriate goods (e.g. Carrier 1990; Lien 1993; Sherry and McGrath 1989). As Alexander notes (1992: 89–91), it is extraordinary how little ethnography has been attempted on, for example, the way in which prices are fixed in fully developed consumer markets. Yet even cursory studies show that quite contrary to the assumptions implicit in the concept of the 'market', prices show remarkably little relation to demand, and are closer to perceptions of 'fair' mark-up.

As an alternative to focusing upon capitalism as the context for modern mass consumption, there has been an equally pronounced concern by anthropologists to use consumption to exemplify conditions of modernity and postmodernity. Partly this builds upon theorists, such as Harvey (1989), who have argued for a more general transition. This would make new modes of consumption symptomatic of new modes of production generally, including both capitalist production and also international finance. The task of anthropologists has been to try and characterise this new state in which flexible 'post-Fordism' is matched by flexible identity creation and new creolised and pluralist forms. The journal *Public Culture* has included numerous articles on this theme and Appadurai (1990) has been particularly influential in using the debates about 'local' and 'global' formations to expand upon these new conditions. Arguments for a kind of macro-shift in identity construction which subsume new forms of consumption have come in a variety of versions such as Friedman (1990) and Strathern (1991). Some of these works have attempted to appropriate new aesthetic forms and literary styles in order to capture the image of this new consumption world within the form as well as the content of their contributions.

Within more traditional anthropological forms of enquiry and presentation there has also been a concern with the relationship between consumption and modernity. Ethnographic work has often been concerned with the manner in which people perceive for themselves the new forms of global power and attempt to both appropriate and ameliorate the conditions under which they might be destroyed by these global influences. A wide range of studies suggest that people often bring to this task earlier forms of 'local' and 'global' distinction such as between rural areas and the town. Tambiah (1984) in Thailand and Rowlands (forthcoming) in Cameroon show how urban entrepreneurs see their successful utilisation of new consumption worlds as dependent upon their not neglecting the spiritual resources and powers that are located in the remote forest ascetics or village ancestral shrines. In a similar vein, recent work on the festival of Christmas (Miller 1993) has examined how both the cosmology of Christmas with its links between domesticity and some transcendent global 'family', and also its involvement in elaborate purchasing and gifting, may be in part a response to the perceived threat posed by materialism to the maintenance of sociality.

Another important series of studies by anthropologists has shown how certain of the key items in modern consumption are themselves used to objectify, and thereby understand, the nature of modernity as social experience. This was because for many people the entry into consumption is also seen as their entry into modernity. Weir's (1985) analysis of the consumption of *Qat* in Yemen concludes on this theme, as have a number of papers by Wilk (e.g. 1990) on Belize. The theme is also taken up by Friedman (1990) in reporting studies of the *sapeur* of central Africa. Other versions of these concerns include a focus upon the key terms used to conceptualise these shifts in consumption (e.g. Moeran 1984) or a focus on what anyway would be regarded as key symbols of modernity, such as the computer (Jules-Rosette 1990) or new communication media (Turner 1992). What several of these studies demonstrate is how societies on the periphery of the industrial world often seize upon new possibilities of consumption with alacrity and use them to embody elements of modernity which as yet are resisted by more metropolitan regions. These portrayals of the Third World as often in the vanguard of new practices of consumption provide thereby a useful complement to earlier studies which tended to emphasise patterns of resistance or the taming of imported goods and images.

It is important, however, that these studies also address other highly problematic areas of consumption such as addictive drugs. An example is contained in a proposal to research the cult of guns, violent videos and the general tendency to violence as 'style' amongst the West African youth currently being recruited to the armies of various warlords in Liberia and elsewhere in West Africa (Richards forthcoming). Often the integration of imported images goes hand in hand with a re-creation (and commoditisation) of the local area as self-consciously distinctive and 'traditional' (e.g. Tobin 1992), or with the construction of an increasingly separate elite class (Sklair 1991). As Foster (forthcoming) notes for a local example in Papua New Guinea, the construction of a cosmopolitan elite class of consumers is often the stimulus to, rather than opponent of, the affirmation of a specific and often nationalistic localism.

To conclude this review, it is evident that for a field that hardly existed a mere decade ago, there is a tremendous surge in research today. It may seem that this is partly because the term 'consumption' rather than being applied narrowly to acts of purchase and use, has rapidly expanded to mean anything from the popular appropriation of state services to the literal translation of ingestion in traditional Hinduism. Such eclecticism, however, is typical of anthropology in which, as Strathern (1991) has pointed out, almost anything can become the context or idiom for almost anything else. This, however, is a strength rather than a weakness of a discipline which is anyway much more successful exemplifying the diversity of human practices through detailed scholarship than arguing about the proper definition of its semantic tools.

III Two case-studies

HOUSES AND HOUSEHOLDS

In an article entitled 'Houses as consumer goods – social processes and allocation decisions', Wilk (1989) examines the dynamics of consumption amongst the Kekchi Maya of southern Belize. In common with a number of other writers on consumption, he simultaneously addresses the constitution of the household as a unit of consumption and the house itself as an object of consumption. This work exemplifies one of the key points of anthropological concern, the inseparability of the material and social processes involved. Wilk compares three villages differentiated by their relative degree of involvement in the cash economy. In the village least involved with commodities, house construction remained a communal and not merely a household task. It was conducted by the village as a whole and was important in coordinating the relationship between the household and the community. Houses were therefore largely identical in form and did not reflect differences in household income and status. In order not to challenge this expression of equality, cash incomes are spent upon personal consumption items such as jewellery or cigarettes, which reflect individuals, rather than on goods that might represent either household or community. By contrast, in a village with more cash involvement, most household income is spent on house furnishing and items, which for the wealthiest meant building for themselves new non-Kekchi style houses. Any further income is spent on household priorities such as educating a child rather than on individual consumption.

In the village least concerned with commodities the sense of corporate community remains powerful; here the main threat to community ideology comes from an overt expression of differences between households. Consumption is therefore channelled into the less threatening arena of individual luxuries. As Wilk notes, the first households to use imported housing material may incur considerable hostility. In areas of greater cash involvement, where this battle against the individual construction of houses by households is lost, the dominant pattern shifts. The unit of concern is usually a set of houses around a compound each consisting of a nuclear family, the whole representing an extended family. The major threat now becomes perceived as the relative contribution of individual members of the household, both in terms of productive labour and income. In particular, individual cash-earning members must be persuaded to subsume themselves within a family economy that includes subsistence farming. The ideal is therefore to channel consumption into household projects such as the house itself or the education of children as against potential individual aggrandisement. The house as a consumption object thereby changes from being the principal threat to communal values to becoming the principal strategy for protecting such values.

Gell (1986) also studied the changing consumption concerns of a tribal group as they enter into the cash economy; in this case, the Muria of Central India. Various new economic opportunities had arisen which resulted in relatively large cash incomes and resources for some families. Once again there was a desire to retain the traditional sense of egalitarianism amongst the community more widely, and therefore a constant search for forms of expenditure that did not pose a threat to core values. Indeed, the wealthiest members of the community were often the most explicitly puritanical and ascetic in their daily consumption. Nevertheless one of the wealthiest families was on its way to building five surplus houses at the time it was studied. This was because for this group the construction of housing could be represented as a merely practical and sensible investment rather than as a form of symbolic consumption *per se*. House-building therefore provided a means for using up surplus money without appearing to indulge in forms of consumption that would have signified social differences and which Gell suggests were simply not seen as attractive to those who maintained the core values of the group.

It is noticeable that in the case of the Muria the ideology of equality that continues to play a major role in their self-definition is not primarily a contrast with some larger Western capitalism assumed to represent a more individualistic and hierarchical society. Rather the salience of equality lies in its opposition to the surrounding Hindu caste villages which (as noted above) put considerable effort into ensuring that consumption is used to express clear hierarchical differences between the various subgroups that inhabit the villages. The Muria are refusing the option taken by many Indian tribal groups in the past of entering into Hindu society, most commonly near the bottom of the established hierarchy. Furthermore although in both Gell's and Wilk's studies the growth of consumption is related to resistance by a core of 'intimate' relationships to being expressed through money or expense, this cannot be assumed. There are many cases where contrary to Western expectation it is the intimate sphere of social relations which has taken easily to using com-modification as idiom while other areas of social life refuse this possi-bility (e.g. Geschiere 1992).

The home has become the core objectification of family life in many times and regions. An eighteenth-century English gentlewoman (Vickery 1993) and contemporary Columbian peasants (Gudeman and Rivera 1990) may show an almost obsessive concern with issues of thrift and the reten-tion of property or the crops grown by the household. Such possessions are strongly articulated with questions of descent and family continuity. The sometimes violent and highly charged disputes over property and inher-itance may therefore relate to much more than either the legalistic or self-interested concerns that are often assumed. In Trinidad some of the most violent intra-family inheritance disputes take place with respect to housing or land that has virtually no monetary value or potential but rather represents the core of family identity and continuity. For the Norwegian working-class housewives, studied by Gullestad (1984), the decoration and maintenance of the house and more generally the daily cleaning and tidying provides the foundation for expansive sociality. The importance of an under-lying egalitarian ethos for the furtherance of this form of sociality is high-lighted by a case in which one housewife felt it was impossible to include a wealthier housewife in her social circle because, despite the protestations intended to assert equality, the latter's home was so clearly beyond the aspirations of the former's network (Gullestad 1992: 61–91).

This close relationship between the constitution of the house and of the basic units of sociality may remain even when there are much more transient concerns operating than these long-term issues of descent. Lofgren (1990), examining the biography of Swedish individuals in terms of their changing ideas and practices of home decoration, relates this to the prob-lem of identity construction during periods when 'what it is to be modern' is itself constantly shifting so that in a sense even to remain the same requires constant change. Studies of media technologies in the home also exemplify the manner in which this emphasis on possessions within the home became the vehicle for the construction rather than the repudia-tion of what has been called the moral economy of the home (Silverstone, Hirsch and Morley 1992) where the relative contributions of household members and their sense of obligation and autonomy can be worked out. This internal solidarity is often based on an opposition to some outside force. Recent work on house decoration examines how the household can thereby constitute itself in repudiation of variously: the state (Miller 1988); competitive individualism in the marketplace (McCracken 1989); the anomie of being amongst the long-term unemployed (Sixmith and Sixmith 1990); a variety of other concerns (Putnam and Newton 1990). Although the term 'consumption' first brings to mind purchased items, in some of these cases the problem is that of living with objects of state provision.

What this work on houses as sites and objects of consumption suggests is that a single arena of consumption may be exploited or not exploited in a variety of ways depending upon social concerns with what might be expressed by consumption patterns. As such, this literature represents two typical anthropological concerns which should have an important contribution to consumption studies more generally. First, they view consumption as arising from social constructions of value rather than universal psychological drives or desires. Second, the implied relativism suggests that even within that set of studies whose context is clearly one of increasing involvement in cash economies and capitalist systems, this may be as much the foundation for new diversities as for the elimination of old ones.

CUSTOMISING TRANSPORT

The town of Chaguanas in Central Trinidad is currently the fastest-growing urban centre within Trinidad and Tobago. There is, however, relatively little manufacture evident in the region and by far the most conspicuous and successful industry appears to be that devoted to upholstery, within which the dominant sector is that of car upholstery. Most recently, under conditions of severe recession, this relates mainly to the re-upholstery of older vehicles such as taxis, but the industry grew up during the oil-boom when the primary business consisted of newly purchased cars. This involved removing the upholstery the cars were purchased with and replacing this with new patterns chosen by the purchaser. Upholstery might at this stage be added to parts of the car (such as the boot/trunk and dashboard) which were not previously upholstered.

To understand why this should have developed as the dominant industry of this region requires some consideration of the imperatives behind the patterns of car consumption on the one hand and upholstery on the other. Although the car only came in reach of most people as a possession with the oil-boom of the late 1970s, it now dominates the Trinidadian self-image, outweighing even clothing in its ability to incorporate and express the concept of the individual. People are constantly recognised through their cars. One is more often directed to the car parked at the house than the house number or the house description. Most people memorise dozens of car number plates and greet passing cars accordingly. Much gossip and innuendo is based upon where a car has been seen parked, though number plates are not used to announce parties or in obituary notices, as reported by Manning (1974) for Bermuda. Street dialogue constantly asserts that men are attractive to women as much through the body of their cars as their own bodies and there are abundant sexual metaphors based on car parts.

The significance of the car also appears in a general unwillingness to walk, once in possession of a car. A queue of cars may form in front of the school gates as each waits to park directly in front of the entrance rather than walk the few yards from a more convenient parking place. There was also an often extreme concern for car care. Anecdotes were common about neighbours who wash the car at least once a day, twice if it has rained, and with particular attention paid to the area within the treads of the tyres. A Hindu pundit might typically in a sermon call for people to pay the same degree of attention to their spiritual life as they do to their car care. In general then, the car provides a key objectification of the individual.

The particular kinds of upholstery used in the car (for example, certain kinds of buttoning or the use of plush (long-haired) materials) is reminiscent of the importance of domestic upholstery in the home, which again is a conspicuous arena of expenditure amongst families who otherwise are relatively impoverished (e.g. within a community of squatters living on the periphery of the town). The other upholstery industry in the same area is found in the funeral parlours, where coffins and the more expensive and luxurious caskets are almost invariably lined in deep recessed upholstery. The car also evokes the living room through the use of maroon elements and the use of transparent plastic covered seats. A study of household interiors suggests that the particular aesthetic is used to construct an image of the larger family unit subsuming individualism into a concern with tradition and descent continuity (see Miller 1994).

While the upholsterers are essentially concerned with car interiors, in the same high street are found other shops that are devoted essentially to the car exteriors. One shop, for example, which advertises itself as customising cars, in effect concentrates on just two operations: the tinting of window glass and the adding of stripes to the exterior. Both of these are extremely common practices as might be extra-wide wheels, new wheel hubs and less commonly the bonnet scoop.

The existence of distinct shops concentrating on car interiors and car exteriors respectively, appeared to be significant from some suggestion that the two activities might appeal to different groups of people. That is, although some might engage in both forms of customising, there were differences which retailers sometimes described in terms of ethnic stereotypes. To quote one: there is the 'Indian with gold on his fingers and hair greased back who wants crushed velvet upholstery but can only afford short pile acrylic but spends ages brushing it the right way'. In contrast there is the image of the black dude, with his mistress projecting loud music from a car with tinted glass and stripes.

Customising the car therefore expresses something of a contradiction. The interior replicates that of the home interior which is most often an objectification of family security and continuity, while the car as a consumption item provides an ideal objectification of individualism and mobility, commonly used in opposition to any association with the home. In some cases this is resolved by splitting the car into its interior and exterior aspects. In so far as the majority of people in this part of central Trinidad are of East Indian origin and a proportionally higher percentage of men tend to own cars, the male Indians are the dominant car-owning group and the majority customers in this area. As a group they appeared to be using the car as a key element in resolving a clear tension expressed by many of them. Although largely positively avowing their own ethnicity, there is a clear emulation of the sense of freedom which is associated with the lifestyle of black males, in particular the supposed more active sexuality of the latter, and their lack of familial constraints.

The younger Indian males constantly asserted their desire for greater freedom as an individualised independence. This was clearly associated with their desperate desire to obtain a car. Once they owned a car there arose at first an equally strong anxiety created by the tension between, on the one hand, a desire for exclusive control and use of the car and, on the other, the traditional claims of friends and relatives to use one's possessions. Much of the fanaticism of car care seemed aggressively aimed at those, including one's family, who might wish to make use of the car. Car ownership often brings to actuality many of the fantasies of those who strive for them. It is the means by which they do indeed escape the scrutiny of their families. It is often a major element in successful seduction and the fulfilment of sexual fantasy, and it is a form of property that can be individualised. The car is a substantial possession which gives its owners the experience of the freedom that was understood to be incompatible with substance. This does not necessarily mean that the driver abandons one set of values for another. As in much consumption, people attempt to retain both sides of an opposition – in this case the security of the interior representing family and religious values, alongside the excitement of the outside with its associations of the event and of freedom. The car thereby becomes that classic instrument of modernity, the means of enabling contradiction.

There have been several studies of the customising of vehicles ranging from elaborately painted public trucks in South Asia to the aficionados of specialist racing vehicles in the United States (Moorehouse 1991). The dynamics of such appropriation were clearly exemplified in Hebdige's study of the transformation of a manufacturer's dualism, where motorscooters were intended as the female equivalent of the male motorbike. In the process of consumption this was transformed into a consumer's distinction between two youth groups in Britain – the mods and the rockers (Hebdige 1988: 77–113).

Several conclusions may be drawn from such analysis. First, if I suggest that car upholstery becomes the dominant industry because it resolves a tension within the moral order of a social group, this has evident affinities to the interpretation of myth by Lévi-Strauss, and there is no reason (as Barthes pointed out) why modern goods should not stand in this analogous role. This does not mean, however, that a symbolic analysis replaces a more material concern for the effect of goods. On the contrary, the implication of this study is that vehicles have the material power to become the form by which people can significantly transform their lives and opportunities, and this is what makes them so appropriate for mythic resolution. Finally there is no need to polarise the interests of manufacturers and consumers since it does not detract from the endless search by manufacturers to exploit such symbolic niches. As might be expected, amongst the richest people in Chaguanas are the car upholsterers. But to ask whether producer or consumer is the primacy instigator of these developments is as pointless as to ask whether the effect is primarily instrumental or symbolic.

Hopefully there will be a considerable variety of contributions to the study of consumption from anthropology, but these examples do demonstrate a specific advantage arising out of ethnography as the traditional approach by the discipline. In contrast to the clichés about consumption documented in the introduction, which specify this or that effect of Western commodities, such studies treat cars and purchased houses much as anthropologists once discussed the place of cattle or spears within social life. Commodities, as other material forms, prove able to act as mythic structures, as taxonomic systems creating homologies between different models of sociality, as expressions of the inalienable, and as the objectification of moral and cosmological values. Of course, commodities may also be mechanisms of alienation, of control by more knowledgeable outsiders, or as symbols of inaccessible distinction. But a mature anthropology recognises that while any of these are possible, none can be presumed.

CONCLUSION

This chapter has argued that the development of an anthropology of consumption is not merely the addition of a neglected area of enquiry, but represents a fundamental metamorphosis of the discipline itself. It is an essential one, which transforms anthropology from a discipline whose purpose is in decline to one whose potential is on the point of becoming revealed. As is typical in anthropological approaches, the topic of consumption is of importance not because it is reified as the ultimate goal to be understood but simply because it is recognised that cultural forms are increasingly employing it as idiomatic. What is rejected is an older suspicion that while the use of kinship was highly creative because it was indigenous, consumption as an often imported practice represented the disintegration of the local in favour of global homogenisation. There is considerable evidence to suggest that as consumption comes to play a greater part in cultural life as against production and exchange, this need not in any sense diminish that dialectical process of societal self-construction which is culture. Indeed, much of its importance might well lie in the struggle by which peoples re-evoke their pluralism in the face of new massive and often distant institutions. This means that consumption may generate in every-day life far more diverse personhoods, social relations and communities than presupposed by the standard theories and terms of sociology or economics.

As noted in the introduction to this volume, the diversity that has grown up in the use of the term consumption and the kinds of studies it has spawned does not preclude us from trying to establish certain priorities or at least suggested areas of emphasis for future research. As we move from the more 'triumphalist' phase of consumer studies to a more mature phase, the detailed research should start to emerge which does not assume the significance of consumption but investigates its social consequences within varied conditions of differential empowerment and resources. Anthropologists who often work in association with development agencies concerned with the relief of poverty have particular reasons to confront assumptions about basic needs and the prioritisation of expenditure that arise in these new studies. Similarly, encouragement should be given to an emergent emphasis on issues of politics and morality, which arise in more affluent contexts. These include green confrontations with materialism, and arguments over the relative role of the state and market in relation to concepts of freedom and responsibility, as well as a questioning of the assumptions made in the use of these standard terms of Western politics and economics. In a period when universalistic political and ideological models are being replaced by much more contingent and modest propos-als for future development, the sensitivities of relativistic but nevertheless committed anthropological research may have a considerable positive role to play in future studies of consumption. By the same token while devel-opment and political issues will not wait for the proper consolidation of theoretical and empirical studies, these longer-term goals must be retained in an area of research whose foundations remain extremely shallow.

ACKNOWLEDGEMENTS

I would like to thank James Carrier and Richard Wilk for comments on an earlier draft of this chapter and suggestions for further reading.

REFERENCES

Abu-Lughod, L. (1990) 'The romance of resistance: tracing transformations of power through Bedouin women', *American Ethnologist* 17 (1): 41–55.

Alexander, P. (1992) 'What's in a Price?' in R. Dilley (ed.) *Contesting Markets*, Edinburgh: Edinburgh University Press, pp. 79–96.

Appadurai, A. (ed.) (1986) *The Social Life of Things: Commodities in Cultural Perspective*, Cambridge: Cambridge University Press.

Appadurai, A. (1990) 'Disjuncture and difference in the global cultural economy', *Theory, Culture and Society* 7 (2–3): 295–310.

Arnould, E. and Wilk, R. (1984) 'Why do the Indians wear Adidas?', *Advances in Consumer Research* 11: 748–752.

Barthes, R. (1973) *Mythologies*, London: Paladin.

Baudrillard, J. (1981) *For a Critique of the Political Economy of the Sign*, St Louis, Mo.: Telos Press.

Bayly, C. (1986) 'The origins of swadeshi (home industry): cloth and Indian society, 1700–1930', in A. Appadurai (ed.) *The Social Life of Things: Commodities in Cultural Perspective*, Cambridge: Cambridge University Press, pp. 285–321.

Bean, S. (1989) 'Gandhi and Khadi, the fabric of Indian independence', in A. Weiner and J. Schneider (eds) *Cloth and Human Experience*, Washington: Smithsonian Press, pp. 355–376.

Bohannan, P. (1955) 'Some principles of exchange and investment among the Tiv', *American Anthropologist* 57: 60–70.

Bott, E. (1987) 'The Kava ceremony as a dream structure', in M. Douglas (ed.) *Constructive Drinking*, Cambridge: Cambridge University Press.

Bourdieu, P. (1977) *Outline of a Theory of Practice*, Cambridge: Cambridge University Press.

Bourdieu, P. (1984) *Distinction*, London: Routledge and Kegan Paul.

Brookfield, H. and Hart, D. (1971) *Melanesia*, London: Methuen

Carrier, A. and Carrier, J. (1991) *Wage, Trade, and Exchange in Melanesia*, London: Harwood Academic Press.

Carrier, J. (1990) 'The symbolism of possession in commodity advertising', *Man* 25 (4).

Carrier, J. (1992) 'Occidentalism: the world turned upside-down', *American Ethnologist* 19: 195–212.

Carrier, J. (1994) *Exchange and Markets: Capitalism since 1700*, London: Routledge.

Cohen, B. (1989) 'Cloth, clothes, and colonialism: India in the nineteenth century', in A. Weiner, and J. Schneider (eds) *Cloth and Human Experience*, Washington: Smithsonian Press, pp. 303–353.

Comeroff, J. (1990) 'Goodly beasts and beastly goods: cattle and commodities in a South African Context', *American Ethnologist* 17: 195–216.

De Certeau, M. (1984) *The Practice of Everyday Life*, Berkeley: University of California Press.

Dilley, R. (1992) 'Contesting markets', in R. Dilley (ed.) *Contesting Markets*, Edinburgh: Edinburgh University Press, pp. 1–34.

Douglas, M. (1958) 'Raffia cloth distribution in the Lele Economy', *Africa* 28: 109–122.

Douglas, M. (ed.) (1987) *Constructive Drinking*, Cambridge: Cambridge University Press.

Douglas, M. (1992) *Objects and Objections*, Toronto: Toronto Semiotic Circle.

Douglas, M. and Isherwood, B. (1978) *The World of Goods*, London: Allen Lane.

Drakulic, S. (1992) *How We Survived Communism and Even Laughed*, London: Vintage.

Fonesca, C. (1991) 'Spouses, siblings and sex-linked bonding', in E. Jelin (ed.) *Household and Gender Relations in Latin America*, London: Kegan Paul International, pp. 133–160.

Foster, R. (forthcoming) 'Print advertisements and nation making in metropolitan Papua New Guinea', in R. Foster (ed.) *National Making in Postcolonial Melanesia*, Ann Arbor, Mich.: University of Michigan Press.

Friedman, J. (1990) 'The Political Economy of Elegance', *Culture and History* 7: 101–122.

Friedman, J. and Rowlands, M. (eds) (1977) *The Evolution of Social Systems*, London: Duckworth.

Gell, A. (1986) 'Newcomers to the world of goods', in A. Appadurai (ed.) *The Social Life of Things*, Cambridge: Cambridge University Press, pp. 110–138.

Gell, A. (1992) 'Inter-tribal commodity barter and reproductive gift-exchange in old Melanesia', in C. Humphrey and S. Hugh-Jones (eds) *Barter, Exchange and Value*, Cambridge: Cambridge University Press, pp. 142–168.

Geschiere, P. (1992) 'Kinship, witchcraft and "the Market"', in R. Dilley (ed.) *Contesting Markets*, Edinburgh: Edinburgh University Press, pp. 159–179.

Gewertz, D. and Errington, F. (1991) *Twisted Histories. Altered Contexts*, Cambridge: Cambridge University Press.

Gilroy, P. (1993) *The Black Atlantic*, London: Verso.

Goodman, J. (1993) *Tobacco in History*, London: Routledge.

Gregory, C. (1982) *Gifts and Commodities*, Cambridge: Cambridge University Press.

Gudeman, S. and Rivera, A. (1990) *Conversations in Colombia*, Cambridge: Cambridge University Press.

Gullestad, M. (1984) *Kitchen-Table Society*, Oslo: Universitetsforlaget.

Gullestad, M. (1992) *The Art of Social Relations*, Oslo: Scandinavian University Press.

Guss, D. (1986) 'Keeping it oral: a Yekuana ethnology', *American Ethnologist* 13: 413–429.

Hamilton, G. and Lai, C.-K. (1989) 'Consumption without capitalism: consumption and brand names in late Imperial China', in H. Rutz and B. Orlove (eds) *The Social Economy of Consumption*, Lanham: University Press of America, pp. 253–279.

Harvey, D. (1989) *The Condition of Postmodernity*, Oxford: Blackwell.

Hebdige, D. (1988) *Hiding in the Light*, London: Routledge.

Hendry, J. (1989) 'To wrap or not to wrap; politeness and penetration in ethnographic enquiry', *Man* 24: 620–635.

Heyman, J. (1990) 'The emergence of the waged life course on the United States–Mexico border', *American Ethnologist* 17 (2): 348–359.

Hirsch, E. (1990) 'From Bones to Betelnut', *Man* 25: 18–34.

Hirsch, E. (1993) 'Negotiated limits. Interviews in South East England', in J. Edwards *et al.* (eds) *Technologies of Procreation. Kinship in the Age of Assisted Conception*, Manchester: Manchester University Press, ch. 3.

Hodder, I. (1982) *Symbols in Action*, Cambridge: Cambridge University Press.

Hugh-Jones, S. (1992) 'Yesterday's luxuries, tomorrow's necessities: business and barter in northwest Amazonia', in C. Humphrey and S. Hugh-Jones (eds) *Barter, Exchange and Value*, Cambridge: Cambridge University Press, pp. 42–74.

Humphrey, C. and Hugh-Jones, S. (1992) (eds) *Barter, Exchange and Value*, Cambridge: Cambridge University Press.

Jelin, E. (1991) 'Social relations of consumption: the urban popular household', in E. Jelin (ed.) *Household and Gender Relations in Latin America*, London: Kegan Paul International, pp. 165–196.

Jules-Rosette, B. (1990) *Terminal Signs: Computers and Social Change in Africa*, Berlin: Mouton de Gruyer.

Kopytoff, I. (1986) 'The cultural biography of things: commoditization as process', in A. Appadurai (ed.) *The Social Life of Things*, Cambridge: Cambridge University Press, pp. 64–91.

Lien, M. (1993) 'From deprived to frustrated: consumer segmentation in food and nutrition', in U. Kjaernes, L. Holm, M. Ekstrom, E. Furst and R. Prattala (eds) *Regulating Markets: Regulating People*, Oslo: Norvus Forlag.

Lofgren, O. (1990) 'Consuming interests', *Culture and History* 7: 7–36.

McCracken, G. (1988) *Culture and Consumption*, Bloomington: Indiana University Press.

McCracken, G. (1989) 'Homeyness', in E. Hirschman (ed.) *Interpretive Consumer Research*, Provo, UT: Association for Consumer Research.

MacKenzie, A. (1991) *Androgynous Objects*, London: Harwood Academic Press.

Manning, F. (1974) 'Nicknames and number plates in the British West Indies', *American Folklore* 87: 123–132.

Mars, G. (1987) 'Longshore drinking, economic security and union politics in Newfoundland', in M. Douglas (ed.) *Constructive Drinking*, Cambridge: Cambridge University Press.

Mauss, M. (1954) *The Gift*, London: Cohen and West.

Miller, D. (1987) *Material Culture and Mass Consumption*, Oxford: Basil Blackwell.

Miller, D. (1988) 'Appropriating the state on the council estate', *Man* 23: 353–372.

Miller, D. (1992) 'The young and the restless in Trinidad: a case of the local and the global in mass consumption', in R. Silverstone and E. Hirsch (eds) *Consuming Technologies*, London: Routledge, pp. 163–182.

Miller, D. (ed.) (1993) *Unwrapping Christmas*, Oxford: Oxford University Press.

Miller, D. (1994) *Modernity: An Ethnographic Approach*, Oxford: Berg.

Miller, D. (forthcoming) 'Capitalism: an ethnographic approach'.

Mintz, S. (1985) *Sweetness and Power*, New York: Viking Penguin.

Moeran. B. (1984) 'Individual, group and Sheishin; Japan's internal cultural debate', *Man* 19 (2): 252–266.

Moorehouse, H. (1991) *Driving Ambitions: an Analysis of the American Hot Rod Enthusiasm*, Manchester: Manchester University Press.

Munn, N. (1986) *The Fame of Gawa*, Cambridge: Cambridge University Press.

Overing, J. (1992) 'Wandering in the market and the forest', in R. Dilley (ed.) *Contesting Markets*, Edinburgh: Edinburgh University Press, pp. 180–200.

Pahl, R. (1984) *Divisions of Labour*, Oxford: Basil Blackwell.

Parry, J. (1982) 'Sacrificial death and the necrophagous ascetic', in M. Bloch and J. Parry (eds) *Death and the Regeneration of Life*, Cambridge: Cambridge University Press, pp. 74–110.

Polanyi, K. (1957) *The Great Transformation*, Boston: Beacon Press.

Price, S. (1984) *Co-Wives and Calabashes*, Cambridge: Cambridge University Press.

Putnam, T. and Newton, C. (eds) (1990) *Household Choices*, London: Futures.

Richards, P. (forthcoming) 'Videos and violence on the periphery', *Institute of Development Studies Bulletin*, ed. S. Davies, Falmer: Sussex.

Rowlands, M. (forthcoming) 'Prestige of presence: negotiating modernisation through tradition', in D. Miller (ed.) *Worlds Apart: Modernity through the Prism of the Local*, London: Routledge.

Rutz, H. (1989) 'Culture, class and consumer choice: expenditures on food in urban Fijian households', in H. Rutz and B. Orlove (eds) *The Social Economy of Consumption*, Lanham: University Press of America, pp. 211–252.

Rutz, H. and Orlove, B. (eds) (1989) *The Social Economy of Consumption*, Lanham:

293

University Press of America.

Sahlins, M. (1974) 'The original affluent society', in *Stone Age Economics*, London: Tavistock, pp. 1–39.

Sahlins, M. (1976) *Culture and Practical Reason*, Chicago: University of Chicago Press.

Sahlins, M. (1988) 'Cosmologies of capitalism: the trans-Pacific sector of the world system', *Proc. of the British Academy* LXXIV: 1–51.

Sahlins, M. (1992) 'The political economy of grandeur in Hawaii from 1810 to 1830', in E. Ohnuki-Tierney (ed.) *Symbols Through Time*, Stanford: Stanford University Press.

Selby, H., Murphy, A. and Lorenzen, S. (1990) *The Mexican Urban Household*, Austin: University of Texas Press.

Shanks, M. and Tilley, C. (1986) *Re-Constructing Archaeology*, Cambridge: Cambridge University Press.

Sharma, U. (1980) *Women, Work and Property in North-West India*, London: Tavistock.

Sharma, U. (1986) *Women's Work, Class and the Urban Household*, London: Tavistock.

Sherry, J. and McGrath, M. (1989) 'Unpacking the holiday presence: a comparative ethnography of two gift stores', in E. Hirschman (ed.) *Interpretive Consumer Research*, Provo UT: Association for Consumer Research.

Silverstone, R., Hirsch, E. and Morley, D. (eds) (1992) *Consuming Technologies*, London: Routledge.

Sixmith, J. and Sixmith, A. (1990) 'Places in transition', in T. Putnam and C. Newton (eds) *Household Choices*, London: Futures, pp. 20–24.

Sklair, L. (1991) *Sociology of the Global System*, Hemel Hempstead: Wheatsheaf.

Spooner, B. (1986) 'Weavers and dealers; the authenticity of a Persian carpet', in A. Appadurai (ed.) *The Social Life of Things*, Cambridge: Cambridge University Press, pp. 195–235.

Strathern, M. (1984) 'Subject or object? Women and the circulation of valuables in Highlands New Guinea', in R. Hirschon (ed.) *Women and Property, Women as Property*, London: Croom Helm.

Strathern, M. (1988) *The Gender of the Gift*, Berkeley: University of California Press.

Strathern, M. (1991) *Partial Connections*, Savage: Rowman and Littlefield.

Swallow, D. (1982) 'Production and control in the Indian garment export industry', in E. Goody (ed.) *From Craft to Industry*, Cambridge: Cambridge University Press.

Tambiah, S. (1984) *The Buddhist Saints of the Forests and the Cult of the Amulets*, Cambridge: Cambridge University Press.

Thomas, N. (1991) *Entangled Objects*, Cambridge, Mass.: Harvard University Press.

Tobin, J. (ed.) (1992) *Re-made in Japan*, New Haven, Conn.: Yale University Press.

Toren, C. (1989) 'Drinking cash: the purification of money in ceremonial exchange in Fiji', in M. Bloch and J. Parry (eds) *Money and the Morality of Exchange*, Cambridge: Cambridge University Press.

Turner, T. (1992) 'Defiant images: the Kayapo appropriation of video', *Anthropology Today* 8 (6): 5–16.

Umble, D. (1992) 'The Amish and the telephone, resistance and reconstruction', in E. Hirsch and R. Silverstone (eds) *Consuming Technologies*, London: Routledge.

Vickery, A. (1993) 'Women and the world of goods', in J. Brewer and R. Porter (eds) *Consumption and the World of Goods*, London: Routledge.

Weiner, A. (1985) 'Inalienable wealth', *American Ethnologist* 12 (2): 210–227.

Weiner, A. and Schneider, J. (eds) (1989) *Cloth and Human Experience*, Washington: Smithsonian Press.

Weir, S. (1985) *Qat in Yemen*, London: British Museum Press.

Weismantel, M. (1989) 'The children cry for bread: hegemony and the transformation of consumption', in H. Rutz and B. Orlove (eds) *The Social Economy of Consumption*, Lanham: University Press of America, pp. 101–120.

Wilk, R. (1989) 'Houses as consumer goods', in H. Rutz and B. Orlove (eds) *The Social Economy of Consumption*, Lanham: University Press of America, pp. 101–120.

Wilk, R. (1990) 'Consumer goods as dialogue about development', *Culture and History* 7: 79–100.

Worsley, P. (1957) *The Trumpet Shall Sound*, London: MacGibbon and Kee.

9

THEORIES OF CONSUMPTION IN MEDIA STUDIES

David Morley

INTRODUCTION

The very development of the field of media studies has been premised on an understanding of the centrality of the process of media consumption in contemporary social and cultural developments. Over time (as detailed below, in section I) the model of media consumption in play within the field has oscillated between two poles. At one pole there have been models of media consumption which stress the power of the media (or the 'Culture Industries') and correspondingly treat media audiences as relatively passive and powerless, 'victims' of various kinds of media effects. Against this, especially in recent years, a variety of approaches has been developed, which lay more stress on media consumption as an active process, in which audience members are understood not only actively to select from the range of media materials available to them, but also to be active in their different uses, interpretations and 'decodings' of the material which they consume. The development of a model of media consumption which can reconcile the necessary concern with various forms of media power, with a recognition that audiences – or media 'consumers' – cannot adequately be treated as mere dupes or 'victims' of the media, is crucial to the development of the field. Indeed, the debate about this issue has been one of the most contentious within media studies, over the last fifteen to twenty years.

It is in this context that the present chapter is written. The argument falls into three sections. Section I engages with the literature on media consumption, media audiences and media effects, tracing the development of debates concerning these issues, from the early work of the Frankfurt School, up to contemporary questions concerning the conceptualisation of the 'active audience'. Section II explores a number of the different dimensions of media consumption, as a material and as a symbolic process, both within the broad framework of the development of consumer society and, more narrowly, in relation to contemporary developments concerning the 'commodification' and

296

'globalisation' of the media. Section III offers two case-studies, based on recent research in which I have been involved, which, in the first place, has explored a number of often neglected issues, concerning the significance of gender as a determinant of domestic processes of media consumption. This work has also attempted to broaden the frame of media studies, and to move beyond the field's traditional focus (on the effects of television, radio and the press) so as to address the contemporary significance of a fuller range of the new information and commentation technologies, from the point of view of their users, or 'consumers'.

I   Consumption in media studies

EFFECTS, USES AND DECODINGS

The history of studies of media consumption can be seen as a series of oscillations between perspectives that have stressed the power of the text (or message) over its audiences and perspectives that have stressed the barriers 'protecting' the audience from the potential effects of the message. The first position is most obviously represented by the whole tradition of effects studies, mobilising a 'hypodermic' model of media influence, in which the media are seen as have the power to 'inject' their audiences with particular messages, which will cause them to behave in a particular way. This has involved, from the right, perspectives that would see the media causing the breakdown of 'traditional values' and, from the left, perspectives that see the media causing their audience to remain quiescent in political terms, or causing them to inhabit some form of false consciousness.

Interestingly, one finds curious contradictions here. On the one hand, television is accused of reducing its audience to the status of 'zombies' or 'glassy-eyed dupes', who consume a constant diet of predigested junk food, churned out by the media 'sausage factory' and who suffer the anaesthetic affects of this addictive and narcotic substance. However, at the same time as television has been held responsible for causing this kind of somnambulant state of mind (as a result of their viewers' consumption of this 'chewing gum for the eyes'), television has, of course, also been accused of making us *do* all manner of things, most notably in the debates around television and violence – where it has been argued that the viewing of violent television content will cause viewers to go out and commit violent acts. One point of interest here is that these 'television zombies' are always other people. Few people think of their own use of television in this way. It is a theory about what television does to other, more vulnerable people.

One of the most influential versions of this kind of 'hypodermic' theory of media effects was that advanced by Adorno and Horkheimer (1977) along with other members of the Frankfurt School of Social Research. Their 'pessimistic mass society thesis' reflected the breakdown of modern Germany society into fascism, a breakdown that was attributed, in part, to the loosening of traditional ties and structures which were seen as then leaving people more 'atomised' and exposed to external influences, and especially to the pressure of the mass propaganda of powerful leaders, the most effective agency of which was the mass media. This 'pessimistic mass society thesis' stressed the conservative and reconciliatory role of 'mass culture' for the audience. Mass culture suppressed 'potentialities', and denied awareness of contradictions in a 'one-dimensional world'; only art, in fictional and dramatic form, could preserve the qualities of negation and transcendence. Implicit here was a 'hypodermic' model of the media, which were seen as having the power to 'inject' a repressive ideology directly into the consciousness of the masses. The passive role attributed to the media consumers is apparent in the language in which Adorno and Horkheimer develop their argument. Thus, they claim that the 'Culture Industry' has automatic ideological effects on its consumers: 'Under the regime of the Culture Industry . . . the film leaves no room for imagination or reflection on the part of its audience . . . the film forces its victims to equate it directly with reality' (Adorno and Horkheimer 1977: 353–354), and again 'the machine rotates on the spot . . . [and] moves rigorously in the worn grooves of association . . . the product prescribes every reaction . . . .The Culture Industry forces its productions on the public' (ibid.: 361–362).

However, against this overly pessimistic backdrop, the emigration of the leading members of the Frankfurt School (Adorno, Marcuse, Horkheimer) to America during the 1930s led to the development of a specifically 'American' school of research in the 1940s and 1950s. The Frankfurt School's 'pessimistic' thesis, of the link between 'mass society' and fascism, and the role of the media in cementing it, proved unacceptable to American researchers. The 'pessimistic' thesis proposed, they argued, too direct and unmediated an impact by the media on its audiences; it took too far the thesis that all intermediary social structures between leaders/media and the masses had broken down; it didn't accurately reflect the pluralistic nature of American society; it was – to put it shortly – sociologically naïve. Clearly, the media had social effects; these must be examined, researched. But, equally clearly, these effects were neither all-powerful, nor simple, nor even necessarily direct. The nature of this complexity and indirectness also needed to be demonstrated and researched. Thus, in reaction to the Frankfurt School's predilection for critical social theory and qualitative and philosophical analysis, the American researchers developed what began as a quantitative and positivist methodology for empirical radio audience research into the 'Sociology of Mass Persuasion'.

Over the next twenty years, throughout the 1950s and 1960s, the over-all effect of this empirically guided 'Sociology of Mass Persuasion' was to produce a much more qualified notion of 'media power', in which media consumers were increasingly recognised to not be completely passive 'victims' of the culture industry. In a review of the field in the early 1970s, Counihan (1973) summarised these developments thus:

> Once upon a time . . . worried commentators imputed a virtual omnipotence to the newly emerging media of mass communication. In the 'Marxist' version . . . the media were seen as entirely manip-ulated by a shrewd ruling class, in a 'bread and circuses' strategy, to transmit a corrupt culture and neo-fascist values – violence, dehu-manised, consumer brain-washing, political passivity, etc. – to the masses. . . . These instruments of persuasion, on the one hand, and the atomised, homogenised, susceptible masses on the other, were conjoined in a simple stimulus–response model. However, as empirical research progressed, survey and experimental methods were used to measure the capacity of the media to change 'attitudes', 'opinions' and 'behaviour'. In turn, the media–audience relationship was found to be not simple and direct, but complex and mediated. 'Effects' could only be gauged by taking account of other factors intervening between the media and the audience member. Further, emphasis shifted from 'what the media do to people' to 'what people do to the media', for audiences were found to 'attend to' and 'receive' media messages in a selective way, to tend to ignore or to subtly reinterpret those messages hostile to their particular viewpoints. Far from possessing autonomous persuasive and other anti-social power, the media were now found to have a more limited and, implicitly, more benign role in society; not changing, but 'reinforcing' prior dispositions, not cultivating 'escapism' or passivity, but capable of satisfying a great diversity of 'uses and gratifications'; not instru-ments of a levelling of culture, but of its democratisation.
>
> (Counihan 1973: 43)

In this passage, Counihan notes the increasing significance, at that time, of a new perspective on media consumption – the 'uses and gratifica-tions' approach, largely associated with the work of the Leicester Centre for Mass Communications Research, in Britain, during the 1960s. Within that perspective, the viewer is credited with an active role, and it is then a question, as Halloran (1970) put it, of looking at what people do with the media rather than what the media do to them. This argument was obviously of great significance in moving the debate forward – to begin to look at the active engagement of the audience with the medium and with the particular television programmes that they might be watching. One key advance, which was developed by the uses and gratifications perspectives was that of the variability of response and interpretation. From this perspective, one can no longer talk about the 'effects' of a message on a homogeneous mass audience, who are all expected to be affected in the same way. However, the limitation is that the 'uses and gratifications' perspective remains individualistic, in so far as differences of response or interpretation are ultimately attributed to individual differences of personality or psychology. Clearly, the uses and gratifications approach does represent a significant advance on effects theory, in so far as it opens up the question of differential interpretation. However, it remains severely limited by its insufficiently sociological or cultural perspective, in so far as everything is reduced to the level of variations of individual psychology.

It was against this background that Stuart Hall's (1973) 'encoding/decoding' model of communication was developed at the Centre for Contemporary Cultural Studies, as an attempt to take forward insights that had emerged within each of these other perspectives. It took, from the effects theorists, the notion that mass communication is a structured activity, in which the institutions that produce the messages do have the power to set agendas, and to define issues. This is to move away from the idea of power of the medium to make a person behave in a certain way (as a direct effect, which is caused by a simple stimulus, provided by the medium) but it is to hold on to a notion of the role of the media in setting agendas and providing cultural categories and frameworks within which members of the culture will tend to operate. The model also attempted to incorporate, from the uses and gratifications perspective, the idea of the active viewer, who makes meaning from the signs and symbols that the media provide. However, it was also designed to take on board, from the work developed within the interpretative and normative paradigms, the concern with the ways in which responses and interpretations are structured and patterned at a level beyond that of individual psychologies. The model was also, critically, informed by semiological perspectives, focusing on the question of how communication works. The key focus was on the realisation that we are, of course, dealing with signs and symbols, which only have meaning within the terms of reference supplied by codes (of one sort or another) which the audience shares, to some greater or lesser extent, with the producers of messages.

The premises of Hall's encoding/decoding model were:

1 The same event can be encoded in more than one way.
2 The message always contains more than one potential 'reading'. Messages propose and prefer certain readings over others, but they can never become wholly closed around one reading: they remain polysemic.
3 Understanding the message is also a problematic practice, however transparent and 'natural' it may seem. Messages encoded one way can always be read in a different way.

300

In this approach, then, the message is treated neither as a unilateral sign, without ideological 'flux'; nor, as in the uses and gratifications approach, as a disparate sign which can be read any way, according to the psychology of the decoder. Reference can usefully be made here to Volosinov's (1973) distinction between sign and signal, and his argument that structuralist approaches tend to treat the former as if they were the latter – i.e. as if they had fixed meanings. The television message is treated as a complex sign, in which a preferred reading has been inscribed, but which retains the potential, if decoded in a manner different from the way in which it has been encoded, of communicating a different meaning. The message is thus a structured polysemy. It is central to the argument that all meanings do not exist 'equally' in the message: it has been structured in dominance, despite the impossibility of a 'total closure' of meaning. Further, the 'preferred reading' is itself part of the message, and can be identified within its linguistic and communicative structure.

Thus, when analysis shifts to the 'moment' of the encoded message itself, the communicative form and structure can be analysed in terms of what the mechanisms are which prefer one, dominant reading over the other readings; what are the means which the encoder uses to try to 'win the assent of the audience' to his preferred reading of the message.

Before messages can have 'effects' on the audience, they must be decoded. 'Effects' is thus a shorthand and inadequate way of marking the point where audiences differentially read and make sense of messages that have been transmitted, and act on those meanings, within the context of their situation and experience. Hall (1973) assumes that there will be no necessary 'fit' or transparency between the encoding and decoding ends of the communication chain. It is precisely this lack of transparency, and its consequences for communication, which we need to investigate, Hall claims. Having established that there is always a possibility of disjunction between the codes of those sending and those receiving messages through the circuit of mass communications, the problem of the 'effects' of communication could now be reformulated, as that of the extent to which decodings take place within the limits of the preferred (or dominant) manner in which the message has been initially encoded. However, the complementary aspect of this problem is that of the extent to which these interpretations, or decodings, also reflect, and are inflected by, the codes and discourses which different sections of the audience inhabit, and the ways in which this is determined by the socially governed distribution of cultural codes between and across different sections of the audience; that is, the range of different decoding strategies and competencies in the audience.

To raise this as a problem for research is already to argue that the meaning produced by the encounter of text and subject cannot be 'read off' straight from 'textual characteristics'. From this point of view the text cannot be considered in isolation from its historical conditions of production and consumption: 'What has to be identified is the use to which a particular text is put, its function within a particular conjuncture, in particular institutional spaces, and in relation to particular audiences' (Neale 1977: 39–40). Thus, the meaning of the text must be thought of in terms of which set of discourses it encounters, in any particular set of circumstances – and how this encounter may restructure both the meaning of the text and the discourses that it meets. The meaning of the text will be constructed differently according to the discourses (knowledge, prejudices, resistances) brought to bear on the text by the reader: the crucial factor in this encounter of audience/subject and text will be the range of discourses at the disposal of the audience. Thus social position may set parameters to the range of potential readings, through the structure of access to different codes; certain social positions allow access to wider repertoires of available codes, certain others to narrower ranges.

In short, the encoding/decoding model was designed to provide a synthesis of insights that had come out of a series of different perspectives – communication theory, semiology, sociology and psychology – and to provide an overall model of the communication circuit as it operated in its social context. It was concerned with matters of ideological and cultural power and it was concerned with shifting the ground of debate, so that emphasis moved to the consideration of how it was possible for meaning to be produced. It attempted to develop the argument that we should look not for the meaning of a text, but for the conditions of a practice – i.e. to examine the foundations of communication, but, crucially, to examine those foundations as social and cultural phenomena.

PSYCHOANALYTIC THEORIES OF THE AUDIENCE: SCREEN THEORY

The growing influence of feminism during the 1970s led, among other effects, to a revitalisation of interest in psychoanalytic theory, given the centrality of the concern with issues of gender within psychoanalysis. Within media studies, this interest in psychoanalytic theories of the construction of gendered identities was one of the informing principles behind the particular approach to the analysis of the media developed by the journal *Screen*. This British journal was heavily influential for a period in the 1970s.

Screen theory was centrally concerned with the analysis of the effects of cinema (and especially the regressive effects of mainstream, commercial, Hollywood cinema) in 'positioning' the spectator (or subject) of the film, through the way in which the text (by means of camera placement, editing and other formal characteristics) 'fixed' the spectator into a particular kind of 'subject-position', which, it was argued, 'guaranteed' the transmission of a certain kind of 'bourgeois ideology' – of naturalism, realism and verisimilitude.

'*Screen* theory' was largely constituted by a mixing of Lacan's (1977) rereading of Freud, stressing the importance of language in the unconscious, and Althusser's (1971) early formulation of the 'media' as an 'Ideological State Apparatus' (even if operating in the private sphere), which had the principal function of securing the reproduction of the conditions of production by 'interpellating' its subjects (spectators, audiences) within the terms of the 'dominant ideology'. Part of the appeal of this approach, to media scholars, rested in the weight which the theory gave to the ('relatively autonomous') effectivity of language – and of 'texts' (such as films and media products), as having real effects in society. To this extent, the approach was argued to represent a significant advance on previous theories of the media (including traditional Marxism) which had stressed the determination of all superstructural phenomena (such as the media) by the 'real' economic 'base' of the society – thus allowing no space for the conceptualisation of the media themselves as having independent (or at least, in Althusser's terms 'relatively autonomous') effects of their own.

Previous approaches, it was argued, had neglected the analysis of the textual forms and patterns of media products, concentrating instead on the analysis of patterns of ownership and control – on the assumption, crudely put, that once the capitalist ownership of the industry was demonstrated, there was no real need to examine the texts (programmes or films) themselves in detail, as all they would display would be minor variations within the narrow limits dictated by their capitalist owners. Conversely, *Screen* theory focused precisely on the text, and emphasised the need for close analysis of textual/formal patterns – hardly surprisingly, given the background of its major figures (Heath 1977/8; MacCabe 1974) in English studies. However, their arguments, in effect, merely inverted the terms of the sociological/economic forms of determinist theory which they critiqued. Now it was the text itself which was the central (if not exclusive) focus of the analysis, on the assumption that since the text 'positioned' the spectator, all that was necessary was the close analysis of texts, from which their 'effects' on their spectators could be automatically deduced, as spectators were bound to take up the 'positions' constructed for them by the text (or film).

The textual determination of *Screen* theory, with its constant emphasis on the 'suturing' (cf. Heath 1977) of the spectator, into the predetermined subject position constructed for him or her by the text, thus allocated central place in media analysis to the analysis of the text. As Moores (1993) puts it, 'the aim was to uncover the symbolic mechanisms through which cinematic texts confer subjectivity upon readers, sewing them into the film narrative, through the production of subject positions' (Moores 1993: 13), on the assumption that the spectator (or reading subject) is left with no other option but to 'make . . . the meanings the film makes for him/her' (Heath 1977/8: 58).

Undoubtedly, it was one of the great achievements of *Screen* theory, drawing as it did on psychoanalysis, Marxism and the formal semiotics of Christian Metz (1975), to restore an emphasis to the analysis of texts which had been absent in much previous work. In particular, the insights of psychoanalysis were extremely influential in the development of later feminist work (see pp. 320–1) on the role of the media in the construction of gendered identities and gendered forms of spectatorship (see e.g. Brunsdon 1981; Byars 1991; Gledhill 1988; Mattelart 1984; Modleski 1984).

However, despite the theoretical sophistication of much of the psychoanalytic-based work, in offering a more developed model of text/subject relations it has, until now, contributed little to the empirical study of the audience. This is for the simple reason that those working in this tradition have, on the whole, been content to 'deduce' audience responses from the structure of the text. To this extent, and despite the theoretical advances achieved by this work in other respects, I would argue that the psychoanalytically based work has ultimately mobilised what can be seen as another version of the hypodermic theory of effects – in so far as it is, at least in its initial and fundamental formulations, a universalist theory which attempts to account for the way in which the subject is necessarily positioned by the text. The difficulty, in terms of audience studies, is that this body of work, premised as it is on universalist criteria, finds it difficult to provide the theoretical space within which one can allow for, and then investigate, differential readings, interpretations, or responses on the part of the audience. This is so quite simply because the theory, in effect, tries to explain any specific instance of the text/reader relationship in terms of a universalist theory of the formation of subjects in general.

From within this perspective, emphasis falls on the universal, primarily psychoanalytic processes through which the subject is constituted. The text is then understood as reproducing or replaying this primary positioning, which is then the foundation of any particular reading. My argument would be that, in fact, we need to question the assumption that all specific discursive effects can be reduced to, and explained by, the functioning of a single, universal set of psychic mechanisms – which is rather like a theory of Platonic forms, which find their expression in any particular instance. The key issue is that this form of psychoanalytic theory poses the problem of the politics of the signifier (the struggle over ideology in language) exclusively at the level of the subject, rather than at the intersection between constituted subjects and specific discursive positions – i.e. at the site of interpellation, where the discursive subject is recognised to be operating in interdiscursive space.

In making this argument, I follow Stuart Hall's (1981) critique of the Lacanian perspective. Hall argues that without further work, further specification, the mechanisms of the Oedipus complex in the discourse of Freud and Lacan are universalist, trans-historical and therefore 'essentialist'. To that extent, Hall argues, these concepts in their universalist forms cannot usefully be applied, without further specification and elaboration, to the analysis of historically specific social formations.

This is to attempt to hold on to the distinction between the constitution of the subject as a general (or mythical) moment and the moment when the subject in general is interpellated by the discursive formation of specific societies. That is to insist on the distinction between formation of subjects for language, and the recruitment of specific subjects to the subject positions of discursive formations through the process of interpellation. It is also to move away from the assumption that every specific reading is already determined by the primary structure of subject positions and to insist that these interpellations are not given and absolute but, rather, are conditional and provisional, in so far as the struggle in ideology takes place precisely through the articulation/disarticulation of interpellations. This is to lay stress on the possibility of contradictory interpellations and to emphasise the unstable, provisional and dynamic properties of subject positioning. It is also to recognise that subjects have histories and that past interpellations affect present ones, rather than to 'deduce' subjects from the subject positions offered by the text and to argue that readers are not merely bearers or puppets of their unconscious positions. It is to insist, with Volosinov (1973), on the 'multi-accentuality of the sign', which makes it possible for discourse to become an arena of struggle.

These are, in my view, the main difficulties with much psychoanalytic work in media studies, in so far as it is a theoretical perspective which presumes a unilateral fixing of a position for the reader, imprisoning him or her in its structure, so as to produce a singular and guaranteed effect. The text, of course, may offer the subject specific positions of intelligibility, it may operate to prefer certain readings above others; what it cannot do is to guarantee them – that must always be an empirical question. This is, in part, because the subject that the text encounters is, as Pecheux (1982) has argued, never a 'raw' or 'unacculturated' subject. Readers are always already formed, shaped as subjects, by the ideological discourses that have operated on them prior to their encounter with the text in question.

If we are to theorise the subject of television or film, it has to be theorised in its cultural and historical specificity, an area where psychoanalytic theory is obviously weak. It is only thus that we can move beyond a theory of the subject which has reference only to universal, primary psychoanalytic processes, and only thus that we can allow a space in which one can recognise that the struggle over ideology also takes place at the moment of the encounter of text and subject and is not 'always already' predetermined at the psychoanalytic level.

305

FACTS, FICTIONS AND POPULAR CULTURE

If, in the British context, media studies was reinvigorated in the early 1970s by what Stuart Hall (1982) has characterised as the 'rediscovery of ideology', this 'rediscovery' also led in the first instance to a focus on the analysis of the ideological structure of 'news', (both on television and in the press) and, more generally, to a focus on the analysis of media coverage of politics and, in particular, media coverage of explicitly 'controversial' issues such as industrial and race relations (Glasgow Media Group 1976, 1980; Gilroy *et al.* 1981).

Some of this work was framed within a more (or less) sophisticated concern with 'bias' (see the work of the Glasgow Media Group, 1976, 1980) while other studies mobilised concepts of ideology derived from the work of Gramsci and Althusser (see e.g. Hall *et al.* 1981). However, while internally differentiated in this respect, much of this work shared two key premises: first, that it was in the field of explicitly political communications that the concern with the reproduction of ideology (and the presumed consequence of the maintenance of social order or 'hegemony') would be most productively focused, and second (partly inscribed in the theoretical model of ideology underpinning the first premise – see Abercrombie *et al.* 1980) that the (ideological) effects of the media could, in effect, be 'deduced' from the analysis of the textual structure of the messages they emitted. To this extent, the media audience was largely absent from these analytical discourses, and the power of the media over their consumers was often taken for granted (Connell 1985).

Both of these premises came to be severely questioned in subsequent years. In the first case, there was a growing recognition of the considerable political significance of a much wider realm of cultural products (partly due to the influence of feminist and anti-racist perspectives on the symbolic process of construction of personal and cultural identities), and a consequent concern with the ideological structure of 'entertainment' media, popular fiction and music. In the second place, there was a growing recognition – dating notably from Hall's seminal paper on the 'encoding' and 'decoding' of TV (Hall 1973) – of the complex and contradictory nature of the process of cultural consumption of media products, both within the realm of TV (e.g. Morley 1980) and within the broader field of popular culture (Hebdige 1979, 1988).

From the mid-1970s onwards, researchers within the media / cultural studies traditions in Britain began to explore the political and ideological significance of the structure of media products outside of the 'news' category. These studies focused on issues such as the construction of gender identities in soap opera (Ang 1985; Hobson 1982), the presentation of racial stereotypes in drama and light entertainment (Cohen and Gardner 1984), the political and cultural values embedded in popular fiction and drama (Bennett and Woollacott 1987; McArthur 1981; MacCabe 1981), and the presentation of knowledge itself in quiz shows (Mills and Rice 1982). In Britain much of this work was collected and summarised in the Open University's influential course on 'Popular Culture' (1981). These studies demonstrated that any concern with the influence of the media in the construction of culture needed to operate with a wider and more inclusive definition of the kind of media texts considered to be relevant. In this context, the study of news and explicitly 'political' media products was then seen to be but a small part of the overall field of materials with which media scholars needed to be concerned.

These developments paved the way for the notable boom in studies of media consumption which occurred during the 1980s. To take only the best-known examples, the body of work produced in that period included, *inter alia*, my own study of the 'Nationwide' audience (Morley 1980); Hobson's study of 'Crossroads' viewers; Modleski's (1984) work on women viewers of soap opera; Radway's (1984) study of readers of romance fiction; Ang's (1985) study of 'Dallas' viewers; Fiske's (1987) study of 'Television Culture'; Philo's (1990) and Lewis's (1991) studies of the audience for TV news, and the work of Schroder (1988) and Liebes and Katz (1991) on the consumption of American TV fiction in other cultures. Towards the end of the decade, much of the most important new material on media consumption was collected together in the published proceedings of two major conferences on audience studies: Drummond and Paterson's (1988) collection *Television and its Audience*, bringing together work on audiences presented at the International Television Studies Conference in London in 1986, and Seiter *et al.*'s (1989) collection *Remote Control: Television, Audiences and Cultural Power*, based on the conference of that name held in Tübingen in 1987.

While this work in the field of media consumption was naturally varied in its particular emphases and concerns, a number of threads of continuity can be picked out. Centrally, almost all of this work was concerned to move away from the Frankfurt School's image of the media consumer as a passive dupe of the all-powerful Culture Industry. The emphasis was on media consumers' choices, actions and forms of creativity. Much of the work was influenced by notions of the consumer of popular culture as an active 'bricoleur' – as evinced most sharply in Hebdige's (1979) formulation of how the process of cultural consumption should be understood:

> Popular culture offers a rich iconography, a set of symbols, objects and artefacts, which can be assembled and reassembled by different groups in a literally limitless number of combinations. The meaning of each selection is transformed as individual objects are taken out of their original, historical and cultural contexts and juxtaposed against other objects and signs from other contexts.
>
> (Hebdige 1979: 104)

307

In a similar vein, Fiske (1986) argued that the Culture Industry could not simply express dominant values, otherwise they would be of no interest to subordinate groups. Fiske's argument was that

> Culture is a process of making meanings that people actively partic-
> ipate in: it is not a set of 'preformed' meanings, handed down and
> imposed on people. . . . The mass produced text can only be made
> into a popular text by the people, and this transformation occurs
> when the various subcultures can activate sets of meanings from it,
> and insert these meanings into their daily cultural experience.
>
> (Fiske 1986: 404)

However, this radical stress on the active nature of cultural consumption was not without its critics, and a number of voices soon began to bemoan what they saw as the trend towards a certain 'romanticisation' of the freedom of the media consumer, in the establishment of a new conventional wisdom in this field, in which the question of media power was in danger of being altogether lost sight of. Thus Modleski complained that

> The insight that audiences/consumers are not completely manipu-
> lated, but may appropriate mass cultural artefacts for their own pur-
> poses has been carried so far that mass culture no longer seems to be
> a problem at all, for some critics.
>
> (Modleski 1986: xi)

Modleski went on to argue that, in their reaction against the Frankfurt School, media scholars, especially those working within a cultural studies perspective, had now entirely lost any critical perspective on popular culture. As she put it:

> If the problem with the Frankfurt School was that its members were
> too elitist, too far outside the culture they examined, many cultural
> studies writers today have the opposite problem – they are so
> concerned not to be 'elitist' that they fall into a mode of populism
> – immersed in popular culture themselves, half in love with their own
> subject, they seem unable to achieve the proper critical distance from
> it, and end up writing apologies for mass culture.
>
> (Modleski 1986: xi)

THE 'NEW' AUDIENCE RESEARCH: REVISIONISM AND INTERPRETIVISM

By the end of the 1980s, it certainly seemed that the new conventional wisdom of media studies was a very 'optimistic' one, so far as the position of the media consumer was concerned, and the passively consuming audience seemed to be, definitively, a thing of the past. Some part of this

'optimism' may have been influenced by a certain technological determination – in which it was assumed that technological advances (the video,
enabling time-shifting; the remote control, enabling channel-hopping) were
empowering the media consumer in important new ways. Thus Erni (1989)
argues bluntly that 'in the context of the enormous changes in television
technology' (such as the increasing use of VCR technology and the development of 'television-computer-telephone hybrids') audience research work
focusing on broadcast television 'becomes somewhat obsolete' (ibid.: 39).
In a not dissimilar vein, Lindlof and Meyer (1987) argue that the
'interactive' capacities of recent technological developments fundamentally
transform the position of the consumer. As they put it:

> with increasing adoption of technological add-ons for the basic media
> delivery systems, the messages can be edited, deleted, rescheduled or
> skipped past, with complete disregard for their original form. The
> received notion of the mass communications audience has simply little
> relevance for the reality of mediated communication.
>
> (Lindlof and Meyer 1987: 2)

The technological advances are often seen to have transformative (if not
utopian) consequences for the TV audience. Thus, in the Italian context,
RAI's publicity at one point claimed that:

> The new telematic services, video recorders and video discs . . . will
> make a more personal use of the medium possible. The user will be
> able to decide what to watch, when he [sic] wants. It will be possi-
> ble, then, to move beyond that fixed mass audience which has been
> characteristic of TV's history: everybody will be able to do his [sic]
> own programming.
>
> (Quoted in Connell and Curti 1985: 99)

The problem here is that many of these arguments run the danger of
abstracting these technologies' intrinsic 'capacities' from the social contexts
of their actual use. In understanding such technological developments, we
could more usefully follow Bausinger (1984) in his concern with the
question of how these technologies are integrated into the structure and
routines of domestic life – into what he calls 'the specific semantics of the
everyday'. However, it was not only a technologically driven form of
optimism that was at stake here: by the late 1980s, it could be argued that
the 'optimism' had became central to the model of media consumption
which had come to dominate the field. Thus, by 1990, Evans noted that
audience work in media studies could largely be characterised by two
assumptions: (a) that the audience is active (in a non-trivial sense) and (b)
that media content is always 'polysemic' or open to interpretation. The
question is, what these assumptions are taken to mean exactly, and what
their theoretical and empirical consequences are (cf. Evans 1990).

As noted earlier, Hall's (1973) formulation of the encoding/decoding model had contained, as one of its central features, the concept of the 'preferred reading' (towards which the text attempts to direct its reader), while acknowledging the possibility of alternative negotiated or oppositional readings. The difficulty is that this model has subsequently been quite transformed, to the point where it is often maintained that the majority of audience members routinely modify or deflect any dominant ideology reflected in media content (cf. Fiske 1987), and the concept of a 'preferred reading', or of a 'structured polysemy', drops entirely from view. In this connection I have to confess a personal interest, as I have been puzzled to find some of my own earlier work (cf. Morley 1980) invoked as a theoretical legitimation of various forms of 'active audience theory' (variously labelled as the 'new revisionist' or 'interpretivist' perspective by other critics). For my own part, while I would argue that work such as the *Nationwide Audience* project (along with that of Ang 1985; Liebes and Katz 1991; and Radway 1984) offers counter-evidence to a simple-minded 'dominant ideology' thesis, and demonstrates that any hegemonic discourse is always insecure and incomplete, this should not lead us to abandon concern with the question of, as Martin-Barbero puts is, 'how to understand the texture of hegemony/subalternity, the interlacing of resistance and submission, opposition and complicity' (Martin-Barbero 1988: 462). That was (and remains) precisely the point of studying audience consumption of media texts, a point which now, with the discrediting of some of the more 'romantic' versions of 'active audience theory' is in great danger of being obscured – as demonstrated, for example, by Seaman's (1992) total failure to understand the significance of what he describes as 'pointless populism' in audience studies. This is by no means to deny the existence of problems in contemporary audience theory. I would agree with Corner (1991) that much recent work in this field is marred by a facile insistence on the polysemy of media products, and by an undocumented presumption that forms of interpretive resistance are more widespread than subordination, or the reproduction of dominant meanings (cf. Condit (1989) on the unfortunate current tendency towards an overdrawn emphasis on the 'polysemous' qualities of texts in media studies). To follow that path, as Corner (1991) correctly notes, is to underestimate the force of textual determinacy in the construction of meaning from media products, and not only to romanticise improperly the role of the reader, but to risk falling into a 'complacent relativism, by which the interpretive contribution of the audience is perceived to be of such a scale and range as to render the very idea of media power naïve' (Corner 1991: 281).

In a similar vein to Corner, Curran offers a highly critical account of what he describes as the 'new revisionism' in mass communications research on media audiences. In brief, his charge is that while 'this . . . "revisionism"

. . . presents itself as original and innovative [it] . . . is none of these things'
(Curran 1990: 135), but rather amounts to 'old pluralist dishes being
reheated and presented as new cuisine' (ibid.: 151). The history Curran offers
is an informative one, alerting us to the achievements of scholars whose work
has been unrecognised or neglected by many (myself included), thus far.
However, my contention is that this is a particular history which could not
have been written (by Curran or anyone else) fifteen years ago, before the
impact of the 'new revisionism' (of which Curran is so critical) transformed
our understanding of the field of audience research, and thus transformed
our understanding of who and what was important in its history. I would
argue that it is precisely this transformation which has allowed a historian
such as Curran to go back and reread the history of communications research,
in such a way as to give prominence to those whose work can
now, with hindsight, be seen to have 'pre-figured' the work of these 'new
revisionists'.

According to Blumler *et al.* (1985: 257) the interpretivist focus on the
role of the reader in the decoding process 'should be ringing bells with
gratificationists . . . because . . . they are the most experienced in dealing with a multiplicity of responses'. Similarly, Rosengren (1985) claims
that Radway's (1984) work 'indirectly offers strong validation of the general
soundness of uses and gratifications research', and he goes on to claim that
'in her way, Radway has reinvented . . . gratifications research' (Rosengren
1985: 278).

The first question, in this connection, as Schroder (1987) notes, is
perhaps whether, rather than constituting evidence of a genuine unity
between cultural studies and uses and gratifications perspectives, what we
see here, in Blumler *et al.*'s argument is, in fact, a misguided attempt to
reduce interpretivist concepts to gratificationist terms. The second (and as
Schroder 1987 notes, rather embarrassing) question is why has it required
a cultural studies scholar to excavate a lost sociological tradition? The answer
that Schroder offers, and with which I for one am inclined to agree, is that
in spite of the tributes now paid by Curran *et al.* to those who can,
retrospectively, be identified as the forgotten 'pioneers' of qualitative media
audience research, 'the fact remains that, until the 1980s, their qualitative
work . . . was . . . the victim of a spiral of silence, because they attempted
to study what mainstream sociology regarded as unresearchable, i.e. cultural
meanings and interpretations' (Schroder 1987: 14).

However, despite my differences with him, concerning the general terms
of his critique, I would agree with Curran that recent reception studies,
which document audience autonomy and offer optimistic/redemptive readings of mainstream media texts, have often been taken to represent not
simply a challenge to a simple 'effects' or 'dominant ideology' model, but
rather as, in themselves, documenting the total *absence* of media influence,
in the 'semiotic democracy' of postmodern pluralism.

311

As Curran observes (1990: 148), Fiske's (1986) celebration of a 'semiotic democracy', in which people drawn from a vast shifting range of subcultures and groups construct their own meanings within an autonomous 'cultural economy', is problematic in various respects, but not least because it is readily subsumable within a conservative ideology of sovereign consumer pluralism. The problem with the concept of 'semiotic democracy', as Murdock (1989) notes, is that this model of 'perfect competition' is as 'useless in understanding the workings of the cultural field as it is in economic analysis, since it is obvious that some discourses (like some firms in the market) are backed by greater material resources and promoted by spokespersons with preferential access to the major means of publicity and policymaking' (Murdock 1989: 438). Hence, as Hall argues, to speak of the cultural field is 'to speak of a field of relations structured by power and difference' in which some positions are in dominance, and some are not, though these 'positions are never permanently fixed' (Hall 1989: 57).

Budd, Entman and Steinman argue that work of this kind now routinely assumes that 'people habitually use the content of dominant media against itself, to empower themselves' (Budd *et al.* 1990: 170) so that, in their analysis, the crucial 'message' of much contemporary American cultural studies media work is an optimistic one: 'Whatever the message encoded, decoding comes to the rescue. Media domination is weak and ineffectual, since the people make their own meanings and pleasures' (ibid.: 170) or, put another way, 'we don't need to worry about people watching several hours of TV a day, consuming its images, ads and values. People are already critical, active viewers and listeners, not cultural dopes manipulated by the media' (ibid.: 170). While I would certainly not wish to return to any model of the audience as 'cultural dopes', the point Budd *et al.* make is a serious one, not least because, as they note, this 'affirmative' model does tend then to justify the neglect of all questions concerning the economic, political and ideological forces acting on the construction of texts (cf. Brunsdon 1989), on the (unfounded) assumption that reception is, somehow, the only stage of the communications process that matters, in the end. Apart from anything else, and at the risk of being whimsical, one might say that such an assumption does seem to be a curiously Christian one, in which the sins of the industry (or the message) are somehow seen to be redeemed in the 'after-life' of reception.

One crucial question concerns the significance that is subsequently given to often quite particular, ethnographic accounts of moments of cultural subversion, in the process of media consumption or decoding. Thus, Budd *et al.* note that, in his account of the ways in which Aboriginal Australian children have been shown to reconstruct TV narratives involving blacks, in such a way as to fit with and bolster their own self-conceptions, Fiske (1986) shows a worrying tendency to generalise radically from this (very particular) instance, so that, in his account, this type of 'alternative' response, in quite particular circumstances, is decontextualised and then offered as a model for 'decoding' in general, so that, as Budd *et al.* (1990: 179) put it, 'the part becomes the whole and the exception the rule' (see also Schudson 1987).

While we should not fall back into any form of simplistic textual determinacy, none the less we must also avoid the naïve presumption that texts are completely open, like 'an imaginary shopping mall in which audience members could wander at will, selecting whatever suits them' (Murdock 1989: 236). I would agree with Murdock that the celebration of audience creativity and pleasure can all too easily collude with a system of media power that actually excludes or marginalises most alternative or oppositional voices and perspectives. As Murdock (1989: 236) argues, 'because popular programmes . . . offer a variety of pleasures and can be interpreted in different ways, it does not follow . . . that attempts to maximise the diversity of representations and cultural forms within the system are redundant'.

The equivalence that Newcomb and Hirsch (1987) assert between the producer and consumer of messages, in so far as the television viewer is seen to match the creator (of the programme) in the making of meanings, is in effect a facile one, which ignores De Certeau's (1984) distinction between the strategies of the powerful and the tactics of the weak (or, as Silverstone and I have argued elsewhere (Morley and Silverstone 1990), the difference between having power over a text, and power over the agenda within which that text is constructed and presented). The power of viewers to reinterpret meanings is hardly equivalent to the discursive power of centralised media institutions to construct the texts which the viewer then interprets, and to imagine otherwise is simply foolish. The problem, as Ang (1990: 247) argues, is that while 'audiences may be active, in myriad ways, in using and interpreting media . . . it would be utterly out of perspective to cheerfully equate "active" with "powerful"'.

II The consumption of television as a commodity

SIGNS OF CONSUMPTION

As noted in the introduction, media studies have long been concerned with debates about the 'effects' of the consumption of television, film, radio, etc. In these debates, it is the audience's consumption of symbols and meanings in media messages which is brought into central focus. Below, I shall explore some of the issues that arise in the context of contemporary developments in the British (and more broadly European) media. I shall argue, in this connection, that we need to look afresh at how we are to understand the audience as consumer, and the process of consumption of TV, at a point at which that process itself is being commoditised – i.e. when the selection of programmes (in the form of pay-per-view or subscription services) begins to take a more closely parallel form to that of the purchase of consumer goods.

However, before addressing these issues, I shall begin with some more elementary (though often ignored) issues, concerning the material and symbolic dimensions of media consumption. In the first place, it is necessary to note that the position of television, considered as an object of consumption, is already a complex one, which needs to be considered as operating, simultaneously, along a number of different dimensions. In the first place, the TV set (along with all the other technologies in the household) is already a symbolic object *qua* item of household furnishing, a choice (of design, style, etc.) which expresses something about its owner's (or renter's) tastes, and communicates that choice, as displayed by its position in the household (cf. Bourdieu 1984; Leal 1990).

This aspect of the process is perhaps most dramatically expressed in Alfred Gell's (1986) account of the Muria Fishermen in Sri Lanka, where the richer villagers now often buy television sets, which are displayed as the centrepieces of their personal collections of 'wealth signifiers', despite the fact that the lack of electricity supply makes the sets inoperable, in any narrowly functional sense. None the less, the objects signify – in powerful ways, just as would my own acquisition of a new flat-screen Japanese TV, quite independently of whether or not I ever switched it on: the presence of the object itself, in my home, would 'mean' something to all who saw it. Indeed, recent advertising campaigns for flat-screen High Definition Television sets, targeted at the up-market 'selective viewer', have taken precisely the theme of the 'less you watch, the higher standards you require when you *do* watch'. Thus, the presence in my home of this particular object would signify both that I was a person who did not watch much TV, and that I was a 'discriminating consumer', with 'high standards' in all things. The symbolic function of objects is not a phenomenon exclusive to the ways of life of other people in strange places. All of which should also alert us to the fundamentally symbolic dimension of these forms of consumption, as opposed to an understanding of them as always/only desired for their 'rational'/functional uses (cf. Douglas and Isherwood 1980).

In this connection Brunsdon (1991) offers a fascinating commentary on the symbolic dimensions of the satellite television dish, in contemporary culture. In Britain, since the demise of the short-lived, upmarket, 'British Satellite Broadcasting' station, with its distinctive 'squariel', satellite television has *meant* 'B Sky B' television – i.e. popular television, designed for a largely working-class audience, supplied by Rupert Murdoch. Brunsdon's point is that, in this context, the erection of a satellite dish on a house functions as a publicly visible sign of the 'low' taste of the household and its occupants. Drawing ironically on Veblen's (1899) theories of 'conspic-uous consumption', Brunsdon argues that 'the satellite dish has come to signify the conspicuous consumption of a certain kind of [taste–DM] poverty' (Brunsdon 1991: 33) and she quotes one press commentator as observing that, in many cities, 'the way to tell the middle-class area from the . . . [working-class area–DM] is that the council houses all have satellite dishes' (Leith, quoted in Brunsdon 1991: 33). Indeed, more recently, Murdoch's B Sky B station, concerned that its down-market image is putting off potential advertisers, has begun to claim, explicitly, that it is not *just* 'council-house television', but also has things to offer to the more 'discerning' consumer. None the less, estate agents continue to use the appearance of satellite dishes in a particular street as a worrying sign that the area is going 'down-market', and that house prices there are about to fall. Such 'abstract' symbols of taste in media consumption can, then, also have very material consequences.

OPPORTUNITIES TO CONSUME

It is well established that, throughout the Western world, for most of its history, television has been dependent for its existence on advertising. Thus, as Smythe (1977) argued long ago, commercial television is principally in the business of selling potential consumers to advertisers: the shows are simply the necessary means to get the viewers in front of the set, to see the advertisements. To this extent, television has to be understood as 'doubly articulated' – in so far as its messages are themselves consumed (with mean-ings that are both predefined in design and marketing and negotiable – of which, more later) and it also enables consumption. Through its combined messages, it brings news of further consumption possibilities, and in some cases, through its interactive capacities, decisions to consume can now be communicated, goods ordered, etc.

Thus, Robins and Webster (1986) have argued that TV can usefully be considered as the 'fourth dimension of advertising', second-best only to having a salesman physically present, as a way for business to enter the homes of the nation, through doors and windows no matter how tightly barred, to deliver its message. Similarly, Peter Conrad argues that

> the [TV] set itself is a trophy of consumerism . . . as well as a the-atre for the cavorting of consumer durables, on the game shows or in the ads. Watching TV, we're dually customers, of the medium (as spectators) and of the goods it's displaying (as potential customers). The screen is a shop window, the box a warehouse.
>
> (Quoted in Robins and Webster 1986: 121–122)

With the development of interactive services, of course, all of this reaches its apogee in programmes like CBS 'Home Shopping Club', in America.

315

Jane Desmond (1989) offers us an arresting account of viewing the 'Home Shopping Club':

> The first time I tuned into the Home Shopping Club I couldn't get out of my chair for three hours. I sat stunned, mesmerised by the parade of neck chains, earrings, china birds, microwaves. . . . It took every ounce of my will not to pick up the phone and dial. . . . Jane, I said, remember the anorexic state of your bank account. Still – two teak serving trays for $10, minus my first-time shopper rebate of $5! I didn't exactly need teak trays . . . but . . . they were a bargain. . . . At last, I thought, the PBS slogan running through my mind, 'TV worth watching'.
>
> (Desmond 1989: 340)

This, of course, is not only an 'American' phenomenon: B Sky B, in the UK, now offers its 'Home Shopping TV network', under the slogan 'The department store you come home to'.

THE COMMODIFICATION OF TELEVISION: AUDIENCES, CONSUMERS AND CITIZENS

Appadurai (1986) offers an analysis of the modalities through which commodities, like persons, enjoy social lives. He is concerned with exploring how the circulation of objects, in space and time, is mediated by different 'regimes of value'. From this point of view, a commodity is defined as 'any thing intended for exchange': the focus is not so much on the internal properties of the thing itself, but rather on the nature of the exchange process. Thus, a commodity is not a certain type of thing; rather, Appadurai suggests, we should focus on the 'commodity potential' of all things, and see things (biographically, as it were) moving in and out of the 'commodity state' over time. So, a 'commodity' is not a class of things (defined by internal properties) but rather, one phase in the life of some things. Similarly, within this category, Appadurai argues that 'luxuries' are not a specific class of things but, rather that 'luxury' is a 'special register' of consumption, so that any particular commodity can move in and out of this 'register' over time (cf. Appadurai 1986: 38).

One could argue that contemporary shifts in the financing of television, away from a flat-rate licensee fee, towards further dependence on advertising finance and subscription (or pay-per-view), involves just such a process – of the commoditisation of television viewing, with concomitant shifts in the dynamics of the 'regime of value' through which exchange is achieved. It is also a process involving the enfranchisement (and disenfranchisement) of different groups (advertisers as opposed to viewers) in the determination of production mechanisms and in the modalities or capacities in which individual viewers relate to this process (as consumers rather than citizens, for example).

A number of commentators have pointed to the fact that, as the availability of TV programmes comes to depend, to an increasing extent, on people's ability to pay for them, the airwaves can no longer be considered as shared public resources. As the provision of information, education and entertainment passes into a 'regime of value' determined by the cash-nexus, television's contributions to a public culture will be increasingly divisive, as between the 'information rich' and the 'information poor'. The much-heralded 'wider choices', offered by these new technologies, will in practice be available only to those who can afford to pay for them. To the extent that access to public information and cultural resources comes to depend on the capacity of citizens to pay, so their capacity to participate effectively in the public realm will be correspondingly differentiated.

Both Peter Golding (1989) and Graham Murdock (1990) have recently argued this case, focusing on the economic determination of unequal access to information (cf. Schiller 1988 for the international version of this argument). As Golding puts it, commenting on the simple correlation of income levels with ownership of media hardware (such as the telephone, video and computer),

> entrance to the new media playground is relatively cheap (as a percentage of total income) for the well-to-do, a small (and easy) adjustment in spending patterns. Conversely, for the poor (and this is of course exacerbated in the U.K. by recent trends in income differentials) the price is a sharp calculation of opportunity cost, access to communication goods jostling uncomfortably with the mundane arithmetic of food, housing, clothing and fuel.
>
> (Golding 1989: 90)

Any mechanism of communication that costs money to use will necessarily produce inequalities of access across social and economic groups. What we see here, according to Golding, is the potential for the dramatic emergence of forms of attenuated citizenship, imposed by information poverty, especially in relation to television, given its centrality in the culture. In Murdock's words, 'Given the steadily widening gap between the top and bottom income groups since 1979, the effect (of pay-per-view, subscription, etc.) is to deny the poorest members of the society access to the full range of resources they need for effective citizenship and full political participation' (Murdock 1990: 87). This is evidenced, in his view, by the recent reorientation of the BBC's view of its audiences, now seen primarily as consumers and honorary shareholders, wanting 'value for money' above all else.

TELEVISION AND POPULAR TASTE

It has frequently been argued that the 'deregulation' of broadcasting, and its increased reliance on advertising revenue, will force the medium down-market, and lead not only to a reduction in the opportunity for genuine viewer choice but also to the end of 'Quality Television' as we know it. Of course, it is also increasingly recognised that, given advertisers' interests in targeting up-market segments of the population, this will not necessarily be the whole story, in so far as various forms of 'quality' or innovative programming may have to be sponsored in order to attract these 'desirable' groups. Nevertheless, so the argument runs, it is only rich minorities who will be served. That is certainly true, but there is also a problem with the implied 'alternative' (traditional) model of public service broadcasting, in so far as the 'public sphere' created by traditional broadcasting in the UK was itself always heavily structured by class (and region). That is the point of Connell's argument (1983) about the 'progressive' dimension of the impact of ITV in the 1950s, in so far as, both in its own programming and in terms of the extent to which the BBC was then forced to compete with it, ITV had a built-in drive to connect with the structure of popular taste, which no public service institution necessarily has. To move to another context, one could also argue that many of the more progressive developments in a whole range of public/welfare institutions over the last few years have precisely been the result of their beginning to take on board elementary considerations of marketing, premised on the need to serve their differentiated client bases, in something other than the traditional forms of 'universal provision'.

Linked in to this issue is, of course, the further question of 'internationalisation'. The fear, in the ex-Director General of the BBC, Alisdair Milne's deathless phrase, is that deregulation will lead to an endless supply of 'wall-to-wall *Dallas*', which will undermine our national culture and identity. To which, clearly, one possible reply is: 'Whose national identity?' The work of writers such as Worpole (1983) and Hebdige (1988), on the extent to which such concepts of 'national culture' have always been heavily structured by metropolitan and class bias, points to the fact that 'foreign' cultural objects (from American crime fiction to Italian motor scooters) have often functioned for working-class people as *positive* cultural icons, cultural resources which could be used to undercut the class structure of national taste precisely by virtue of their vulgarity, as defined by 'established' taste patterns. Thus, Collins (1988) quotes a 'World Film News' survey, from the 1930s, which reported that cinema distributors in working-class areas of Scotland were

> on the whole satisfied with the more vigorous American films . . .
> but practically unanimous in regarding the majority of British films
> as unsuitable for their audiences. British films, one Scottish exhibitor

writes, should rather be called English films, in a particularly parochial sense; they are more foreign to his audience than the products of Hollywood, over 6,000 miles away.

(Collins 1988: 7)

From this perspective we may better be able to understand how local cultures are produced, differentially, in their articulation with and by means of their consumption of global forms (cf. Miller's (1992) analysis of the process of appropriation and 'indigenisation' of American television in Trinidad). To return to Brunsdon's analysis of the consumption of satellite television, the point, she argues, in this connection, is that the erection of a satellite receiving dish functions as a 'concrete and visible sign of a consumer who has bought into the supranational entertainment space, who will not necessarily be available for the ritual, citizen-making moments of national broadcasting (Scannell 1988; Chaney 1979)' (Brunsdon 1991: 38).

III   Case-studies

In recent years the debate, noted above, concerning the question of media consumption as an active process, and how that activity is to be conceptualised in relation to questions of media power, has been paralleled by another debate, this time concerning how the process of media consumption itself should best be studied. Much of this debate has focused on the potential contribution of ethnographic (and other qualitative) approaches (cf. Ang 1991; Lul 1987; Silverstone 1990) to the development of our understanding of such seemingly simple, but actually rather complex, activities as the domestic watching of television in the family (cf. Goodman 1983; Lindlof and Traudt 1983). This focus on the domestic setting, as the context of consumption of television and other media, has also served to highlight a series of hitherto largely ignored questions concerning the nature of the home as a gendered space, and the significance of gender relations in the consumption of television and other media.

I offer below both an account of the overall development of feminist work in this field, concerned with gender and the media, as well as accounts of two particular research projects focused on these issues, with which I have been involved. I do this because I would argue that while debates such as those about the activity/passivity of the media audience, as a general issue, are instructive up to a point, such matters can never be resolved in the abstract. It is only by looking more concretely at such issues, as they are played out in particular contexts and circumstances, that research can really advance. It is this spirit that I offer the material and case-studies below.

TELEVISION, TECHNOLOGY AND GENDER

Between the point, in the early 1940s when Herta Herzog did her path-breaking analyses of the specific responses and behaviour of women listeners to daytime radio serials in the USA (Herzog 1944) and 1982, when Dorothy Hobson's study of British women viewers of soap opera was published, media research largely ignored the question of gender in its analyses of media audiences. In recent years writers such as Spigel (1986) and Haralovich (1988) have begun, retrospectively, to address the fascinating issues which surrounded the introduction of domestic television in America in the 1950s. As they point out, given the centrality of advertisers' concerns to reach an audience of housewives as the economic motor of the whole enterprise, it is, in retrospect, remarkable that issues of gender should have been so consistently evaded. In short, as they note, if television could not be made to appeal to housewives, then commercial television was not going to work at all, as a domestic medium. Moreover, as Spigel notes, it was women who were assumed to have the moral responsibilities for 'managing' the disruptions to family life introduced by the new medium – thus it was in women's magazines that many of the key issues concerning the 'effects' of television, especially on children, found their first public airing.

When attention to issues of gender began to develop in media studies, under the impact of feminism, in the mid-1970s, that attention was initially directed towards the textual analysis of 'women's genres' (melo-drama in film studies, soap opera in television studies). Initially, this attention was focused on questions of gender identity and the gendering of visual pleasure (voyeurism, etc.) as identified in the Lacanian psycho-analytic perspective developed by writers such as Mulvey (1981). Subsequently Modleski (1984) and Brunsdon (1981) have analysed the specificity of material which appeals particularly to feminine audiences, relating the issues of genre and gender, in their analyses both of the post-war modes of feminine cultural competencies and, in Modleski's case, through an analysis of the connections between the textual characteristics of genres such as soap opera (cyclical, fragmented) and the conditions and rhythms of the housewife's domestic labour. In a different context, Ang (1985) has explored the political issues surrounding women's identification with soap opera, as one of the most despised forms of popular culture, in an interesting attempt to develop an analysis of the specific pleasures of the 'popular'.

However, it is the work of Hobson (1982) and Radway (1984) which has begun to explore these issues from an empirical perspective, investigating the ways in which women's particular position in the domestic sphere structures their relation to the media. Thus Hobson offers a fascinating account of the ways in which housewives use the media to counter their isolation, and Radway analyses women's reading of romantic fiction as a mode of preserving a 'private world' of pleasurable fantasy within the pressures of their domestic role. It is in the context of the debates opened up by these studies that I want to offer an account of two research projects in which I have been involved – the 'Family Television' study (Morley 1986) and, more recently, the study of the 'Houschold Uses of Information and Communication Technology' based at Brunel University (see Morley and Silverstone 1990).

FAMILY TELEVISION

The 'Family Television' study was designed to explore, through interviews with family members, the issues arising once one takes the family (or household), rather than the individual viewer in isolation, as the effective 'unit of consumption' of television. Immediately a whole set of issues concerning power relations in the family is necessarily brought into focus – concerning, for instance, the differing power of family members (a matter both of gender and of age) to choose what is to be watched (at least on the household's main set). This approach is, to an extent, influenced by anthropological analyses of the power relations invested in domestic rituals, and is concerned to situate television consumption within the context of what Sean Cubitt (1985) has called 'the politics of the sitting room' – where, if the camera pulls you into involvement with the screen, the dynamics of family life are equally likely to disrupt your attention. This approach also follows Bausinger (1984) in focusing on the ways in which the uses of domestic media inevitably get intertwined with household relationships – e.g. in his example of a man who switches on the television principally in order to avoid having to talk to his wife, and the various ways in which people use 'audio-visual walls' to create personal space and to separate themselves from other members of their household. The point is very simple. Once one takes seriously the fact that television is a domestic medium (and is characterised by programme forms specifically designed for that purpose), it becomes clear that the domestic context of television viewing is not some secondary factor, which can subsequently be sketched in. Rather, the domestic context of TV viewing, it becomes clear, is constitutive of its meaning. Once one considers TV viewing in the context of domestic relations, one inevitably raises the question of power relations, and within the domestic sphere these power relations are principally constructed by gender. The fundamental issue concerns the differential positioning of men and women in the sphere of 'leisure' (whether as a temporal phenomenon – 'time off'; or a spatial phenomenon – 'at home'). For many men, the home is principally a site of leisure and rest (in contrast to their work obligations in the public sphere); for many women (if not most) the home is a site

321

of labour (both physical and emotional) and responsibility, at least as much, if not more, than it is a site of leisure – whether or not they also do paid work outside the home. The point is perhaps put best by one of my woman interviewees. When asked about her favourite TV programmes, she began to list the programmes she liked – and then stopped herself, saying, 'Oh, do you mean *sitting down* watching'? For her (unlike her husband), TV watching was something she usually did while moving about the household, attending to the housework or the children, and 'sitting down watching' was a minor subcategory of her viewing activity, largely reserved for 'special occasions'.

Before going on to outline the major findings of the 'Family TV' study, one or two contextualising points should be made. The study was conducted within the limits of an urban lower-middle-class/affluent working-class, white culture – it is an account of how gender relations affected TV consumption in that particular cultural context, *not* a generalisable model for all other contexts. Moreover, the issues at stake are those of gender, not sex – i.e. it is a question of the effects of culturally acquired modes of masculine and feminine subjectivities, not of characteristics which are the essential qualities of men and women as biological beings.

That said, the differences between the relation to TV on the part of the men and the women in my study were quite notable, in a number of different ways. First, men seemed to have much more power and control over which programmes were to be watched. In many households this power took the form of the man keeping the automatic channel control device in his hand, or on the arm of his chair – rather as a mace might have featured as an (equally phallic) physical symbol of authority, in an earlier time. Second, it was only the men, on the whole, who planned their viewing in advance, the women tending to have a more 'take it or leave it' attitude to TV. Third, it was the men who viewed more attentively, more often. For most of the women to 'just watch' TV, without sewing or ironing, or doing something 'useful' at the same time, made them feel so guilty as to negate any pleasure they gained – except in the case of their particular 'special' programmes. Moreover the problem for them in watching, for example, a soap opera in their husband's company, is also that they feel that their viewing takes place against a disparaging background of cynical criticism. One of the women explained that in order to avoid this, she gets one of her children to video-tape the soap operas for her (she can't work the video herself – cf. Gray 1992) and she gets up early on Saturday mornings, when her husband and sons are still in bed, so as to be able to watch 'her' programmes in peace. (For further details of gendered viewing patterns, see Morley 1986.)

The issue of gender and technology raised by the example of video is of considerable interest. Ann Gray (1987, 1992) has explored the ways in which video seems to have been incorporated into a masculinised domain of leisure in many households – as yet another 'boy's toy'. Clearly, this is no simple matter of 'technological incompetence' on the part of the women concerned, who are 'unable' to work the video, but who routinely operate more complex forms of domestic technology, such as automatic washing machines (which their husbands are correspondingly 'unable' to operate). The issues arising here can serve us as a bridge to a brief account of the project on the 'Household Uses of Information and Communication Technology' mentioned earlier.

THE HOUSEHOLD USES OF INFORMATION AND COMMUNICATION TECHNOLOGY

The rationale for this project (directed by Roger Silverstone at Brunel University, 1987–1990) was that, in the context of current technological changes, in which the TV set can be used for many other purposes (video, video games, teletext services, computer link-ups) besides that of receiving broadcast television, it makes little sense to study the consumption of TV in isolation. Rather, we should begin to look at TV consumption in the broader context of the 'technological culture' of the household – looking also at the use of other ICTs such as radio, hi-fi, computing and telephone services. Much has been written about the effects of IT in 'transforming society'. The premise of this study was that such perspectives often fall into a kind of 'technological determinism' and that we need to examine *how* these technologies are taken up, and their potentialities explored (or not) in different ways, both as between households of different types (e.g. in terms of class or ethnicity) and between different individuals (e.g. in terms of gender or age) within a given household.

In relation to gender, the central issue is how different technologies are incorporated into particular, gender-designated domains of culture competence – according to cultural rules defining their 'appropriateness' for individuals, in relation to gendered modes of subjectivity. Thus as Gray (1987, 1992) and Lull (1988) have noted, the video recorder has, on the whole, been 'masculinised' in contemporary Western cultures: on its initial appearance, for many women, it was simply not a technology which 'fitted' into their own sense of 'their' world. As Skirrow has argued (1986) the same is true of video games, .on the whole, because the games (and their meaning) articulate the cultural meanings of the technology through a set of predominantly masculinised images and meanings (action, horror and adventure genres; modes of combat, survival and quest: all the classical modes of 'masculine' film and TV genres). The same is true, argues Turkle (1988) in the case of the computer. According to her analysis, the reluctance she identifies, on the part of many women, to engage with 'computer culture', takes the form of what she calls 'computer reticence'. She argues that these women see the dominant culture of computing as expressing, principally, a set of masculine values (abstract formal systems; retreat from personal relationships to a relation with a machine; 'risky' strategies in computer 'hacking' culture, etc.) which they perceive as antithetical to their own sense of their feminine identity. Clearly, the point relates back for the more fundamental antipathy felt by many teenage girls towards maths and science subjects (cf. Walkerdine 1988). These areas become problematic because they are culturally defined as masculine spheres, and thus not 'worlds' in which many women feel able (or willing) to participate.

It would be possible, but probably not profitable, to enumerate many further examples of the 'gendering' of technologies. Clearly, in the context of current debates about the centrality of ICT in determining the future of the British economy, these issues need to be highlighted. However, I will end by attempting to draw out one further, and in some ways, more fundamental aspect of these issues. Beyond the question of how gender affects the consumption of TV, or the take-up of new technologies, there lies a fundamental issue concerning the ways in which the new ICTs are transforming the relationship between the public and private spheres of society. Thus, we currently witness the decline of public forms of leisure, such as the cinema, and the increasing privatisation of leisure in the home (witness the rise of video, etc.). ICTs offer the potential for tele-shopping, tele-banking and computerised home-working – all of which presage major transformations in the relationship between the spheres of work and leisure, public and private. Given the differential positioning of men and women in the domestic sphere and given the fundamental nature of the 'cultural equations' of public = masculine and private = feminine, in our culture, we must ensure that these issues remain in central focus in the further development of communications and media studies, now that the forty-year 'silence' on these questions has been broken.

REFERENCES

Abercrombie, N., Hill, S. and Turner, B. (1984) *The Dominant Ideology Thesis*, London: Allen and Unwin.

Adorno, T. and Horkheimer, M. (1977) 'The culture industry: enlightenment as mass deception', in J. Curran, M. Gurevitch and J. Woollacott (eds) *Mass Communication and Society*, London: Edward Arnold.

Althusser, L. (1971) 'Ideological state apparatuses', in L. Athusser, *Lenin and Philosophy*, London: New Left Books.

Ang, I. (1985) *Watching 'Dallas'*, London: Methuen.

Ang, I. (1990) 'Culture and Communication', *European Journal of Communications* 5 (2–3).

Ang, I. (1991) *Desperately Seeking the Audience*, London: Routledge.

Appadurai, A. (ed.) (1986) *The Social Life of Things*, Cambridge: Cambridge University Press.

Bausinger, H. (1984) 'Media, technology and everyday life', *Media, Culture and Society* 6 (4).

Bennett, T. and Woollacott, J. (1987) *Bond and Beyond: the Political Career of a Popular Hero*, London: Macmillan.

Bennett, T., Boyd-Bowman, S., Mercer, C. and Woollacott, J. (eds) (1981) *Popular Television and Film*, London: British Film Institute.

Blumler, J., Gurevitch, M. and Katz, E. (1985) 'Reaching out: a future for gratifications research', in K. Rosengren *et al.* (eds) *Media Gratification Research*, Beverly Hills, California: Sage.

Bourdieu, P. (1984) *Distinction*, London: Routledge and Kegan Paul

Brunsdon, C. (1981) 'Crossroads: notes on a soap opera', *Screen* 22 (4).

Brunsdon C. (1989) 'Text and audience', in E. Seiter, H. Borchers, G. Kreutzner and E.-M. Warth (eds) *Remote Control*, London: Routledge.

Brunsdon, C. (1991) 'Satellite dishes and the landscape of taste', *New Formations* 15.

Budd, B., Entman, R. and Steinman, C. (1990) 'The affirmative character of American Cultural Studies', *Critical Studies in Mass Communications* 7 (2).

Byars, J. (1991) *All that Hollywood Allows*, London: Routledge.

Centre for Contemporary Cultural Studies (1982) *The Empire Strikes Back*, London: Hutchinson.

Chaney, D. (1979) *Fictions and Ceremonies*, London: Edward Arnold.

Cohen, P. and Gardner, C. (eds) (1984) *It Ain't Half Racist, Mum*, London: Comedia.

Collins, R. (1988) 'National culture: a contradiction in terms', paper presented to International Television Studies Conference, London, July.

Condit, C. (1989) 'The rhetorical limits of polysemy', *Critical Studies in Mass Communications* 6 (2).

Connell, I. (1983) 'Commercial broadcasting and the British left', *Screen* 24 (6).

Connell, I. (1985), 'Blaming the Meeja', in L. Masterman (ed.) *Television Mythologies*, London: Comedia.

Connell, I. and Curtis, L. (1985) 'Popular broadcasting in Italy and Britain', in P. Drummond and R. Paterson (eds) *Television in Transition*, London: British Film Institute.

Corner, J. (1991) 'Meaning, genre and context', in J. Curran and M. Gurevitch (eds) *Mass Media and Society*, London: Edward Arnold.

Counihan, M. (1973) 'Orthodoxy, revisionism and guerilla warfare in mass communications research', mimeo, Centre for Contemporary Cultural Studies, University of Birmingham.

Cubitt, S. (1985) 'The politics of the living room', in L. Masterman (ed.) *Television Mythologies*, London: Comedia.

Curran, J. (1990) 'The "new revisionism" in mass communication research', *European Journal of Communications* 5 (2–3).

De Certeau, M. (1984) *The Practice of Everyday Life*, Berkeley: University of California Press.

Desmond, J. (1989) 'How I met Miss Tootsie: the Home Shopping Club', *Cultural Studies* 3 (3).

Douglas, M. and Isherwood, B. (1980) *The World of Goods*, Harmondsworth: Penguin.

Drummond, P. and Paterson, R. (1988) *Television and its Audiences*, London: British Film Institute.

Erni, J. (1989) 'Where is the audience?', *Journal of Communication Enquiry* 13 (2).

Evans, W. (1990) 'The interpretive turn in media research', *Critical Studies in Mass Communication* 7 (2).

Fiske, J. (1986) 'Television: polysemy and popularity', *Critical Studies in Mass Communication* 3 (1).

Fiske, J. (1987) *Television Culture*, London: Methuen.

Gell, A. (1986) 'Newcomers to the world of goods: consumption among the Muria Gods', in A. Appadurai (ed.) *The Social Life of Things*, Cambridge: Cambridge University Press.

Glasgow Media Group (1976) *Bad News*, London: Routledge and Kegan Paul.

Glasgow Media Group (1980) *More Bad News*, London: Routledge and Kegan Paul.

Gledhill, C. (1988) 'Pleasurable negotiations', in E. Pribram (ed.) *Female Spectators*, London: Verso.

Golding, P. (1989) 'Political communication and citizenship', in M. Ferguson (ed.) *Public Communication*, London: Sage.

Goodman, I. (1983) 'Television's role in family interaction', *Journal of Family Issues*, June.

Gray, A. (1987) 'Behind closed doors: women and video', in H. Baehr and G. Dyer (eds) *Boxed in: Women in and on Television*, London: Routledge and Kegan Paul.

Gray, A. (1992) *Video Playtime: the Gendering of a Leisure Technology*, London: Routledge.

Hall, S. (1973) 'Encoding and decoding in the TV discourse', reprinted in S. Hall, I. Connell and L. Curti (1981) (eds) *Culture, Media, Language*, London: Hutchinson.

Hall, S. (1981) 'Theories of language and ideology', in S. Hall, I. Connell and L. Curti (eds) *Culture, Media, Language*, London: Hutchinson.

Hall, S. (1982) 'The rediscovery of ideology', in M. Gurevitch *et al.* (eds) *Culture, Society and the Media*, London: Methuen.

Hall, S. (1989) 'Ideology and communication theory', in B. Dervin, L. Grossberg, B. J. O'Keefe and E. Wartella (eds) *Rethinking Communication*, vol. 2, London: Sage.

Hall, S., Connell, I. and Curti, L. (1981) 'The unity of current affairs TV', in T. Bennett, S. Boyd-Bowman, C. Mercer and J. Woollacott (eds) *Popular Television and Film*, London: British Film Institute.

Halloran, J. (1970) *The Effects of Television*, London: Panther.

Haralovich, M. (1988) 'Suburban family sitcoms and consumer product design', in P. Drummond and R. Paterson (eds) *Television and its Audiences*, London: British Film Institute.

Heath, S. (1977/8) 'Notes on Suture', *Screen* 18(4).

Hebdige, D. (1979) *Subculture: the Meaning of Style*, London: Methuen.

Hebdige, D. (1988) *Hiding in the Light*, London: Comedia/Routledge.

Herzog, H. (1944) 'Daytime serial listeners', in P. Lazarsfeld and F. Stanton (eds) *Radio Research*, New York: Duell, Sloan and Pearce.

Hobson, D. (1982) *Crossroads*, London: Methuen.

Jensen, K. (1987) 'Qualitative audience research', *Critical Studies in Mass Communication* 4 (2).

Lacan, J. (1977) *Ecrits: A Selection*, London: Tavistock.

Leal, O. (1990) 'Popular taste and erudite repertoire: the place and space of television in Brazil', *Cultural Studies* 4 (1).

Lewis, J. (1991) *The Ideological Octopus*, London: Routledge.

Liebes, T. and Katz, E. (1991) *The Export of Meaning*, Oxford: Oxford University Press.

Lindlof, T. and Meyer, T. (1987) 'Mediated communication: the foundations of

qualitative research', in T. Lindlof (ed.) *Natural Audiences*, Norwood, NJ: Ablex.
Lindlof, T. and Traudt, P. (1983) 'Mediated communication in families', in M. Mander (ed.) *Communication in Transition*, New York: Praeger.
Lull, J. (1987) 'Audience, text and contexts', Critical Studies in Mass Communication, 4 (1).
Lull, J. (ed.) (1988) *World Families Watch Television*, London: Sage.
McArthur, C. (1981) 'Historical drama', in T. Bennett, S. Boyd-Bowman, ·C. Mercer and J. Woollacott (eds) *Television and Film*, London: British Film Institute.
MacCabe, C. (1974) 'Realism and the cinema', *Screen* 15 (2).
MacCabe, C. (1981) 'Days of Hope', in T. Bennett *et al.* (eds) *Popular Television and Film*, London: British Film Institute.
Martin-Barbero, J. (1988) 'Communication from culture', *Media, Culture and Society* 10.
Mattelart, M. (1984) *Women, Media, Crisis*, London: Comedia.
Metz, C. (1975) 'The imaginary signifier', *Screen* 16 (2).
Miller, D. (1992) 'The young and the restless in Trinidad', in R. Silverstone and E. Hirsch (eds) *Consuming Technologies*, London: Routledge.
Mills, A and Rice, P. (1982) 'Quizzing the popular', *Screen Education*, 41.
Modleski, T. (1984) *Loving with a Vengeance*, London: Methuen.
Modleski, T. (ed.) (1986) *Studies in Entertainment*, Bloomington: Indiana University Press.
Moores, S. (1993) *Interpreting Audiences*, London: Sage.
Morley, D. (1980) *The Nationwide Audience*, London: British Film Institute.
Morley, D. (1981) 'Texts, readers and subjects', in S. Hall, I. Connell and L. Curti (eds) *Culture, Media, Language*, London: Hutchinson.
Morley, D. (1986) *Family Television*, London: Comedia.
Morley, D. and Silverstone, R. (1990) 'Domestic communications: technologies and meanings', *Media, Culture and Society* 12 (1).
Mulvey, L. (1981) 'Visual pleasure', in T. Bennett, S. Boyd-Bowman, C. Mercer and J. Woollacott (eds) *Popular Television and Film*, London: British Film Institute.
Murdock, G. (1989) 'Cultural studies: missing links', *Critical Studies in Mass Communication* 6 (4).
Murdock, G. (1990) 'Television and citizenship', in A. Tomlinson (ed.) *Consumption, Identity and Style*, London: Comedia.
Neale, S. (1977) 'Propaganda', *Screen* 18 (3).
Newcomb, H. and Hirsch, P. (1987) 'Television as a cultural forum', in W. Rowlands and B. Atkins (eds) *Interpreting Television*, Newbury Park, California: Sage.
Open University (1981) *U203: Popular Culture Course*, Milton Keynes: Open University Press.
Pecheux, M. (1982) *Language, Semantics and Ideology*, London: Macmillan.
Philo, G. (1990) *Seeing and Believing*, London: Routledge.
Radway, J. (1984) *Reading the Romance*, Chapel Hill: University of North Carolina Press.
Robins, K. and Webster, F. (1986) 'Broadcasting politics', *Screen* 27 (3–4).
Rosengren, K. (1985) 'Growth of a research tradition', in K. Rosengren L. Wenner and P. Palingreen (eds) *Media Gratifications Research*, Beverley Hills, California: Sage.
Scannell, P. (1988) 'Radio Times', in P. Drummond and R. Paterson (eds) *Television and its Audiences*, London: British Film Institute.

Schiller, H. (1988) 'The erosion of national sovereignty by the world business system', in M. Taber (ed.) *The Myth of the Information Revolution*, London: Sage.

Schroder, K. (1987) 'Convergence of antagonistic traditions?', *European Journal of Communications* 2.

Schroder, K. (1988) 'The pleasure of *Dynasty*', in P. Drummond and R. Paterson (eds) *Television and its Audiences*, London: British Film Institute.

Schudson, M. (1987) 'The new validation of popular culture', *Critical Studies in Mass Communication* 4 (1).

Seaman, W. (1992) 'Active audience theory: pointless populism', *Media, Culture and Society* 14.

Seiter, E., Borchers, H., Kreutzner, G. and Warth, E.-M. (eds) (1989) *Remote Control*, London: Routledge.

Silverstone, R. (1990) 'Television and everyday life', in M. Ferguson (ed.) *Public Communication*, London: Sage.

Silverstone, R. (1991) 'Beneath the bottom line: households and ICTs', *PICT* Policy Research Paper no. 17, Swindon: Economic and Social Research Council.

Skirrow, G. (1986) 'Hellivision: an analysis of video games', in C. MacCabe (ed.) *High Theory/Low Culture*, Manchester: Manchester University Press.

Smythe, D. (1977) 'Communications: blindspot of Western Marxism', *Canadian Journal of Political and Social Theory* 1.

Spigel, L. (1986) 'Ambiguity and hesitation: discourses on television and the housewife in women's magazines', paper to International Television Studies Conference, London, July.

Spigel, L. (1992) *Make Room for TV*, Chicago: University of Chicago Press.

Turkle, S. (1988) 'Computational reticence: why women fear the intimate machine', in C. Kramarae (ed.) *Technology and Women's Voices*, London: Routledge.

Veblen, T. (1899) *The Theory of the Leisure Class*, New York: Macmillan.

Volosinov, V. (1973) *Marxism and the Philosophy of Language*, New York: Academic Press.

Walkerdine, V. (1988) *The Mastery of Reason*, London: Routledge.

Worpole, K. (1983) *Dockers and Detectives*, London: Verso.

INDEX

329

7. Oct. 02   HKP   33.95   86078